Apocalypse in Islam

The publisher gratefully acknowledges the generous support
of the General Endowment Fund of the University of
California Press Foundation.

Cet ouvrage publié dans le cadre du programme d'aide à la
publication bénéficie du soutien du Ministère des Affaires
Etrangères et du Service Culturel de l'Ambassade de France
représenté aux Etats-Unis.

This work, published as part of a program of aid for
publication, received support from the French Ministry
of Foreign Affairs and the Cultural Service of the French
Embassy in the United States.

Apocalypse in Islam

Jean-Pierre Filiu

Translated by M. B. DeBevoise

UNIVERSITY OF CALIFORNIA PRESS
Berkeley · *Los Angeles* · *London*

University of California Press, one of the most
distinguished university presses in the United States,
enriches lives around the world by advancing
scholarship in the humanities, social sciences, and
natural sciences. Its activities are supported by the
UC Press Foundation and by philanthropic contributions from individuals and institutions. For more
information, visit www.ucpress.edu.

University of California Press
Berkeley and Los Angeles, California

University of California Press, Ltd.
London, England

Library of Congress Cataloging-in-Publication Data

Filiu, Jean-Pierre.
   [Apocalypse dans l'islam. English]
   Apocalypse in Islam / Jean-Pierre Filiu ; translated by
M.B. DeBevoise.
     p. cm.
   Includes bibliographical references and index.
   ISBN 978-0-520-26431-1 (cloth : alk. paper)
   1. Eschatology, Islamic. 2. Political messianism—
Islamic countries. 3. Islamic fundamentalism.
4. Islam and politics. 5. Jihad. I. DeBevoise, M.B.
II. Title.
   BP166.8.4513 2011
   297.2'309—dc22

                      2009049780

Originally published as *L'Apocalypse dans l'Islam* by
Jean-Pierre Filiu, © LIBRAIRIE ARTHÈME FAYARD, 2008.

Manufactured in the United States of America

20 19 18 17 16 15 14 13 12 11
10 9 8 7 6 5 4 3 2 1

This book is printed on Cascades Enviro 100, a 100%
post consumer waste, recycled, de-inked fiber. FSC
recycled certified and processed chlorine free. It is acid
free, Ecologo certified, and manufactured by BioGas
energy.

Let's begin with that piece [by Celāl Bey] so many people call a classic: "When the Bosphorus Dries Up." The signs of the apocalypse—aren't they all lifted from the Koran's verses on the Day of Judgment and from Ibn Khaldun and Ebu Horasani? All describe days of destruction that will precede the arrival of the Messiah; Celāl Bey does the same by plundering their words. To this he adds a vulgar tale about a gangster.

—Orhan Pamuk, *The Black Book*

"Good evening. Your question?"
"Good evening, sir. I would like to know: if, at six o'clock, French time, this war [in Iraq] begins, might it be a world war, . . . and, if so, could it possibly be the end of the world?"

—Sampled radio call-in from Mano Negra, "Machine Gun"

Contents

Plates follow page 120

Preface to the English-Language Edition

For more than thirty years now I have traveled the lands of Islam, worked in them, and been fascinated by them. They are the sources of some of my most precious memories, particularly the years in Damascus, where my two sons spent their early childhood. One of our greatest pleasures was to wander about the suqs, delighting in their colors and smells, and stocking up on spices and candies before making our way to the Great (or Ummayad) Mosque. My little boys delighted above all in the mosque's vast courtyard, where they shouted themselves hoarse running after the indefatigable pigeons. They took rather less interest than I did in the brilliance of the mosaics and the majesty of the columns— mute witnesses to the innumerable ceremonies of worship that had been performed in this place over so many centuries.

The hours slipped by between two calls to prayer. Inside, the shrine's thick carpets invited visitors to pause for a moment, perhaps for a brief nap, or to exchange whispered confidences amid the muffled chatter that filled the air. Outside, the sun played on the shimmering facets of the façade. In the courtyard, friends and strangers happily passed the time in conversation. Someone came along and pointed out one of the corner minarets, the famous white Minaret of Jesus, where Muslim tradition locates the son of Mary's return to earth. I was then regaled once again with the tale of this supernatural descent, and of the battle that would rage with the Antichrist, perched on the opposite minaret. My companions sought to outdo one another in evoking memorable incidents of this apocalyptic duel—as though, by doing this, they could postpone the moment of its occurrence until some comfortably distant time in the future. Here, in the shadow of the Umayyad Mosque, the end of the world was an occasion for playful storytelling, not a source of dread and anxiety.

This was in the late 1990s—the end of the second millennium of the Christian era, or the beginning of the fifteenth century of the Islamic calendar. The countdown to the year 2000, and the collective doubt and existential worry it stimulated in the West, left the majority of Muslims utterly indifferent, for the West's troubles did not trouble them. In the street stalls and on the sidewalks I did, of course, notice booklets announcing the end of the world, wedged among guides to the interpretation of dreams and moralizing manuals on conjugal happiness, but they scarcely seemed worth lingering over. Over time, however, these apocalyptic pamphlets, with their garish and blood-filled cover illustrations, came to take up more and more space in general-interest bookstores and on the book racks in shopping centers. Intrigued, I began to collect them. What had been a marginal novelty soon found itself transformed by the attacks of 11 September 2001 in New York and Washington, and to an even greater degree by the American invasion of Iraq in March 2003, into a mass-market phenomenon. A new and hugely popular genre, apocalyptic fiction, was now rapidly spreading throughout the Muslim world.

For a long time I hesitated to throw myself into a detailed study of this literature. As a scholar, I would have to overcome academic prejudices against a subculture that had grown up around self-educated authors and cheaply produced books. Beyond that, there was a risk of conferring undue importance on authors having no recognized social or religious authority. I nonetheless continued to collect dozens of works from every part of the Islamic world; from each of my trips I brought back additional proof of a growing and disturbing tendency. Eventually my Arab colleagues convinced me of the necessity of taking this frenzied expression of apocalyptic feeling seriously, and I devoted myself to further research for several years. In the present work I have tried to place the most recent period of ferment in historical perspective, examining the roots of Muslim prophecy and retracing the chains of transmission of those traditions that are most commonly cited today. In this way it becomes possible, or so I hope, to illuminate the connections of current ideas with the past while at the same time bringing out the importance of foreign contributions to Islamic thought.

The Muslim vision of the end of the world incorporates two important strands of the Judeo-Christian heritage: messianism, an idea that is intimately associated with the Jewish faith, and millenarianism, a central element in the Christian economy of salvation. Additionally, the Muslim vision appropriates the figure of Jesus, not only glorifying him as the penultimate prophet of Islam, but also predicting his return to earth, in Damascus, and his apocalyptic combat with the abominable leader of the forces of Evil, the Antichrist. The army of the faithful will then be led by the Mahdi, a distant descendant of the Prophet Muhammad, who will seal the triumph of Islam over the heathen. Messianic expectation is concentrated on this latter figure, the Mahdi. The reverence that he inspires among Sunnis, profound though it manifestly is, nonetheless reaches its height in the piety of the Shi'a, who honor the Mahdi as the Master of the Age, believing that his imminent appearance will mark the advent of an epoch of universal justice, itself the prelude to the end of the world. On this view, messianic and millenarian expectations are inextricably linked.

The history of Islam is punctuated by revolutionary movements, which typically irrupt at the instigation of a self-proclaimed mahdi or of his avowed representatives. Where they are successful, such uprisings culminate in the establishment by the supposed messiah of a new line of leaders, populated in most cases by his descendants. Although this form of dynastic institutionalization is invariably accompanied by harsh repression of the movement's earliest supporters and the brutal resolution of internal quarrels, the messianic spark is never quite extinguished, setting in motion fresh cycles of challenge and dissent. The majority of Mahdist rebellions end up in bloody failure, however, and the rewriting of history by the victors has surely caused the actual number of mahdis who rose up against rulers they reviled as tyrants and apostates to be underestimated. Moreover, the revolutionary impulse is intensified with the arrival of a new century in the Islamic calendar, each one thought to be more favorable than the last to the appearance of a messiah who will bring salvation. The beginning of Islam's fourteenth century, in 1883, saw the conquest of Sudan by a mahdi born in the eastern part of the country; in 1979, with the onset of the fifteenth century, a messianic insurrection in Mecca plunged the entire Muslim world into mourning.

Few authors of apocalyptic fiction today, if any, are animated by a comparable sense of revolutionary urgency. Even so, their conviction that the end of the world is near cannot be doubted. In providing ordinary believers with an alternative picture of the world's future, a competing grand narrative, they have, inadvertently or not, worked to restore the original Greek sense of "apocalypse," once again understood as a revelation—an unveiling, or uncovering, of a true state of affairs that has been hidden from view by a coalition of evildoers. These authors seldom belong to the religious hierarchy; indeed, their overriding purpose is to turn a vengeful reading of history, and especially of its end, against the clergy itself. In order to fill in what they regard as gaps in Islamic tradition, they draw freely from Jewish and Christian prophecies, giving the protagonists of these accounts an important place in their own inventions. But whereas the ancient Hebrew prophets Ezekiel, Daniel, and Zechariah are called upon to corroborate the most dramatic claims of present-day Muslim authors, the Apocalypse of Saint John—better known as the Book of Revelation—is distorted to suit the purposes of a new vision, in which the Paraclete is revealed to be the Prophet Muhammad, and the New Jerusalem, Mecca.

The result of this exercise in reinterpretation is an apocalypse of unceasing struggle that stigmatizes Zionism, identified with the Beast, and America, avatar of the decadence of Rome. Even the concept of Armageddon, wholly absent from Islamic scripture, may be found in fundamentalist pamphlets. But the most prolific authors do not limit their borrowing to Judeo-Christian prophecy. They also rummage through the predictions of Nostradamus, delve into the mysteries of the Bermuda Triangle, and discourse at length on extraterrestrials and flying saucers. Speculations of this kind cannot help but call to mind the sinister forecasts of Western writers such as Hal Lindsey, in *The Late Great Planet Earth,* and Tim LaHaye and Jerry Jenkins, whose *Left Behind* series has captured the imagination of millions of Christian readers throughout the world. By a fascinating sort of mirror effect, these bestsellers are now cited as authoritative references by propagandists of the Islamic apocalypse—just as the sermons of American televangelists on the Day of Judgment, and of the rapture that it heralds, are taken literally by apostles of revenge from Casablanca to Jakarta. There is, after all, no reason why globalization should spare the apocalypse.

More than twenty years ago, in 1987, in a review of the French translation of Bernard Lewis's *Semites and Anti-Semites,* I observed that anti-Semitism in modern Muslim societies was less the product of a local religious heritage than a consequence of the importation of European hate literature. The sudden growth of apocalyptic apprehension in the Islamic world since then marks a new step in this process, shrouding familiar works such as *The Protocols of the Elders of Zion* in a gnostic aura. More troubling still, their obsessive quality has now been further accentuated by conspiracy theories that place renewed emphasis on the stock figure of the scheming and cosmopolitan Jew. With the perceived imminence of the end of times, hatreds have been rendered inexpiable and compromise inconceivable. The absolute violence and appalling cruelty of Islamist apocalyptic fictions are sustained by the prospect not only of more and larger massacres, but also of genocide. The disappearance of the Jewish people, either by conversion or extermination, is celebrated in advance, and with a fervor that is more commonly associated with eulogists of ethnic cleansing than with doctors of religious law.

This anti-Semitic fanaticism is sadly modern, for it has arisen as part of a new kind of eschatological account having no recognized theological basis. In explicitly distancing itself from official dogma, apocalyptic fiction confronts the clerical hierarchy with a dismaying alternative: either to feign indifference toward plainly deviant—indeed, delirious—writings, and so risk letting them multiply without hindrance; or to refute them more or less formally, with the danger of offering marginal authors a platform that otherwise they could not hope to enjoy. Perhaps the most worrisome aspect of the thriving trade in apocalyptic provocation we are witnessing today is the nearly total liberty taken with the scriptural corpus of Islam by populist entrepreneurs eager to turn the call to combat against a clergy they consider unwilling to fully embrace the messianic cause. For the moment, apocalyptic militancy represents a greater challenge to the 'ulama than it does to established political authority. But although it assumes several different forms in the Sunni and Shi'i branches of Islam, it carries a devastating potential for wider revolt, as the experience of the past three decades, from Mecca in 1979 to Najaf in 2007, makes abundantly clear.

Messianic outbursts can be encouraged by opportunistic leaders. The apocalyptic impulse typically animates "honest fanatics"—to borrow the expression of James Darmesteter, speaking at the Collège de France in 1895 about the Sudanese mahdi who had recently risen up against Great Britain and Egypt. The guilelessness of such figures is the gravest menace of all, for they have not the slightest interest in compromise. President Ahmadinejad, who in 2005 famously claimed to be shrouded in the light of the Hidden Imam, persists in his messianic beliefs. Following his controversial reelection in June 2009, demonstrators chanted: "You, who saw the light [of the Imam]—why didn't you see our vote?" Their protests against electoral fraud were swept aside with violence. Official repression in Iran no longer spares even the clerical leadership, whose disavowal of state-sponsored messianism has further aggravated the inclination to dissidence.

As for Muslim apocalyptic pamphleteers, all of them forecast victory by John McCain in the U.S. presidential election of 2008, for it agreed with their vision of a demoniacal alliance between the American Antichrist and Christian Zionism. Barack Obama's election took them by surprise, no less than it did bin Laden and his followers in al-Qaida, who share the same blindness regarding the nature of the United States. But the grand apocalyptic narrative soon regained its familiar self-assurance by exalting the eschatological dimension of Khurasan, the Afghan-Pakistani borderland where it is supposed the black banners of Islamic vengeance will gather in preparation for their ultimate triumph over the forces of impiety. With the approach of the end of the world, all manner of cleverness in rewriting the past is permitted, and with it every imaginable reversal of expectation.

I was living in the United States when the attack in Oklahoma City took place in April 1995. Since then the horror of 168 persons massacred in the bombing of the Federal Building there has been supplanted in collective memory by the trauma of 11 September 2001. The author of the carnage in Oklahoma City turns out to have been not only a right-wing extremist, but also an enthusiastic subscriber to a whole culture of conspiracy that draws inspiration from the loonier realms of science fiction. This does not make every believer in flying saucers a potential terrorist, of course. But it does throw an unsettling light on the trivialization of the death wish promoted by unhinged minds whose urgent messages are too often regarded simply with contempt, and suggests at least one very good practical reason for taking apocalyptic literature seriously, however difficult, frustrating, or tedious the task may be.

From the scholarly point of view there are additional motivations for studying the messianic impulse in contemporary Islam, which presents a novel mechanism for both the transmission and the invention of scriptural tradition. The pioneering work of David Cook at Rice University on Sunni apocalyptic literature has its counterpart in Shiʻi studies with the investigations of Abdulaziz Sachedina at the University of Virginia and Abbas Amanat at Yale. Outside the United States, younger scholars are increasingly interested in adopting an interdisciplinary and comparative approach to a phenomenon that remains very largely unexamined. Closer attention to individual authors, as well as critical analysis of publishers' lists and of their readers' beliefs, will make it possible to measure the appeal of apocalyptic prophecy more accurately. In the meantime I can only hope that the present book will answer more questions than it raises.

Very far away, night has begun to fall in Damascus. The suqs are now empty, and the calm of the streets is disturbed only by the conversation of neighbors and the insistent murmur of televisions. The last call to prayer sounded long ago. In front of the Umayyad Mosque, two passersby can be seen by the light of the moon that illuminates the white minaret above them. Wordlessly, they point to the evanescent tip of the minaret, where Jesus will descend to wage the battle of the end of the world—many, many centuries from now. Until then, may peace reign.

Paris
January 2010

Acknowledgments

Gilles Kepel generously agreed to act as my advisor at Sciences Po (Institut d'Études Politiques de Paris), where I undertook this research in satisfaction of the requirements for the *diplôme d'habilitation*. I am indebted in the first place to him, but also to the members of my thesis committee, to its chairman, Ghassan Salamé, as well as to Henry Laurens, Bernard Hourcade, Mercedes García-Arenal, and David Cook.

I hasten also to thank Ammar Abd Rabbo, Emma Aubin-Boltanski, Aurélie Daher, Stéphane Lacroix, Jean-François Legrain, François Nicoullaud, and Ahmad Salamatian. Their comments, suggestions, and insights have been invaluable to me.

I could not have completed this work without the hospitality shown to me by the capable and diligent staff of research libraries in several countries: the library of the graduate school of the Sciences Po, and also of the Institut du Monde Arabe in Paris, the University of Leiden, and the Netherlands Institute for the Near East in Holland, and, in Spain, the School of Arab Studies (Casa del Chapiz) of the Consejo Superior des Investigaciones Científicas de Granada.

I am grateful, finally, to all the persons who assisted me during my stays in Amman, Sharjah, Damascus, Dubai, Jerusalem, Kota Bharu, Kuwait, Kuala Lumpur, Ramallah, and Riyadh in assembling the collection of apocalyptic literature that forms the basis of this book.

Prologue

The End of the World Draws Near

Islam, no less than the two other monotheisms, has nourished a rich and impressive vision of the Final Judgment. It has developed, in particular, an apocalyptic narrative in which small "signs of the Hour," succeeded by great signs, set in motion a terrifying sequence of events. The decay of the Muslim faith and the distortion of Muslim values will be only the prelude to the advent of the Mahdi, a descendant of the Prophet, who will do battle with the heathen at the head of the armies of Islam. Jesus will then come down to earth to combat the Antichrist, first in Damascus, then in Palestine. The havoc wrought by the damned of the earth, the return of the Beast, and the devastation of Mecca will serve to announce the moment of universal resurrection and the punishment of human souls in accordance with Islamic teaching and precept.

This vivid account is based on the Qur'an and the classical sources of Islamic tradition. It has nonetheless had a mixed posterity, having been revived only on the occasion of great trials during the medieval period: Christian reconquest of Andalusia, Crusades in the Levant, Mongol invasions of the Mashriq. In the meantime, alongside Sunni ortho-doxy, Shi'i schismatics constructed a competing revelation in which the Mahdi—the last of the mystical line of imams, concealed from the view of mankind since the ninth century—is cast as the central figure, the "Master of the Age." Until recently these apocalypses occupied the domain of popular superstition rather than of theological speculation. Then suddenly, in the space of a few weeks, everything changed. Toward the end of 1979, the partisans of a self-proclaimed Saudi mahdi forcibly seized the Great Mosque in Mecca. The uprising was bloodily suppressed. Shortly afterwards the Soviet Union invaded Afghanistan—the Khurasan of medieval legend—and the international forces of jihad began at once to assemble there, raising the banner of Islam in an unrelenting struggle against godlessness and blasphemy.

The past twenty-five years have seen an extraordinary growth in Muslim apocalyptic literature. One school of interpretation, messianic and radical in equal parts, finds signs of the Hour in numerological divination and reports of unidentified flying objects. Another school, more punctilious in matters of dogma, combats borrowings from biblical sources, but at the same time joyfully endorses the most sickening conspiracy theories, citing *The Protocols of the Elders of Zion* as its authority. In the meantime, the emergence of al-Qaida has been accompanied by a millenarian rereading of jihadist terrorism that considers the Taliban sanctuary in Afghanistan to be only a first step toward the establishment of a universal caliphate. On this view America is the Beast, whose demented hordes hurl themselves in waves onto the lands of Islam and whose arrogant towers collapse under the blows of the faithful. The Hour is near. The signs are there for all to see.

This apocalyptic sense of urgency was aggravated by the American invasion of Iraq in 2003, which gave new life to Shi'i messianism. The following year a "Mahdi Army" was raised against the occupier and soon became the most important militia in the country. In neighboring Iran a new president, Mahmud Ahmadinejad, was persuaded of the immanent appearance of the Hidden Imam, whose luminous radiance he sensed surrounding him like a halo when he addressed the General Assembly of the United Nations in New York in September 2005. These tragic visionaries share with the most farsighted of American neoconservatives the conviction that an implacable conflict is foretold in prophecy. It is therefore less a clash of civilizations that is now beginning to take shape than a confrontation of millenarianisms. In seeking to make sense of this symbolic vigil of arms, one must nonetheless be careful to avoid two opposite but related errors: on the one hand, exaggerating the political importance of messianic imprecations in the Islamic world; and, on the other, dismissing apocalyptic anxiety as an inconsequential preoccupation limited to the working classes in Muslim society.

In the pages that follow I have not wished to insist on a strict distinction between the terms "messianic" and "millenarian." It is customary among historians of religion to contrast the messianism dominant in Judaism with more typically Christian forms of millenarianism. Yet apocalyptic writings in Islam are remarkable for combining the two, so that messianism, associated with the expectation that a redemptive and supernatural figure will one day appear, is inseparable from millenarianism, marked by a restless search for signs of the end of the world and an obsession with numerological divination. Although the overwhelming majority of Muslims today pay no heed to delusional prophecy, its gruesome fantasies furnish the basis for a paradoxically modern and increasingly influential ideology that relentlessly demonizes America as the absolute enemy of Islam. In the minds of the most impassioned believers, each bloody defeat draws the moment of ultimate and total triumph that much nearer.

The end of the world is a serious matter—especially for those who are busy preparing for it.

PART ONE

True and False Messiahs of Islam

CHAPTER I

Archeology of the End of the World

Apocalypse is, historically, a Christian concept whose etymology (Greek ἀποκάλυψις, Latin *apocalypsis*) refers to the disclosing or revelation of hidden realities within an eschatological perspective. Whereas Arabic translations of the term "apocalypse" (both *jilliān* and *sifr al-ro'ya* are common) carry over the fundamental Christian sense of uncovering, the Islamic concept of revelation *(wahīī)* is indissolubly linked to the descent *(inzāl)* of the Qur'anic message. In order to understand the meaning of apocalypse in Islam, and in particular the notion of the end of times *(ākhir al-zamān)*, a way of overcoming this dogmatic obstacle will need to be found.

Classical biographies of the Prophet Muhammad relate the tale of his encounter, at the age of nine (or perhaps twelve) years, with an Arab Christian hermit named Bahira. This meeting is said to have taken place in Bassora (present-day Basra), in the southern part of Syria, where Muhammad had traveled from Mecca with his family's caravan. The monk, recognizing in the young Muhammad the sign of prophecy, warned his parents against the malice of the Jews and the violence of the Byzantines *(Rūm)*.[1] The reality of this prediction is no longer disputed in Islamic lands, and the Monastery of Bahira, as it is known, still attracts visitors to Basra. Nor is Bahira's historical existence a matter of doubt for Christian polemicists, although his Nestorian allegiance leads them to see Bahira as a heretical figure who exerted a decisive (and deleterious) influence on the Qur'anic message. An Apocalypse (or

"Vision") of Bahira, originally disseminated in both Syriac and Arabic, continues to give rise to contradictory arguments and claims.[2]

THE SACRED TEXT

Revealed to the Prophet Muhammad in Mecca and Medina between 610 and 632 C.E., the Qur'an is composed of 114 suras, or chapters, which themselves are divided into 6,235 verses. The Arabic word designating these verses, *ayāt,* is also one of the terms used to describe the premonitory "signs" of the Hour *(sā'a),* the exact moment of which is known to Allah alone. This is the most impenetrable mystery of Islam, fatal to unbelievers and infidels:

> They ignore every single sign that comes to them from their Lord. . . . But all they are waiting for is a single blast *[sayha]* that will overtake them while they are still arguing with each other. They will have no time to make bequests, nor will they have the chance to return to their own people.
> The Trumpet will be sounded and—lo and behold!—they will rush out to their Lord from their graves. They will say, "Alas for us! Who has resurrected us from our resting places?" [They will be told,] "This is what the Lord of Mercy promised, and the messengers told the truth." It was just one single blast and then—lo and behold!—they were all brought before Us. "Today, no soul will be wronged in the least: you will only be repaid for your deeds."[3]

Allah is spoken of in the first sura of the Qur'an not only as "the Lord of Mercy" *(ar-rahmān)* and "the Giver of Mercy" *(ar-rahīm),* but also as "Master of the Day of Judgment" *(al-malik al-yawm al-dīn,* literally "day of religion"). This Day of Judgment—or Day of Resurrection *(al-yawm al-qiyāma)*—will see the gathering together *(hashr)* of all of humanity, summoned to appear before the Almighty. The dead will come out from their tombs and Muhammad will have delegated to him the full powers of intercession enjoyed by the prophets who have preceded him. Islam recognizes no intermediate category between the paradise promised to the faithful (including martyrs fallen "in the path of Allah") and the hell of infinite torments:

> There will be no good news for the guilty on the Day they see the angels. The angels will say, "You cannot cross the forbidden barrier," and We shall turn to the deeds they have done and scatter them like dust. But the companions in the Garden will have a better home on that Day, and a fairer place to rest. On the Day when the sky and its clouds are split apart and the angels sent down in streams, on that Day, true authority belongs to the Lord of Mercy. It will be a grievous Day for the disbelievers.[4]

Apocalypse in Islam therefore covers the confused period, marked by a succession of violent auguries, that leads up to the Last Hour. Jesus occupies a central place in this preparatory time: the Qur'an calls him "the Messiah, Issa, son of Mariam."[5] He is the eleventh of the twelve messengers of Allah and takes his place in the mystical line that begins with Adam and ends with Muhammad, seal of the prophets. Yet Jesus's crucifixion was only a sinister omen: he has yet to complete his mission. For Jesus incarnates the inevitability of the Hour, whose secret he harbors. He has already come to earth with "clear signs" *(bayyināt)*,[6] and he will come back to close the cycle of Creation: "[Jesus] gives knowledge of the Hour: do not doubt it. Follow Me for this is the right path; do not let Satan hinder you, for he is your sworn enemy."[7] Jesus the prophet, like Muhammad the messenger of God, has been granted the privilege of obtaining access to the divine mystery that believers can apprehend only through their message.

Cosmic signs will announce the nearness of the end, even if infidels persist in denying the obvious: "The Hour draws near; the moon is split in two. Whenever the disbelievers see a sign *[ayāt]*, they turn away and say, 'Same old sorcery!' They reject the truth and follow their own desires—everything is recorded. . . ." First there will be smoke, mentioned in a sura of the same name, the forty-fourth: "[Prophet,] watch out for the Day when the sky brings forth clouds of smoke for all to see. It will envelop people. They will cry, 'This is a terrible torment!'" Then from the bowels of the earth will spring forth a creature known as the Beast *(dābba)*: "When the verdict is given against them, We shall bring a creature out of the earth, which will tell them that people had no faith in Our revelations." This creature is mentioned only one other time in the sacred text, in the course of an obscure verse concerning the "family of David": "Then, when We decreed Solomon's death, nothing showed the jinn he was dead, but a creature of the earth eating at his stick—when he fell down they realized. . . ."[8]

By contrast, the Qur'an abounds in descriptions of the natural catastrophes that will foretell the final state of the world. Thus chapter 84 ("Ripped Apart") begins: "When the sky is ripped apart, obeying its Lord as it rightly must, when the earth is leveled out, casts out its contents, and becomes empty, obeying its Lord as it rightly must. . . ." In addition to the Call, a trumpet blast will ring out: "When the Trumpet is sounded a single time, when the earth and its mountains are raised high and then crushed with a single blow, on that Day the Great Event will come to pass. The sky will be torn apart on that Day, it will be so frail."[9]

Other suras announce "a Day when the heavens will be like molten brass and the mountains like tufts of wool. . . ." This will be "the Day when the sky sways back and forth and the mountains float away," when "the earth will be torn apart," when "We shall roll up the skies as a writer rolls up [his] scrolls." On this Last Day, "the sun is shrouded in darkness [and] the stars are dimmed," and "the seas boil over."[10]

The Qur'an accords a particular place in these cataclysmic last times to the monstrous peoples known as Gog and Magog *(ya'jūj wa ma'jūj)*. To halt their depredations ("[they] are ruining this land"),[11] the "Two-Horned One" *(dhū 'l-qarnayn, sometimes identified with Alexander the Great)[12] had been assigned the task of raising a rampart of iron and molten metal against them.[13]

> "But [said the Two-Horned One] when my Lord's promise is fulfilled, He will raze this barrier to the ground: my Lord's promise always comes true." On that Day, We shall let them surge against each other like waves and then the Trumpet will be blown and We shall gather them all together. We shall show Hell to the disbelievers, those whose eyes were blind to My signs, those who were unable to hear.[14]

Rich though it is in descriptions of the Final Judgment and of hell and heaven, the Qur'an provides few clues regarding the apocalyptic calendar. It was instead the oral "traditions"—the sayings attributed to the Prophet, collectively known as *hadīth* (literally, "news" or "reports" of Muhammad and his companions)—that were to complete the Islamic vision of the end of the world, giving it color and depth. The genuineness of individual hadiths was nonetheless fiercely contested—an indication of the tension between customary behavior *(sunna)* and orthodoxy that characterized Islam during its formative stages.

THE GREAT SCHISM

The death of Muhammad, struck down by a sudden illness in 632, plunged the young Muslim community into disarray. He left no political testament, no instructions to his followers regarding the collective management of the faith after his death. The institution of the caliphate *(khilāfa,* a term of Arabic origin meaning "succession") fairly quickly came to be established by means of a more or less settled, and on the whole pragmatic, consensus. The caliph was understood to be nothing more than a successor of the Prophet, and no other title augmented his power, supreme though it was.

The first four caliphs, Abu Bakr, 'Umar, 'Uthman, and 'Ali are tra-ditionally referred to as "rightly guided" *(rāshidūn),* and with the pas-sage of time the three decades of their rule in Medina (632–661) have come to acquire the aura of a golden age. But this reputation survives only by a willful neglect of the severe strains that marked the period of the "Great Dissension" *(al-fitna al-kubrā)* that set Muslims against one another,[15] amounting to a civil war whose legacy of hatred and incom-prehension was to bring about a lasting divorce, fraught with conse-quence, between Sunnis and Shi'a.

Following the brief caliphate of Abu Bakr, who died after only two years, 'Umar's decade-long reign witnessed a formidable expansion of Islam outside the Arabian Peninsula, with the defeat of the Byzantine and Sassanid empires as well as the conquest *(fath)* of Egypt. But ten-sions grew under 'Uthman, an eminent figure of the powerful Umayyad clan from Mecca. Unlike the majority of the members of this tribal aristocracy, who rallied to the Prophet's cause only after having fought against him for many years, 'Uthman had been one of Muhammad's first companions. On becoming caliph, 'Uthman nonetheless favored the strengthening of family privileges over the spreading of the faith by arms. The undisguised nepotism over which he presided gave rise to complaints from the military leaders camped in the garrison cities of Kufa and Bassora, in Iraq, as well as in Fustāt, near present-day Cairo. Yet the Umayyad governor of Damascus, Mu'awiya, unreservedly sup-ported the caliph, to whom he was related by blood.

The crisis erupted in 656 with the siege of Medina by rebel forces. A contingent from Egypt assassinated 'Uthman, and 'Ali, the Prophet's cousin and son-in-law, was elevated to the caliphate with the support of most of the generals of Islam. But Mu'awiya accused 'Ali of having encouraged the uprising and demanded that his kinsman's murderers be punished. Relations between Syria, under Umayyad control, and Iraq, bastion of the partisans of 'Ali *(shī'at 'Ali,* source of the name Shi'a), quickly deteriorated. The two camps mobilized their forces in anticipa-tion of a clash that took place the following year, in 657, at Siffin in the valley of the middle Euphrates. Just when defeat seemed inevitable, Mu'awiya's troops negotiated a cessation of hostilities by raising copies of the Qur'an high in the air, spiked on the tip of their lances. The ensu-ing arbitration, though on its face favorable to 'Ali, in fact signaled his political demise, for some of his allies rejected any idea of conciliation and turned against a caliph whom they considered too accommodating. This armed rebellion on the part of the Kharijites ("Seceders") soon came to absorb the better part of 'Ali's energies: the following year he managed to crush their forces south of Baghdad; three years after that, however, in 661, he was fatally stabbed by a revanchist at Kufa. In the interval Mu'awiya had been patiently working to consolidate his influence in the various lands of Islam, and succeeded finally in convening at Jerusalem an assembly of Arab leaders who proclaimed him caliph. This title was no longer contested after 'Ali's assassination—all the less since Hasan, 'Ali's son, publicly renounced any ambition of seeking supreme power for himself.

The two decades of Mu'awiya's caliphate saw the marginalization of the Arabian Peninsula and the vassalization of Iraq, both to the profit of Damascus, now effectively the capital of the empire. The Umayyad clan found strong support there among the Banū Kalb, an Arab tribe originally from Yemen that had settled on the Syro-Mesopotamian steppe before the arrival of Islam. But the pace of conquest, dazzling at first, now came to a standstill, Mu'awiya having proved to be a more skillful politician than military strategist. After protracted negotiations with Arab chieftains, he managed to have his son Yazid designated as his successor, thus substituting a hereditary principle for the earlier custom of reserving the choice of a new caliph to the leaders of the community.

On Mu'awiya's death in 680, anger at the Umayyad monopolization of power was growing in Iraq. Husayn, 'Ali's younger son and a grandson of Muhammad on his mother's side, raised the standard of the family of the Prophet. 'Ali's followers accused agents of Damascus of poisoning Husayn's older brother, Hasan. Having taken refuge in Mecca, and refusing to pledge his allegiance to Yazid, Husayn tried instead to make his way to Kufa. But the road was blocked by Umayyad forces, which encircled the rebel heir and seventy of his loyalists in the middle of the desert, and then massacred them in a place called Karbala.

Husayn's martyrdom at Karbala fatally ruptured relations between the majority Sunnis, who considered that Muslim (in the event, Umayyad) rule continued to enjoy legitimacy, and the Shi'a, downcast in the aftermath of this horrible event and despondent at their powerlessness to prevent it. The ensuing and inexorable dissension (fitna) led on to a dreadful cycle of sacrilege: the Umayyads having mutilated the remains of Husayn and his followers, the Shi'a reacted by heaping ritual abuse on the companions—in their eyes, the felons—of the Prophet (saab al-salaf). Each camp proclaimed itself the Messenger of Allah and produced quotations from the Prophet in support of its claim, often the same ones, only now subject to the most varied interpretations.

These troubled times encouraged a disposition toward apocalyptic prophecy. Two hadiths that enjoyed great popularity in Medina during the Umayyad era were used to justify ambitions on both sides. The first, which says "at the end of My community there will be a caliph who will spend money without counting," was cited in defense of every kind of official extravagance and favoritism; but it was also pointed to in bringing charges of corruption against the Damascene dynasty. The second says, "The Hour will not come until a man from Qahtan appears and drives the people with his stick."[16] Qahtan had given its name to the ancestor of the Arabs who came from the southern part of the peninsula, in particular the Kalb tribe, pillar of the Umayyad throne. This hadith made it possible to represent the Umayyads both as guardians of the order imposed on the descendants of Qahtan and as harbingers of the chaos that these same descendants would one day sow.

The political and religious landscape became still more complicated in 683, when, in addition to the Shi'i challenge in Iraq, Damascus had to confront a rebellion in Medina led by 'Abd Allah ibn al-Zubayr, grandson of the first caliph, Abu Bakr. Yazid dispatched a powerful army from Syria to suppress the revolt, and the historian al-Tabari relates that Medina was "given over to plunder for three days [and] the blood flowed." But Ibn al-Zubayr and his followers fell back to Mecca, where they were besieged for two months by the Syrian expeditionary corps. Catapults hurled stones and "pots of flaming naphta" onto the Ka'ba—a blasphemy so shocking that it was popularly believed to be the act of "an infidel, an Abyssinian,"[17] himself killed by fire blown back from the burning shrine. The Black Stone was broken into three pieces and the Ka'ba, damaged by the bombardment, resembled "the heaving bosom of a woman in mourning."[18]

The Umayyad troops retreated ingloriously from Mecca, and Ibn al-Zubayr was proclaimed caliph in the "noble sanctuary" or "sacred enclosure" (al-haram al-sharīf) within the city. Although his anti-caliphate exerted little influence outside central Arabia, Ibn al-Zubayr retained control of the holy city for almost ten years. It was only in 692 that Umayyad troops, having finally restored order in Iraq, turned their attention back upon Mecca. The holy city endured a merciless siege of seven months, punctuated by bombardment on a scale that was massive for the time. Abandoned by thousands of his supporters, Ibn al-Zubayr himself was slain while fighting in the vicinity of the Ka'ba. The ferocious combat both around and within Medina, as well as Mecca, inspired many hadiths of a more or less political character;[19]

and the sacrileges committed in the course of this civil war were later to be recast as elements of new apocalyptic episodes.

The Shi'a, for their part, refused to endorse either the caliph in Damascus or the anti-caliph in Mecca, instead proclaiming the supremacy of the Imam (the Leader—literally, "the one who stands [or walks] in front"). This person could only be the "rightly guided" one, the Mahdi, charged by Allah with the task of reestablishing justice on earth and of punishing both infidels and impious Muslims, which is to say members of the opposing Sunni camp. In order to make up for the absence of a pretender to the caliphate, the Shi'i conception of the Imam had to be fortified by the theme of concealment: shut away in an inaccessible mountain stronghold protected by wild beasts, the Mahdi was preparing the day of his return, when he would march from the east beneath black banners and supervise the destruction of the enemies of Islam.[20]

The compensatory value of such assurances only increased with the crushing of the anti-caliph and the suppression of various Shi'i insurrections. By the time of Hisham's caliphate (724–743), Umayyad power seemed to have been durably established. The regime's many opponents had been driven underground, but they had not been rooted out, and after Hisham's death they resumed their subversive activities with renewed vigor, relying on quotations that were conveniently ascribed to the Prophet. One hadith then popular in Kufa claimed: "Members of my family will suffer reverses, banishments, and persecutions until people come from the east with black banners. They will ask for charity, but they will be given nothing. Then they will fight and they will be victorious." At Bassora, another highly political hadith enjoyed great favor: "Three men, one of them the son of a caliph, will fight in front of your treasure house. None of them will gain control over it. Black banners will then be raised from the east. . . . When you see him, pledge him allegiance, even if you must wait in the snow, for it is him, the Mahdi."[21]

Still lacking an uncontested leader, Shi'i propaganda continued to promote the idea of an anonymous imam—the "chosen one of the family of Muhammad" *(al-ridā min āl Muhammad)*. This indecision well suited the designs of a revolutionary of genius, Abu Muslim, who in 747 launched an anti-Umayyad uprising in Khurasan, formerly a satrap of the Sassanid Empire, on the borders of Persia and Afghanistan. Skillfully manipulating apocalyptic symbolism, Abu Muslim marshaled his troops under the dark standards associated with the return of the Mahdi. In less than two years he had seized control of Persia, going on to cross the Tigris and then the Euphrates. His entry into Kufa was celebrated by the

Shi'a as a posthumous victory for Husayn, whose great-grandson Ja'far was nominated for the caliphate. At this moment Abu Muslim showed his true intentions by revealing a prior commitment to the cause, not of the descendants of 'Ali, but of another clan originally from Mecca, the 'Abbasids, kinsmen of the Prophet's uncle.

In 749 Abu'l-'Abbas al-Safah became the first caliph of the new line. The Umayyad family was liquidated; only one of its dignitaries escaped the massacre, taking refuge first in North Africa and then in Spain. But this amounted only to replacing one dynastic principle by another, for Abu'l-'Abbas's half-brother, Abu Ja'far, succeeded him in 754 under the name of al-Mansur ("the Victorious"). During the twenty years of his reign the second 'Abbasid caliph provided a firm and lasting basis for the dynasty's claim to power. He ordered the murder of the overly cunning Abu Muslim and entrusted to his own son, Abu Abdallah, command of the army of Khurasan. Voices of Shi'i dissent were stifled, one after another. To put an end to the endemic unrest in Kufa once and for all, however, al-Mansur in 762 founded a new capital at Baghdad, where he died twelve years later. Scarcely had Abu Abdallah inherited the throne than he moved to exploit the symbolic value of his campaigns in Khurasan, under the black banners of the dynasty, by assuming the name of al-Mahdi. It is significant that the new caliph felt sufficiently sure of his power to adopt a conciliatory policy toward Shi'i notables, with the paradoxical consequence that messianic accounts now came to recognize the legitimacy of 'Abbasid rule.

Complicating this situation further was the apocalyptic dimension associated with Byzantium. A hadith announcing the fall of Constantinople to a caliph bearing the name of a prophet justified three determined expeditions against the Byzantine capital within a half-century. Umayyad forces laid siege to it by both land and sea between 666 and 673, without managing to break the Christian will to resist. In 716, Caliph Sulayman (the Arabic version of Solomon, recognized as a prophet of Islam), having first instructed his eulogists to present him as the saving Mahdi, dispatched his own brother to direct an assault on the city.[22] But Sulayman was forced to order a retreat at the end of a year of unfruitful hostilities. The 'Abbassids had better luck. On seeing enemy troops beneath the walls of Constantinople in 782, Empress Irene quickly agreed to pay tribute to the caliphate in Baghdad. A truce was signed, and the Muslim troops promptly departed.

These military adventures were subsequently placed in an eschatological perspective by means of a hadith listing six harbingers or signs of the Last Hour, five of which had already come to pass: the death of the Prophet Muhammad, the conquest of Jerusalem, a frightful epidemic (identified with the so-called plague of Amwas under 'Umar's caliphate), an abundance of superfluous goods (associated with the corruption and nepotism that were rampant under 'Uthman), and a devastating fitna (corresponding to the Great Dissension brought about by 'Uthman's murder).[23] The final sign was to be the violation by the Byzantines of the truce they had concluded with the Muslims, who would find themselves the target of a massive offensive. The hadith relating these things reflected a fear that the balance of forces, for the moment favorable to Baghdad, would one day tilt to the advantage of Constantinople, potentially the most serious threat to 'Abbasid power, at the northern boundaries of the empire.

Finally, the prophetic sayings inspired by the revolt of the anti-caliph at Mecca between 683 and 692 were belatedly to have great influence. Owing to a complex interplay of positive and negative identifications, the rebel of the holy city, Ibn al-Zubayr, was transformed into an ambiguous mahdi, whereas his adversary, sent from Syria, took on the traits of a mythical figure known as the Sufyani (after the name of a ruling branch of the Umayyads in Damascus). Defamed by both Shi'i and 'Abbasid propagandists as a satanic incarnation, the Sufyani assumed by contrast the aspect of a national hero in Syria, where his legend intermittently galvanized Umayyad resistance to the caliphate of Baghdad.[24] An enigmatic figure of apocalypse, the Sufyani emerged only by extrapolation from hadiths that were themselves bitterly disputed.

All parties during these years of conflict looked to prophetic tradition for inspiration, arguments, and rallying cries.[25] The messianic impulse was prominent in the various uprisings of the seventh and eighth centuries, each side claiming to carry out the purposes of the Mahdi in order to cast its adversaries back into the camp of the devil. The result of these furious polemics, marked by the unrestrained production of quotations from the Prophet and a corresponding stream of suitably biased commentaries, was great doctrinal confusion. The time had come for orthodoxy to provide itself with a set of scriptures less open to challenge.

THE TWO AUTHENTIC COLLECTIONS

Almost two centuries were to pass after the death of Muhammad before a definitive selection was finally made from the immense corpus of traditions attributed to the Prophet. The controlling criterion was the validity of the chain of transmission *(isnād)* of a given saying, which in order to be considered wholly reliable had to reach back, from one chronicler to another, as far as the companions of the Prophet himself. Tens of thousands of hadiths of doubtful provenance were therefore set aside, when they were not actually stigmatized as pure and simple fabrications.

A dozen monumental anthologies were compiled during the second half of the ninth century, while the 'Abbasid caliphate still shone in all its glory in Baghdad. The end of times was generally treated under the rubric of dissension *(fitan,* plural of *fitna),* for quarrels among Muslims, it was believed, must inevitably accompany and precipitate an apocalyptic course of events. The singular form *fitna,* which signifies both discord and unrest or insurrection, refers not only to the great schism in Islam between Sunnis and Shi'a, but also to any of the episodes of armed combat that unfolded from the time of the Patriarchal Caliphate until the consolidation of 'Abbasid rule. To the custodians of the prophetic heritage, dissension in all these related senses stood out as the direst threat facing Islam.

The two most respected collections of hadiths, each titled *Al-Sahīh* ("Authentic" or "Genuine"), are the work of a pair of Persians who had been Arabized by long stays in 'Abbasid Iraq, Arabia, and Egypt: Muhammad ibn Isma'il al-Bukhari, born in Bukhara in 809 and buried near Samarkand in 870; and Abu al-Husayn Muslim, born in 816 at Nishapur, where he passed away some sixty years later, having completed an equally heroic labor of recension. Bukhari claimed to have seen himself in a dream fanning the Prophet and driving away the flies that disturbed his peace of mind. From this Bukhari concluded that henceforth his duty was tirelessly to chase away the lies that disfigured prophetic tradition. Of the hundreds of thousands of hadiths he had collected, only one in every hundred met the tests of authenticity. Muslim was no less rigorous in his selection.[26]

Bukhari reports the solemn warnings of Muhammad to his followers: "When I will no longer be here, do not go back to idolatry, and do not kill each other."[27] The direction from which the final catastrophe shall come is known, for "the Messenger of Allah has said, his face turned toward the east: 'Is the insurrection not here, from the side where the horn of the devil appears?'" Contemplating Medina, the Prophet uttered this premonition: "I see dissension falling among your dwellings as does the rain."[28]

According to Bukhari, again, the Prophet preached neutrality—indeed, passivity—as the antidote to the enmity among Muslims: "There will be troubles. Whoever remains seated will be more worthy than he who stands up. Whoever stands up will be more worthy than he who marches [into battle], whoever marches will be more worthy than he who incites others [to violence]. Whoever lays himself open to [these temptations] will perish. May whoever is able to find asylum or shelter take refuge in it. . . . Every time two armed Muslims come to blows, both will go to hell." But everything will go from bad to worse until the advent of the Hour: "They will be the worst of men who are alive when the Last Hour comes. . . . You will have no time that will not be followed by another that is worse until you meet your Lord."[29]

A famous hadith intimately links the worsening of unrest with the end of the world:

The Last Hour will not arrive before two figures come to blows and a great struggle takes place between them; both will preach the same thing. It will not arrive until some thirty false messiahs appear, all of them pretending to be the messenger of Allah. It will not arrive until [religious] knowledge has disappeared, until unrest has spread, until the length of a day is near unto the length of a night, until the unrest is manifest and until murder [herj] has become frequent. It will not arrive until wealth, which has become so great among you, grows greater still, so that no one can any longer be found who will accept alms. Whomever is offered alms will say to the one who has offered them: I do not need any. It will not arrive until people build buildings that are too high and until whoever passes by a tomb says: I wish to Allah that I were in the place of the one buried here.[30]

This hadith predicts the sudden appearance of false messiahs—literally, "charlatans" or "imposters" (dajjāl; pl. dajjālūn). But the harm they will cause is as nothing compared to that which will be done by one of them, the Antichrist (ad-Dajjāl), who contends with Jesus for the title of Messiah (al-Masīh): "The Antichrist will make his camp at a place near Medina. The city will tremble three times, and after that the infidels and hypocrites will go out [of Medina] to the Antichrist." Fortunately, "Medina will not have to dread the terror inspired by the Antichrist messiah, for that day it will have seven gates, each one guarded by two angels." Carrying with him "a mountain of bread and a river of water," the Antichrist "will be blind in the right eye, like a grape protruding from the socket," and between this blind eye and his good eye will be "written the word: infidel [kāfir]."[31]

Bukhari ratifies the prediction of other apocalyptic signs, for they too come from the mouth of the Prophet: "The Last Hour will not arrive until a fire shoots up from the land of Hijaz. The glow from this fire will throw light on the necks of camels as far as Bassora,"[32] in the south of Syria; that is, a supernatural fire rising from the shores of the Red Sea and illuminating a good part of the Middle East. The moment is also near "when the Euphrates will [part to] reveal heaps of gold. Whoever will be present [at that moment] should take only a small amount." But the greatest catastrophe, in Bukhari's account, will be the rupture of the barrier that holds back Gog and Magog. These accursed peoples will rush forth and break like a wave over the "wretched Arabs," who face annihilation despite the virtue of the faithful in their midst, for "the iniquities will have become too many."[33]

The fifty-second book ("Book of Dissension and Portents of the Hour") of Muslim's *Sahīh* devotes 143 hadiths to the last days of the world. For the most part Muslim concurs in the apocalyptic traditions approved by Bukhari. But he expands the chronology of the major signs *(ayāt)* and portents of the Hour, organizing them in a sequence of ten events. First there will be three entombments *(khasf)*, which is to say three places—in the east, in the west, and in the Arabian Peninsula—where the earth will open up and people will be buried alive. These events will be followed by the appearance of smoke, and then of the Antichrist. The Beast will then crawl out of the earth, followed by Gog and Magog, who will break through the wall that isolates them from the civilized world and run wild. The three last signs will be the rising of the sun in the west, the supernatural fire originating in Yemen, and finally the gathering together of humanity, driven by the fire to the place of the Final Judgment.[34]

The figure of the Antichrist, the subject of only a handful of hadiths in Bukhari's *Sahīh*, acquires considerably greater stature in Muslim's compilation. There the Dajjāl is intent on making the confusion of the faithful more acute by transposing the usual properties of water and fire: "When the Antichrist will appear, he will have alongside him water and fire. What people take to be water will in truth be blazing fire, and what they take to be fire will in truth be cool and pure water." The Antichrist will be "followed by seventy thousand Jews from Isfahan," whose heads will be covered by a veil *(taylassan)* made from a kind of satin found in Persia. Throughout the whole of human history, from Adam until the resurrection, no thing or person will have caused greater turmoil than the Antichrist.[35] Muslim also confirms a detailed hadith concerning the Dajjāl's repudiation by a follower of Muhammad:

> On seeing him the believer hastened to alert those around him: "O people, this is none other than the Antichrist against whom the Prophet has warned

us." The Antichrist will then order [the people] to throw him down on the ground and strike him with blows on his back, after which he will say [to the believer]: "Do you not therefore believe in me?" [The believer] will reply to him: "You are only a blind imposter." The Antichrist will then order [the believer] to be cut in two with a saw and he will walk between the two parts, and then he will say: "Stand." The believer will then stand upright. The Antichrist will say to him: "Do you not therefore believe in me?" The believer will say: "I am only more sure of your deceitfulness," and then tell those around him: "After this he shall no longer be able to perform such a trick with others." The Antichrist will then take hold of [the believer] and try to strangle him, but his neck will be protected by [a] lead [collar] and [the Antichrist] will not be able to achieve his purpose. He will then take hold of [the believer] by the hands and feet and throw him [into the air]. The people will believe that he has been cast into Hell, whereas in truth he will have been hurled up into Paradise.[36]

According to Muslim, the Antichrist will dominate for "forty days, forty months, and forty years" before he meets up with Jesus. In these troubled times, "the Byzantines [Rūm] will be the most numerous of men," whereas the Arabs, caught unawares first by the Christian menace, and then by the Antichrist, will be "very few."[37] Their apocalyptic combat occurs as part of an involved sequence of events in which the Byzantines will threaten the Muslims at one of two places in the north of Syria before finally losing Constantinople:

> The Last Hour will not come until the Byzantines attack A'amaq or Dabiq. A Muslim army consisting of some of the best men on earth at this time will be sent from Medina to thwart them. Once the two armies come face to face with each other, the Byzantines will cry out: "Let us fight our brethren who have converted to Islam." The Muslims will respond: "By Allah, we will never let our brothers fall." Then the battle will be joined. A third part of the [Muslim] army will admit defeat; Allah will never forgive them. A third will die; they will be excellent martyrs in the eyes of Allah. And a third will conquer: they will never have been tested and they will [go on to] conquer Constantinople. Then, when they will have hung their swords on the olive trees and divided up the spoils, the devil will falsely spread this word among them: "The Antichrist has taken your place in your homes." They will then hasten to leave and, once arrived in Syria [Shām], the Antichrist will come out. The Muslim soldiers will then prepare themselves to do battle against him and draw up their ranks.[38]

The Muslims will be able to ward off the spells of the Antichrist by reciting chapter 18 of the Qur'an ("The Cave").[39] The scene will have been set for the apocalyptic clash:

Then Allah will send the Messiah, son of Mary, who will descend [from heaven] to the white minaret on the east side of Damascus, wearing two saffron-colored garments and placing his hands on the wings of two angels. When he lowers his head, beads of perspiration will fall from it, and when he raises it, beads like pearls will flow from it. Death will strike every infidel who breathes the odor of the Messiah, and [Jesus's] breath will extend as far as he can see. Jesus will search for the Antichrist until [he reaches] the gate of Ludd, where he will kill [the Antichrist].[40]

Ludd is the Arabic name for Lod, in Palestine, where Saint George, one of the principal figures of Eastern Christianity, was laid to rest, having been martyred in 303. A veritable cult grew up around his remains, and his victory over the dragon came to be regularly celebrated. In addition to this popular veneration, ancient Jewish traditions of the False Messiah persisted as well. During the Islamic conquest of Lod in 636, a Jew of that city is said to have predicted to Caliph ʿUmar the murder of the Antichrist "a bit more than ten cubits from the gate of Lod."[41] Since then, scholars have emphasized the role played by Jewish and Christian influences in the emergence of Lod in Islamic eschatology as the place where the Antichrist meets his death at the hands of Jesus.

The execution of the Antichrist is accompanied by the extermination of all those Jews who have persevered in impiety rather than convert to Islam: "The Last Hour will not come until the Muslims fight against the Jews and kill them. And when a Jew will hide behind a [stone] wall or a tree, the wall or tree will cry out: "O Muslim! O servant of Allah! There is a Jew behind me." And [the Muslim] will come to kill him. Only the *gharqad* [will remain silent], for it is the tree of the Jews."[42] This supernatural intervention of minerals and plants to eliminate any Jewish presence made a considerable impression in the Islamic world. The "tree" mentioned in the hadith is a thorny bush native to the region of Jerusalem,[43] inseparably linked in the popular mind with the notion of Jewish resilience.

Having achieved total victory over the Antichrist and his allies, Jesus will comfort the surviving and sorely tested Muslims. He will lead them into the calm haven of Tur *[al-Tūr]*. The word *Tūr*'s general meaning— "mountain"—has given rise to scholarly disagreement over the location of the refuge chosen by Jesus for the Muslims. The most widely shared view today places it atop the Mount of Olives *(Tūr Zayta)*, on the east side of Jerusalem, though Mount Thabor *(Jabal al-Tūr)*, near the Sea of Galilee, and Mount Gerizim *(al-Tūr)*, to the south of Nablus, are also considered. Other commentators lean toward Mount Sinai, which indeed is twice associated with "al-Tūr" in the Qur'an itself.[44] However this may be, it is clear that such a sanctuary was supposed to be essential in preserving the Muslims from the new apocalyptic catastrophe. For "Allah will then send Gog and Magog, who will swarm down from every slope"[45] and drain Lake Tiberias to slake their monstrous thirst. Gog and Magog will next lay siege to the Messiah and his followers, who have taken refuge atop Tur:

> Jesus and his companions will beseech Allah and He will send insects to bite the peoples of Gog and Magog in the neck, so that in the morning they will all be dead. Jesus and his companions will come down [from the mountain] and will find every corner and recess of the earth filled with the stench of their putrefaction. They will pray again to Allah, who will send birds that resemble the necks of camels. [These birds] will snatch up the bodies of Gog and Magog and throw them where Allah wishes. Allah will send rains that no house or tent can keep out and in this way the earth will be washed so thoroughly it will look like a mirror.[46]

Syria is classically spoken of as the "land of *Shām*," a phrase that refers both to Syria in the broad historical sense (including Palestine and Lebanon) and to its capital, Damascus. Muslim's *Sahīh* assigns great importance to the region as a whole. Target of the Byzantine offensive, base for the counterattack on Constantinople, theater of the struggle between Jesus and the Antichrist, and the scene of devastation by Gog and Magog, ancient Syria is central to this apocalyptic account. The Antichrist, in particular, "will appear somewhere between Syria *[Shām]* and Iraq, before spreading terror on all sides," and Jesus "will come down to the white minaret on the east side of Damascus *[Dimashq]*."[47]

Finally, Muslim accepts a structurally complex hadith in which the Prophet endorses the account given by a convert to Islam named Tamim al-Dari, from Hebron, of an extraordinary encounter with the Antichrist.[48] Tamim relates that, while still a Christian, he had set out to sea with thirty other merchants. A violent storm stranded their ship on an island. There Tamim and his companions found an astonishingly hairy creature, who introduced himself to them as "the Spy" *(al-jassāsa)* and bade them to go to see a huge man, whom they found in chains. This was the Antichrist, who questioned them about Muhammad's victory over the people of Mecca and foretold that Lake Tiberias would soon dry up. The Antichrist added that he himself would travel throughout their land for forty nights, but that he could not enter either Mecca or Medina. According to Muslim, the Prophet cited this account as proof of the inviolability of the two holy cities in the face of the Antichrist—all the more since the evaporation of Lake Tiberias confirmed other forecasts regarding Gog and Magog. The great popularity enjoyed by this hadith for its colorful descriptions of the Spy and the Antichrist made it a founding myth for the Tamimi, one of the leading families of Hebron.[49]

As not only the Islamic archetype of the converted Christian, but also as a vehicle for transmitting eschatological traditions, Tamim al-Dari is a fascinating figure. A native of Palestine, he was one of the great travelers of the period, on both land and sea, and sold wine (among other things) before embracing Islam. Tamim became a companion of the Prophet (even though the other members of his family remained Christians and paid the capitation tax that fell upon *dhimmi*), and, having had regular commercial contacts with Mecca following his conversion, transferred the base of his activities to Medina after Muhammad's migration there, known as the Hegira *(hijra)*. Muhammad's unqualified approval of the "hadith of the Spy" is exceptional for revealing the profound influence of a defector who was reputed also to have introduced two incontestably Christian innovations—oil lamps and, still more notably, the pulpit *(minbar)*—in the Prophet's own mosque in Medina, where they were Islamized.[50]

Alongside certain elements already found in the Qur'an (the Smoke, the Beast, Gog and Magog), both Bukhari's and Muslim's collections incorporated new supernatural phenomena, such as tremors that open up the earth and bring widespread destruction, the rising of the sun in the west, and a fire covering the entire Arabian Peninsula. But most striking of all is the figure of the Antichrist, absent from the Qur'an, who emerged only in the two centuries that followed the death of the Prophet—and this on the authority of the most respected Islamic sources.[51] The similarity with Christian tradition is especially intriguing, considering the absence of the Antichrist from the Book of Revelation, on the one hand, and his mention in the two epistles attributed to John and his popularization in the second and third centuries by Tertullian, Irenaeus, and Origen.[52]

TRADITIONS AND VALIDATIONS

A relatively detailed examination of the apocalyptic tradition literature can hardly be avoided if we are to understand the debates within Islam, past and present, over the end of the world. The two anthologies of authentic hadiths compiled by Muslim and Bukhari have been continually cited in the interval, from medieval commentaries to modern-day pamphlets. Despite the lack of any mention of the Dajjāl in the Qur'an, the uncontested authority of these two arbiters guaranteed the Antichrist and his death at the hands of Jesus, Allah's messenger, a pivotal place in apocalyptic narratives, further emphasized by contemporary commentators on prophetic tradition.

The jurist Nu'aym ibn Hammad (771–843) was one of the first to specialize in the critical analysis of the hadith literature. Born in Khurasan, at Merv, Ibn Hammad became Arabized over the course of a long and itinerant apprenticeship that finally took him to Egypt. Toward the end of his life, under the caliphate of al-Mu'tasim (833–842), his support for the doctrine of the uncreated Qur'an (according to which the Word of Allah has always existed) brought him into conflict with the reigning orthodoxy. Transferred to Iraq, he was forced to submit to interrogation and finally imprisoned in Samarra, where he died while still in custody. His *Kitāb al-fitan* (Book of Dissension), written during the period of al-Mu'tasim's rule, is nonetheless characterized by a profoundly quietist messianism,[53] notable above all for the importance it attaches to traditions concerning the Sufyani and for its unalterable animosity toward this figure, reviled as an agent of Umayyad subversion. At a time when an independent base of Umayyad power was being consolidated in Andalusia, Ibn Hammad sought to heighten popular anxieties over the prospect of a Berber insurrection originating in the west and advancing eastward behind a line of yellow standards. His work can therefore be seen as a distinctive form of apocalyptic legitimism, though this did not spare him an ignominious death in the shadow of the 'Abbassid caliphate.

Ibn Hammad was not alone in advocating the doctrine of the uncreated Qur'an. Despite threats of official sanction, the most conservative of the four canonical schools of Sunni Islam, founded by Ahmad ibn Hanbal (780–855), relentlessly defended it as well. The steadfastness of the Hanbali school in the face of state repression and its ultimate triumph over more liberal factions made Ibn Hanbal a major figure of fundamentalist Islam; indeed the rise of Saudi Wahhabism in recent times has owed much to Hanbali dogma. But Ibn Hanbal was also the compiler of a collection *(musnad)* of traditions that remains among the most respected anthologies. It lays stress, in particular, on the religious and moral decadence that will announce the arrival of the Hour, marked by the reign of ignorance, fornication, and drunkenness.[54]

Ibn Hanbal also assigned an important place to the Antichrist, who would be mounted on an ass in his journeys.[55] Despite all the blasphemers and hypocrites who follow him, the Antichrist will succumb in the end to Jesus. Ibn Hanbal located the place of his death not at Lod, however, but at Aqabat Afiq, a mountain pass near Lake Tiberias, in the Golan Heights, through which the Antichrist will travel in going from Damascus to Jerusalem: "The Antichrist will roam the earth as far as Medina, but he will not be permitted to enter [that city]. . . . From there he will roam until he reaches the country of Shām. Jesus will then descend and by his hand Allah will kill the Antichrist near Aqabat Afiq."[56]

Abu Dawud (817–889), one of the most zealous disciples of Ibn Hanbal, to whom he dedicated his own collection of oral traditions, the *Kitāb al-Sunan*, claimed to have selected its 4,800 hadiths from an initial corpus of a half-million.[57] This was not enough, however, to silence recurrent complaints that his method was unrigorous. Thus, for example, Abu Dawud validated a controversial account that bore unmistakable evidence of the conflicts of the Umayyad era:

> A disagreement will occur with the death of a caliph. An inhabitant of Medina will flee his city toward Mecca. People from Mecca will go out to find him and make him rebel against his will. They will put him under oath between the corner [rukn] of the Ka'ba and the Station [maqām] of Abraham. An expedition will be dispatched against him from Syria, but it will be buried in the desert, between Mecca and Medina. When people see that, the righteous of Syria will come to him, as well as groups of Iraqis, to pledge their allegiance to him. Next there will appear a man from the Quraysh [tribe], whose maternal uncles belong to the Kalb [tribe]. He will send an expedition against them, but it will be vanquished. This will be the expedition of the Kalb, and disappointment will overcome those who do not share in their spoils. Next he will distribute money and treat the people in conformity with customary behavior [sunna]. He will firmly establish Islam on earth. He will stay for seven years, then he will die, and the Muslims will pray at his grave.[58]

This hadith became widely known in Iraq in the aftermath of the anti-Caliph revolt in Mecca of 683–692. Its first part recycles certain typical features of such accounts: a quarrel over the very legitimacy of the caliphate, flight of the rebel from Medina to Mecca, a futile expedition ordered by the Umayyads (a branch of the Quraysh tribe linked by marriage to the Kalb tribe), and so on. But the same hadith at the end conflates the rebel and the reformer, without the name of the Mahdi ever being mentioned. Perhaps owing to its confusion of rebellion with restoration, this tradition became one of the most popular of the messianic style, and its validation by Abu Dawud severed the link to memories of the tragic uprising of Mecca. The same process is at work in Abu Dawud's *Kitāb al-mahdī* (Book of the Mahdi), which upholds another hadith having its origins in the Umayyad wars. According to this proph-ecy, the Mahdi would be named Muhammad ibn Abdallah (Muham-mad, son of Abdallah), like the Prophet himself.[59]

Apocalyptic exegesis owes a very particular debt to the great histo-rian Abu Ja'far Muhammad ibn Jarir al-Tabari, who was born in the Persian town of Amol in 839 and died in Baghdad in 923. By the age of seven Tabari had learned the whole of the Qur'an by heart. In addi-tion to the unrivaled influence exerted by his monumental *Kitāb ta'rīkh al-rusul wa-al-mulūk* (History of Prophets and Kings), the dogmatic and normative deductions contained in his commentary *(tafsīr)* on the Qur'an, thousands of pages long, continue to stimulate contemporary scholarship. Tabari also sought to renew the study of oral traditions in a work titled *Tahdhib al-athār* (Classification of Transmitted Reports). Unfortunately left unfinished at his death, it not only classified prophetic utterances according to their chain of transmission, but also scrutinized their philological and juridical implications—a striking departure from the restrained and deferential method observed by the two *Sahīh* com-pilations and the *Musnad*.[60]

In his analysis of apocalyptic accounts, Tabari lays particular empha-sis on the Beast, mentioned only in passing in the Qur'an, and finds grounds for authenticating the hadith in which it is foretold that the Beast will emerge from Safa, one of the two hills of Mecca, notwith-standing that Jesus and the Muslims will have already made the ritual seven turns *(tawāf)* around the Ka'ba. The ears of the Beast, Tabari says, will be no less hirsute than the crown of its head. Nor will anyone be able to escape the Beast (who, he adds, will speak Arabic). It will divide people into two groups, causing the visages of believers to shine like stars while stigmatizing the foreheads of the ungodly with the black mark of infamy. Not content to "make men ashamed of their impiety and their hypocrisy," the Beast will itself bear the sign of universal death, which the imam of the mosque of Mecca will eventually recognize. Tra-ditionists who came after Tabari embellished his picture of the Beast by adding to it the rod of Moses (used to pick out believers) as well as the seal of Solomon (for branding infidels).[61]

Abu Bakr Muhammad ibn Hibban (884–965) was raised in an Arab family in the southern part of Afghanistan. Although his reputation as a scholar hardly matched that of Tabari, he nonetheless traveled as far as Egypt to collect and validate prophetic reports. From these Ibn Hibban drew his own *Sahīh*, the eighth book of which treats the last days of the world and reverses the chronology of the ten major signs: the rising of the sun in the west now opens the cycle, followed by the arrival of the Antichrist (against the backdrop of fighting between Muslims and Byzantines),[62] the Smoke, the return of Jesus, the appearance of the Beast, the sudden resurgence of Gog and Magog, the earth's three swallowings of humanity, and, ultimately, the Fire. The Antichrist, Ibn Hibban adds, will emerge from an island (not from Khurasan) and only Mecca and Medina will escape ruin, thanks to the intervention of angels who will defend the two holy cities.[63]

THE SOURCES OF SHI'I MESSIANISM

Whereas Sunni orthodoxy established a scriptural canon concerned with the habits and religious practice *(sunna)* of the Prophet during the third century of Islam, the terms of Shi'i dissidence were thrashed out in quarrels over legitimacy among the various descendants of 'Ali. The acceptance of the 'Abbassid caliphate by the sixth imam, Ja'far al-Sadiq, notwithstanding that he was Husayn's great-grandson, intensified the confusion surrounding an already mystical genealogy, with a schismatic minority holding that only Ja'far's son, Isma'il, could be revered as the next imam. For many years to come the Isma'ili challenge to Shi'i orthodoxy was able to further its cause only by clandestine means.

Legitimist Shi'ism, for its part, continued to issue pronouncements in the matter of imamate lineage. To 'Ali, the first imam, it attributed a "Sermon of the Great Declaration" *(khutba al-bayān)* having prophetic overtones: "I am the sign of the Almighty. I am the gnosis of the mysteries. I am the threshold of thresholds. I am the companion of the radiance of the divine majesty. I am the first and the last, the manifest and the hidden. I am the face of Allah and I am his mirror."[64] The succession of Shi'i imams, inaugurated by 'Ali, was carried on by his sons Hasan and Husayn. Husayn's younger son, 'Ali, was venerated as the fourth imam under the title of Zayn al-'Abidin ("Adornment of the Worshipers" [of Allah]), and his own son, Muhammad, bore as fifth imam the title of Baqir al-Ilm ("Source of Knowledge"). Ja'far was revered as the sixth imam, and his refusal to claim the caliphate for himself was elevated into a model of integrity—whence his epithet al-Sadiq ("The Truthful").

The last three imams lived and died in Medina, but the 'Abbasids preferred to have greater control over their descendants. Indeed the seventh imam, Musa al-Kazim ("The One Who Swallows His Anger"), earned a reputation for forbearance by uncomplainingly submitting to the will of Caliph Harun al-Rashid. Musa's son and successor

'Ali, styled al-Rida ("The Chosen One"), was buried next to Harun al-Rashid in northeastern Iran, where a city of pilgrimage, Mashhad, sprang up around their tombs.

'Ali al-Rida's son, Muhammad, became the ninth imam under the epithets al-Jawad ("The Generous") and al-Taqi ("The Respectful" [of Allah]). He was laid to rest next to his grandfather in Baghdad. The two imams who came after him lived on the margins of the 'Abbassid court, installed in the caliphate's new capital, Samarra, north of Baghdad: 'Ali, the tenth, called al-Hadi ("The Guide"), and his son Hasan, the eleventh, known as al-Askari since his life was confined to the military camp *('askar)* of the Commander of the Faithful. Hasan al-Askari died without issue in 873, or so it appeared. According to his followers, however, he had left behind in a closely guarded hiding place a four-year-old son, Muhammad.[65]

Although the boy Muhammad was thereafter venerated as the twelfth imam, only a handful of initiates were allowed to have contact with him. Charged in the first instance with protecting a vulnerable minor, over time they became the exclusive interpreters of the doctrine of the Hidden Imam *(al-madhī al-ghā'ibh)* for the rest of the faithful. This was the period of the Lesser Occultation *(al-ghayba al-sughrā)*, during which Muhammad received the attributes of the Mahdi and communicated with his followers through a series of four "ambassadors" *(sufarā)*. In 941 the last of these agents (or "mediators") declared that the Hidden Imam, now reckoned to be seventy-two years of age, had resolved to sever his remaining ties with the world and to disappear from it completely: "Henceforth this is the business of Allah alone."[66] Thus began the Great Occultation *(al-ghayba al-kubrā)*, in whose shadow Shi'ism has lived until the present day.

The Hidden Imam had now become the Awaited Mahdi *(al-mahdī al-muntazar)*, yet his continuing physical absence prevented neither his radiant beauty nor his long black hair and dark beard from being described. One day, it was believed, the Mahdi would manifest himself as the Master of the Age *(al-sāhib al-zamān)*, and his return would mark the end of the cycle of creation. But the Mahdi is also the Master of the Sword *(al-sāhib al-sey)*, for he will mercilessly punish the enemies of Islam. This dual conception integrated the residual elements of three centuries of millenarian anxiety, dramatized by means of the theme of occultation, which emerged during the darkest times of Umayyad oppression. But it was only in the course of the tenth century that this view achieved precedence over other interpretations of the imamate and that the expression "Twelver Shi'ism" (referring to the belief in a sacred line of twelve imams) came into common use.[67]

Shi'i theologians themselves insisted on the connection between this sacralization and the mystical aura of the number twelve in the Judeo-Christian tradition (the twelve tribes of Israel, the twelve apostles of Jesus, and, in the Book of Revelation, the twelve gates of the New Jerusalem). The refulgent brilliance of Creation, they held, was divided into twelve lights corresponding to the twelve imams as well as to the twelve houses of the zodiac, the twelve months of the year, and the twelve hours of the day and night.[68] Additionally, as the French scholar of Islam Henry Corbin has pointed out, this enumeration also agrees with the twelve millennia of Zoroastrian cosmogony.[69]

In order to saturate the suspended time of this Great Occultation, Shi'i theologians endorsed a saying of the Prophet previously validated by Sunni tradition: "If the world had only one day of existence left to it, Allah would prolong this day until there appears a man descended from me, whose name will be my name, and whose surname my surname. He will fill the world with harmony and justice, just as it will have been filled until then with violence and oppression."[70] In Shi'i dogma the Great Occultation corresponds to this day, which will not come to an end until the Mahdi returns.

An attempt was therefore made to draw up an encyclopedic inventory of the sayings attributed not only to the Prophet, but also to each of the twelve imams. Like the Sunni interpreters of oral tradition of the previous century, Shi'i exegetes performed a colossal labor of selection and commentary. In Baghdad, Shaykh Muhammad ibn al-Nu'man earned the epithet al-Mufid ("The One Who Instructs") for a collection of validated quotations called *Kitāb al-irshād* (Book of Guidance). Moreover, his receipt of a personal letter from the Hidden Imam, proof of the trust placed in him by the Mahdi at the height of his occultation, conferred exceptional authority on the shaykh's compilation.[71] From 1017 until his death in 1022 Shaykh Mufid trained Muhammad ibn al-Hasan at-Tusi, later known as Shaykh at-Tusi and perhaps the most important author of Twelver Shi'ism, who published in his turn *Tahdhīb al-ahkām* (The Rectification of Judgments), one of the four canonical Imami hadith collections.

In the meantime the city of Kufa, cradle of Arab Shi'ism, had gained in prestige from its proximity to Najaf and the tomb of the first of the imams, the incomparable 'Ali. Husayn, the martyred imam, had been laid to rest in Karbala, the other holy city of Iraq. Shi'ism also put down deep roots in the Iranian city of Qum through the work of emigrés from Kufa who became Persianized in the course of their stay there, and subsequently enjoyed great popularity throughout the Iranian high plateau, where jurists composed treatises in Arabic with the purpose of refuting extreme deviations from orthodoxy *(ghulāt)* associated with the influence of anti-Islamic, Zoroastrian, and gnostic doctrines.

Under the direction of Shaykh Mufid, in particular, the Shi'i apocalyptic account acquired greater detail and assurance.[72] The return of the Mahdi is to be preceded by a series of cataclysms, including eclipses in the midst of Ramadan and ravaging swarms of locusts. The Euphrates will then overflow its banks and rise in the streets of Kufa, where the wall of the great mosque will crumble. A rain of reddish fire will fall on Baghdad and Kufa. Syria will be laid waste by fighting between Arab rebels from Egypt, cavalrymen stationed in Al-Hira, and the troops who will suddenly have come out of Khurasan beneath black banners. The Turks will occupy the middle valley of the Euphrates (the Jazira), while the Byzantines will attack the Palestinian city of Ramla (not far from Lod). As in the Sunni traditions, the sun will rise in the west, the infidels will seem to triumph, and the chaos will be aggravated by the appearance of dozens of false messiahs *(dajjālūn)*. Shaykh Mufid adds that a wave of "twenty-four successive storms" will rid Muslims of the miasmas emanating from the epidemics ("the red death and the white death") that are to come in the wake of so much bloody strife.[73]

It is therefore at this moment that the Mahdi will appear in the sacred grounds of Mecca, between the Ka'ba itself and the place *(maqām)* where Abraham stood to contemplate it: "The Shi'a will come to him from the ends of the earth, crowding together in great numbers to pledge him their allegiance."[74] No Shi'i student of prophetic tradition ventured to predict exactly when the occultation would draw to a close, but a consensus grew up around the idea that this moment would fall during an even year of the Islamic calendar, on the anniversary of the massacre of Husayn and his followers (Ashura, the tenth day of the Muslim month of Muharram). On that day the Mahdi will leave Mecca in the company of five thousand angels, with Gabriel on his right and Michael on his left, and go first to Medina, and then to Kufa, where he will massacre "all the hypocrites" and destroy their palaces and mosques. The mausoleums of 'Ali in Najaf and of Husayn in Karbala will then miraculously be linked together by a canal. Finally, after conquering "Constantinople, China, and the mountains of Daylam [south of the Caspian Sea]," the Mahdi will institute a period of the most perfect justice lasting seven or nineteen years, depending on the account, and in this way prepare the world for the Resurrection and the Final Judgment.[75]

In compiling their anthologies, Shi'i traditionists enumerated the "five signs" (al-alamāt al-khams),[76] or apocalyptic heralds, of the Mahdi's appearance: the return of the Sufyani, the Mahdi's sworn enemy, identified with Umayyad tyranny; the rising up against him of the Yemeni, who, as the Mahdi's ally, is implacably opposed to the Sufyani; the Call—not the Qur'anic summons to the Final Judgment, but the heavenly rallying cry of the partisans of the Mahdi[77]—which will be answered by the demoniacal roar of his enemies issuing from the bowels of the earth (this battle of rival exhortations will last for the entire month of Ramadan); the assassination of the Mahdi's messenger, known by the name of the Pure Soul;[78] and the swallowing up (khasf) by the earth, probably between Mecca and Medina, of an army sent out against the Mahdi.[79] This premonitory sequence of five signs proceeds by a terrible dialectic between Satanic successes (the revolt of the Sufyani and the murder of the Pure Soul) and Mahdist victories (the Yemeni's counterattack and the entombment of enemy forces) and against the echoing clamor of the celestial and infernal calls. The apocalyptic scenario of Shi'i tradition therefore rests on a balance of terror that only the sudden appearance of the Mahdi himself can resolve.

The consolidation of Twelver Shi'ism was accompanied by a transfiguration of the return of the Mahdi. In coming back to earth to avenge Husayn and the martyrs of Karbala, the Mahdi will put an end to a cycle of violence inaugurated in 624 by the Prophet Muhammad's first victory, at Badr. Just as Muhammad was joined there by three hundred and thirteen warriors and assisted by a cohort of angels, so the Mahdi will lead an army of three hundred and thirteen faithful, escorted by the same angels that had helped Islam to triumph at Badr.[80] This Mahdi Army (jaysh al-mahdī) will also be an army of wrath (jaysh al-ghadab), for between the Hidden Imam and the Arabs "there will only be the sword."[81] The intensity of anti-Arab feeling in the hadiths that tell of the Mahdi Army's progress is striking.[82] Once again apocalyptic narrative was used to settle very immediate quarrels, against the background of a growing identification of Persian nationalism with Twelver Shi'ism (which was nevertheless to remain a minority faith in Iran until the sixteenth century).

Having embarked upon the conquest of Hijaz, Iraq, Syria, and Egypt, the Mahdi Army will then turn against the Byzantines with the object of taking Constantinople.[83] At this point, with the sudden appearance of the Antichrist and the intervention of Jesus, Shiʻi traditions come into alignment once more with the Sunni apocalyptic calendar. But just the same it is the Mahdi who will set Islam back on the straight and true path from which it had strayed: each of his fighters will carry a sword engraved with "a thousand words, each one of which gives access to a thousand others,"[84] and the Mahdi himself will disclose the twenty-five letters of knowledge that remain secret to this day, only two letters yet being known to humanity.[85] The apocalypse, quite literally, is an act of revelation, an unveiling.

. . .

We are now in a position to briefly characterize the apocalyptic sensibility that took shape in the three centuries following Muhammad's death. The following features are conspicuous:

- The Qur'an has rather little to say about the end of the world, and still less about the omens of the Last Hour, whose prediction and description later came to be based on prophetic reports.
- The apocalyptic narrative was decisively influenced by the conflicts that filled Islam's early years, campaigns of jihad against the Byzantine Empire and recurrent civil wars among Muslims.
- The emergence of this narrative at a time of tumult and violence sharpened the tensions that grew up between Syria (al-Shām), Iraq, and the two holy cities of Mecca and Medina.
- The acts of sacrilege provoked by the uprising of the anti-caliph in Mecca were too numerous and too painful to be accommodated even by a schismatic heritage, and therefore had to be recast as a series of apocalyptic episodes.
- The figure of the Antichrist (Dajjāl), absent from the Qur'an, was authorized by Sunni tradition, and his death at the hands of Jesus located in Palestine.
- Shiʻi tradition, for its part, granted a central place to the Mahdi, an eleventh-generation descendant of the Prophet Muhammad, who triumphs over the combined forces of evil; like the Antichrist, he is nowhere mentioned in the Qur'an.
- The black banners, insignia of the Mahdi on his westward march from Khurasan, were initially associated with the messianic perspective of Shiʻism; later, owing to their reappropriation by

'Abbasid agitators and subsequently by the caliphate in Baghdad, they came to be incorporated in Sunni symbolism as well.

- The final state of the world is a matter on which Sunnism and Shi'ism profoundly disagree, not as it is described in their respective apocalyptic accounts, but for what it implies about the scope and mechanics of human salvation.

- There is an abiding tendency within Islam as a whole to consider widespread impiety as a sign of the end of the world, and to hold that it must precede the ultimate revenge of faith. In much the same way, Shi'i quietism maintains that no temporal power is legitimate so long as the Mahdi remains hidden, and that the human usurpation of divine political authority carries within it the seeds of tyranny. Paradoxically, then, apocalyptic beliefs encourage Muslims to endure the unendurable.

The desire to rehabilitate the fundamental tenets of Islam, shared by both Sunnis and Shi'a, must be examined more closely if we are to make sense of the production of apocalyptic prophecies on the massive scale seen today. More than a simple rereading of ancient texts, it amounts to a reinvention of Islamic tradition by means of a process of selection whose very arbitrariness is claimed to be an incontrovertible proof of authenticity. The fierceness of the faith's original disputes over doctrine was deepened, as we have seen, by the harshness of the world in which an apocalyptic corpus was first assembled. In many respects the modern discovery of the end of the world sees itself as a return to sources, and therefore as requiring the development of two kinds of argument, one concerned with textual justification, the other in support of armed combat. But this discourse has been shaped in its turn by two decisive things: on the one hand, the canons of the great medieval exegetes, and, on the other, the actual experience of messianic insurrection.

CHAPTER 2

Grand Masters
of the Medieval Apocalypse

The Sunni world entered the Middle Ages with a developed and validated body of apocalyptic doctrine that appeared to leave little room for either informed speculation or fantastical departures from orthodoxy. With the approach of each new century of Islam, of course, millenarian passions—accompanied by messianic condemnation of the ambient corruption of the age—became intensified. But above all, the general sense of anxiety was nourished by infidel aggression. The Crusades that gave Christians possession of Toledo in 1085, and of Jerusalem in 1099, were thought to constitute the Byzantine offensive that had been promised to occur at the end of times. The Mongol invasion that later descended upon Baghdad, in 1258, was identified with the cataclysmic resurgence of Gog and Magog, predicted to come from the east as well.

Five authors stand out among the mass of writers during the medieval period by virtue of the depth and the originality of their eschatological vision. What is more, their command of prophetic traditions and mastery of the science of hadith allowed them to mark out the landscape of the end of the world with enduring authority. Two of these masters, Ibn 'Arabi and al-Qurtubi, were Andalusians exiled in the East; another, Ibn Khaldun, wandered the lands of Islam in every direction, finally encountering Timur (Tamerlane) beneath the walls of Damascus. Ibn Kathir, a native of Syria, and al-Suyuti, an Egyptian, were less adventurous, though this did not prevent their prestige from extending far beyond the Levant. The apocalyptic thought of all these thinkers was enriched and fortified by encyclopedic learning. Coming after the founders of the prophetic tradition of the Islamic faith, they heralded an era of interpretation.

THE MYSTICAL APOCALYPSE OF IBN 'ARABI

Muhyi ad-Din ibn al-'Arabi (1165–1240) is unquestionably the most celebrated of all the mystics of Islam. Born in Murcia, he acquired a sound basic training in theology in Seville, completed by further study with the foremost teachers of Andalusia and the Maghrib from 1194 to 1201. But it was in the East that his reputation was destined to grow. Friend of princes and dervishes alike, he lived in Arabia, Egypt, Iraq, and Anatolia before settling permanently in Damascus, in 1230. Ibn 'Arabi exalted "the oneness of the world" *(wahdat al-wujūd)* and the primacy of the Word. His rejection of dogma aroused the incomprehension, and indeed the hostility, of religious and legal scholars *('ulama; sing. 'alim)*, but mystics saw in him the power of the legendary "red sulphur" *(al-kibrīt al-ahmar)*, or philosopher's stone. To his admirers he came to be known as "the supreme master" *(al-shaykh al-akbar)*.

Ibn 'Arabi published a condensed version of Bukhari's *Sahīh,* in addition to hundreds of his own books. Surprisingly, perhaps, the works of his youth, imbued with the mysteries and the delights of esotericism, are more impenetrable than those of his maturity. Nowhere is this more true than in his *'Anqā' mughrib fī sifat khatm al-awliyā wa shams al-maghrib* (Astounding Phoenix on the Seal of the Saints and the Sun of the West). The sun referred to in the title may be one of the signs of the Hour, the sun that rises in the west, or else a veiled allusion to the Mahdi. The notion that the Master of the Age would first appear in Islam's westernmost domain enjoyed a special vogue in medieval Andalusia, where the Mahdi was awaited as the "seal of the saints," just as Muhammad had been the "seal of the prophets."

But it was in his major work, the immense *Al-futūhāt al-makkiyya* (Meccan Illuminations), that Ibn 'Arabi extended and refined his thinking about the end of the world. These illuminations comprise six sections, the fourth of which is devoted to the initiatory stages *(manāzil,* literally "dwellings") of the spiritual traveler's journey and divided into 114 chapters. Each chapter corresponds to a sura of the Qur'an. The one on the Mahdi's ministers *(wuzarā,* sometimes translated as "advisors" or "helpers") is associated with sura 18, "The Cave," whose invocation is prescribed for resisting the Antichrist.

Ibn 'Arabi accepts the classical traditions concerning the appearance of the Mahdi in the sacred enclosure of Mecca, which, he adds, the people of Kufa will celebrate with a very special joy. The Mahdi will be followed by "seventy thousand Muslims, all descended from Isaac." Together they will besiege Constantinople, chanting "Allah is great" *(Allāh akbar)*. In Arabic this homage to divine majesty is called *takbīr*. "When they pronounce the first *takbīr* the first third of the ramparts of the city will crumble; during the second, the second third [will crumble], and during the third, all the rest of the ramparts will collapse. They will therefore conquer it without using the sword."[1]

The apocalyptic calendar in Ibn 'Arabi's version is condensed by comparison with some others:

> The conquest of the Byzantine City, which is [to say] mighty Constantinople, the Great Battle *[al-malhama al-uzmā]*, which will provide the occasion for the Feast *[ma'daba]* on the plain of Acre, and the [invasion] of the Antichrist—these events will take place over a period of seven months. Between the fall of Constantinople and the appearance of the Antichrist, eighteen days will elapse. The Antichrist will come from Khurasan, in the East, where the insurrections will take place. He will be followed by the Turks, and the Jews, who will join him at Isfahan, will themselves alone number seventy thousand.[2]

To the Mahdi's seventy thousand Muslim partisans will therefore be opposed an equal number of Jewish warriors. Although this massive confrontation with the forces of the Antichrist (and the ensuing Feast) follow closely on the taking of Constantinople, Ibn 'Arabi gives few further details. Syria retains its central place in the apocalyptic account: Jesus will descend from heaven to the white minaret in Damascus, and the Sufyani will be crushed in the Ghuta, the fertile plain surrounding the city. Ibn 'Arabi does insist, however, on the avenging mission of the Mahdi, "brother of the sword," warning that "whoever refuses to follow him will be executed." This holy violence will be directed not only against the enemies of Islam, but also against the 'ulama, who are blinded by ideological conformism: "They will then reluctantly submit to his authority from a fear of his sword and of his power, and also from a desire to enjoy his favor. The ordinary Muslim will rejoice in his coming more than those who hold an official position."[3]

Ostracized by a part of the religious hierarchy, Ibn 'Arabi took heart in the knowledge that he was held in great respect by the people. His vision of the Mahdi is permeated by this sense of personal frustration at the hands of the 'ulama, and also by the spirit of messianic populism that compensated for it: "When the Mahdi appears, his worst enemies will be the jurists, for they will lose their powers and privileges in relation to the ordinary believers. . . . If he did not possess the sword, the jurists would have sentenced him to death, but Allah will cause him to appear with the sword and nobility. [They] will also submit out of fear and accept his legal opinions, without believing in them, [for] in their heart of hearts these jurists will be convinced that the Mahdi is in error." The Mahdi's ministers are likewise the possessors and protectors of secret knowledge. They will assist the Mahdi in his divine mission among human beings, jinns, and animals. The ministers will not themselves be Arabs, although they will speak only in Arabic, the language of Qur'anic revelation. They will be between five and nine in number, which is to say will be equal to the number of years of the Mahdi's reign.[4]

Ibn 'Arabi attaches special importance to a new episode in the apocalyptic sequence, the Great Battle and the Feast that follows it on the plain of Acre. Whereas Muslim's *Sahīh* mentions the death of a third of the Muslims fighting at Constantinople, Ibn 'Arabi, as we have seen, predicts the fall of the Byzantine capital without any blood being spilled. But it is the Great Battle afterward that will constitute the decisive and merciless clash. Only one of the Mahdi's ministers will survive this carnage "on the plain of Acre, where Allah will set the divine table *[al-ma'ida al-ilāhiyya]* for the vultures and lions."[5]

This emphasis on Acre ('Akka) is almost certainly associated with recent memories of the Crusades. Already a victim of the wars with the Byzantines, Acre was occupied by the Crusaders from 1107 to 1187. Its reconquest by the combined forces of Philip Augustus and Richard the Lionheart in 1191 was accompanied by appalling massacres of the Muslim population. When Ibn 'Arabi was composing the *Illuminations*, the city stood as the last surviving emblem of Christian power in the East under the name of "Saint-Jean d'Acre," itself a tremendous gesture of defiance toward Islam. It was only in 1291, a half-century after Ibn 'Arabi's death, that the Crusaders were finally to be expelled from Acre. Present-day events in the Middle East have given the great Andalusian mystic's apocalypse great historical resonance—all the more since he envisaged the next coming of the Mahdi.[6]

The sacred counterpart in this account to the plain of Acre, where the Mahdi's victory will be celebrated, is the gate of Lod, where Jesus will strike down the Antichrist. We have seen that Lod first acquired eschatological significance from the time of its conquest by Caliph 'Umar in 636. During Ibn 'Arabi's lifetime Lod had remained more or less under the control of the Crusaders, whose fortress-cathedral there was dedicated to Saint George. The apocalyptic triumph of Islam, inaugurated in Damascus, therefore had to be concluded at Lod with the crushing of Evil.

Ibn 'Arabi's refusal to align himself with a particular brotherhood gave him a measure of authority in every branch of Muslim mysticism. Henry Corbin notes the integration of elements of Ibn 'Arabi's thought in Shi'i mysticism, remarking that Iranian theologians have devoted more than a hundred commentaries to his work.[7] In Anatolia his tradition was carried on by the followers of the Persian poet Jalal al-Din Rumi. Western medievalists emphasize the influence of Ibn 'Arabi's apocalyptic vision on the Catalan philosopher Ramón Llull (and indeed on Dante in *The Divine Comedy*),[8] while among Sufi mystics its effect has continued to be felt up to the present day.

AL-QURTUBI AND THE MAHDI OF THE MAGHRIB

Abu 'Abd Allah Muhammad ibn Ahmad al-Ansari al-Khazraji al-Andalusi was born on an unknown date at the beginning of the thirteenth century in Córdoba—whence the name al-Qurtubi (the Cordovan) under which he has passed into history. His family could claim an eminent Arab lineage that went back as far as the Prophet's first helpers *(ansār)* in Medina. Far from being an outsider like Ibn 'Arabi, al-Qurtubi was a cleric and a scholar *('alim)* associated with the Maliki school, dominant in the western lands of Islam.

In 1236, al-Qurtubi suffered the humiliation of seeing his native city reconquered for Christendom by Ferdinand VII of Castille. The loss of Andalusia was gradual, but irreversible, with the fall of Valencia in 1238 and then of Seville ten years later. By the middle of the thirteenth century all that was left to Islam was the Nasrid emirate of Grenada, which protected its independence by multiplying gestures of good will toward the sovereigns of Castille. The Moroccan jihad, which for two centuries had fueled resistance to the *reconquista,* was exhausted as a consequence of its own internecine quarrels: the Almohads, who had supplanted the Almoravids, were now challenged in their turn by the Marinids, to whom they were forced to give up Fez in 1248, the same year that saw the loss of Seville.

It was against the background of these deeply disquieting events that al-Qurtubi, having lived for many years in the East, settled in Upper Egypt and there composed *Tafsīr al-jāmi' li-ahkām al-Qur'ān,* the commentary on the Qur'an that was to make him famous. From this he drew a volume entitled *Al-tadhkira fī ahwāl al-mawtā wa umūr al-ahkīra* (Remembrance of the Affairs of the Dead and Matters of the Hereafter), a synthesis of Islamic eschatology that, in addition to upholding classical doctrines about the Resurrection and the Judgment, contains a quite personal vision of the Last Hour and of its premonitory signs.

Al-Qurtubi accepted the hadiths, earlier attributed to the Prophet by Bukhari and Muslim, that urged neutrality as the least objectionable attitude in the face of dissension among believers.[9] He cites Muslim's *Sahīh* in finding that two Muslims who come to blows are both doomed to hell, no matter what may have been the reason for their disagreement. Yet this warning against the dangers of partisanship scarcely concealed al-Qurtubi's hostility toward the Umayyads: "They contradicted the family of the Prophet, took the female descendants of his family captive, destroyed their dwellings, and spilled their blood. [The Umayyads] therefore contradicted custom [*sunna*] and the testament of the Prophet." Al-Qurtubi showed particular bitterness toward the assassins of Husayn, whose martyrdom he describes in detail.[10]

Despite this undisguised animosity with regard to the Umayyads, al-Qurtubi rejected any suggestion of sympathy for Shi'ism, and presented himself instead as an unwavering supporter of the 'Abbasids. Egypt, during the time he lived there, was the seat of the Mamluks, emancipated military slaves converted to jihad who had welcomed the surviving members of the 'Abbasid caliphate from Baghdad and succeeded in halting the advance of the Mongol hordes in 1260 at Ayn Jalut, in northern Palestine. Al-Qurtubi seems therefore to have felt a typically Sunni reverence toward established authority. But he knew perfectly well that the fall of Andalusia was due to the negligence and corruption of Muslim leaders, and indeed he approved a highly controversial hadith on the duty of rebellion in the face of official overreaching: "When the governor becomes a despot and disregards divine precept and custom [*sunna*], rise up against his authority. To die in the name of Allah is better than to survive in humiliating disobedience to His orders."[11] Apparently taken aback by his own daring, however, al-Qurtubi promptly reverted to his habit of counseling a prudent docility: "The governor will rely upon the Qur'an to vanquish his people and subjugate them, to the point that they are made into slaves. And the reciters of the Qur'an, by obeying the whims of the rulers, encourage them in their despotism. In this case the people must show patience."[12]

For the most part al-Qurtubi adopted prior descriptions of the apocalyptic calendar. He mentions the forecast of Mecca's devastation by
"an Abyssinian," and goes on to argue that this sign of the Hour had
already been manifested during the revolt of the anti-caliph Ibn Zubayr
in the late seventh century. By contrast, however, al-Qurtubi dwells at
some length on the satanic uprising of the Sufyani, who will dispatch
two armies from Damascus: one to Baghdad and Kufa, both of which
will be taken after long and unimaginably brutal fighting; the other to
Medina, which will fall after only three days. This second army of the
Sufyani will nevertheless be struck down on the road to Mecca by divine
intervention, with the fatal result that his soldiers will be swallowed up
by the earth *(khasf)* or else transformed into animals or monsters.[13]

Al-Qurtubi's most original contribution to apocalyptic dramaturgy is
his contention that the Mahdi will emerge in Morocco and pass the first
ten years of his return preaching there. The Mahdi's standards will be
white and yellow, emblazoned with the name of Allah. He will receive
the allegiance of "all the tribes" in Morocco, which is to say eighty thousand mujahedin, and the Muslims of Spain will cry out to him for help.
At that juncture "the combatants will cross the sea and come to Seville,
where the Mahdi will deliver an astonishing sermon, after which he will
be recognized by the faithful of Andalusia as their leader. They will then
set out all together toward the country of the Byzantines, where they
will invade seventy cities and seize control of the Church of Gold."[14]

Al-Qurtubi's hostility toward the Jews, whom Jesus will punish without forgiveness, is particularly virulent:

> Allah has caused them to fall into an ignominious state, which is why, since
> the advent of Islam, they have never raised an army. No longer do they have
> any authority whatsoever on earth, nor any power or dominion. Thus they
> will remain until the end of times, and with the appearance of the Antichrist,
> though he is the worst of sorcerers, they will pledge their allegiance and
> serve in his army in the hope of taking their revenge, through him, against
> the Muslims. At this moment Allah will send down to earth the one whom
> they swear they have killed. . . . Allah will help [Jesus] to triumph and . . . on
> that day there will no longer be any way out left to them; whether they hide
> under a rock or a tree or a wall, the[se] things will cry out: "O Spirit of Allah!
> Here! Here hides an enemy!" Under the yoke of the sword, [the Jew] will be
> commanded to convert or to die.[15]

Al-Qurtubi proceeds to chart an apocalyptic geography in which the
Antichrist suddenly appears in Khurasan and the Mahdi in the Maghrib,
with Jesus descending from the heavens in Damascus to confront the

False Messiah. He asserts, moreover, that the Beast (also called "the Spy") is a hairy monster who, on emerging in Mecca, will mark infidels on their forehead with the seal of Solomon and brighten the visages of believers by brandishing the rod of Moses. The Prophet and his companions, al-Qurtubi claims, though they were "well informed" about future events and the end of the world, "told no one of these things so as not to spread terror among Muslims; they gave voice only to the hadiths that explain the obligations of the faithful."[16]

Despite the impression of humility al-Qurtubi gives, that of a humble commentator who limits himself to collecting bits and pieces of apocalyptic prediction, without purporting to give a complete picture of the end of the world, the striking role he assigns the Mahdi of the Maghrib is plainly a very personal and millenarian response to the loss of Andalusia. The jihad waged by the Almoravids, and then by the Almohads, is transfigured in his account, foretelling the day when the Muslims of Spain will once again be united. Although al-Qurtubi was fated to die in exile in Egypt, in 1272, too soon to have witnessed Islam's revenge in its western domains, Morocco would yet give birth to more mahdis than any other Arab land.

IBN KATHIR AND THE APOCALYPSE OF REVENGE

Imad al-Din Isma'il ibn 'Umar ibn Kathir was born in 1300 in the south of Syria, not far from Basra. He was only six years old when the death of his father obliged the family to settle in Damascus. On reaching adolescence Ibn Kathir entered upon a formal course of religious study and, after becoming acquainted with the doctrines of the various schools of law, committed himself to the body of teaching codified in the ninth century by Ahmad ibn Hanbal. This was the strictest of the four canonical schools of Sunni Islam, as we have seen, affirming the uncreated character of the Qur'an and rejecting the possibility of free interpretation, which placed it in irreconcilable opposition to Shi'ism.

In Damascus Ibn Kathir studied with Taqia al-Din Ahmad ibn Taymiyya (1263–1328), the unrivaled champion of Hanbali literalism. Marked less by the Crusades than by the Mongol invasion, Ibn Taymiyya broadened the ban on Shi'i customs to include any practice that in his view deviated from Sunni orthodoxy, particularly the Sufi cult of holy men. In so doing he laid the foundations for an aggressive and predatory campaign, directed primarily against "bad Muslims," that angered both the 'ulama and the Mamluk government. Imprisoned in the citadel of

Damascus, first in 1321 and then again in 1326, Ibn Taymiyya remained very popular among both clerics and the common people of Syria.

On the death of his teacher, Ibn Kathir devoted himself to historical and exegetical work. His panoramic account of Islam from the earliest times, *Al-Bidāyah wa-al-nihāyah* (The Beginning and the End), was recognized as authoritative, along with his commentary *(tafsīr)* on the Qur'an. In the matter of hadiths, Ibn Kathir enlarged the collection *(musnad)* due to Ibn Hanbal by incorporating the contributions of subsequent students of oral prophecy, and began a treatise on Bukhari's *Sahīh,* left unfinished at his death in 1373. He was buried alongside Ibn Taymiyya, having taught at the Umayyad Mosque in Damascus for the last seven years of his life.

Ibn Kathir's apocalyptic vision was closely allied with the Hanbali anathema that fell upon the vast majority of Muslims. Thus in the *Ashrāt al-sā'at* (Signs of the Hour), for example, he approves a doubtful hadith according to which "the Jews will be divided into seventy-one sects: only one will go to heaven, and seventy to hell. The Christians will be divided into seventy-two sects: seventy-one will go to hell, and only one to heaven. In the name of the One who possesses my soul, my community will be divided into seventy-three sects: only one will go to heaven, and seventy-two to hell."[17] It is true, of course, that traditionists before Ibn Kathir had claimed to authenticate this saying. Even the great mystic Ibn 'Arabi commented on it in the *Tadhkirāt,* and concurred that the Muslims who will be saved will, "despite their number, constitute a single group."[18]

But Ibn Kathir was clearly less tolerant than his predecessors. The Last Hour, he held, will be announced by the corruption of morals in the lands of Islam: "The signs of the Hour are, among others, the disappearance of knowledge and the appearance of ignorance. Adultery will spread and the drinking of wine will become commonplace. The number of men will diminish and that of women will increase, until only one man looks after fifty women." These, however, are only the minor signs of the Hour. The first of the major signs will be the coming of the Mahdi, who is unequivocally distinguished from the Hidden Imam of the Shi'a: the Mahdi, Ibn Kathir says, will appear after the reign of the 'Abbasids; he will be descended from Muhammad by the Prophet's daughter, Fatima; he will emerge "from the east";[19] and it will be in Mecca that believers will pledge him their allegiance.

With the approach of the Last Hour, disputes *(fitan)* among Muslims will assume an apocalyptic dimension. Ibn Kathir lays particular emphasis on the conflicts arising from the discovery of gold in the Euphrates, and in this connection modifies a hadith validated earlier by both Bukhari and Muslim:[20] "The Hour will not come until the Euphrates reveals a mountain of gold that will be fought over. Of one hundred persons who contend for this gold, ninety-nine will die, but each one will say he has a chance of being the one who will survive."[21] The confusion that will reign in the community and in the minds of the faithful is daunting: "Woe to the Arabs for the great evil that will soon come upon them: it will be like the tattered cloak of darkest despair! A man will wake up a believer and by nightfall will have become an unbeliever (kāfir). People will sell their religion for a few earthly goods. Whoever clings to religion that day will resemble one who grasps a burning coal—or a handful of thorns."[22]

Ibn Kathir adopted the idea—widespread, as we have seen, since the eighth century—of an apocalyptic struggle against the Byzantines, who will attempt to seize the initiative by violating the truce they had concluded with the Muslims and lining up in a row "eighty banners, each one followed by twelve thousand men." This vast tide of Christian warriors will nevertheless be overwhelmed by the Muslims, who after giving thanks to Allah and chanting his almighty name (Allāh akbar) will take possession of Constantinople. But whereas Ibn 'Arabi forecast the crumbling of the walls of Constantinople under the force of Muslim invocations alone, Ibn Kathir predicted "very fierce battles."[23] Al-Qurtubi, it will be recalled, had sidestepped this eschatological trap by foreseeing two sieges of Constantinople, one peaceful, the other violent, and both crowned by success.[24]

In Ibn Kathir's apocalyptic scenario, as in that of his predecessors, the conquest of Constantinople opens the way to the sudden appearance of the Antichrist (Dajjāl):

> The Antichrist will be allowed to appear at the end of times after the conquest of Constantinople by the Muslims. He will appear first of all in the Jewish quarter of Isfahan, followed by 70,000 Jews, all armed, as well as 70,000 Tatars and people from Khurasan. At the beginning he will set himself up as a tyrannical king, then he will pretend to be a prophet, and finally a lord. Only the most ignorant men will follow him: upright people and those guided by Allah will turn away from him. He will begin to conquer the world country by country, stronghold by stronghold, region by region, city by city: no place will escape injury, apart from Medina and Mecca. . . . Allah will allow him to perform many miracles, which will lead astray those whom He wishes [to be misled], but which will strengthen the faith of the believers.[25]

The moment now comes in Ibn Kathir's account to summon Jesus:

> He will come down to the [white] minaret on the east side of Damascus. The believers and the true servants of Allah will rally to him. He will bring them within sight of the Antichrist, who will then head off toward Jerusalem [bayt al-maqdis]. Jesus, son of Mary, will overtake him at Aqabat Afiq. The Antichrist will flee, but Jesus will catch up with him outside Lod. [Jesus] will kill him with his spear just when [the Antichrist] tries to get clear of it. [Jesus] will say to him: "You will not be able to escape me; you cannot escape me." Just when the Antichrist is confronted by Jesus, he will begin to dissolve like salt in water. Then Jesus will kill him with his spear at the gate of Lod.[26]

In synthesizing various prophetic reports, Ibn Kathir sometimes finds it necessary to reconcile differing versions of an event. Whereas Ibn Hanbal situates the Antichrist's death at Aqabat Afiq, not far from Lake Tiberias, for example, Ibn Kathir transforms it into a manhunt whose conclusion, at the gate of Lod, nevertheless agrees with the classical narrative. So, too, he amalgamates hadiths in which the Antichrist disappears on being confronted by Jesus with others in which Jesus disembowels him with his spear. This technique enables Ibn Kathir not only to establish a sequence of events calculated to appeal to a broad audience, but also to resolve the contradiction posed by the eschatological centrality of the Antichrist, notwithstanding his absence from the Qur'an: "The Antichrist is not mentioned in the Qur'an because he is very insignificant. He claims to be divine, but he is only a human being. His affairs are not important enough to be mentioned in the Qur'an. The prophets, faithful to Allah, warned their people against the Antichrist, against the dissension he sows and his miraculous duplicities. It is enough for us to be acquainted with the many accounts concerning him."[27]

In Ibn Kathir's version, not only will Jesus kill the Antichrist, he will also win over the last Christians to Islam: "The son of Mary will descend [from heaven] and will be a just leader. He will destroy the cross and kill the swine. Peace will everywhere reign and swords will be used as sickles."[28] As in earlier traditions, Jesus will be the instrument by which all other religions are abolished and the universal reign of Islam inaugurated. He will also be the one who puts an end to the ravages of the "Turkic" peoples known as Gog and Magog,[29] who "will rush down in all directions, sowing corruption, uprooting [crops] and killing people. When Jesus will pray against them, Allah will send a kind of worm in their neck, which will kill all of them."[30] Jesus will next confront "Dhu'l-Suwayqatayn, who will come from Abyssinia and destroy the Ka'ba to steal its treasure."[31] Bald-headed, with short legs (suwayqatayn) and deformed wrists, this vandal will at once set about attacking the sanctuary "with his spade and his pickaxe." But "Allah will send Jesus at the head of a vanguard of seven to eight hundred men. Then they will march toward Dhu'l-Suwayqatayn [and] Allah will send from Yemen a breeze that will delight the soul of each believer. Only the worst men will be left and they will begin to copulate like animals."[32]

After Jesus's vanquishing of the blasphemous Abyssinian will come the time of the Beast. Ibn Kathir validates earlier traditions that portray the Beast as bearing the seal of Solomon and the rod of Moses, which it uses to mark infidels and believers, respectively. But whereas al-Qurtubi identifies the Beast with the Spy (al-jassāsa), Ibn Kathir distinguishes between the two. The Spy, he says, is "a creature so hairy [that it is impossible] to tell its front from its rear."[33] It remains in any case a marginal figure, both from the point of view of dogma (the sole mention of the Spy occurs in the story told by Tamim al-Dari, the Christian merchant who converted to Islam) and of topography (all versions of the story agree that the Spy resides on an island off the coast of Yemen; most hold that the Antichrist left the island at some point after his encounter with Tamim and that he will reappear later in Khurasan as the leader of the armies of Evil).

Finally, in his commentary on the Qur'an, Ibn Kathir distinguishes three "blasts" of the supernatural trumpet: "The Blast of panic, the day when the angel Raphael will blow the trumpet . . . , the Blast of striking down [by lightning or thunderbolt], which will annihilate all living beings, followed next by the Blast of the resurrection."[34]

Ibn Kathir's account is notable above all for its great strength of conviction—another legacy of Hanbali literalism—and for the lack of any critical distance. In addition to more or less disputed hadiths, his apocalyptic vision incorporates elements that reflect the harsh experience of Islam's first century (particularly the devastation of Mecca by the "Abyssinian" during Ibn Zubayr's uprising and the founding myth of the Tamimi), all of which are combined in a colorful narrative having great evocative power. The undeniable popularity enjoyed by Ibn Kathir's synthesis stands in stark contrast to the complex esotericism of Ibn 'Arabi's apocalypse.

THE RATIONAL MESSIANISM OF IBN KHALDUN

The vast and extraordinary scholarship of 'Abd al-Rahman ibn Khaldun (1332–1406) is so closely associated with a certain style of modernity in the Arab world that it may seem incongruous to make him a key figure in the medieval panorama of apocalyptic thought. But Ibn Khaldun's intellectual integrity, together with the variety of his political experience in the courts of the Maghrib, Andalusia, and Egypt, permitted him to put the millenarian impulses that inspired revolutionaries, disturbed the powerful, and gripped the imagination of ordinary people in a longer perspective. Giving messianic movements their proper place in the great cycles of Islamic history meant, above all, going back to the least contestable traditions.

Ibn Khaldun entertained no doubt whatever regarding the apocalyptic fate of mankind: "There is, first of all, that which is mentioned [in the Qur'an] in connection with the Hour and its signs, with the era when [these] harbingers will appear, with the number of the guardians of hell. . . . None of this, as I am well aware, is subject to the least ambiguity. Indeed, no equivocal utterance is to be found there, nor anything of the sort. It is simply a question of the timing of these events, foreknowledge of which is reserved to Allah [alone], as this is explicitly indicated in His book and expressed through the mouth of His prophet."[35] It is on the basis of this profession of faith that Ibn Khaldun endorses the classical scenario of the last times:

> Plainly it has always been known, among the Muslims, that at the end of times a man from the family of the Prophet must come to rescue religion and cause justice to triumph. The Muslims will follow him and he will subject all the lands of Islam to his authority. He will be called the Mahdi. After him will appear the Antichrist, as well as all the signs of the Hour, as these are laid down in the *Al-Sahīh* [of Bukhari and of Muslim]. Next Jesus will come down to earth and kill the Antichrist. Or Jesus will come down with the Mahdi, help him to kill the Antichrist and take [the Mahdi] as Imam in his prayers.[36]

The tone of this passage is sober and restrained, displaying none of the emphatic flourishes that are customary in writing of this kind. With characteristic methodicalness, Ibn Khaldun proceeds to make a rigorous selection from the apocalyptic literature. The only works finding favor in his eyes are the "authentic" collections of Bukhari and Muslim: "There is, in fact, a consensus among traditionists concerning the contents of these two works. . . . Moreover, there is general and uninterrupted agreement in the Muslim community regarding the practice of accepting [these works] and of conforming to their contents. This consensus constitutes the best protection and defense [against error]. There are no other works that enjoy a comparable position."[37] This privilege was denied to other anthologies of apocalyptic traditions, whose chains of transmission Ibn Khaldun showed to have been truncated, where they were not actually falsified. He subjected to particular scrutiny the highly politicized hadiths of the Umayyad era, casting doubt on the famous prediction regarding the black banners of the Mahdi Army,[38] and diligently traced Shi'i influences on the millenarian heritage of Islam, so that they might be permanently excluded from it. The verdict sustained by this meticulous labor of textual examination and comparison is unequivocal: "The reader may judge: few, indeed very few [of these traditions], escape criticism."[39]

Ibn Khaldun showed greater leniency toward what he called the "fragile foundations" of Sufi eschatology, whose esoteric orientation won his approval. Ibn 'Arabi, for example, associated silver with the Mahdi, but gold with the Prophet—a mystical hierarchy Ibn Khaldun found pleasing. He also took an interest in the astrological calculations and numerological forecasts of Andalusian savants, and reported speculations regarding the ideal line of the twelve caliphs and the date of the Mahdi's return. Depending on the source, he noted, the future reign of the Mahdi may be reckoned to have a total duration of between three and nine years, or else ten, forty, or even seventy years. But these were minor details. In Ibn Khaldun's view, the essential issue lay in the profound popular resonance of the theme of the Mahdi:

> The simple people of the lower classes . . . believe for the most part that the Mahdi will suddenly appear in some distant province, or some region at the end of the world, such as Zab in Tunisia or Sus in Morocco. . . . This is a belief that rests on no foundation, apart from the strangeness of these nations . . . and the situation of [a] remote province that eludes the control of the authorities. All the more firmly, then, do people imagine that the Mahdi will suddenly appear where he will be beyond the reach of government, law, and force. There is no basis for this conjecture. Many weak-minded people go to [such] place[s], thinking they will help a cause that, through the suggestion of Satan or owing to madness, they hope to see succeed. In this way a great many of them go to their deaths.[40]

The argument is masterful. Whereas al-Qurtubi encouraged Andalusian nostalgia and sought to justify outbursts of millenarian enthusiasm in Morocco, Ibn Khaldun challenged not only the soundness but the sanity of such messianic pretensions. The unrest in these parts he interpreted instead as the result of altogether earthly quarrels, instigated by rebellious tribal leaders in the peripheral regions of Islam who hoisted the standard of the Mahdi in order to rally errant believers to their side.

This wholly unsentimental analysis of millenarian anxiety follows from a very clear conception of faith as an instrument of political combat (one of the chapters of Ibn Khaldun's *Book of Examples* is titled "The Arabs Obtain Power Only by Relying upon a Religious Movement")[41] that forms part of a pessimistic and cyclical view of history in which marginalized social groups, taking advantage of the opportunity presented by the decadence of a dominant class, gradually succeed in strengthening their solidarity *('assabiyya)* and then, on seizing power for themselves, experience the very same dissolution of their collective values.

It is important, finally, to keep in mind that Ibn Khaldun includes in his universal geography the apocalyptic peoples called Gog and Magog, whose existence, having been confirmed by the Qur'an, therefore seems to him indubitable. He locates them at the extreme northeastern corner of the Euroasiatic land mass (in an area bounded by "the mountains of Qūfuya" and, still more significantly, by "the Wall constructed by Alexander") and, in agreement with Ibn Kathir, says that they "belong to the Turkic peoples."[42] It is precisely this alliance of practical outlook and unshakable faith in the truth of scriptural revelation that gives Ibn Khaldun's contribution to the Muslim vision of the end of the world its distinctive character.

AL-SUYUTI AND THE TENTH CENTURY OF ISLAM

Jalal al-Din al-Suyuti (1446–1505) came from a family of notables having ancient roots in Middle Egypt (their name means "from Asyut"). His father was among the teachers at the 'Abbasid court who had sought refuge in Cairo following the fall of Baghdad in 1258. Now that the Mamluk sultans held Egypt and the Levant in an iron grip, having contained the Mongol invasion and eliminated the last Crusader strongholds, Arab caliphs exercised merely symbolic power in the shadow of a warrior aristocracy of converted slaves.

According to one of his biographers, al-Suyuti was born in the family library, where his mother had gone into labor. It was there, in any case, that the young scholar earned the epithet "son of books" *(ibn al-kutūb),*[43] for already by the age of eight he had memorized the whole of the Qur'an. He composed his first book at fifteen and began to teach in Cairo two years later.

Al-Suyuti achieved a reputation as a jurist skilled in the science of hadith very early in his career. He regularly received foreign delegations, either on their way to Mecca or coming back from it,[44] and published a great many legal opinions *(fatāwā;* sing. *fatwā)* on a range of questions, including political and religious disputes in an African emirate.[45] These proofs of international prestige naturally aroused the jealousy of his Egyptian colleagues, and gave rise to attacks in the mosques of Cairo. Al-Suyuti did nothing to appease his critics: linking the annihilation of Islam in Andalusia (marked by the fall of Grenada in 1492) with the advent of Islam's tenth century the following year,[46] he aspired to play the part of the reformer *(mujaddid)* who would help the faith regain its rightful position of preeminence.[47]

Al-Suyuti sharply dissented from the ideological conformism of his time. Initiated into various brotherhoods, while no doubt finding the Shaziliyya the most congenial among them, he imbued the traditional treatment of legal matters with a Sufi sensibility, and exhibited a fierce independence with regard to the Mamluk sultanate. In his determination to restore to its former glory the Arab caliphate of the 'Abbasids, for the moment languishing in exile under Turkish guard in Cairo, he lay great store by the following quotation from the Prophet: "The worst of the punishments on the Day of Resurrection will be that of the iniquitous leader."[48]

In the immense corpus of works left behind by al-Suyuti,[49] two stand out: a compilation of several hundred thousand hadiths *(Jame' al-jawāmi')* and a treatise on fatwas *(Al-ḥāwī lil-fatāwī).* As a distinguished jurist he was accustomed to publishing comprehensive and detailed responses to the written questions of his followers. One of these replies, dealing with "the descent of Jesus, son of Mary, at the end of times,"[50] contains the essence of al-Suyuti's apocalyptic vision. The approach of the end of the world, he says, will be marked by the growth of faithlessness, indeed of apostasy. Considerable importance is attached in this regard to one hadith in particular: "The Hour will not come so long as groups within my community will not have joined with the polytheists, going so far as to worship idols. In my community there will be a succession of thirty imposters, each one pretending to be a prophet."[51] These thirty false messiahs, announced in Bukhari's *Sahīh,* serve the sole apocalyptic purpose of preparing the way for the Antichrist.

Al-Suyuti adopts the classical traditions concerning the Antichrist and affirms that he will be denied access to the holy cities of Islam: "[The Antichrist] will pass near Mecca, where he will find an extraordinary creature. 'Who are you?' the Antichrist will ask, and the creature will answer him: 'I am Michael, and Allah has sent me to prevent you from reaching its sacred grounds [haram].' Then the Antichrist will pass near Medina, where he will find [another] extraordinary creature. 'Who are you?' the Antichrist will ask, and the creature will answer him: 'I am Gabriel, and Allah has sent me to prevent you from reaching its sacred grounds.'"[52] Bukhari's Sahīh, it will be recalled, mentions only the angelic protection of Medina, whereas al-Suyuti includes Mecca as well. But the devastation caused by the Antichrist will not be any less horrible for that: "Never, from the creation of Adam until the final Hour, will Allah send down a greater trial [fitna] than that of the Antichrist."[53]

The Mahdi will then appear to restore true Islam for a period of seven years: "The traditions report that the Mahdi will come before Jesus, son of Mary, and that he will spread justice over the earth, which will have been filled until then with iniquity. Jesus will then return to approve the work of the Mahdi, who will have given back to the Muslims all those things which are rightfully theirs but to which the Turks, by their power, have helped themselves."[54] This is because the holding of property in perpetuity (waqf), a practice "reserved to kings, princes, and their descendants," is "illegal and illegitimate, contrary to religious law, and Jesus will abrogate it."[55] The charge of impiety brought by al-Suyuti against the Mamluks was a very serious one, justifying once more the resort to apocalyptic prophecy as an instrument of propaganda against a corrupt Muslim government.

In the matter of Jesus, al-Suyuti upholds a long tradition of Islamic apologetics in refusing to believe in his martyrdom: "They crucified someone other than Jesus, taking him for [Jesus], so great was the illusion of their resemblance. But Allah [had] brought [Jesus] up to Him alive." Citing the authority of Ibn Hanbal, al-Suyuti adds that "the Antichrist will stay on earth as long as Allah wishes it. Then Jesus, son of Mary, will come from the west, attesting the veracity of Muhammad and of his religion, and he will slay the Antichrist. Only then will the Hour arrive." Once descended to the white minaret in Damascus under the escort of two angels, and after having pursued the Antichrist, Jesus will kill him at the gate of Lod. Al-Suyuti adds that Jesus will ensure the ultimate glory of Islam by abolishing all other religions: "He will destroy the cross, he will kill the swine, he will make harmony reign, and he will drive out enmity [among men]."[56] For whatever catastrophic events may intervene, the triumph of Islam is inevitable, al-Suyuti says, citing Muhammad in this connection: "How could a community perish in which I come at the beginning, and Jesus son of Mary at the end, and the Mahdi, the issue of my descendants, in between?"[57]

Like the majority of authors concerned with eschatology, al-Suyuti is torn by two conflicting temptations: on the one hand, of deploying the full arsenal of apocalyptic prophecy against the Muslim target of the moment, in this case the Mamluks; and, on the other, of pushing the Last Hour back into the indefinite future, on the ground that the accumulation even of a great many minor signs cannot be considered to authorize immediate messianic expectations. In the event, al-Suyuti chose to combat the literalist millenarian claim that the end of the world would occur in the thousandth year of Islam, which is to say during the year 1591 of the Christian calendar. Creation, he believed, would last for seven thousand years, the Qur'anic revelation having occurred during the second half of the sixth millennium.[58] The last days could therefore be located between the eleventh and the fifteenth centuries of Islam—probably nearer to the end of the fifteenth.[59]

Whether or not al-Suyuti was unconsciously redirecting a sense of frustration at not having been recognized as the one called upon to reform Islam in the tenth century of the Hegira, he managed to postpone the prospect of apocalypse only by half a millennium: the Hour was now forecast to coincide with the approach of A.H. 1500, or not later than 2076 C.E. But this was enough to bequeath to apocalyptic agitators in our own time a calendar within their reach.[60] As a consequence, his influence has never been greater than it is today.

With al-Suyuti's death at the beginning of the sixteenth century of the Christian era, the line of the medieval masters of the Muslim apocalypse came to a close—just when Christianity was beginning once again to mine its own apocalyptic vein, with the advent of the Reformation. Both Luther and Calvin drew upon it in elaborating their indictments of Rome, the former denouncing the pope as the Antichrist, the latter condemning him as the Beast.[61] In the minds of Catholics and Protestants alike, the increasingly urgent threat represented by the Ottoman Empire was now arrayed with the attributes of Gog and Magog, though "Mahomet" was generally seen as no more than an auxiliary of the Antichrist, not as the great deceiver himself. The Christian apocalyptic tradition of the early modern period inhabited a parallel world to that of the medieval Muslim tradition, and exploited a parallel register of ideas and images; there was no exchange, either positive or negative, between them.

· · ·

The end of the world was never to be quite the same in Sunni Islam. The reason for this is not that the great medieval thinkers called into question the fundamental categories of the standard apocalyptic account. It has to do instead with the extraordinary reputation that their readings and commentaries came to acquire. Each of the dominant families of apocalyptic interpretation acknowledges the authority of one of these authors: mystics continue to revere the gnosticism of Ibn 'Arabi; liberal thinkers pay homage to Ibn Khaldun (making him, if anything, more secular than he ever was), while conservative clerics lay claim to the heritage of al-Suyuti; believers who are bewildered by the course of current events look for guidance to al-Qurtubi, and those who insist upon the duty of moral cleansing echo the punitive forebodings of Ibn Kathir.

These masters of the medieval apocalypse nevertheless exerted little influence over the course of messianism in their own time. Leaving aside al-Qurtubi's endorsement of the opinion that the Mahdi would appear in the West, their speculations seldom strayed far from orthodox Sunni belief, and therefore found themselves deprived of any active political consequence. Revolutionary millenarianism was to depend instead on dissident movements and popular unrest.

CHAPTER 3

Avatars of the Mahdi

The first centuries of Islam saw the consolidation of a standard apocalyptic account under the influence of civil strife that very quickly tore apart the community of believers. Once the two main branches of the faith had been durably established, the vision of the Last Hour came to be colored by sectarian differences over doctrine, with the result that the perceived imminence of the end of the world varied with the degree of divergence from orthodoxy. Nevertheless, the figure of the Mahdi remained at the heart of the millenarian dynamic.

The dissident Shi'i movement known as Isma'ilism embodied the messianic impulse of Islam in its most elaborate form. But mainstream Shi'ism, itself hardly less persecuted than its heretical offshoot, was not immune to the temptations of apocalyptic speculation; indeed, this facet of its appeal was largely responsible for making it the official religion of Iran. Sunnism, on the other hand, achieved stability by relegating the millenarian perspective to its doctrinal and geographical margins. For it was in the extreme western lands of Islam *(al-maghrib al-aqsā)*, in territories belonging to present-day Morocco, that most of the tragic mahdis of Sunni wrath were to emerge.

FROM ISMA'ILI SUBVERSION TO THE FATIMID CALIPHATE

We have seen that the Isma'ili schism dates back to the middle of the eighth century and the overthrow of the Umayyads by the 'Abbasids.

When Ja'far as-Sadiq, the sixth Shi'i imam, refused to claim the caliphate, a dissident minority condemned his quietism and revoked his title, granting it instead to his son Isma'il, from whom they took their name. Isma'il's son, Muhammad, was subsequently revered by his followers as the seventh and last imam, whose date of death was unknown and whose return was awaited under the signs and powers customarily ascribed to the Mahdi.

By the middle of the ninth century a distinctive Isma'ili doctrine had been formalized and equipped with a network of propagandists charged with spreading the faith (da'wa, literally "preaching"), levying a fifth part of personal incomes in the name of the Hidden Imam, and stockpiling arms in anticipation of the Mahdi's return. Although the sect was based in Salamiyya, a small town in central Syria not far from Palmyra, Isma'ili missionaries ranged over a vast territory extending from North Africa to the province of Sind in the lower Indus Valley that included secondary settlements north of Aden and at Qatif, on the eastern coast of Arabia.

In 899, the leader of the sect, 'Abd Allah Sa'id, proclaimed himself the Mahdi in Salamiyya. This dramatic gesture triggered a new wave of revolutionary evangelism in the Maghrib and Syria, but the Isma'ilis of Iraq and Arabia, as well as a part of the community of Yemen, persisted in the belief that the seventh imam, the one and true Mahdi, remained in occultation. Divisions quickly became insurmountable between the partisans of the Mahdi of Salamiyya and his opponents, the Qaramita (or Carmathians), whose principal bastion was Bahrain, the medieval name for the Arabian coast of the Persian Gulf. In 929 the Qaramita conducted a daring raid on Mecca and seized the Black Stone, sacred for its link to the prophets Adam and Abraham. The following year they conquered Oman, and even occupied Kufa for almost a month in 931.

It was then that Abu Tahir, the leader of the Qaramita, professed to recognize a young prisoner originally from Isfahan as the awaited Mahdi and yielded power to him, proclaiming the advent of the "true religion."[1] This murky episode, which occurred in the middle of Ramadan, harkened back to a pre-Islamic type of Iranian messianism that held the Mahdi to be a magus—indeed, a descendant of the kings of Persia—and forecast his appearance to coincide with the 1,500th anniversary of the death of Zoroaster.[2] Isfahan itself was associated by astrologers with an Iranian dynasty that would overthrow the Arab caliphate. In the event, the new Persian mahdi urged his followers to vilify previous prophets and celebrated fire—an obvious echo of Zoroastrian practice. These sacrileges, together with his incitements to debauchery and the

pronounced anti-Arab character of his preaching, led Abu Tahir to dis-
avow him as an "imposter" and to have him put to death.[3]

The Qaramite community was deeply shaken. A number of Iraqi
tribes renounced their allegiance to it and joined the ranks of the Sunnis,
but Abu Tahir nonetheless survived the crisis. Having managed to preserve the main part of his rebel state, he negotiated an agreement with
the 'Abbasid caliphate in 939 for the protection of pilgrims to Mecca,
and more than a decade was to pass before his successors consented to
return the Black Stone, in exchange for a substantial tribute, in 951. The
Qaramite emirate prospered for another half-century, at which point its
population gradually came to accept Twelver Shi'ism.

In the meantime the authority of the mahdi from Salamiyya had
been invoked by Isma'ili insurgents, who seized control of the whole
of central Syria in his name, in 903, before finally being crushed by
Iraqi troops. Pursued by the 'Abbasid police, 'Abd Allah al-Mahdi fled
to Egypt and from there took refuge in the High Atlas Mountains of
Morocco. His followers had more success in the Maghrib, where the
spirit of revolt spread rapidly among the Berber tribes. With the fall of
Qayrawan in 909, the Mahdi settled in the conquered city and took the
title of caliph under the name of 'Abd Allah.[4] He claimed moreover to
be a descendant of Fatima, daughter of the Prophet and wife of 'Ali, and
though this genealogy was vigorously contested,[5] it furnished the basis
for what was commonly referred to as the Fatimid caliphate.

Once again, as during the 'Abbasid revolution, messianic mobilization led to the establishment of a new dynastic line of succession. But
'Abd Allah was quite incapable of deploying even the least of the supernatural powers attributed to the Mahdi by his eulogists; those whom he
found too insistent or demanding were dismissed, and in some cases put
to death. Before long he quit Qayrawan in order to supervise construction of a city on the Tunisian coast commensurate with the scale of his
divine mission, called Mahdia, and conferred on his son the titles of
prophetic glory. Rebels who unsuccessfully laid siege to the new capital were portrayed as agents of the Antichrist; the leader of the revolt,
Abu Yazid, was captured and executed in 947, and his corpse stuffed
with straw and borne aloft in triumph by Fatimid troops. The date of
the apocalypse was nonetheless indefinitely postponed, having been
rescheduled to occur at the end of a new cycle of imams. Until then,
Qur'anic faith remained in force.

The Fatimid caliphate subsequently abandoned millenarian rhetoric
altogether and devoted itself to military expansion: Sicily was taken in

948, North Africa unified under the Mahdi's authority in 959, and the Nile Delta conquered in 969. Having transferred its capital to the new city of Cairo (*al-Qāhira*, "the Victorious"), the caliphate then proceeded to extend its power over Palestine and, less securely, Syria. In all of this empire building, however, Isma'ili militants looked in vain for any trace of the new law that had been promised with the arrival of the Mahdi.

Then came the caliph al-Hakim, whose long habit of eccentricity during a reign that spanned a quarter-century (996–1021) seemed to his most devout followers to display a divinely inspired impulsiveness. Nocturnal cease-fires, the liquidation of all dogs, and the prohibition of music were of less lasting consequence, however, than the destruction of churches ordered by Hakim. Together with the enforcement of discriminatory measures against Jews and Christians, this campaign gained fresh impetus with the coming of Islam's fifth century during the year 1009 of the Christian era, when it was believed that the whole of humanity would convert to the Muslim faith. Hakim's unpredictable commands were carried out with extreme violence—and occasionally rescinded with equal suddenness. In the apocalyptic atmosphere of the age, a fervent minority became convinced of Hakim's divinity and founded an initiatory cult under the direction of a man by the name of Muhammad ibn Isma'il al-Darazi. Thus came into being the Druze religion, which disappeared from Egypt with the death of Hakim and today is confined to the Golan Heights and neighboring areas in Palestine and Lebanon (Galilee, Jebel Druze, the Shuf Mountains, and the western Biqa' Valley).

Chastened by Hakim's scandalous and capricious excesses, his successors forswore millenarian temptation and set about consolidating the political power of the Fatimid line. Preoccupied by the continual erosion of its territories in both the Maghrib and the Levant, however, the caliphate in Cairo gradually relinquished its supranatural claims, taking on the trappings of a mere earthly power in both its official conduct and its ceremonial rituals. "The seeds of doubt and dismay concerning the ideal character of the Isma'ili state had been planted in people's minds," observed the French historian Maxime Rodinson. "Disappointment could not fail to make itself felt, despite the militants' stubborn determination to cling to their faith, under the most trying circumstances, by resigning themselves to lowered expectations."[6]

A crisis erupted with the death of the Fatimid caliph al-Mustansir in 1094. His son and designated successor, Abu Mansur Nizar, was pushed aside by Mustansir's vizier al-Afdal, commander of the Fatimid army, and replaced by the late caliph's docile son-in-law. A revolt led by Nizar was crushed at Alexandria the following year. Meanwhile the commander of the Isma'ili forces in Iran, Hasan-i Sabba, refused any longer to recognize Cairo's authority and proclaimed instead the new preaching (da'wa; Persian da'vat). From his citadel in Alamut, Hasan fomented instability throughout the east of Iran while disseminating his own dogma westward into Syria. In the decades that followed, Isma'ili sicarians—the hired killers immortalized by Western chroniclers under the name of the "Assassins"—spread terror both among the 'Abbasids and at the Fatimid court in Cairo. In 1121, the imam Nizar's death was avenged by the murder of Mustansir's vizier, Afdal. In 1130, the Fatimid caliph al-Amir was stabbed to death. And finally, in 1135, the 'Abbasid caliph al-Mustarshid likewise fell victim to Hasan-i Sabba's agents, along with his son and heir, al-Rashid, three years later; in both cases the assassination of the supreme authority of Sunnism was celebrated in Alamut for seven days and seven nights.[7]

By the middle of the thirteenth century, however, this wave of revolutionary terrorism had subsided. The same sense of disappointment that had taken hold among militants in Fatimid Cairo now began to intrude upon the deceptive calm of Alamut. "In the virtual stalemate and tacit mutual acceptance between the Ismaili principalities and the Sunni monarchies," Bernard Lewis notes, "the great struggle to overthrow the old order and establish a new millennium, in the name of the hidden Imam, had dwindled into border-squabbles and cattle-raids. . . . Among them there were still some who harked back to the glorious days of Hasan-i Sabbah—to the dedication and adventure of his early struggles, and the religious faith that inspired them."[8]

The new master of Alamut—whose given name, like that of the sect's founder, was Hasan—chose to respond to these attacks by acting in the name of the Hidden Imam. In the middle of the fasting month of Ramadan in A.H. 559 (1164 C.E.), on the anniversary of 'Ali's death, Hasan gathered his followers in the heart of the citadel. He announced to men, jinns, and angels the coming of the Hour, the end of the Occultation (ghayba), and the advent of the Resurrection (qiyāma).[9] The holy law of Islam no longer had any force. Sacrilege took its place: the assembled loyalists turned their backs toward Mecca, and the ritual fast was violated by a banquet whose merriment reached its height under the afternoon sun. This millenarian inversion of values was not merely symbolic, for the observance of Muslim rites was now liable to the most severe punishment. But so great was the resistance it aroused that Hasan was stabbed to death by his own brother-in-law in 1166.

In Cairo, the Fatimid caliphate was now little more than a shadow of its former self. Emptied of its Isma'ili substance, the dynasty had exhausted itself in competition with the 'Abbasids, to the point that it was obliged to consider forming an alliance with the Crusaders against them. In the event, however, it was the jihad launched by the Seljuk governor, Nureddin, ruling from Damascus, and his general Saladin, sent to conquer Cairo in 1171, that sealed the fate of the Fatimids and united the forces of Islam under the banners of a single and undisputed caliphate, now restored to Baghdad. In Alamut, Islamic law was reinstituted with the death of Hasan's son—too late to prevent the sect's strongholds from crumbling in the middle of the thirteenth century in the face of the Mongol invasion.

SHI'I ANXIETIES AND HATREDS

The same Mongols who sounded the death knell for Isma'ili radicals in Iran were welcomed by Twelver Shi'i scholars. Once again the basic apocalyptic narrative was interpreted in opposite ways by Sunnis and Shi'a: in the eyes of 'Abbasid orthodoxy, the Mongols were none other than the doomsday peoples from the east, Gog and Magog, mentioned in the Qur'an, who were to break through a great barrier erected by divine command and swarm over the lands of Islam; from the perspective of Shi'i millenarianism, these invaders had been announced by the first Imam, 'Ali ("individuals with small eyes and faces like shields covered with skin, draped in iron, bald and beardless"),[10] and were the instrument of divine vengeance upon Baghdad and its godless potentates.

In this connection special mention must be made of Nasr ed-Din at-Tusi (1201–1274), a man of universal genius (in Henry Corbin's phrase)[11]—mathematician, astronomer, philosopher, politician, and the author of dozens of scholarly treatises. Despite his Twelver Shi'i convictions, Tusi entered into the service of Isma'ili princes and composed in Alamut two fundamental expositions of Sevener doctrine.[12] With the approach of the Mongol army, Tusi was dispatched to negotiate with Hulagu Khan, grandson of Chingiz Khan. But instead of obtaining assurances of clemency toward the Isma'ili citadel, Tusi betrayed his masters. Alamut was delivered to Hulagu's forces and destroyed in 1256.

In many ways Nasr ed-Din at-Tusi embodied the Shi'i embrace of the Mongol invasion, ultimately becoming (in the words of the German orientalist Rudolf Strothmann) Hulagu's "éminence grise—one is tempted to say, éminence noire."[13] Tusi accompanied Hulagu on his devastating offensive through the whole of Iran and subsequently, in Iraq, urged Hulagu to march on Baghdad, which he seized in 1258, and convinced him to execute the 'Abbasid caliph al-Muzta'sim.[14] But the Shi'i quarters of Baghdad were not spared in the massacre that followed, and only the voluntary surrender of the Shi'i town of Hilla, further to the south on the Euphrates, made it possible for the sanctuaries of Najaf and Karbala to be saved.

Five centuries after Abu Muslim's dazzling campaign of conquest in the East, the specter of apocalypse led Shi'i strategists to commit a similar error. Convinced that the forces of divine retribution would suddenly appear in Khurasan, they set out in 747–749, and then again in 1256–1258, to conquer Persia and Iraq—in the first instance, to help bring about the overthrow of the Umayyads by the 'Abbasids; in the second, to assist the Mongols in expelling the 'Abbasids. But the Shi'a were no more victorious in the thirteenth century than they had been in the eighth: Hulagu's son favored the Buddhists and Nestorians instead,[15] and when the Mongol leaders finally converted to Islam, in 1295, they opted for Sunni orthodoxy. It was only for a brief period, from 1310 to 1316, that a Mongol khan, Uljaytu, professed Shi'ism. The Sunni reaction, barely contained during Uljaytu's lifetime, erupted into violence immediately following his death.

This fatal miscalculation, largely due to a biased interpretation of the apocalyptic calendar, did not forestall the publication of a copious Sunni literature accusing the Shi'a of having betrayed Islam for the sake of infidel invaders and, by handing over Baghdad to them, of having spread ruin and desolation. A similar charge of betrayal was to be brought by Sunni polemicists against the Shi'i community some seven hundred years later, during the American invasion of Iraq in 2003.

By the beginning of the fourteenth century, Shi'ism had entered into an era of clandestine dissidence in Iraq and Iran, both dominated by the Mongols. Many cities nevertheless cultivated a regular and ostentatious ritual of waiting for the Mahdi. Ibn Battuta, who embarked from Tangiers in 1325 on a series of travels that over the course of almost three decades took him to the furthest boundaries of the Muslim world, tells how the faithful of Hilla, the main center of Shi'i learning, prepared each day for the return of the Hidden Imam:

> Each day, after the afternoon prayer, one hundred townsmen, swords drawn, go to the emir and receive [from him] a horse or a mule, saddled and bridled. Drums are beaten and trumpets and bugles sounded before the mount, which is preceded and followed by fifty men, while the others surround it on the right

and the left. Thus the procession makes its way to the "sanctuary of the Master of the Hour," halts at the gate, and cries: "In the name of Allah, Master of the Hour, in the name of Allah, come, for disorder is rampant and iniquity rife! This is the moment for you to appear! Through you, Allah will make known the true [and separate it] from the false!" They continue this ritual until the evening prayer, sounding bugles and trumpets and beating the drum.[16]

Similar ceremonies of aggressive messianism, marked by the arming of the faithful and the preparing of the Mahdi's mount, were reported in Iran as well.[17]

The disintegration of the khanate after 1335 liberated the millenarian energies of Shi'ism. Their principal vehicle was a group of itinerant brotherhoods whose members propagated the Shi'i version of the popular spirituality associated with Sufism. Foremost among these orders was the Shaykhiyya-Juryya, which announced the imminent coming of the Mahdi and called upon the Shi'a to take up arms in anticipation of this event. Its proselytizing met with great success in the east of Iran and constituted the official creed of the independent principalities of Sabzavar and Amol, which the Turco-Mongol invasion under Timur finally managed to subdue between 1381 and 1392.

The sudden appearance of this new conqueror did not calm messianic agitation; quite to the contrary. The Iranian shaykh Fazlallah al-Astarbadi (b. 1339), known for most of his life only as a modest hatter with a talent for interpreting dreams, one day happened himself to dream that his right eye had absorbed the supernatural brilliance of an eastern star,[18] and in 1386 he proclaimed himself the "manifestation of divine glory"[19] and possessor of the attributes of the "Master of the Age."[20] Because he claimed, moreover, that the hidden meaning of the letters of the alphabet (hurūf; sing. harf) had been revealed to him, his gnostic doctrine came to be known as Hurufism (hurūfiyya). Fazlallah was executed in 1394 on the order of one of Timur's sons, but his disciples continued to venerate him as a divine incarnation and awaited his return under the signs of "the Master of the Sword." Shaykh Fazlallah's murderer was identified with the Antichrist,[21] and the Turkmen prince who later killed this assassin aroused great hopes among the Hurufists—hopes that were quickly disappointed.[22] The sect was hounded on all sides for heresy and gradually disappeared from Iran and Syria. Its members found refuge at last in Anatolia, where they were assimilated by the Sufi brotherhood of the Bektashis.[23]

The Turkish novelist Orhan Pamuk, a recent Nobel Laureate for literature, devotes a large part of his *Kara Kitap* (The Black Book, 1990) to an explicitly Hurufist tale in which the writings of a popular Istanbul newspaper columnist supply the means for interpreting the city itself, and indeed the lives of the book's characters. Pamuk reflects upon the tragic career of Shaykh Fazlallah, and wonders what will be the fate of all "the surveyors, gas bill collectors, sesame roll sellers, junk dealers, and beggars . . . all the poor souls who've counted up the numerical values of [the] letters [of the alphabet] to calculate the day when the Messiah will appear on our cobblestone streets, to save our piteous nation, to save us all."[24] Pamuk traces a complex and ironic genealogy in which the Hurufist method of interpretation was adapted, under the Ottoman Empire, to the rites of the Bektashi order of Sufi dervishes (and of the Janissaries who made up a large part of its membership), before finally being transfigured in the modern era as the basis for the rituals of Albanian Marxist-Leninism.[25] I have placed an excerpt from Pamuk's book as an epigraph at the head of the present work, since the entire novel magnificently exploits the dramatic possibilities of the apocalyptic sensibility.

The execution of Shaykh Fazlallah and the scattering of his disciples did not curb the millennialist impulse, however. A generation later, in what is now Tajikistan, a Sufi master of the Kubrawiyya order called Ishaq al-Khuttalani proclaimed one of his followers, who had become known by the name of Nurbakhsh ("The Gift of Light"), the awaited Messiah. The movement grew in size and influence, and after a failed revolt Sultan Murad II ordered the execution of Shaykh Khuttalani and dozens of his initiates in 1425. The Ottoman sovereign spared Nurbakhsh, officially in cognizance of his youth, though more probably in order to avoid making a martyr of him. In the event, this rare display of restraint robbed the movement of its momentum. After a second unsuccessful uprising, Nurbakhsh was imprisoned in Herat, and later in Shiraz; on his release he was allowed to study in the holy cities of Iraq. Subsequently Nurbakhsh established his own order in Kurdistan, at Shariyar, but found himself forced to publicly renounce any claims to the imamate.[26] Thus deprived of political influence, he passed away in 1464.

At the same time that Nurbakhsh was identified as the Mahdi in Tajikistan, Muhammad ibn Falah (1400–1465/66) proclaimed himself the "friend" *(walī)* of the Mahdi in the south of Iraq (by analogy with Imam 'Ali, regarded by Shi'a as the *walī* of Allah). By 1436 Ibn Falah's messianic appeals had attracted a following in Khuzestan, in southwestern Iran, where he delivered an "address of the Mahdi," now claiming to be the seventh imam's ultimate incarnation.[27] Anger at such heresy began to grow in the holy cities of Iraq, and in 1453 Ibn Falah moved to silence his enemies by laying waste to Hilla and Najaf, where not even 'Ali's tomb was spared desecration—a sacrilege that did not prevent Ibn Falah from establishing an emirate in Khuzestan ruled by his descendants, who survived as provincial governors following conquest by the Safavids in 1508. Once again, after a period of serious disturbance, a millenarian insurrection had given rise to a new dynastic power.

This phenomenon was reproduced throughout Persia as a whole with the advent of the Safavid dynasty. Probably of Kurdish origin, the family took its name from the Safawiyya, a Sufi order that had converted to Shi'ism in the fifteenth century. For military support it relied mainly on the fanatical Turkmen tribes that ceaselessly waged war on the borders of the Caucasus. Their Turkish name "Qizilbash" (Red Heads) came from the color of their twelve-tasseled caps, supposedly designed in honor of the twelve Shi'i imams. The death in combat of their leader, Haydar, hastened the succession in 1499 of his youngest son, a twelve-year-old boy named Isma'il.

Strongly influenced by the teachings of one of Nurbakhsh's disciples,[28] Isma'il gave an eschatological interpretation to the raids carried out by the Qizilbash, stressing that he was the awaited Mahdi, the incarnation of the twelve imams, and the mantle of the divine light,[29] and used apocalyptic rhetoric to justify the savagery of his Turkmen fighters, whose paganism and shamanism were made still more ominous by reports of ritual cannibalism.[30] The military efficiency of the Qizilbash was in any case impressive, and Isma'il was able to seize Baku in 1500 and Tabriz the following year. Having granted himself the Persian royal title of shah, the young monarch imposed Shi'ism as the official religion and ordered the Sunni caliphs to be cursed in all the mosques of the land. Isfahan and Shiraz fell to his forces in 1503, followed by Baghdad five years later. Although the Qizilbash everywhere succeeded in shattering Sunni resistance to the new state religion, Shi'ism remained a minority faith among the people of Iran. What it lacked in the way of doctrinal authority was made up for by unremitting displays of military power, reinforced by apocalyptic reverence for the shah as the Mahdi.

Isma'il's supernatural pretensions were nevertheless dealt a fatal blow in 1514 at Tshaldiran, near Tabriz, where Ottoman artillery routed the Safavid contingents. This first but nonetheless ignominious defeat—sustained, moreover, at the hands of a Sunni sultan—ruined the sovereign's reputation for invincibility. Unable any longer to pose as the Mahdi, he now claimed to be an ambassador of the Hidden Imam.

The Anatolian origins of the Safavid family were conveniently forgotten and replaced by a prophetic ancestry that allowed the dynasty to represent itself as the instrument of the twelfth imam during the course of the Great Occultation. A minority of Qizilbash nonetheless continued to consider the shah to be the Mahdi himself. Isma'il's son and successor, Tahmasp, suppressed this expression of heresy in 1555,[31] with the result that Safavid legitimacy came to be concentrated in the person of the sovereign as intercessor of the Hidden Imam, and protector and guarantor of the state religion.

We have seen that the 'Abbasids were the first, in 749, to turn a millenarian uprising to the advantage of their own dynastic designs. In that case, at least, the kinship of Abu al-Abbas with the Prophet Muhammad was undeniable. The Mahdi 'Abd Allah had a somewhat harder time validating a Fatimid line that went back to the Prophet's daughter, the wife of 'Ali, since his own proclamation as caliph, at Qayrawan in 909, crowned decades of subversion. The same process of genealogical transformation was at work with the Safavids and their imposition of Shi'ism as the official religion of the Persian Empire.

SUNNI MAHDIS AND REVOLUTIONARIES

Whereas the apocalyptic figure of the Mahdi is at the heart of Shi'i eschatology, it occupies a much less central place in Sunni orthodoxy. Yet we have noted that one hadith, popular among both Sunnis and Shi'a, announced that a descendant of the Prophet, bearing the same name, Muhammad, will come to restore justice on earth.[32] This tradition has formed the chief doctrinal basis for intermittent messianic claims to authority in the Sunni world.

Muhammad ibn 'Abdallah ibn Tumart (1078/1081–1130) was a complex and obscure figure. Born into a Berber tribe of the Anti-Atlas Mountains in Morocco, he traveled extensively in both the Mashriq and in Andalusia. At the end of his voyages he elaborated a doctrine of divine oneness *(tawhīd)* that thereafter came to be known as "almohad" (from the Spanish corruption of al-Muwahhidūn, the name Ibn Tumart gave to its adherents, meaning the unitarians). This monism was as rigorous as it was exclusive, being interpreted to justify the rejection of all the rival legal schools of Islam. Ibn Tumart condemned the Almoravid dynasty then reigning in Morocco and Andalusia for its anthropomorphization of Allah, and lashed out at the corruption of morals that had been allowed to go unchecked under its rule. The indictment of

Almoravid perversion was drawn up in apocalyptic terms, with the purpose of demonstrating that the signs of the Hour were already manifest.[33] The perceived imminence of the Last Hour provoked an uprising on the part of Ibn Tumart's followers, who acclaimed him as the Mahdi Muhammad in 1121.

From his eyrie in the mountain village of Tinmallal (Tinmel or Tin Mal), in the High Atlas, Ibn Tumart carefully superintended the dissemination of revolutionary and messianic propaganda throughout Morocco. The territory under Almohad control gradually grew in extent, and the mujahedin of the sect tolerated no challenge when the probability of a triumphant outcome in armed combat favored them. But it was to no avail that the Mahdi personally led the assault of his troops against Marrakesh in 1130. Once again, a military defeat undermined his messianic pretensions to invulnerability and, shortly before his death, Ibn Tumart designated his lieutenant, a fellow Berber named 'Abd al-Mu'min, as his successor (or caliph).[34]

Thus came into being the Almohad dynasty, by an opposite process to the one that brought the founders of the Fatimid dynasty to power two centuries earlier. At that time Isma'ili warriors, victorious on the field of battle, had offered the conquered city of Qayrawan to their Mahdi as the capital for his dynasty. In this case, the Mahdi Ibn Tumart, humiliated outside the capital of his godless enemies, passed the torch of messianic insurrection to a trusted associate, the future founder of the Almohad dynasty, who managed to capture Marrakesh only in 1146. From that point onward, however, Almohad expansion was irresistible, crossing the Mediterranean from Morocco to Andalusia. In 1160, at Gibraltar, the caliph acknowledged the submission of the Spanish emirs, and his victory was celebrated in messianic terms: "To conduct the war against evil, ['Abd al-Mu'min] received Allah's sword from the greatest of guides: the pommel being firmly grasped by the hand of the Mahdi, his blade achieved its purpose."[35] By this it was meant that the caliph was the political and military instrument of the Mahdi's designs, and his bellicosity therefore an emanation of divine vengeance.

The millenarian impetus of this moment was nevertheless not strong enough to withstand the dynastic interest in continued and indefinite expansion. In 1230, the ninth Almohad caliph officially renounced the doctrine of Ibn Tumart.[36] Exactly a century after his death, then, the charismatic leader of Tinmallal was denied the title of Mahdi by the very dynasty that he himself had brought to power. So great, in fact, was the Almohad determination to undermine Ibn Tumart's credibility, and actually to erase his memory, that only Jesus managed to retain his original importance in the apocalyptic formula of belief authorized by Marrakesh.[37]

The same dialectic of messianic impulse and dynastic ambition was still at work in Morocco during the sixteenth century. The Banū Saʿid, a family claiming descent from the Prophet, came forth to oppose Portuguese penetration of the southern region of Sus. With the armed support of the most powerful brotherhood in the region, the Shaziliyya, the Banū Saʿid prevailed, and its leader was proclaimed sovereign of Sus in 1509. Having been given the name Muhammad al-Mahdi—literally, the Mahdi Muhammad—at birth, his followers saw in him the realization of the famous hadith attributed to the Prophet. Before long the millenarian audacity of a local family of *sharifs,* aided by the systematic use of firearms, gave rise to a dynasty. In 1550 the Saʿids seized control of the capital, Fez, and more or less completely dominated Morocco for most of the following century.

In the person of Ibn Abi Mahalli (1559–1613), the millenarian dynamic in Morocco achieved its full tragic purity, for in this case the cause of revolution, instead of triumphing as it had among the Almohads and the Saʿids, was bloodily suppressed. Born in Sidjilmassa into a family of scholars and trained in Fez by Sufi masters, Ibn Abi Mahalli became one of the closest disciples of ʿAbd al-Qadir Abi Samha, a holy man revered in the desert of western Algeria under the name of Sidi Shaykh. In 1602, however, the two men had an irreparable falling out, with Ibn Abi Mahalli angrily denouncing Sidi Shaykh as an imposter *(dajjāl),* a term by now famously associated with the Antichrist.

In addition to attacking his former teacher, whom he accused of reprehensible innovations in doctrine, Ibn Abi Mahalli castigated the Saʿid dynasty for what he saw as its lax attitude toward the Spanish. He drew an apocalyptic picture of Christianity as a monstrous and insatiable beast having two heads—Malta and Oran, the staging points for the raids against Islamic lands[38]—and, by railing against the Antichrist of Shallala and encouraging millenarian apprehensions of conquest by the infidel, hinted that he himself might be the Mahdi. He also cast opprobrium on the mahdis who had previously appeared in the Maghrib, charging the Fatimids with Zoroastrianism and dismissing the Almohads as mere illusionists.[39]

The surrender of Larash to the Spanish in 1610 presented Ibn Abi Mahalli with the opportunity he had been seeking. Proclaiming himself the Mahdi at Sidjilmassa, he marched on Marrakesh, which soon opened its gates to his forces. But the Sa'did counterattack in 1613 was unrelenting and merciless. Ibn Abi Mahalli was killed by enemy fire, and his followers, having seen their faith in his invincibility disproved, fled in panic. The head of Ibn Abi Mahalli was hung from the ramparts of Marrakesh, until finally it disintegrated. A part of the population in the south of Morocco nevertheless refused to accept his death, believing instead that the Mahdi had hidden himself from public view.

More than two centuries later the same tragic fate awaited the insurrection of an Algerian mahdi named Bu Ziyan. This time, however, the messianic jihad was not directed against Muslim leaders vilified for their complicity with Christians, but against the infidels themselves—the French, who had occupied Algeria since 1830. Emir 'Abd al-Qadir's surrender in December 1847 ratified French hegemony, but it also gave new life to the millenarian longings of a distraught people and accelerated the spread of rumors predicting the appearance of the Master of the Age, much to the concern of colonial administrators.[40]

During the guerrilla insurgency, Bu Ziyan had served as 'Abd al-Qadir's representative at the oasis of Za'atsha, not far from Biskra. In early 1849 the Prophet Muhammad appeared in a series of dreams to Bu Ziyan, three times commanding him to assume the duties of the Mahdi and to drive out the French invader. Many members of the strongest local Sufi brotherhood, the Rahmaniyya, gave him their support, despite the hesitations of the order's leadership, and the revolt erupted to cries of "The Christians will no more enter Za'atsha than they will Mecca."[41] After a gruesome siege lasting fifty-two days, the French army gained entry to the oasis and massacred the population, mounting the head of Bu Ziyan on the tip of a pike at the entrance to the devastated village. As in the case of Ibn Abi Mahalli, word spread through the Sahara that the Mahdi—or at least one of his sons—had escaped alive.

The succession of Sunni mahdis was then continued in East Africa. Muhammad Ahmad ibn 'Abd Allah (1844–1885) had been initiated in Sudan as an adolescent into the Sufi rites of the Sammaniya, and went on to distinguish himself through years of rigorous asceticism under the tutelage of the grand master of the order, Shaykh Muhammad Sharif. During the interval the disciple's puritanical quickness to anger grew more pronounced, however, and after sharply criticizing the venerable shaykh for his toleration of licentiousness he found himself expelled from the Sammaniya in 1878.[42] This crisis, which recalls Ibn Abi Mahalli's condemnation of Sidi Shaykh, left Muhammad Ahmad free to organize his own order. In the meantime the Anglo-Egyptian condominium in Sudan had aroused both popular protest and millenarian unrest. Citing colonial rule as justification for mobilizing the forces of apocalypse, Muhammad proclaimed himself Mahdi in 1881. He announced that he had been enthroned in a dream by the Prophet himself, the first four caliphs acting as witnesses, and presented by Azrael—the angel of death—with a dazzlingly white banner to take with him into battle.[43]

The advent of the fourteenth century of Islam further encouraged such speculation. Muhammad Ahmad now sought the support of Sayyid al-Mahdi, the powerful leader of a Libyan order known as the Senussiya, who controlled a vast Saharan network of commerce and influence. Sayyid al-Mahdi already had quite enough to do, however, trying to restrain the millenarian enthusiasms of his own followers, and left Muhammad's missive unanswered.[44] As it happened, this was of little consequence to the Sudanese mahdi, who in November 1883—the year 1300 of the Islamic calendar—captured El-Obeid and established control over the surrounding province of Kordofan. The Mahdi Muhammad then predicted that soon he would say prayers in Khartoum, and thereafter in Mecca, Medina, Cairo, and Jerusalem, before finally praying in Kufa.[45]

James Darmesteter, in a sensational lecture two years later inaugurating his chair in Persian language and literature at the Collège de France, compared Mahdist Sudan to France in 1793: "The revolutionary idea among us and the messianic idea among the Muslims share the same instinct, the same aspiration—among us in a secular form, among them in a religious form; among us withered, in abstract formulas and theoretical arguments, among them [vibrant], in the native and radiant state of supernatural visions." Warming to his theme, Darmesteter went on to emphasize that "the Mahdi is not a politician in the European sense of the word; he is something both more and less; he is an honest fanatic."[46]

The rebel messiah had in fact declared his intention "to destroy this world in order to construct the other world,"[47] and the defeat of the Anglo-Egyptian army at Khartoum in January 1885 seemed to confirm his apocalyptic prophecies. In the aftermath of this stunning victory Muhammad Ahmad led solemn prayers in the country's largest mosque, and proceeded to found the capital of a Mahdist state at Omdurman, on the opposite bank of the Nile. But to the utter consternation of his followers, convinced that he could not die before having reached Kufa,[48] he passed away a few months later. Over the objections of his own family, Muhammad was succeeded by one of the three whom he had designated as caliph, a disciple named 'Abdallah ibn Muhammad. This familiar tension between the messianic dynamic and dynastic ambition contributed to the gradual weakening of the Mahdist state, which failed in its attempt to quell the endemic revolt in Darfur and finally collapsed in 1898, under the joint assault of forces dispatched by London and Cairo.

. . .

The events I have just briefly sketched conform in the main to a pattern of political behavior first identified by Ibn Khaldun.[49] The embrace of a messianic doctrine by a small group of revolutionaries enables them to form a united tribal and territorial front with the purpose of forcibly seizing power. In the event that this armed rebellion succeeds, the movement's initial millenarian impetus is gradually absorbed by a process of dynastic institutionalization. If it does not succeed, however, the first military defeat often turns out to be the last one for the self-proclaimed Mahdi, whose reputation for invincibility is suddenly shattered and whose followers, overcome by doubt and fear, subsequently defect. In either case, the life span of the movement is limited.

Sunnis and Shi'a remained divided even with respect to the phenomenon of Mahdist fervor. The darkness of the Great Occultation came to envelop the outlook of believers in the Hidden Imam; indeed it was this shadow alone that permitted Twelver Shi'ism to take root in Persian lands. As for the Isma'ili schismatics, even if they managed to sustain their original millenarian inspiration, only twice did they bring about a radical reversal of values, first in 931 at Qatif, and then in 1164 at Alamut—moments that were as ephemeral as they were violent. Moreover, Isma'ilism as a political movement survived the disappearance of the Fatimid caliphate by no more than a few decades.

Revolutionary messianism typically took aim at the Muslim government of the day, accusing it of corruption and debauchery. This theme, long dominant in apocalyptic rhetoric, was later developed by incorporating a further indictment of collaboration with the infidel. The Sa'dids made it the major weapon of their conquest of power in Morocco, before seeing it turned against them by Ibn Abi Mahalli; and with the advent of colonial expansion by the European powers, Muslim peoples soon found themselves on the front lines of the struggle against godless foreigners. Once an instrument of mobilization within Islam, the millenarian impulse became strengthened now that its focus had been enlarged and redirected; and the apocalyptic calendar was invested with a new vigor, since proofs of Christian deceit and the invasion of Christian armies on a massive scale now had to precede the appearance of the Mahdi, whose urgency was therefore all the more pronounced. The modern messianisms were to emerge from exactly this circumstance, in which the need to reestablish the purity of Islam and the duty to exact revenge against the West amounted to one and the same thing.

In the preceding pages we have seen how Islamic eschatology grew out of the turmoil of the first centuries of the faith, how the medieval doctors magnified this or that aspect of apocalyptic doctrine, and how messianic movements generated a dynamic that was both popular and institutional. But whereas the symbolic potential of the apocalyptic impulse was regularly and successfully exploited for the purposes of expanding dynastic control and resisting foreign penetration, the anti-colonial uprisings of the nineteenth century—excepting the interlude of the Sudanese mahdi—produced only defeat and despair. We shall now examine the reasons why for much of the twentieth century, with the formation of modern states in the Middle East, the apocalyptic element of Islamic eschatology came to be neutralized in both the Sunni and the Shi'i worlds.

PART TWO

Apocalypse Now

CHAPTER 4

Dawn of the Fifteenth Century of Islam

Cairo, and the prestigious university attached to its famous mosque, al-Azhar, have long been associated with the preeminent authorities of Sunni Islam, especially after the abolition of the Ottoman caliphate by Atatürk in 1924. For many years Egyptian religious leaders successfully discouraged all outbursts of millenarian fervor, and with all the more determination as their principled hostility was reinforced by yet vivid memories of the Sudanese mahdi, who had risen up against Egypt no less than the British Empire. Indeed, the moralizing and legitimist literature that emanated from al-Azhar was expressly intended to forestall any inclination to messianic rebellion.

In May 1942, for example, Shaykh Mahmud Shaltut, then vice dean of the faculty of religious studies at al-Azhar, decreed a fatwa in response to a question regarding the return of Jesus. It was just this kind of juridical exercise that had led al-Suyuti, almost five centuries earlier, in 1481, to develop an eschatological doctrine of lasting influence. Shaykh Shaltut, for his part, attempted to preempt debate by invalidating the most colorful—but also the most doubtful—prophecies. The view that Jesus is now alive in heaven and will come down to earth at the end of the world, for example, depends on "various uncertain and contradictory traditions dealing with the descent of Jesus after the appearance of Al-Dajjāl [The Anti-Christ]. There is no means of reconciling these contradictory traditions. Most of them emanate from Wahb ibn Munabbih and Kaʻb al Akhbar, who were Jews who became Muslims."[1] Suspicion of traditions that appeared to have been infected by Jewish mysticism *(isra'īliyyāt)* was as old as the science of hadith itself, of course, but the ruling issued by Shaykh Shaltut was notable for a degree of clarity that bordered on ruthlessness.[2]

This extreme caution in the face of apocalyptic forebodings was not the monopoly of al-Azhar and the clerical authorities. It is also found in the work of Sayyid Qutb (1906–1966), widely regarded as the father of contemporary Islamicism.[3] Whereas Gamel Abdel Nasser's regime promoted Shaykh Shaltut to the rectorship of al-Azhar,[4] it threw Sayyid Qutb in prison, finding him guilty of agitating on behalf of the Muslim Brotherhood. It was during these ten years of incarceration, from 1954 to 1964, that Qutb composed the better part of his monumental commentary on the sacred text, *Fī zilāl al-Qur'ān* (In the Shade of the Qur'an). Although he could scarcely obscure the apocalyptic message of the eighteenth sura ("The Cave"), Qutb is very careful not to pronounce on the identity of the "Two-Horned One," or on the precise nature of Gog and Magog, the monstrous peoples who were kept apart from the civilized world by an extraordinary fortification. Qutb allows the revelation to Muhammad to preserve all of its mystery, noting that "everything that is said [on this subject] is probable, without having been proved." And it is only in a footnote that Qutb ventures to situate the Qur'anic barrier on the outskirts of Termez, in present-day Uzbekistan, astride a mountain pass called the "Iron Gate."[5]

Historically, then, neither orthodox nor dissenting Sunnism has shown much tolerance for millenarian speculation. Works intended for a popular audience, colored with superstition, did, of course, continue to keep a certain messianic spirit alive, but until recently its impact on political and theological thinking was practically nil. Shi'i dogma, for its part, has traditionally found very little place for human volition in the supreme designs of the Master of the Age. And even the Khomeynist revolutionaries of the Islamic Republic were to prove noticeably reluctant to exploit the millenarian impulse.

THE REVOLUTIONARY IMAM

Ruhullah Khomeyni (1902–1989) skillfully and methodically climbed his way up the Shi'i hierarchy in Qum, until finally at the age of fifty he gained admission to the exclusive circle of ayatollahs (literally, "the signs of Allah"). From among the twenty or so most respected members of this group a handful of "grand ayatollahs" were recognized, whose company Khomeyni aspired to join in order to become a model for imitation *(marja'-e taqlīd)*. He at once adopted a line that marked a radical departure from the quietism of his peers, and he was one of the few ayatollahs to officially endorse the intolerance of the Hojjatieh Society, a politico-religious sect founded in 1953 by Shaykh Mahmud Halabi for the purpose of eradicating Baha'ism, a syncretic offshoot of Shi'ism that had appeared in Iran in the mid-nineteenth century.

The history of Baha'ism is itself very closely bound up with millenarian anxieties. Indeed, the execution of its founder on the order of the shah, in 1850, was portrayed as the work of the Antichrist.[6] A period of fierce repression followed, encouraged by the Shi'i clergy, and led to the exile of the spiritual leader of the Baha'is, Baha' Ullah, first to Iraq, then to Turkey, and finally to Palestine, where he died in 1892. His tomb in Haifa subsequently became the principal site of pilgrimage for Baha'is, a circumstance that after the founding of the state of Israel in 1948 inevitably gave rise to charges of collusion with Zionism. In 1956, in reaction against Mohammad Reza Shah Pahlavi's complacency toward the Baha'i faith, Khomeyni announced his support for Hojjatieh's resolute campaign against it, and the next year he published a fatwa condemning the drinking of Pepsi Cola, whose agent in Iran was a Baha'i.

Seven years later, in 1963, Ayatollah Khomeyni openly defied the shah's regime in denouncing the reform program known as the White Revolution, which promised, among other things, to fill positions in public administration without regard to religion and to promote the emancipation of women. When violent demonstrations broke out, he expressed approval of the protesters' aims, a crime for which he was punished only by house arrest in Teheran. On returning to Qum, in 1964, Khomeyni renewed his attacks, now rebuking the government for having granted diplomatic immunity to hundreds of American military advisors. By this point official patience was exhausted, however, and the ayatollah paid for his insubordination with exile to Turkey. Closely watched by the Kemalist regime, Khomeyni quickly grew restless and in the fall of 1965 obtained permission to settle in the holy city of Najaf, in Iraq, where he composed a number of theological studies.

In Iraq, Khomeyni was in frequent contact with Ayatollah Muhammad Baqir al-Sadr, who had made Najaf the center of resistance to the dictatorship of the Ba'th Party. Khomeyni must have noted with bitterness that his calls in 1970 for a boycott of the ceremonies of the 2,500th anniversary of the Persian Empire were largely ignored. In the meantime, however, his clandestine network of supporters in Iran had steadily grown in size and influence, and his lectures drew increasingly large audiences in Najaf, where in 1971 he published *Hokumat-e islami: Vilayat-e faqih* (Islamic Government: The Authority of the Jurisprudent). These twin concepts were to shape an unprecedented revolutionary movement that broke once and for all with the grand ayatollahs' longstanding refusal of political responsibilities. In 1977, Khomeyni promulgated a fatwa stripping Mohammad Reza Shah of any claim to legitimacy. By symbolically deposing the sovereign, Khomeyni elevated himself to the status of an "imam" and became the political and religious figurehead of the riots that followed, in the course of which hundreds of demonstrators died, later to be venerated as martyrs.

In the autumn of 1978, with Iran teetering on the edge of revolt, Saddam Hussein expelled the rebel ayatollah to France. In response, Khomeyni's supporters sought to dramatize his confrontation with the shah by appealing to apocalyptic sensibilities. A "Prayer for the Return of Ayatollah Khomeyni" was widely broadcast in poetic form, explicitly likening the imam to the awaited Mahdi:

> The Imam must come back
> So that Good will be installed on its throne,
> So that Evil, betrayal, and hatred
> Will disappear for ever and ever.[7]

Soon the rumor spread that the ayatollah's visage would be visible on the face of the moon during the night of 27 November 1978, and millions of believers claimed that they were in fact able to make out the imam's features that night.[8] Khomeyni's allies then proceeded to extend the messianic metaphor in the hope of stirring up popular feeling further, with the result that the appearance of the ayatollah's face on the moon came to be identified with the rising of the sun in the west, and therefore regarded as a sign of the Hour. But the chief purpose of this campaign was to counteract the growing opposition of the other grand ayatollahs, who feared the threat to their power of widespread popular support for the revolutionary imam. In the event, this was to be his sole venture onto millenarian terrain, but it was no less fraught with consequence for that.

Ayatollah Khomeyni's return to Teheran in February 1979 literally toppled the shah's regime. An Islamic Republic was overwhelmingly approved by referendum (with the support of 98.2 percent of the voters) that April. The principle of *vilayat-e faqih*—affirming the authority, which is to say the regency, of the religious judge—was nonetheless not mentioned, nor did it figure in the first constitutional proposals submitted by Ayatollah Khomeyni later in the spring.[9] An assembly of experts *(majiles-e khobregan)* was elected in August in balloting marked by irregularities and demonstrations, and even a boycott by some of the grand ayatollahs.[10]

Fifty-five of the seventy-two elected experts were followers of "the Imam's Line" *(khatt-e imam)* and elaborated a program based on the absolute character of the principle of *vilayat-e faqih*. Its most ardent supporters were Ayatollah Bihishti, president of the Islamic Republic Party, and Ali Khamenei, who had not yet attained the rank of ayatollah. Controversy divided Shi'i hierarchs, and the grand ayatollah Shariatmadari, whose revolutionary commitment was indisputable, nonetheless challenged the very idea of rule by a religious judge.[11] But the occupation of the United States embassy by the Muslim Student Followers of the Imam's Line, in November, and the crisis created with Washington by the taking of hostages allowed the Khomeynists to withstand internal disunity. In December 1979, a referendum on the new Constitution was approved by a majority no less overwhelming than the one that concurred in the proclamation of the Islamic Republic.[12]

Article 5 of the first chapter of this Constitution, part of a preliminary statement of principles prepared and presented by Ayatollah Bihishti himself, placed the new office of the Guide of the Revolution, held by the religious judge, under the immanent authority of the Hidden Imam: "During the occultation of His Holiness the Master of the Age (may Allah the Almighty hasten his reappearance), the executive regency and the leadership of the Islamic community of believers in the Islamic Republic of Iran belong to the just and virtuous *faqih*, who is fully aware of the problems of his time, courageous, resourceful, wise, recognized and accepted as Guide by the majority of the people."[13] This supreme power therefore emanated from the expected messiah, the Mahdi, whose authority the Guide exercised in an absolute manner.

The establishment of an Islamic Republic marked a new era within Twelver Shi'ism. But the conceptual revolution it represented was not really experienced in an apocalyptic way, partly for calendrical reasons: the passage of time is reckoned in Iran according to the solar months of the Persian calendar, rather than the lunar months of the Islamic calendar, and the Constitution of the Islamic Republic stipulated that "the records of state administration will be based on the solar calendar." Notwithstanding that the Christian year 1979 corresponded to the year 1358 of the solar calendar of the Hegira, Iranian legislators nevertheless made a point of associating the adoption of the Islamic Constitution with "the dawn of the fifteenth century of the Hegira."[14] This entry into a new century of Islam, now solemnized by constitutional ceremony in Teheran, was to be celebrated in blood in Mecca.

THE MESSIANIC UPRISING OF MECCA

The first day of the fifteenth century of Islam fell on 20 November 1979. The Hegira year begins just after the lunar month of *dhū al-hijja,* during which the *hajj*[15]—the pilgrimage to Mecca, one of the five pillars of Islam—takes place. Coming immediately after the dramatic challenge issued by Imam Khomeyni in the form of an Islamic, Shi'i, and anti-American revolution, this last pilgrimage of the fourteenth century presented King Khalid bin Abdul Aziz with an ideal opportunity for restoring the reputation of the Saudi monarchy. For Wahhabism, the kingdom's official denomination, found its fundamental justification in the organization and sponsorship of the *hajj,* which enabled it to speak and act in the name of Islam, or at least of Sunnism, in such a way as to cause Muslims to overlook the fact of Saudi Arabia's multiform alliance with the United States, the protector and defender of Israel.

At dawn this day, 20 November 1979, just as the venerable imam of the Great Mosque of Mecca was preparing to lead tens of thousands of the faithful in prayer, two or three hundred armed rebels blocked off the routes of access to the sacred grounds, overpowering the security force assigned to guard the enclosure. One of the insurgents then came forward and made his way toward the corner of the Ka'ba facing the station *(maqām)* of Abraham. There, at the urging of his followers, he proclaimed himself the awaited Mahdi.

The unthinkable had just occurred—before an incredulous Muslim world and an astounded Saudi Arabian nation. Taking the apocalyptic traditions of Islam literally, an underground organization had spent months preparing a messianic uprising.[16] Its charismatic leader, a former member of the National Guard named Juhayman al-'Utaybi, came from a family that had long borne witness to the vexed relations between the royal family and the Bedouin tribes: his grandfather had taken part in the Wahhabi raids that prepared the way in the early twentieth century for the formal establishment of Saudi Arabia; his father was a member of the tribal militia known as the Ikhwan (literally, "the Brothers") that, having helped to consolidate the Sa'uds' dynastic ambitions, later rose up unsuccessfully against King Abdul Aziz al-Sa'ud, in 1929, at a moment when jihad had been suspended for reasons of state; and Juhayman himself was born seven years later, in 1936, in one of the Ikhwan's dilapidated camps in the Nejd Desert. After his demobilization from the National Guard in 1973, 'Utaybi went to Medina, where he joined a puritanical and sectarian group of young unmarried men, most of Bedouin origin, though some were foreign students at the university there. Four years later, in 1977, he took control of the group, in effect an exile community within the nation's borders, and gave it the symbolic name of Ikhwan.

The extremism of the latter-day Ikhwan did not escape the vigilant notice of the state security services. 'Utaybi nonetheless managed to avoid being taken into custody, thanks to tribal connections within the police force, and took refuge in the Nejd, where for two years he lived a nomadic life, moving from one hiding place to another. Following upon the internal urban exile of the Ikhwan in Medina, this prolonged retreat in the Arabian desert deepened 'Utaybi's preoccupation with the classical sources of Islam, driving him to formulate an increasingly revolutionary message. In a series of eleven open letters distributed in the form of pamphlets, he denounced the corruption of the House of Sa'ud, its criminal suspension of jihad, and the nation's subjection to the Christian West. The fact that the ruling dynasty was not originally from Mecca furnished incontrovertible proof of its illegitimacy in 'Utaybi's eyes, and he scoured the prophetic traditions for evidence of the Mahdi's imminent vengeance.

The fifth of these open letters, "Tribulations *[fitan]*, the Mahdi, the Descent of Jesus, and the Signs of the Hour," argued that all such signs "are without exception associated with the Arabian Peninsula."[17] Interpreting the convulsions surrounding the birth of Saudi Arabia in pre-apocalyptic terms, 'Utaybi retroactively invested the original militia of the Ikhwan with the supreme mission of abolishing the forces of evil. The Sa'ud family having wickedly interrupted this struggle against "hypocrisy," it fell to the Ikhwan's present-day successors to bring it to fruition with explicit reference to apocalyptic prophecy, and this on the incomparably historic terrain of Arabia. 'Utaybi declared that he had devoted eight years to the study of the relevant hadiths. From these he made a very personal selection that accorded great importance to the traditions of Abu Dawud on the Mahdi, who will bear the name Muhammad Ahmad ibn 'Abd Allah, on his appearance in Mecca between the station of Abraham and the nearest corner of the Ka'ba, and on the entombment of the army sent from the north to subdue the messianic insurrection.[18]

In late 1978, 'Utaybi reported having received confirmation in a dream that one of the Ikhwan, his brother-in-law Muhammad al-Qahtani, was in fact the Mahdi. He laid emphasis on the fact that Qahtani was descended from the Prophet, that he was named Muhammad ibn Abdallah, like the Prophet himself, and that he exhibited certain physical characteristics that were consistent with the indications of the classical hadiths. Many of 'Utaybi's followers rejected these claims and quit the organization. Those who remained continued to stockpile weapons, with the reputed Mahdi's brother, Said al-Qahtani, coordinating transactions with Yemeni arms dealers. In the meantime, as munitions and supplies were being smuggled into the sacred grounds of Mecca, the conspirators underwent intense military training in the region of Hijaz.

While it is clear enough what 'Utaybi and his followers were trying to achieve, their choice of methods and their expectations are rather perplexing. Millenarian fervor became translated into angry anathemas rather than practical demands. Plainly the insurgents desired the overthrow of the ruling dynasty, as well as the punishment of all those 'ulama who, in their view, had corrupted Islam by serving the interests of the Sa'uds. 'Utaybi's hostility toward America and the West was absolute, and he insisted that oil revenues be used to combat the infidels.[19] In the event, even though all communications with the Ka'ba had been cut on the morning of the assault, this revolutionary message spread like wildfire throughout the kingdom. But to the rebels' immense dismay and incomprehension, no movement of solidarity emerged outside Mecca, for the simple reason that the sacrilege they had committed seemed unpardonable. They were no less shocked by the absence of any military response originating in northern Arabia—'Utaybi having placed his trust in a hadith, approved by Abu Dawud, announcing that hostile forces north of Mecca would launch an offensive immediately following the proclamation of the Mahdi.

The first counterattacks mounted by the security forces were quickly suppressed by the insurgents, who lay securely in ambush on all sides of the sacred enclosure. Most of the civilians who had been trapped inside by the uprising were allowed to leave, lest they interfere with the rebels' freedom of maneuver, although an unknown number were kept as hostages. The most zealous of 'Utaybi's men believed that the ones who had been freed, having first been provided with copies of the group's manifesto, could be counted on to transmit the Mahdi's preaching throughout the kingdom. Instead, a mood of despondency and dejection hung over the Saudi people three days later, on 23 November, when the call to prayer and the weekly Friday sermon were broadcast not from the Great Mosque under siege in Mecca, but from the mosque of Medina.

That same day, King Khalid obtained from Shaykh Abdelaziz ibn Baz, head of the High Council of 'Ulama,[20] a fatwa authorizing the use of force to liberate the holy precincts.[21] Blame for the sacrilege therefore fell exclusively on the partisans of the false messiah, who were now considered to be infidels. Artillery barrages, launched by the National Guard, and a helicopter raid by the Saudi Army had little effect, however. The rebels had succeeded in smuggling a considerable arsenal into the underground passages of the complex, and their suicidal determination was unshakable. To avoid any risk of identification, they went to the trouble of disfiguring the corpses of their fallen comrades-in-arms by gunfire.[22]

Prince Sultan, the minister of defense, and his nephew Prince Turki, head of the intelligence services, were put in charge of crushing the insurrection. By the end of the fourth day of the siege, two of the four minarets of the Holy Mosque had been reconquered, along with most of the upper floors. But the insurgents' stocks of munitions seemed to be inexhaustible, and fierce clashes continued. Salim bin Laden, the construction magnate whose family company had constructed the complex, furnished detailed plans of the labyrinth of tunnels, and with Prince Turki at his side made an inspection of the areas reconquered by the security forces. Together they studied the possibilities of further counterattack. At the time, the Bin Laden family shared the Saudi people's horror at the violence perpetrated in the name of the false mahdi. Later, however, Salim's brother, Usama bin Laden, refused to condemn 'Utaybi.[23]

King Hussein of Jordan, whose great-grandfather had been expelled from Mecca by the Sa'uds, offered the aid of his special forces, but the memory of previous disagreements prevented the Wahhabi sovereign from giving serious consideration to this proposal. Initially the Saudi security services had considered flooding the underground passageways, not with the idea of drowning the insurgents, but rather of electrocuting them. Difficulties in putting this stratagem into effect caused it to be abandoned. The plan that was finally settled upon, of introducing an incapacitating gas, required extremely careful preparation. Responsibility for carrying out this first phase of the operation was entrusted to French commandos from the Groupe d'Intervention de la Gendarmerie Nationale, sent at the request of Prince Turki and formally converted to Islam before going into action. In a second phase, openings having been bored through the vaults of the subterranean compound, grenades and explosives were hurled at the surviving rebels inside, forcing them to come out into the line of sight of a team of elite marksmen positioned around the courtyard. Order was finally established after two weeks of siege, but the sanctuary was soiled and the damage extensive. It took the Saudi authorities months to complete repairs in anticipation of the next pilgrimage.

The loss of human life, according to official estimates, was heavy: one hundred twenty-seven members of the security forces and a dozen of the faithful, on the one side; one hundred seventeen rebels, on the other. Other sources speak of a thousand dead, even more.[24] The shock in Saudi Arabia was tremendous. The Mahdi Qahtani seems to have been killed during the first days of the fighting, and there can be no doubt that his demise came as a severe blow to the insurgents.[25] 'Utaybi, for his part, emerged alive from the bowels of the mosque. The royal family was resolved that the surviving insurgents should meet with a spectacular death, and a series of executions was promptly scheduled to take place in several provinces of the country. On 9 January 1980, 'Utaybi and sixty-two of his men were sent to eight cities to be publicly decapitated; forty-one were Saudis, but twenty-two were foreigners (ten Egyptians, seven Yemenis, three Kuwaitis, one Iraqi, and one Sudanese). No matter that the authorities had their own reasons for emphasizing the imported character of the uprising, 'Utaybi's revolutionary messianism had unquestionably resonated beyond Saudi borders. Even within Arabia itself, the conviction was long to endure in some millenarian circles that the Mahdi had not been killed in Mecca, but that he had gone into hiding to escape the forces of evil.

· · ·

The year 1979 marked a decisive point for the Islamic world. The overthrow of the pro-American regime of the shah and the triumph of Imam Khomeyni reoriented the political axis of polemic and struggle in several fundamental ways: nationalist and progressive forces, dominant during the preceding generation, now found their influence reduced by the rise of Islamist movements; Arab anti-imperialists, regularly thwarted in their ambitions for decades, were suddenly obliged to acknowledge the success of the Iranian revolution; and Sunnism, in both its conservative and radical branches, was forced to take into account the existence of a profoundly Shi'i Islamic Republic that showed signs of interest in pursuing an expansionist foreign policy. This shift in the regional balance of power was accompanied by a transfer of supernatural legitimacy, Ayatollah Khomeyni having granted himself, as Guide of the Revolution, the powers of the Hidden Imam's representative. These powers were essentially the same ones that the Safavid sovereigns had enjoyed five hundred years earlier. Like Shah Isma'il, Khomeyni succeeded in appropriating qualities ascribed to the unseen Mahdi, whose advent was indefinitely postponed by a sort of institutionalized occultation.

In the case of Juhayman al-'Utaybi's uprising in Mecca, even more striking than its sense of revolutionary urgency is the messianic fervor that propelled it forward. Unlike Khomeyni, 'Utaybi concluded that the signs of the Hour were now so obvious and so plentiful that they justified rebellion in the most sacred space of Islam. In certain respects, his exaggerated devotion to Sunni piety and his radical critique of official Wahhabi doctrine recall the revolt led by Ibn Zubayr, grandson of the first caliph of Islam. Certainly 'Utaybi was no less hostile to the Shi'a than Ibn Zubayr had been in opposing those in Kufa who nostalgically cultivated the memory of 'Ali; and in both cases, the crushing of an insurrection in the shadow of the Ka'ba was accomplished by means of sacrilegious violence that could be conveniently attributed to foreign infidels (on the one hand, the flame-throwing "Abyssinian" of medieval chronicles, and, on the other, the French commandos). The stimulus to the eschatological imagination provided by such outrages is plain. Ultimately, however, it was the Soviet invasion of Afghanistan that was to be chiefly responsible for reviving the apocalyptic dynamic, with Khurasan, the mythical land where the appearance of the Messiah had been foretold, restored to its traditional role as the front line in the final conflict between Islam and the forces of evil.

The fifteenth century of Islam was therefore inaugurated by three almost simultaneous shocks: the triumph of the Shi'i revolution in Iran, the messianic uprising in Mecca, and the Soviet invasion of Afghanistan. Violence on this scale was enough to rouse the apocalyptic impulse from the lethargic state induced by generations of clerical contempt and, more recently, by the rise of nationalist sentiment; but the impulse did not find expression at once, either in the Sunni world, where for a number of years the Meccan sacrilege silenced millenarian enthusiasm, or in the Shi'i world, where the constitutional allegiance to the Hidden Imam in the Islamic Republic of Iran for the most part quieted messianic longings. Although black banners had once more been raised in the east, whether they signaled the approach of the Hour remained unclear to many.

CHAPTER 5

Pioneers of the Contemporary Apocalypse

On invading Afghanistan in late December 1979, the Red Army at once ran up against determined resistance from local forces united by the cause of jihad against an infidel occupier. The bloody and drawn-out Afghan war of liberation gradually attracted to its margins a cosmopolitan and radical clustering of foreign soldiers of fortune—a sort of mujahedin international dominated by Arab extremists that established itself in the tribal areas of Pakistan and made no attempt to hide its contempt for what it saw as the unconventional and derelict piety of the Afghan population.[1] But even though Afghanistan had long been identified with Khurasan,[2] apocalyptic readings of this episode of "godless" aggression at the beginning of the fifteenth century after the Hegira were few.

THE END OF THE WORLD POSTPONED

A few months after the failure of the insurrection in Mecca, a Kuwaiti Islamist named Muhammad Salama Jabir completed a work entitled *The Signs of the Hour and Their Secrets,*[3] whose principal thesis is that "the Hour will come 1,909 years after the Hegira." This dating pushed the eschatological horizon back by five hundred years. Doomsday is to be brought about by "a destructive world war that will cause civilization to disappear," for there is no question that the conflict will be "nuclear" and as devastating "in the East as in the West."[4] The essential point, to Jabir's way of thinking, is that because none of the great signs *(al-'alāmāt al-kubrā)* has yet occurred, apocalyptic speculation is utterly unfounded. It is not an accident, by the way, that such a refutation of millenarianism should have come from Kuwait, where the opposition press had published 'Utaybi's open letters against the Saudi royal house. Jabir, for his part, confirmed his lack of interest in immediate political questions by publishing a new book on the prophecies of Nostradamus.[5] In the emirate of Qatar, which shares Arabia's allegiance to Wahhabi dogma, Shaykh Abdallah ibn Zayd al-Mahmud, president of the Shari'a Courts and Religious Affairs, took matters further by issuing a categorical rebuke of messianic credulity, summarized by the formula "There is no Mahdi to be awaited."[6] In defense of this shocking claim Mahmud produced a very disputed hadith, according to which "there is no other Mahdi than Jesus."[7] In the event, his attempt to throw out the mahdist baby with the millenarian bathwater seems to have been almost universally ignored.

The Russian invasion of Afghanistan gave Arab Islamists additional grounds for attacking nationalist regimes traditionally allied with the Soviet Union. The Muslim Brotherhood in Syria, engaged in an implacable struggle with the ruling Ba'th Party, chose the path of violence. In obedience to their spiritual leader Said Hawwa, who, on taking refuge in Iraq, had declared that "certain signs of the Hour have already appeared, some are emerging at the present moment, and the other announced signs may be expected [to appear],"[8] the order's members rose up in armed rebellion in the city of Hama in March 1982, only to be drowned in their own blood. The following summer, in Beirut, the Israeli army laid siege to thousands of Palestinian fighters, abandoned to their fate by the Arab states, which cared less about the fate of the Palestinian Liberation Organization than about the conflict unleashed by Baghdad against Teheran. Ba'thist Syria having allied itself with the Islamic Republic of Iran, Saddam Hussein proclaimed Iraq the shield of the Arab nation against a new Persian invasion. Bogged down in the marshes of Mesopotamia, each camp accused the other of harboring Zionist designs.

Saudi Arabia seemed paralyzed by these developments. With the death of King Khalid at the height of the siege of Beirut, in June 1982, the throne passed to his half-brother Fahd. In the theological domain, however, the religious hierarchy, in its eagerness to erase the sacrilegious heritage of year 1400 of the Hegira, had moved quickly to reassert its authority, notably through the publication in Medina, in 1981, of *The Reply to the Lie about the Authentic Hadiths concerning the*

Mahdi.[9] The annual International Book Fair, inaugurated the same year at Imam Muhammad ibn Sa'ud Islamic University in Riyadh, furnished the occasion for promoting a literature of dogmatic restoration, and it was there that the publication of *The Concepts of Geography in the Qur'anic Account of the Two-Horned One* was first announced.[10] The author, a professor of geography in Riyadh named Abdelhalim Abderrahman Khodr, claimed to employ an Islamic methodology in pursuing "scientific and objective studies."[11] Khodr sought to rebut the quite widespread belief that the Great Wall of China had been erected by superhuman means as a barrier against Gog and Magog, while at the same time rejecting Sayyid Qutb's argument regarding Termez. Instead he situated the Qur'anic wall in the Caucasus, and more specifically along the Daryal Pass.

One of Khodr's colleagues, a Kurd named Muhammad Kheir Ramadan Yusuf, extended this line of thought the following year, in 1982, concentrating on the Two-Horned One rather than on Gog and Magog. Despite devoting more than four hundred pages to the topic,[12] Yusuf was careful not to claim to have discovered the exact identity of the *dhū al-qarnayn*. He left open three possibilities: Cyrus the Great, the first Achaemenid emperor of Persia, who built a wall across the Caucasus that may have been the Qur'anic barrier;[13] Alexander the Great, of Macedonia; or a nameless Himyarite sovereign of ancient Yemen. Neither Khodr nor Yusuf, it is important to note, ventured to draw any conclusions regarding present or future events. Their reluctance had the advantage of deflecting apocalyptic anxieties, now safely relocated in a chronological and geographical elsewhere, but it seemed curiously detached from the pressing realities of a world that now was filled, to the point of overflowing, with violence.

Two bombings, several months apart from one another, soon demonstrated the extreme vulnerability of Muslim states to displays of Israeli-American power. In October 1985, Israeli planes struck almost 1,500 miles from their bases, decimating the headquarters of the Palestinian leadership in a southern suburb of Tunis and killing seventy-three people. In April of the following year, American F-111s carried out a nighttime raid against Tripoli in retaliation for the bombing of a discotheque in Berlin. The many victims included the adoptive daughter of Colonel Muammar Qadafi, who was to be profoundly disturbed by the loss. During this same period, the successive revelations of what came to be known as the Iran-Contra affair disclosed the extent of the military support provided by the United States and Israel for the Islamic

Republic in its war against Iraq. Weakened by impotent and corrupt nationalist regimes, the Arab world appeared at best threatened and besieged, at worst divided and betrayed. It was in this atmosphere of humiliation and disarray that a second-rate pamphleteer established his reputation by inventing a novel type of protest literature that was to enjoy an almost unimaginable popularity.

THE APOCALYPSE ACCORDING TO JOB

By signing a peace treaty with Israel in March 1979, Egypt had forfeited its dominant position in the Arab world. It is true that the whole of the Sinai had been restored to it, indeed the full measure of its territorial integrity, and that it had succeeded in negotiating generous terms of financial and military assistance from the United States. But for this Egypt found itself expelled from the Arab League, whose seat was now transferred to Tunisia, and its influence in managing regional crises was considerably reduced. Cairo's condemnation of the bombings of Tunis and Tripoli was muted. Although Islamist terrorists had not been able to create a revolutionary dynamic after the assassination of President Sadat, they continued to carry out spectacular attacks, even in the center of the Egyptian capital. Government security forces were powerless to eradicate this threat, in large part because they were busy tearing themselves apart. Hundreds died in February 1986 when the army crushed a rebellion by the police in Cairo.

Amid the confusion and tumult, an obscure journalist with a background in literary criticism set out to completely revise the standard apocalyptic account. In August 1986, Said Ayyub finished composing *The Antichrist* (in Arabic, *Al-Masīh al-Dajjāl*—literally, The False Messiah), a work meant to provide, in the words of its subtitle, a political interpretation of the foundations of the great religions (see Plate 1). Notwithstanding his claims for the "objectivity"[14] of his "research,"[15] it is plain that the righteous and long-suffering author (whose name, Ayyub, happens to correspond to the Hebrew name we know from the Bible as Job) is obsessed by a single idea, namely, that the history of humanity is only a succession of nefarious maneuvers by the "Jewish" Antichrist,[16] leading up to the moment when Islam, his sworn enemy, will bring against him the decisive and apocalyptic battle.

Ayyub does not shrink from grandiloquence. He begins by making an "appeal to all political and religious leaders in the West, to all Jewish leaders, political and religious [alike], and to every man concerned with the future of humanity." By this exhortation Ayyub sought to make his Arab and Muslim readers believe in the universality of a message that in fact is addressed exclusively to them. For the book is dedicated to the Prophet Muhammad, whom Christian propaganda accuses of being the Antichrist,[17] and its subject is the future of Islam, permanently under assault but ultimately triumphant. Ayyub writes:

> The Jews have placed themselves in the hands of the Antichrist. They have considered him as one of their princes, they have forged a strategy for [carrying out] his purposes, and they have held to it. They have used all the means at their disposal to realize this supreme goal. They have infiltrated political and diplomatic activity in many places in the world, and they have penetrated societies through channels of communication that they control. And all that for the Antichrist! This Antichrist lives in our midst today, in our world! He knows the frontiers reached and occupied by Israel, and it is from this place [i.e., Israel], where he lives, that he will venture forth.[18]

The Antichrist's first intermediary, Ayyub says, was Saint Paul himself, who betrayed Jesus's message by both words and deeds. Jesus was a human being, endowed like Moses and Muhammad with prophetic powers, and the divinization of his person by Saint Paul therefore represented "the first catastrophe." It was followed by the scattering of Christians throughout the world, a stratagem for preserving Jewish domination over Jerusalem. This first "tactical phase" was completed by a second: "Paul founded in Jesus's name a religion that Jesus would not have understood when he was alive . . . and that he will not understand when he returns at the end of times." The new "fetishism" associated with this religion operates through the worship of "idols," making it possible to "establish an apocalyptic cult of the Antichrist."[19]

To illustrate the nature of the duplicity practiced by Paul, outwardly a Christian but in fact militantly Jewish, Ayyub quotes misleadingly from the Jesuit theologian Jean Cardinal Daniélou and Maurice Bucaille, a French physician whose patients included King Faysal of Saudi Arabia.[20] References to Western authors, brandished like talismans against every criticism, are essential to Ayyub's argument, which in the space of a paragraph manages to invoke the authority of Arnold Toynbee, Bertrand Russell, and even V.I. Lenin. The sacred texts of the "peoples of the Book" are regularly quoted as well, above all the prophecies of Daniel and the Apocalypse of "Master John."[21] Yet Ayyub's truncated and fanatical reading is not limited to the Judeo-Christian scriptures. Islamic traditions are typically repeated at second hand, but in the event that they are taken from classical accounts, they are never ones that have been validated by Bukhari, and only very rarely by Muslim. This habitual reliance on doubtful hadiths is coupled with frequent citations to Ibn Kathir and his teacher Ibn Taymiyya, and, nearer our own time, to Sayyid Qutb.

After Saint Paul's diabolical manipulations came the treachery of Emperor Constantine, who "saw the cross in the sky" and "reinforced the citadel of the Antichrist, built by the Jews, in adding to it a perilous dimension—the emergence of the Crusader state in the service of the Jews. This Crusader state survived Constantine and endured throughout history." Ayyub goes on to express his conviction that "in all the great transformations of thought, there is a Jewish factor, avowed and plain, or else hidden and secret." This unequivocal causality makes it possible to detect the Antichrist's influence on both "the bishop of Cluny, foreman of the Crusades" and Luther, "whose Jewish inclinations led him to enthusiastically study Hebrew." It was for this reason that "the thinking of the Messiah awaited by the Jews came to be firmly anchored in the Protestant movement."[22]

"Freemasonry," Ayyub says, "is the oldest of the secret organizations that the Jews have created to control events on behalf of the Antichrist." Ayyub takes literally the myth of a "masonry" going back to Solomon's temple, and reveals that the fusion between Judaism, Protestantism, and Freemasonry came about in the New World:

> The Protestants and the Jews fled to America, where they found Indians and gold and proceeded to divide them up: the Protestants fought the Indians in order to appropriate their lands, while the Jews furnished [the Protestants] with the means for conducting this warfare and monopolized the search for gold. Freemasonry prospered in America. And Hebrew culture spread over this land, so much so that Jews throughout the whole world regarded America as the new Canaan. As for the Protestants, they gave their children names from the Old Testament, and named their towns after those in the Bible. For the Bible had acquired legislative authority in America. [Together] this Jewish renaissance and American Protestant theology created messianic expectations throughout the American continent.[23]

However, Ayyub continues, "the Antichrist had [many] years of deceit yet to look forward to." Even as America was gradually coming under his sway, he hastened to make his influence felt on all sides: Napoleon Bonaparte was only one of the Antichrist's instruments when, in 1798, he called upon "all the Jews of Africa and Asia to join together in restoring the ancient kingdom of Jerusalem," a dream that was to be disappointed at Acre; Karl Marx, for his part, did no more than give his name to "a Jewish doctrine developed four centuries before his birth," for "the Jews use Communism to realize their secret ambitions" and "Communism bound man to his daily bread, since the Antichrist was to bring with him a mountain of bread"; and as for Atatürk, he "rendered the greatest service to the Jews and to the enemies of Islam by abolishing the Ottoman state."[24]

Nonetheless the Judeo-Christian alliance presently in power in the United States constitutes the gravest menace facing Islam. From the notes of an "advisor to President Johnson" Ayyub deduces evidence of an ineluctable "conflict between Muslim civilization and Christian civilization." America is attempting to impose the "way of the Antichrist" on the Muslim peoples by "threatening" to cut off aid to them or obliging them to submit to the will of the World Bank. Ayyub also reports Ronald Reagan's conviction that "the Messiah had taken him by the hand to lead him to victory in the battle of Armageddon."[25] The evident intensity of the American-Soviet rivalry cannot be allowed to obscure the fact that a general war against Islam is taking shape. The signs of this, Ayyub says, are to be found in "Israeli-American strategic cooperation" and "the demand to make Israel a part of NATO." To be sure, "the peace treaty between Israel and Egypt will remain in force until the coming of the Antichrist," but "Egypt and Israel will go to war with each other at the end of times,"[26] Ayyub declares, relying in this instance on the authority of the prophets Isaiah and Daniel.

All these things will prepare the way for an inevitable conflagration between "the two camps" of faith and impiety. In the former camp, resolutely opposed to the Jewish and Christian partisans of the Antichrist, are the followers of Islam, who trust in the return of the Mahdi to strike down the "false messiah." Citing the testimony of Sayyid Qutb, Ayyub repeatedly emphasizes that satanic attempts to "dissolve [Islamic] dogma" and force conversions must be answered by the absolute condemnation of "apostasy."[27] Muslims have no alternative but to close ranks and steel themselves against a massive assault that will be both direct and merciless.

"Earthquakes, volcanic eruptions, and droughts will precede the appearance of the Antichrist," and "the temperature will rise perceptibly," provoking new catastrophes. The false messiah will long remain hidden in Palestine, a desolate land "where every imaginable form of artillery will be concentrated, as well as every conceivable means of espionage and destruction." The portent of these signs is plain: "The Jews are planning the Third World War in order to eliminate the

Islamic world and all opposition to Israel"—all of this, of course, for the greater glory of the Antichrist. Then the "crown of battles" will break out, the Great Battle of the medieval apocalypses. "Blood will flow and even the 'ulama [sic] of the peoples of the Book say that the battle will not be limited to Israel." Ayyub suggests that a "tall building" will be at the heart of these clashes, for its three stories will represent respectively the cult of the Antichrist, his military force, and his preaching (da'wa).[28]

Ayyub closely associates the Crusades with the Christian prophecy of Armageddon. "The war of the beginning of times and the war of the end of times," he says, "are two sides of the same coin"—whence his indomitable optimism with regard to the outcome of this ghastly conflict: "In truth, the road that was opened up to Cluny and paved by the expulsion of the Crusaders from Jerusalem is the same road that will be followed by the global Crusaders and the Jews of our era; their corpses will be delivered up to the birds of Armageddon, and their flesh will be scattered about the skies."[29] This carnage will mark the end of Israel, and with the reconquest of its capital "the command of the Islamic camp, first installed in Damascus, will be transferred to Jerusalem." In vain will the Antichrist summon the ten horsemen of the Apocalypse, for the moral corruption will be so great among his followers that they "will no longer respect any value or limit, indeed they will fall to the level of monkeys and swine."[30]

These novel insights are interspersed with apocalyptic quotations, many of them taken from Ibn Kathir. Tamim al-Dari's meeting with the Antichrist, in the version transmitted by Abu Dawud, is commented on at length, allowing Ayyub to describe the Palestinian geography of the apocalypse in detail. Unburdened by any very great concern for consistency, he goes on to assert that "the Antichrist will appear in Khurasan as the head of an expansionist state" and as "a dictator steeped in hatred and jealousy toward the Islamic world"—and then quickly disposes of this obvious contradiction in his account by concluding that "the appearance of the Antichrist will sow discord on the right and on the left of the surface of the planet."[31]

The Islamic forces, directed from Jerusalem, will have three regional commands: one in Damascus, responsible for Syria; another in Hira, for Iraq; and the third in Bahrain, for the Persian Gulf. The Antichrist's troops, equipped with chemical weapons, will gather in the Iranian city of Kerman to launch a dual offensive, on the one hand toward the Strait of Hormuz, aiming at Mecca, and on the other toward southern Iraq, in the direction of Jerusalem. Medina, in keeping with Islamic tradition,

will be protected by angels. Ayyub seems to envisage a successful flank-
ing maneuver by the partisans of the Antichrist, taking as his authority
a highly contested hadith: "The rest among you shall fight the Antichrist
on the Jordan, you on the east bank and you others on the west." But
this is in any case of little importance, for "the aims of Islam are global
in scale,"[32] and its final triumph will be total.

Even the briefest summary of *The Antichrist* is bound to arouse a
profound sense of unease, not least for its wild exaggerations and reck-
less allegations. But it was just these things that helped make it a pioneering work. Displaying a haughty disregard for earlier apocalyptic
accounts, and permitting himself the most unorthodox speculations
imaginable, Ayyub ruptured the organic link between Islamic tradition
and the last days of the world. In doing this he invented a new genre,
apocalyptic fiction, whose purpose was both educational and propagan-
distic, and whose influence was destined rapidly to spread throughout
the lands of Islam.

Perhaps the most unsettling aspect of *The Antichrist* is its obsessive
anti-Semitism. Ayyub quotes frequently from Western writers such as
Gustave Le Bon and William Guy Carr to support what he is pleased
to call his "argument."[33] The charge against the Jews is chronically and
systematically reiterated, together with denials of the Holocaust and
various other vile slanders from which not even the pope, who stands
accused of having betrayed the Catholic faith by visiting a synagogue, is
exempt. Ayyub's own professions of honorable intent do little more than
add insult to injury: "We have nothing against the Jews! But why does
Israel attack Arabs, who are [themselves] Semites, and wage war against
Muslims, the chosen people of Allah *[sha'ab Allāh al-mukhtār]*?"[34]

Readers will have been given fair warning, however, by the cover
illustration of *The Antichrist*, which reproduces the crudest stereotypes
of anti-Semitic imagery: a helmeted monster with a protuberant and
hooked nose, the Star of David hanging from his neck, and, sewn on
his uniform, American and Soviet emblems (Plate 1). With the appearance of this seminal work the Islamic apocalypse collided with current
events, henceforth serving as a backdrop to the indictment of Egypt as
a puppet of the United States and Israel. The "Jewish siege of Beirut"
during the summer of 1982 reached its climax at Sabra and Shatilla,
Ayyub says, with "the worst massacres of the twentieth century" under
"the smiling gaze of the Statue of Liberty."[35] The Iran-Iraq war, on the
other hand, which was in its seventh brutal year when Ayyub finished
writing his book, is nowhere mentioned, not even in the discussion of

Khurasan. This should not come as a surprise, perhaps, for Palestine and Arab dishonor at the hands of the Jews furnish the author with the main elements of his sinister fable.

THE COUNTEROFFENSIVE OF THE CLERICS

The Antichrist enjoyed an impressive and lasting success not only in Cairo but throughout the Arab world, where the publishing industry continued to be dominated by Egyptian titles. Slackening demand in the domestic market in Egypt, long a source of concern to local publishing houses, was eventually compensated for through targeted investment and an aggressive campaign to promote Egyptian books abroad.[36] As a leading beneficiary of this effort, and encouraged by the popularity of his first book, Said Ayyub went on to write a half-dozen others having an apocalyptic theme, notably *The Doctrine of the Antichrist in the Religions* and *The Trials of Nations*.[37] What is more, he inspired imitators. Two of them, Ayyub's countrymen Muhammad Izzat Arif and Muhammad Isa Dawud, were to enjoy even greater success.

By contrast with the apparent tolerance shown by Egyptian political authorities, the religious authorities plainly could not remain indifferent to the liberties taken by Ayyub with dogma and tradition. Nor could the counteroffensive be led officially by al-Azhar, since the Sorbonne of Islam, as it is sometimes called, could scarcely be seen as stooping to respond to a mere pamphleteer, and a layman at that. Instead the task was confided to a man named Abdellatif Ashur, who claimed to speak on behalf of "the various departments of Islamic research at al-Azhar" and who boasted of his "balanced [Qur'anic] commentary *[tafsir wasīt]*."[38] Ashur published two books in rapid succession, *The Three Whom the World Awaits: Jesus, the Antichrist, and the Mahdi* (1987) and *The Antichrist: The Reality, Not Fantasies* (1988).[39] The argument of these works is carefully developed, and the pertinent prophetic traditions are methodically reviewed. In this regard the second work, which gives a precise reference for each citation, is more rigorous than the first, from which footnotes are almost wholly absent.

Despite his avowed faithfulness to classical orthodoxy, Ashur largely fails in his purpose since, like the very author he attacks, he is concerned to advance a conspiracy theory. Whereas Ayyub's compulsive anti-Semitism is based on the idea that the Jewish Messiah and the Antichrist are one and the same, Ashur denounces three false prophets who he believes have already sought to lead Islam astray:[40] the nineteenth-century Sudanese mahdi Muhammad Ahmad ibn Abdallah, whom the intelligentsia of Cairo never forgave for having triumphantly resisted Anglo-Egyptian domination; Mirza Hussayn Ali Nuri (1817–1892), the true founder of the Baha'i religion in Iran, sent into exile first to Iraq, then to Turkey, and finally to Palestine; and Mirza Ghulam Ahmad Qadyani (1839–1908), who proclaimed himself in British India both the Mahdi and the new Jesus, having convinced the members of his sect (known as the Ahmadiyya) that Jesus was dead and buried in Kashmir.[41] Ashur is determined to show that the Baha'is and the Ahmadis were working actively or passively on behalf of the Antichrist, whose advent they prepared by undermining the foundations of Islam; but in yielding to the same paranoid temptation as Ayyub, and notwithstanding his rhetorical restraint, Ashur disqualifies himself for the assignment of combating the claims of *The Antichrist*.

A more serious attempt to reassert control over the standard apocalyptic account was made by two other authors, Muhammad Bayyumi and Magdi Muhammad Shahawi. Both enjoyed a certain measure of academic credibility (though Bayyumi had closer ties to al-Azhar than Shahawi) while at the same time writing for a popular audience. Both were published by Maktabat al-Imam (The Library of Faith) in Cairo, and both could plausibly be regarded as demonstrating the advantages of a sound religious training by comparison with the untutored and dangerous eccentricities of an author such as Ayyub. Moreover, having already published short books on astrology, the interpretation of dreams, and the world of jinns, both had proven their ability to discuss the chief topics of popular superstition in a more or less strictly orthodox manner. For just this reason, however, the possibility of a conflict of interest cannot be excluded, since by undermining Ayyub's credibility they would be in a stronger position to defend their share of this increasingly profitable niche in the religious publishing market.

The principal accusation made by these authors against Ayyub concerns his degraded treatment of Islamic traditions, often cited at second hand and, still more troublingly, placed on the same level as the Christian prophets and Western anti-Semitic literature. Bayyumi devoted three works to a detailed reconsideration of the classical hadiths, which alone, he held, are capable of illuminating the corruption of modern societies.[42] Shahawi chose a quite different method, preferring to refute the more than three hundred dense pages of *The Antichrist* by means of a slender booklet of only eighty pages entitled *The Antichrist and Gog and Magog*.[43] The typography and page layout of this study (dirāsa) are admirably clear, with questions framed by boxheads and replies underlined; the hadiths are set in boldface, and summaries are presented at the end of each chapter. On the cover, in place of Ayyub's quasi-Nazi imagery, Shahawi's publisher insisted on a more sober design, or in any case one that was more in keeping with the customary Islamic stereo-type of the Antichrist: a one-eyed man, bald and bearded, with the word "infidel" written on his forehead (Plate 2).

Whereas Ayyub's preoccupation with the Jewish roots of Christian messianism leads him to neglect Jesus's apocalyptic role, Shahawi moves at once to restore the direct and symmetrical opposition between the two messiahs: Jesus, "the messiah of the right path" *(masīh al-hudā)*, and the Antichrist, "the messiah of deviation [from the right path]" *(masīh al-dhahāla)*. Although Shahawi does consider the possibility that the Antichrist might appear at Kufa, it is instead the classic conception of the false messiah's emergence in Khurasan, flanked by seventy thousand Jews from Isfahan, that finally meets with his approval. As for Jesus, he will indeed descend upon "the white minaret on the east side of Damas-cus" and give chase to the Antichrist, killing him at the gate of Lod.[44]

While it is true that Shahawi cites the "authentic" collections of Bukhari and Muslim at every possible opportunity, he is more comfort-able quoting from Ibn Hanbal and his disciple Abu Dawud, who lead on in turn to Ibn Taymiyya and Ibn Kathir—an intellectual genealogy that exposes Shahawi to the potentially fatal charge of trafficking in counterfeit hadiths. Nonetheless he is very careful to guard against any extraneous digression regarding the present whereabouts of the Anti-christ. Shahawi slips only once, when he comes to consider the matter of Gog and Magog: he holds that their names are "Persian in the extreme"; that the Turks, alone among the twenty-two tribes that constitute these abhorrent peoples, have escaped being shut in behind the wall built to contain them; and that this wall still stands in the Caucasus, at the Daryal Pass.[45] Shahawi recoils from drawing the logical conclusion of such a line of reasoning, namely, that Gog and Magog live on the other side of this pass, in present-day Georgia—rather than in modern Uzbekistan (as Qutb believed) or somewhere even further to the east.

Hassan Zakarya Fulayfil's pamphlet *Gog and Magog,* published in 1991, is hardly more convincing.[46] Notwithstanding that Sayyid Qutb figures among the authors he cites, this rather readable essay amounts to little more than a detailed exposition of the classical sources on the two nations of the damned, supplemented by the commentaries of Ibn Kathir and of al-Suyuti. Fulayfil says nothing very novel or daring. He notes that "Gog and Magog are the symbols of corruption that announce the coming of the Hour," and associates the two nations with the Mongols and the Tartars.[47] But there is no attempt to look forward, and readers hoping for apocalyptic insight into their current predicament are bound to be disappointed. They will experience the same frustration on turning to Okasha Abdelmannan al-Tibi's *The Whole Truth about the Antichrist,* also published in 1991.[48] Although the cover is no less outlandishly illustrated than Fulayfil's book, this "critical study" *(dirāsa naqdiyya)* turns out to be just as resolutely preoccupied by classical tradition and a bygone past (Plate 3). Tibi repeated the same formula a few years later in *The Agony of the Resurrection,*[49] a work whose cover shows a poor wretch howling in terror while buildings collapse around him, and whose main interest consists in its enumeration of forty-five different names for the day of resurrection. As for Hamza Faqir's *Gog and Magog,*[50] the little crimson devils on the cover once again do little to camouflage the tedious rehashing of familiar quotations inside.

THE BERMUDA TRIANGLE AND FLYING SAUCERS

This conservative apocalyptic literature, inspired by al-Azhar if not actually sponsored by it, was distributed to the book trade via the same outlets as Ayyub's *Antichrist* and quickly found an audience of its own throughout the Arab world. More generally, the revival of millenarian speculation gave rise to a whole popular subculture whose superstitions and violent prejudices now enjoyed the imprimatur of respectable publishing houses. In the meantime, messianic anxieties had been aggravated by the Iraqi invasion of Kuwait, in August 1990, and by the profound split among Arab nations that occurred in response to this, with Yemen and Sudan supporting Saddam Hussein against Egypt and Syria—allies of the petromonarchies and so, by extension, of the United States as well.

The success of the new genre produced surprising changes of professional interest among established authors. The Cairo writer Muhammad Izzat Arif, for example, abandoned religious history in order to devote himself to the theme of apocalypse and to predict the end of Saddam in a short book of the same name.[51] In this he was encouraged by his publisher, the venerable Dar al-I'tisam (The House of Refuge), which was casting around for a way to boost flagging sales.[52] Arif was only too happy to oblige, and depicted the Iraqi dictator as an Israeli agent with instructions to set in motion a vast Jewish conspiracy to shatter the united front of Islam. In the wake of Iraq's defeat at the hands of the U.S.-led coalition formed to liberate Kuwait, Arif immediately came out with another pamphlet entitled *The End of the Jews.*[53] This was followed some years later by *Does the Antichrist Rule the World?* (Plate 4), which claimed that "the Antichrist is the spiritual father of the Jews."[54] Already masters of America, the Antichrist's Jewish representatives and their Masonic henchmen also control the Vatican, as formerly they had controlled world communism, for it is their "secret hand that directs conspiracies and revolutions." Cinema and satellite television, the favored instruments of this "cultural invasion," pose a particularly worrisome threat to Muslim children, who now find themselves subject to the baleful influence of Ninja Turtles.[55]

In the meantime a young friend of Arif named Muhammad Isa Dawud had managed to push the boundaries of anti-Semitic delirium still further. Once an anonymous journalist on the staff of the Cairo daily *Al-Akhbar,* Dawud made a name for himself working for the Saudi press, in whose columns he published an open letter to a Christian woman who had converted to Islam and, rather more remarkably, an interview with a "Muslim jinn." Armed with the self-awarded title of "professor" *(ustāz),* Dawud now rushed into the apocalyptic breach in 1991 with a book entitled *Beware: The Antichrist Has Invaded the World from the Bermuda Triangle*[56] that was notable for its undisguised hostility toward Hollywood (a sentiment shared with Arif) and, in particular, the films of Burt Lancaster and Clint Eastwood. But Dawud's suspicions of worldwide conspiracy acquired a new dimension in his next book, *The Hidden Links between the Antichrist, the Secrets of the Bermuda Triangle, and Flying Saucers* (1994),[57] the cover of which bears the notice "Warning to All Mankind" in red lettering (Plate 5).

Dawud has frequent recourse in this work to the classic texts of Western anti-Semitism, notably *The Protocols of the Elders of Zion,*[58] as well as the hateful polemics of Count Cherep-Spirodovich[59] and William Guy Carr,[60] and incorporates their vision of an enormous Jewish conspiracy in a paranoid historiography in which Satan assumes the traits of the "Samaritan," founder of the cult of the Golden Calf and subsequently the corruptor of Sodom and Gomorrah.[61] In Dawud's telling, the spawn of this demoniacal creature was forced to take refuge on an island off the coast of Yemen, where the Beast gave him much comfort and instruction. Once grown to maturity and become the Antichrist, he managed to insinuate himself in the court of the Pharaoh, where he humiliated Moses. Following the failure of various schemes aimed at consolidating his rule over the world, the Antichrist came back to the home of his youth and there fell into the clutches of the Beast. At this juncture in a rather rambling account Dawud introduces Muslim's hadith regarding Tamim-al-Dari's encounter with the Antichrist and the Beast. Some time after this mythical interview, the Antichrist was able to recover his freedom of movement and, in the eighth century, sailed as far as North America, where his fondness for island life led him to make Bermuda his home base. From here he dispatched spies throughout the entire world, under the false identity of harmless merchants. Eight centuries later, the Antichrist left Bermuda to foment the French Revolution and to install his agents at the head of the new regimes that were to come to power in its aftermath.[62]

In the present day the Antichrist reserves a special hatred for Egypt, which he has made the target of a "major Jewish plot"—for this "richest country in the world [is] the key to the Islamic caliphate." He has therefore sent squads of elite commandos to patrol the Egyptian skies aboard flying saucers. "The Bermuda Triangle," Dawud assures his readers, "is the point of departure and return for the flying saucers, and a [huge] labor force is busily employed there" for the purpose of achieving world domination through its superior command of advanced technologies— a claim that is helpfully accompanied by a table describing the various models of flying saucer.[63] But all this satanic energy has only one objective, namely, the Antichrist's victorious return to Jerusalem. Jewish and Christian Zionists are presently working hand in hand to bring about this sinister state of affairs, together with the royal family of Jordan, which for tactical reasons has concealed its Jewish origins and faith.[64] Dawud concludes by quoting the American televangelist Jerry Falwell: "The Camp David accords [between Israel and Egypt] will not last. . . . For there will be no real peace in the Near East until the Messiah once again sits on the throne of David in Jerusalem."[65]

Muhammad Fuad Shakir, a professor at the University of Suez, likewise sought to combat "worldwide Zionist Christianity" in a book that appeared the same year under the title *The Antichrist: Messiah of Deviation* (1994). By "exculpating the Jews of the murder of Jesus," Shakir argued, Christians laid the foundations of an unshakable alliance meant to "eliminate Islam." George H. W. Bush was a leading architect of this alliance even before his accession to the presidency, having, for example, supervised the removal of Ethiopian Jews to Israel via Sudan as vice president under Reagan. Convinced that "the strengthening of the state of Israel will hasten the return of the Messiah," and that "the world must be run from Jerusalem," Zionist Christians therefore gave their unconditional support to the Jewish state, even seeing in it "the key to the permanence of America." And just as Dawud had done, Shakir used the hadith relating Tamim al-Dari's encounter with the Antichrist on an island off the coast of Yemen as an argument for locating the Antichrist today in one of the islands that make up Bermuda ("the islands of the Devil"),[66] from which he rules America and the world. The cover of Shakir's book shows a one-eyed Uncle Sam, with the classical features of the Antichrist, brandishing a false dove of peace inside of which lurks a crowd of caricatured Jews.

Two years later another Egyptian pamphleteer by the name of Atif Lamada set to work mining this same furiously anti-Semitic vein of invective. The uncluttered page design and generously leaded typography of his book *What Is Known about the Antichrist?* (1996)[67] recall Shahawi's pedagogical ambitions (though here, to forestall the least chance of confusion, even the chapter heads are framed by boldfaced arrows). Additionally, like Ashur before him, Lamada speaks not of the *masīh*, but of the *masīkh*—the messiah become monster—which makes it possible to directly oppose Jesus *(masīh)* to the Antichrist *(masīkh)*.[68] And whereas Ayyub dedicated his book to the highest authorities of the revealed religions, Lamada betrays a certain provincialism by invoking the names of his nephews, friends, and in-laws.

More precise than Ayyub in his citation of the prophetic traditions, Lamada is also more radical in his absolute hatred of the Jewish people, which he says has been "damned by its Lord." For this reason it is necessary to "look into the dark history of the sons of Israel," and to "examine international events going back a very long ways in order to recognize [the Jews'] hand in crimes perpetrated in all times and in all places." One chapter bears the title "The Followers of the Antichrist Are the Jews, May They Be Damned by Allah." Lamada joins Ayyub in accusing Saint Paul of hijacking the Christian religion on behalf of Jewish interests, in asserting that "the Jews manipulate kings and presidents behind the scenes," and in incessantly calling down curses upon them, "for they sow the earth with ruin, destruction, war, and conflict—all this to prepare the way for the Antichrist." Finally, Lamada finds words no less wounding than the ones used by Ayyub to greet with "derision" the claim of the Jews to be the "chosen people," since it is plain that the "chosen people of Allah" are the Arabs, who were chosen to receive the Revelation, and, more generally, the community of Muslims.[69]

In the face of this flood of apocalyptic propaganda, and the subversive challenge that it embodied to orthodox teaching, a new counterattack was launched by a pair of Cairo publishing houses. In 1996, Maktabat al-Sunna (The Library of Tradition) published a lecture entitled "The Awaited Mahdi" that had been given some twenty years earlier in Arabia by Shaykh al-Abbad at the request of the grand mufti, Ibn Baz.[70] Evidently the honor conferred on the author by so eminent a cleric was supposed to recommend a text that otherwise, in view of its scrupulous citation of the classical and medieval references on the subject, held little appeal for a popular audience. Additionally, under the title *The Antichrist,* Maktabat al-Sunna distributed a selection of the apocalyptic writings of Ibn Kathir.[71]

A second publishing house, Al-Tawfiqiyya (The Mediator), hired an author named Amin Muhammad Gamaleddin to write a series of booklets on "the impending appearance of the Mahdi." Identifying himself only as an "engineer," Gamaleddin nonetheless claimed to be a graduate of the "Faculty of Islamic Preaching *[da'wa]*" at al-Azhar, having pursued "advanced studies in Islamic preaching and culture" there—doubtful credentials that appeared on the cover of his first book, *The Revelation of the Minor Signs of the Hour* (1997).[72] Methodically and precisely Gamaleddin proceeds to recapitulate these signs, all seventy-nine of which, he says, have already come to pass. Of this number he distinguishes six, which occurred during the first centuries of Islam, from seventy-three others that occurred later, up until the spring of 1997, when he completed his book.

Among these consummated omens it is unsurprising to find the construction of taller and taller buildings (sign 9), the spread of adultery and fornication (10), and the increasing consumption of alcohol (12). But some items in Gamaleddin's pre-apocalyptic catalogue are less frequently encountered, such as the participation of women in the work and business of their husbands (29), the increasingly general use of automobiles (48), and, interestingly, the rise in the noise level inside mosques (67). In this latter connection the author seems to be disturbed by the lack of vocal restraint on the part of worshipers, rather than the growing reliance of the clergy on loudspeakers.[73]

Unlike Shahawi, however, Gamaleddin permits himself the luxury of candid and uninhibited commentary on the most pressing issues of the day, and includes in his inventory of the minor signs of the Hour a number of events that took place after the Gulf War: the "siege of Iraq, threatened by hunger" (sign 72) and the sanctions similarly imposed on Syria (73); the "dissension in all the houses" (75); the "fighting between the Turks and Iraq" (sign 78); and, finally, "the truce *[hudna]* and the reconciliation *[mussālaha]* between the Muslims and the Byzantines *[Rūm]*" (sign 79).

Gamaleddin finds no excuse for Saddam Hussein, who invaded Kuwait through "stupidity," and thus permitted the "Byzantines, which is to say America, to gain a foothold in our lands and to officially establish military bases in conformity with international law. They then struck Iraq in its strategic heart and destroyed the eastern wing of the Islamic nation." What Gamaleddin calls the siege of Iraq, first instituted in 1991, was formalized five years later by the United Nations "Oil for Food" program; the land of Shām (or Syria, which once included present-day Lebanon, Palestine, and Jordan) endured comparable suffering. To complete the disaster, secular Turkey, which had buried the caliphate and allied itself with Israel, with the blessing of the United States, now opposed Iraq by building a dam on the upper course of the Euphrates.[74]

Such an accumulation of dire signs would appear to point to the same conclusion as the one drawn earlier by Ayyub. But then at the last moment, on coming to his seventy-ninth and final sign of the Hour, Gamaleddin utterly inverts the apocalyptic perspective. With regard to what he sees as the lasting peace, ratified by formal accords, recently concluded between Muslim nations, on the one hand, and Europe and America, on the other, Gamaleddin cites the hadith on the truce with the Banū al-Asfar, whom he identifies with the "Western Christians of today."[75] The apocalyptic battle of Armageddon will indeed occur, but Muslims, Europeans, and Americans will now form a single "coalition" against Communism and Shi'ism. Gamaleddin compensates for this surprising lapse into at least partial religious tolerance by railing against Jewish warmongers, and concludes by forecasting in poetic terms the restoration of the caliphate, when the Mahdi will at last be recognized as the sole and final caliph.[76]

This stunning reversal aptly summarizes the result of a decade of confrontation between two Egyptian schools of millenarian prophecy. Ayyub created an undeniably popular genre of apocalyptic fiction whose radical messianic dimension was subsequently enlarged by Arif, Dawud, and Lamada. The unbridled imagination of these pamphleteers inevitably provoked a sharp response from Islamic conservatives, who had no choice but to try to reinforce the ramparts of classical tradition. Almost certainly with the support of the clerical leadership, but in any case owing to a profound attachment to Islamic dogma, these authors sought to combat the radical messianic recourse to various Christian apocalypses while at the same time indulging virulent anti-Semitic prejudices that came to contaminate virtually the whole of their output. Gamaleddin, in holding Saddam Hussein mainly responsible for Arab misfortunes and proclaiming his faith in a durable peace with the Christian West, while excluding the Jewish people from any such accord, is the perfect illustration of this tendency.

THE END OF THE WORLD AS SEEN FROM THE LEVANT

For ten years the apocalyptic domain was dominated in both its subversive and traditional branches by a massive and hugely popular wave of Egyptian publications. During this time Levantine publishers had been uncharacteristically slow to carve out their own niche in the market. It is striking to note that just as Egypt, signatory of the first peace treaty with Israel in 1979, was succeeded by Jordan, which concluded a second peace treaty with Israel fifteen years later, in 1994, so too it was in Amman that the first attempt was made to join Cairo houses in meeting the growing demand for messianic speculation. Unlike in Egypt, however, where the Muslim Brotherhood was outlawed, in Jordan this Islamist fraternity supported the Hashemite throne and exerted some degree of influence within the religious hierarchy. Represented in parliament, and from time to time in the government itself, by the Islamic Action Front (IAF), the Muslim Brotherhood, though it was hostile to the peace with Israel, was careful never to overstep the tacit boundaries of acceptable behavior in its dealings with King Hussein. In the years that followed, this deep-seated ambivalence was to suffuse Jordanian apocalyptic.

The first work to attract attention was a slender volume entitled *Clarifications Regarding the Events of the End of Times* (1994), by Shaykh Ali Ali Muhammad, whose sole claim to originality lay in its development of the theme of "the golden mountain of the Euphrates,"[77] which Jordan's proximity to Iraq made more or less obligatory. Equally classical in its approach was *The Last Day* (1996) by Abdelaziz ibn Badwa,[78] an abridged version of lectures given in 1987–1988 at the Great Mosque in Sahab, an industrial suburb to the east of Amman. Yusuf Amr's work on "the fate of the Beast," published in 1997 with a preface by the inspector of Islamic courts in Jordan, addressed the prospect of ultimate apocalyptic triumph with greater vigor, though not less confidence in the final outcome:

> The relation of forces that rules the earth today will not be eternal, for Allah has promised that all this will change. To be sure, the Muslims are too weak today to conquer their enemy on the field of battle: the pagans combine

their forces in waging war against us, whereas we are divided. How can our divided nation triumph over their united nation, all the more since the infidel West is more developed and better armed than we are? . . . But the twenty-first century will witness the disappearance of Jewish impiety and of those who support it, with the return of Islam to power.[79]

The compensatory motivation of this argument is clear enough, considering that the author is a subject of an Arab kingdom whose ruler, a descendant of the Prophet, had entered into a historic peace treaty with Israel. Palestinian opponents of Yasir Arafat who fought to obstruct the implementation of the accord concluded at Oslo in 1993 between Israel and the Palestinian Liberation Organization (PLO) faced a similar predicament. The following year Hamas, the Palestinian branch of the Muslim Brotherhood, rebelled against the agreement permitting self-rule in Jericho and Gaza that brought about the repatriation of PLO headquarters from Tunis, and an extremist fringe distributed pamphlets proclaiming the inevitable destruction of Israel in apocalyptic terms. But whereas the works of Ayyub and his Egyptian imitators were saturated with Western-inspired anti-Semitism, Palestinian authors laid greater emphasis on Qur'anic exegesis and sacred numerology.

The case of the radical imam Shaykh Bassam Jarrar, a native of Jenin who presided over a mosque in El-Bireh, on the outskirts of Ramallah, is instructive in this regard. A self-styled Islamist intellectual who refused any affiliation with Hamas or other organizations,[80] Jarrar was nonetheless expelled along with 416 other Palestinians from the occupied territories to southern Lebanon in December 1992. The order for this collective banishment came from Prime Minister Rabin himself. Rabin was determined to punish Hamas in particular, and Islamists in general, for the killing of an Israeli border guard. But Lebanon demurred, not wishing to create a precedent by welcoming the deportees, who were therefore left to camp out in the no man's land of Marj al-Zohur. The United Nations Security Council condemned the expulsion, and American diplomats negotiated the return of a hundred exiles in two months' time, and then of the remaining three hundred within a year. Jarrar was part of this second group, in which members of Hamas, a majority, came into contact with Palestinian ultras of the Islamic Jihad and, perhaps even more significantly, established an enduring relationship with Hizbullah in Lebanon.[81]

It was during this exile to Marj al-Zohur that Jarrar composed a "little book" *(kitaib)* entitled *The Disappearance of Israel in 2022* (see Plate 21a). Brought out in 1995 by a publishing house in Beirut with close ties to Hizbullah, this work gives a numerological interpretation of the seventeenth chapter of the Qur'an, "The Night Journey" *(Al-Isra')*, which relates the mystical voyage made by the Prophet Muhammad from the Ka'ba in Mecca to the al-Aqsa Mosque in Jerusalem.[82] The numbers associated with the verses, words, letters, and signs of this sura, Jarrar claimed, reveal the fate reserved by Allah for the Temple on the Mount, and therefore for the modern Hebrew state that it represents.

Jarrar assigns preeminent value to the number 19,[83] on the basis of which he proceeds to develop an elaborate argument fortified by suitably contrived equations. From these it emerges that Israel will last for seventy-six lunar years from its founding in 1948 (the lunar calendar being used by both Jews and Muslims). These seventy-six years are themselves divided into four sequences of nineteen years apiece: the first two are marked by the rise of Jewish power (with the conquest of East Jerusalem in 1967 forming the symbolic hinge of this era of transient ascendancy) and the last two by the inexorable thrust of Islamic reconquest, culminating in the annihilation of Israel in 2022. The passage from the first part of the cycle to the second occurred in 1986, the year in which the Movement of Islamic Resistance—better known by its Arabic acronym of Hamas—was founded.

Ceaselessly moving back and forth between the ancient past and the immediate present, Jarrar attributes the destruction of the first temple of Israel, in 582 B.C.E., to "the Assyro-Chaldeans, Arab tribes settled on the Euphrates."[84] Curiously, however, he mentions no Arab role in the destruction of the second temple, in 70 C.E., or in the razing of Jerusalem at the end of the Second Revolt in 135, and he attaches little importance to these events in his apocalyptic forecasts. Finally, and in a rather confused way, Jarrar incorporates elements associated with Halley's comet and its various transits through the Earth's orbit. "It is amazing," he remarks, "that Halley's most recent cycle began in 1948"[85]—the year of the founding of the state of Israel.

The success of *The Disappearance of Israel in 2022* went well beyond the circle of Hamas and Hizbullah sympathizers, while at the same time prompting another Palestinian extremist to revisit his own prophecies concerning Israel's fate. Shaykh Assad Bayyud al-Tamimi, a native of Hebron and a graduate of al-Azhar, had taken part in the founding of the Islamic Liberation Party (ILP), a fiercely antinationalist group advocating the restoration of the caliphate, in Jordan in 1952. He was later expelled from the party, but retained a profound aversion to nationalist movements and regularly criticized the PLO as well as its component groups. During the Israeli-Egyptian peace negotiations he took issue with al-Azhar itself, declaring that President Sadat had no right to put an end to jihad. This conviction led Shaykh Tamimi in 1980 to form the Palestinian Islamic Jihad, a small group with which he split ten years later, having defected to the cause of Saddam Hussein, whose invasion of Kuwait he wholeheartedly supported, whereas the Palestinian Islamic Jihad sided with Iran. Now freed from all direct political responsibility, Shaykh Tamimi was able to devote himself to "scientific research" *(bahth 'ilmī)*[86] showing that "the disappearance of the state of Israel is inevitable according to the Qur'an"—the title of a lecture that he had already published in booklet form in Lebanon, and that was translated in both Turkey and Iran. Shaykh Tamimi worked on revisions to the essay right up until his death in 1998. The definitive version of *The Disappearance of the State of Israel Is Inevitable* appeared later that year.[87]

The classical form of this commentary *(tafsīr)*, which takes as its subject the very same chapter of the Qur'an that inspired Jarrar's numerological maunderings, could not conceal the exceedingly tendentious character of Shaykh Tamimi's reading. He detects special significance in the following verses of chapter 17:

> We declared to the Children of Israel in the Scripture, "Twice you will spread corruption in the land and become highly arrogant." When the first of these promises was fulfilled, We sent against you servants of Ours with great force. . . . And when the second promise was fulfilled, [We sent them] to shame your faces and enter the place of worship as they did the first time, and utterly destroy whatever fell into their power. Your Lord may yet have mercy on you, but if you do the same again, so shall We. . . .[88]

Most Muslim commentators feel that the two promises mentioned in this chapter correspond to the two destructions of the Jewish temple in Jerusalem. But Shaykh Tamimi concludes from the Qur'anic anachronism of the term "mosque" that the two divine promises are actually addressed to Muslims. The first is the conquest of Jerusalem in 636 (and its reconquest by Saladin against the Crusaders in 1187), and the second will involve the destruction *(tadmīr)* of Israel: "On account of the promise of a second destruction of their pride ['ulū], the Muslims will once again enter the al-Aqsa Mosque, as they conquered it once before, and they will destroy the material and moral pride of the Jews."[89]

Shaykh Tamimi's posthumous assurances nonetheless fell far short of the apocalyptic expectations aroused throughout the Middle East by Egyptian millenarian authors. Syria banned all original apocalyptic speculation until 1996, when it broke off peace negotiations with

Israel, and for a long time authorized only commentaries by authors who had been dead for centuries.[90] The deficit in messianic production began to be remedied in 1998 with the appearance in Damascus of the final revised edition of *The Disappearance of the State of Israel Is Inevitable*. That same year Muhammad Munir Idlibi published *The Antichrist Invades the World*, whose back cover perfectly summarizes the work's purpose: "This analytical and documented study of the Qur'an, of hadiths, and of scientific realities proves that the Antichrist has in fact appeared and that he is currently spreading his corruption on Earth, in keeping with the prophecies of Muhammad."[91]

The depravity of Christianity and the rise of modern capitalism and imperialist expansion, Idlibi holds, allowed the Antichrist to propagate his agents throughout the world. Idlibi dates this satanic diaspora from the establishment of the first British "colonial bases" in India in 1611, which is to say, one thousand years after the beginning of the revelation of the Qur'an to Muhammad. Colonial pillage has been the work of the Antichrist, as the two world wars of the twentieth century have been. Carried away by his own enthusiasm, Idlibi then declares that Gog and Magog are presently in the service of the Antichrist and take the form of those "Christian Western nations . . . that are conspicuous for lighting the fires of war and turmoil *[fitan]*." In saying this much, Idlibi imagines that he will assuage his readers' feelings of impotence, but the weakness of his argument can plainly be seen in the already finished character of the signs of the Hour. By prematurely introducing Gog and Magog, Idlibi disrupts the millenarian dynamic while preserving only its paranoid mechanism. This abusive reworking of the standard apocalyptic account did not prevent his book from going through six editions in eight years, however.[92]

. . .

By the end of the two decades that separate the advent of Islam's fifteenth century and the beginning of the third millennium of the Christian era, the Sunni domain of Muslim apocalyptic had been profoundly shaken by a series of alternately convergent and contradictory events:

- The development of a radical messianic literature that broke with the conventions of classical tradition, drew freely from the various Christian apocalypses, and absorbed Western fantasies regarding UFOs and the Bermuda Triangle;
- The dissemination, in reaction to this, of a conservative Islamic literature that sought to recapture for itself a part of the popular

success enjoyed by radical messianic works, with a view also to purging them of dogmatic Christian influences;

- The validation of anti-Semitic conspiracy theories by these two apocalyptic schools, combined with a recycling of the themes of the classic Western works of this genre, chief among them *The Protocols of the Elders of Zion;*
- The related obsession with figures of destruction such as the Antichrist and Gog and Magog, the horror of whose future ravages is sublimated in the certainty of the ultimate victory of Islam;
- The compensatory function served by messianic writings in those Arab countries that had made peace with Israel, above all Egypt and, to a lesser degree, Jordan.

This dramatic alteration of the apocalyptic landscape was not taken seriously either by observers of current events in the Middle East[93] or by policy makers, for it seemed to have little consequence beyond a popular and superstitious subculture. Nonetheless it created an atmosphere in which a literature explicitly associated with jihad was soon to flourish.

CHAPTER 6

The Horsemen of Apocalyptic Jihad

The trauma of the messianic uprising of 1979 inhibited apocalyptic longings in Saudi Arabia for many years. While Egyptian millenarian writings found an audience there, as they did in the rest of the Arab world, the clerical hierarchy exercised much firmer control over unorthodox speculation about the end of the world than its counterpart in Cairo, with the result that Arabia brought forth no native equivalent of Said Ayyub or Muhammad Isa Dawud.

CLERICAL RESISTANCE AND TERRORIST AMBITIONS

The spread of apocalyptic in Arabia was curbed by the constant reminder of centuries-old traditions, reinforced by a clear Wahhabi preference for the critical heritage transmitted by Ibn Hanbal through Abu Dawud and Ibn Kathir. Commentaries and booklets very seldom bore any evidence of the personal opinions of their authors, and the range of acceptable topics was highly circumscribed, as the caution of titles such as *The Authentic [Collection] of the Signs of the Hour* and *The Encyclopedia of Weak or Fabricated Hadiths concerning the Mahdi* suggests.[1] Against the background of so much standardized production, the appearance in 1996 of *Gog and Magog: Strife* [Fitna] *in the Past, Present, and Future*[2]—a hybrid work that mixed Islamic tradition and Western sources (the *Cambridge Ancient History* having happily supplanted *The Protocols of the Elders of Zion,* long cherished by Egyptian pamphleteers)—could not fail to raise eyebrows, and all the more since the author, Al-Shafi' al-Mahi Ahmad, professor of Islamic Culture on the faculty of King Sa'ud University in Riyadh, had published it in Lebanon, rather than Arabia.

Al-Mahi Ahmad's book is curiously schizophrenic. On the one hand, he places at the heart of his argument the Qur'anic verses (18:94–102) concerning Gog and Magog, whose ancestry he traces back to Yaphet, son of Noah, and he locates the wall erected by Alexander the Great in Georgia.[3] On the other hand, he undertakes a chronological inventory of seven invasions *(khurūj)* by Gog and Magog in the course of history (a crucial departure from the scriptural account, which mentions only one invasion), these peoples having successively assumed the form of Scythians, Huns, and Mongols. Appealing to the authority of both Herodotus and Ezekiel, al-Mahi Ahmad discourses at length on the building of the Great Wall of China and the tribulations endured on the Danubian frontier. Gog and Magog seem to emerge from an inexhaustible vein of Asiatic subversion, of which the Mongol hordes of Chingiz Khan in the thirteenth century were the most barbarous example. Al-Mahi Ahmad describes the devastation of Khurasan at their hands, not omitting to emphasize the Shi'i courtier Nasr ed-Din at-Tusi's treachery in support of the invaders.[4] This, Gog and Magog's "seventh sortie," ended in disaster for the Arabs with the fall of Baghdad in 1258 and the murder of the 'Abbasid caliph.[5]

These Mongol hordes live among us still, al-Mahi Ahmad says. Their tribes are divided between the Independent Republic of Ulan Bator and Chinese Inner Mongolia, and their eighth and "last invasion . . . will coincide with the approach of the Hour and of the Day of the Resurrection." Following Jesus's victory over the Antichrist, they will once again break out from their captivity and swarm down over the lands of Mesopotamia and the Levant, where they will besiege in vain the Muslim forces entrenched on the mountain of Tur *(al-Tūr)* and succumb to a series of lightning epidemics. In seeking to discover the apocalyptic implications of this chronic onslaught, al-Mahi Ahmad inquires into the "constant characteristics"[6] of each of the raids, past and future, launched by Gog and Magog. In every case, he finds, these gruesome marauders triumph by arms and spread unrivaled corruption with frightening speed, but their terrifying arc of ruin is nonetheless fated to contract just as rapidly as it expands.

However reassuring such a conclusion may seem, it does not save al-Mahi Ahmad from the fatal objection that Shahawi and other Egyptian authors had run up against before him: to assert the continuing physical, historical, and geographical existence of Gog and Magog entails both the affirmation of Qur'anic prophecy and its denial, for the Mongols—no more than the Georgians or any of the other incarnations that these satanic races have been imagined to undergo—have manifestly not been engaged in the incessant sabotage of a barrier built two millennia earlier to contain them.[7]

In this same year of 1996, as al-Mahi Ahmad was laboriously explicating the menace of Gog and Magog for his readers, a Saudi outcast named Usama bin Laden issued a declaration of jihad from eastern Afghanistan. For this first public announcement of al-Qaida's mission to "liberate" the sacred land of Arabia, bin Laden chose "the mountains of the Hindu Kush, Khurasan."[8] In this instance, however, the use of the term "Khurasan" to refer to Afghanistan seems to be an archaism rather than evidence of a preoccupation with apocalyptic toponymy—all the more since the two names are used interchangeably in the jihadist lexicon. Al-Qaida was in any case engaged in a much broader struggle, one that opposed it not only to the "near enemy" (corrupt Muslim regimes, foremost among them Saudi Arabia), but also to the "distant enemy" (the United States). The selection of targets for terrorist attack was made in response to tactical and symbolic opportunities (the American embassies in Kenya and Tanzania, for example, struck on the eighth anniversary of the arrival of U.S. troops in Arabia), with no regard for millenarian considerations. It is nonetheless true, however, that the mounting excitement in Christian messianic circles in anticipation of the year 2000 did stimulate the imagination of certain terrorist cells that operated independently of al-Qaida.

During the month of December 1999, major bomb attacks were foiled in Los Angeles (where the airport was targeted) and in Amman (where the Jordanian jihadist Abu Musab al-Zarqawi had been assigned the task of blowing up a large hotel and several nearby tourist sites).[9] Although no millenarian ideology guided these particular terrorist attempts, their purpose was clearly to profit from the presence of large numbers of Christians in these places and the intense media coverage that accompanied the approach of the new millennium. What was sought, in other words, was a maximum impact, measured in terms of the number of victims and the amount of publicity.

THE COUNTERAPOCALYPSE OF SHAYKH HAWALI

Shaykh Safar al-Hawali had long been one of the major figures of the movement of Islamist political and religious dissent known as al-Sahwa (literally, "The Awakening") in Saudi Arabia. In 1988, he became head of the Department of Islamic Doctrine *('aqīda)* at Umm al-Qura University in Mecca, a position he quickly exploited for the purpose of disseminating a rigorist vision of Islam that was highly critical of the Sa'uds. Two years later, in 1990, he berated the royal family for inviting hundreds of thousands of American soldiers to use Saudi territory as a base from which to liberate Kuwait from the Iraqi occupation, and the next year he reacted violently against the Israeli-Arab peace conference in Madrid, denouncing the "Zionist plan of universal domination, above all in the Islamic world."[10]

Shaykh Hawali's radicalism inspired a whole generation of jihadist militants. In the wake of the Israeli-Palestinian accords and the Israeli-Jordanian treaty of 1993–1994 he sharpened his attacks, to the point that the Saudi government could no longer allow them to go unanswered. Along with the other leaders of the Sahwa he was thrown in jail in 1994.[11] Imprisoned for five years, Hawali repudiated none of his opinions and made a point of emphasizing that his release, in 1999, was unconditional. The eruption in October 2000 of the second Palestinian intifada appeared to him to be the most striking possible confirmation of his earlier pessimism regarding the outcome of negotiations with Israel: "When Zionist forces fired on Muslim crowds inside the al-Aqsa compound, they delivered the death blow for the peace process, this miscarriage whose protracted labor had [already] been lengthened by several years. When Israeli helicopters bombed buildings occupied by Arafat's Palestinian Authority, they utterly smashed the Oslo accords to pieces."[12]

These events led Hawali to compose a pamphlet brimming over with fury and rage, *The Day of Wrath* (2001). Its main target is "Christian Zionism, the most dangerous of all contemporary movements for humanity, [for] it has managed to control the minds of a third of the population of the most powerful nation in the world,"[13] the United States. No degrading epithet for the Jews was neglected,[14] but Hawali's chief obsession remained fundamentalist Christianity, now ascendant "in the White House and the Pentagon" under George W. Bush.[15] He rebuked the televangelists Jerry Falwell, Pat Robertson, and Jimmy Swaggart,[16] declaring that the "fundamentalist movement [is] so crazed that it seeks to hasten the return of Christ. . . . But these [ministers] are not monks who have retired from the world, as was the case during the first centuries of Christianity. To the contrary, they exert a remarkable influence on society, just as they possess a media arsenal and control high-level cabinet posts in the government."[17]

Shaykh Hawali goes on to formulate six principles that, in his view, guide Christian Zionism:

1. The establishment of the state of Israel is a harbinger of the return of Christ.
2. The peace process retards [the fulfillment of] God's promise.
3. All of Jerusalem must be under Israeli control.
4. Israel is blessed: blessed be those who bless it and damned those who damn it.
5. The Palestinians (and the Arabs in general) are contemptible pagans, the party of Gog and Magog.
6. The Millennium is near, but [it will arrive] only once the believers have been called to heaven, whereas the pagans will disappear in the battle of Armageddon.[18]

Notwithstanding his obligation to cite the Qur'an and the prophetic traditions, Hawali's primary interest is in turning the Christian apocalypses back against the American partisans of Israel. He therefore devotes two entire chapters to the prophecy of Daniel, developing what he takes to be irrefutable arguments concerning Christian eschatological symbolism. Not content merely to identify the five kingdoms that appeared in a dream to Nebuchadnezzar,[19] Hawali proceeds to decode the signs of the apocalypse, whose key he delivers "as a gift to the Jews and the Christians": New Jerusalem is Mecca; the Paraclete is the Prophet Muhammad (who is also the Son of Man); the messiah is Jesus (the nearest to Muhammad of all the prophets); the Antichrist is the false messiah; the Beast is Zionism "in its Jewish and Christian forms"; the false prophets are Paul and his popes; the "small horn, or the abomination of desolation, is the state of Israel";[20] the New Babylon is Western culture in general, and American culture in particular; and, finally, the new Roman Empire corresponds to the United States.

Armed with this special insight, Hawali draws on Christian sources in order to reveal an inexorable sequence of apocalyptic events at the end of which divine wrath will engulf the "small horn" of Israel, bringing down the irresistible might of the "army of the mujahedin" upon both the "Zionist" Beast and the "Western" New Babylon.[21] Additionally, he heaps scorn on the Zionist Christian belief in the conversion of the Jews following Christ's return,[22] for they will be "divided into two halves: one half will be killed within the army of the Antichrist and the other half will follow Jesus into Islam."[23] Revising the calculation in the Book of Daniel (8:14), he reckons that the abomination of desolation will last not 1,010 days, but forty-five years. Since the occupation of Jerusalem began in 1967, it follows that the destruction of Israel will occur in 2012. Nevertheless, perhaps taken aback by his own daring, Hawali is careful to insist that no date can be considered absolutely certain, even if the ultimate victory of Islam is beyond all doubt.[24]

Shaykh Hawali was not the first millenarian pamphleteer to take an interest in North American fundamentalists. Muhammad Isa Dawud had first called attention to Jerry Falwell in 1994,[25] and five years later vilified Christianity as the "slave of fanatic Zionism."[26] Indeed, many radical messianic writers were delighted to ransack Christian apocalyptic in search of material that could be used in devising their own theories. Thus, for example, the Egyptian author Abdelwahab Tawila conceived the introduction to his *The Awaited Messiah and the End of the World* (1999) on the model of a thirteen-page essay on Armageddon by a Texas evangelist (though he was shocked to learn that cameras had been installed in the walls of Jerusalem to film the return of the Messiah);[27] and Tawila's countryman Ridha Hilal reserved a part of his *The Jewish Messiah and the End of the World* (2000)[28] for a discussion of fundamentalist networks of influence in the United States. But their method of selective quotation and indignation failed to meet with the approval of Shaykh Hawali, whose ambition lay in a wholly different direction. Hawali's aim was to master the entire Christian Zionist corpus and then, by exposing its fallacies, to construct a complete and unassailable counterapocalypse.

Just as Ayyub had created a genre of crudely anti-Semitic apocalyptic fiction, Hawali some fifteen years later developed an anti-American eschatology that sought to turn against the United States the very texts of Christian apocalypse in which it placed its faith. Not only did this new doctrine engender a feeling of theological superiority among Islamist pamphleteers, whose repertoire of references was now enlarged by more or less predatory looting of the enemy's own holy books; Hawali's jubilation at having understood the real message of the Christian scriptures better than the American televangelists themselves was also to have a profound resonance in the jihadist sphere, where the Saudi shaykh was revered as the triumphant unifier of a set of apocalyptic perspectives that until then had been quite separate.

THE SHOCK OF 11 SEPTEMBER

The attacks perpetrated by al-Qaida in New York and Washington on 11 September 2001 were greeted by Jerry Falwell and Pat Robertson as divine punishment for America's sins.[29] These attacks unleashed a wave of apocalyptic speculation throughout Christendom that could not help but stimulate literary production in the Islamic world. Radical messianic propagandists, quicker than their rivals to seize upon an unexpected opportunity, promptly exploited the possibilities of the moment. Muhammad Isa Dawud, who had just completed a new book that summer, moved at once to modify the introduction, place a picture of the two burning and smoke-filled towers on the cover (Plate 6), and give the book a new title, *The Surprise*.[30] He took further advantage of the sudden turn of events by changing publishers in the hope that his readers would forget the bold prediction of his last book in 1999, in which he foresaw the bombing of New York—by French missiles![31]

Dawud used this occasion to revive and reemphasize his anti-Semitic obsessions, accusing "Talmudic organizations" of having sowed terror in the United States on 11 September in order to unleash a new war against Islam. Dawud bitterly regretted that the chance of a "union between Islam and Christianity against their common enemy" had therefore been ruined, but there was no helping it: America, "a racist and terrorist state," could not avoid paying the price for its iniquity in Afghanistan, where it will suffer a "second Vietnam" at the hands of Muslims threatened with "extermination [*ibāda*]."[32] This paranoid and revanchist vision of 11 September enjoyed a considerable success, at least in Egypt, where *The Surprise* sold through two reprintings within a few weeks.

The bombings of 11 September and the anti-Taliban offensive that followed also produced the stunning defection of a leading Egyptian pamphleteer from the conservative Islamic camp to the radical messianic side. Amin Muhammad Gamaleddin, who, as we have seen, had enumerated seventy-nine signs of the Hour four years earlier, completed a sensational volume entitled *Armageddon* on 19 October 2001,[33] twelve days after the beginning of military operations in Afghanistan by Western powers. The subtitle ("Final Declaration, O Nation of Islam") could not have been more alarming, nor the warning in the introduction against the "Third World War" (which is to say "the terrifying, black, and oppressive wars, the blind and accumulated hatreds . . . that will haunt Syria [Shām], darken Egypt, assail Iraq, and engulf the [Arabian] peninsula") more ominous.[34]

Gamaleddin once more rehearsed a familiar litany of apocalyptic conjectures, only now in the certainty that Saddam Hussein was indeed the Sufyani, the ambiguous figure who would precipitate the promised catastrophe in the lands of Islam—and this owing to his prior invasion of Kuwait: "The Sufyani Saddam is the bearer of good and evil. If the Mahdi appears, then all that is good will disappear [in Saddam], who will now only be evil." The persistence of the Ba'th regime after the Gulf War meant that in Iraq "the love of the people for its president is proportional to the blood spilled by the Coalition." Frustrated at not having overthrown Saddam, "a new coalition, organized by America in response to the destruction visited upon New York and Washington, will inevitably strike Iraq again, after having struck Afghanistan, all in the name of tracking down the terrorists and eliminating terrorism."[35]

In the meantime the apocalyptic cycle of the Great Battle (al-malhama al-uzmā) had commenced in the autumn of 2001. The emergence of the Taliban in "Khurasan" was easily fitted into a precise eschatological calendar: between the taking of Kabul by Mullah Omar, in September 1996, and the appearance of the Mahdi, six years would elapse—the "black banners" of the Afghan forces being the clearest sign of the Mahdi's imminent manifestation in the East. Moreover, the "Crusader war" now set in motion by America and its allies was directed by a "lame chief of staff," General Richard Myers, exactly as a hadith validated in the ninth century by Nu'aym ibn Hammad had prophesied: "The sign of the appearance of the Mahdi will be the raising in the West of an army commanded by a cripple."[36]

The battle taking place in Afghanistan, Gamaleddin says, is only the prelude to "the most violent and the most ruthless war in history, [whose name will be] Armageddon." After the inevitable rout of the Taliban by a far larger force, it will be Iraq's turn: "America and Great Britain will strike Iraq on the pretext that it is reconstituting its nuclear capability, or that it is involved in a biological terrorist attack on America, or Europe, or Israel, or . . . or . . . or, and Iraq will respond, on the advice of Russia and China, by firing missiles on Israel." The conflict will then become global, but Israel will soon be destroyed. Gamaleddin considers Hawali a great pessimist for delaying the extinction of

Zionism until 2012, even though "the Mahdi is at our gates," and for good measure cites the prophet Zechariah in support of his conviction that "the majority of the Jews will die during Armageddon."[37]

Warming to his subject, Gamaleddin proceeds to discuss the millenarian uprising of 1979 in Mecca and the power struggles within the Saʿud family by way of calling attention to the precariousness of the position of King Fahd, whom he styles the "caliph of the moment" *(khalīfat al-waqt)*. It was known that the guardian of the two holiest mosques of Islam had effectively ceded power to the crown prince, Abdullah, during the course of a long illness. Gamaleddin announces that "the death of the Saudi caliph" will bring about a new round of military escalation, in response to which the Mahdi will personally lead the troops of Islam against "Crusader America and Europe," before going on to conquer Russia, India, and China. Additionally, the capture *(fath)* of Constantinople will be necessary in order to bring Turkey, led astray from the true path by secularism, back into the Islamic fold. In view of all these developments, Gamaleddin is moved to issue an urgent "call to the Muslims of America and Europe: come back to your country and to your land, pack your bags and wind up your affairs."[38]

The extent of Gamaleddin's radicalization becomes plain if one recalls that as late as 1997 he foresaw an alliance of Muslims and Westerners, lasting through the battle of Armageddon itself, that would pit this Islamo-Christian coalition against Communism and Shiʿism.[39] The events of 11 September and the war in Afghanistan having eliminated the possibility of such an alliance, Islam and Christianity now found themselves face to face, irrevocably locked together in remorseless combat. A profound sense of geopolitical fatality gripped the entire radical messianic movement, whose messengers looked to one another for support and inspiration. Just as Dawud paid tribute to the "giants" *('amāliqa)* who came before him, foremost among them Ayyub,[40] so too Gamaleddin, the newest convert to their ranks, acknowledged a dozen authorities of apocalypse in contemporary Islam.[41]

Several Egyptian publishing houses sought to profit from the radical messianic vogue by launching new series of apocalyptic titles or by adding to existing collections, such as Dar al-Fajr's "Series of the Hereafter." In addition to quoting from Christian apocalypses and ranting about UFOs, these titles made more and more frequent reference to the prophecies of Nostradamus (who had been of service to Gamaleddin himself by putting 11 September into eschatological perspective).[42] The crowded and cumbersome format favored by Dawud, whose books effortlessly exceeded five hundred pages with the insertion of sketches and photocopies, was far less popular than the familiar softcover booklet, lighter to carry, easier to read (because printed in large characters), and conveniently purchased in street stalls. Thus, for example, Amro Gomaa's recycling of the theme of the Bermuda Triangle, the den of the Antichrist on earth, was very successfully marketed in Cairo as a pamphlet with a suitably garish cover.[43]

Jordanian publishers followed the lead of their Egyptian counterparts, most notably with a booklet by Hisham Muhammad Abu Hakima entitled *The Antichrist and the Battle of Armageddon* (2002).[44] Relying heavily on Ayyub, the author describes the polarization of the world between "the camp of faith and the camp of godlessness," and their implacable antagonism: "The Islamic forces, believing in Allah and in Him alone, will be found in Syria *[Shām]* and in the Arabian Peninsula, whereas the stalwarts of the forces of the Antichrist will be the Jews and their henchmen."[45] In placing an image of Saint George slaying the dragon on the book's cover, the publisher unwittingly betrays the Christian influence exerted on the apocalyptic scenario described inside (Plate 8). Earlier we saw that the Islamic tradition of Jesus's slaying of the Antichrist at Lod is very strongly marked by the ancient myth of Saint George, long a dogmatic element of Eastern Christianity.

THE COUNTERATTACK
OF THE RELIGIOUS ESTABLISHMENT

Gamaleddin's defection to the radical messianic camp dealt a serious blow to Islamic conservatives, who had no choice but to respond. A conscientious refutation in the matter of Armageddon was delivered in 2002 by Shaykh Sirsawi,[46] in a book introduced by another eminent Egyptian cleric, Shaykh al-Ya'qub, who warned against the "danger" of Gamaleddin's writings. Both Ya'qub's foreword and the body of the text are filled with quotations from unquestioned authorities. The demonstration of Gamaleddin's deviations from orthodoxy depends primarily on citation to two of the leading Syrian figures of contemporary Islam, the Muslim Brother Said Hawwa (d. 1989) and the hadith specialist Nasreddin Albani (d. 1999). Once again, the painful lesson of the millenarian uprising in Mecca, in 1979, is invoked to remind readers of the dire consequences of allowing oneself to be "led astray" by warped forecasts of the end of the world. And as for Constantinople, it must be completely abandoned by Islam before it can be reconquered.[47]

Above all, Shaykh Sirsawi is at pains to partially or wholly invalidate the hadiths on which Gamaleddin relies to construct his eschatology. The hadith concerning the "black banners" is judged to be "very weak," like the other prophetic traditions adduced with regard to Afghanistan and Saddam Hussein; Gamaleddin's recourse to the Judeo-Christian apocalypses, and especially to Isaiah, is condemned for its wholesale reproduction of Dawud's "fabrications"; and the call for Western Muslims to return home at once is dismissed as utterly impractical.[48]

There is no reason to believe that this meticulous attempt at refutation did much to discredit Gamaleddin's book, which remained popular for many years. By devoting an entire work to it, a pair of renowned clerics placed themselves in the awkward position of paying tribute to a lay pamphleteer. The book's cover design reflects this ambiguity by giving the word "Armageddon" the same prominence that it enjoys in the title of Gamaleddin's booklet. What is clear, however, is that the challenge to Sunni orthodoxy was judged to be at least as serious as the one posed by Ayyub fifteen years earlier. And now that the commercial stakes were much greater than before, a number of Egyptian houses that until then had hesitated to enter the radical messianic market finally committed themselves to publishing conservative Islamic works.

Apart from Maktabat al-Islamiyya (The Islamic Library), which published Shaykh Sirsawi's rebuttal, Maktabat al-Safa (which takes its name from the hills of Mecca) brought out in rapid succession an apocalyptic pamphlet,[49] a reissue of The Agony of the Resurrection by Imam Bughawi (d. twelfth century),[50] and a commentary on The Book of Dissension by Ibn Hammad (d. ninth century).[51] In a more scholarly vein, Maktaba Mekka (The Library of Mecca) published a weighty collection of apocalyptic hadiths, with the elegant design and precise typography customarily associated with such works,[52] and a publishing house in Alexandria brought out a legal analysis of the "signs of the Hour" that warned against "false teaching" and an "infatuation with the bizarre."[53]

In 2001, Maktabat al-Turath al-Islami (The Library of Islamic Heritage) belatedly moved to stem the messianic tide by publishing a posthumous collection of writings by a very popular Cairo preacher named Shaykh Muhammad Metwalli Shahrawi (1911–1998). In the simple and clear style that had made him famous, notably on television, Shahrawi patiently reviewed each of the eternal and unchanging signs of the Hour.[54] He brushed aside anachronistic interpretations of the apocalyptic hadiths (dismissing, for example, the possibility that the "gold of the Euphrates" was "black gold," or oil) and pushed back the appearance of the Mahdi, his combat with the Antichrist, and the return of Jesus into a future that was both distant and indistinct; the "fire of Hijaz" was similarly postponed.[55] But Shahrawi refrained from examining radical messianic arguments in any real detail in this uncontroversial survey of the eschatological horizon, apparently in order to avoid stooping to the level of authors whose prestige was much less than his own.

THE NEW JIHADIST CRITIQUE

Caught in the crossfire of the conservative Islamic and radical messianic camps, another Cairo publisher, Dar al-Aqida (The House of Doctrine), hoped to find some profitably neutral ground by issuing a critical analysis of Gamaleddin's recent book that appeared to be independent of the religious hierarchy. For this purpose it enlisted the aid of Said Abdelazim, an Egyptian pamphleteer who had crossed swords with Gamaleddin before, in 1999. Their disagreement was renewed and updated under the title *The Signs of the Hour* (2002), rather modestly advertised by the small print on its cover as an "appraisal of the book *Armageddon*" (Plate 9).[56]

Abdelazim's appraisal was in fact nearer to an indictment, for it pointedly accused Gamaleddin of "corruption" *(fasād)* in his interpretation of the canonical sources. Broadening his attack to include all radical messianic writings, Abdelazim heaped special abuse on desperate apocalyptic claims concerning the Bermuda Triangle. To the contrary, far from lurking off the coast of the Carolinas, the Antichrist is now lying in ambush in "the Sea of Syria" *(bahr al-Shām)*.[57] No less remarkably, the eschatological hadith that finds greatest favor with Abdelazim bears the prophecy, reported originally by al-Qurtubi, that stones and trees will betray the presence of Jews hiding behind them to the triumphant Muslims.[58] But speculation lacking a sound basis in tradition is just that—speculation. "It is not permissible to conjecture," Abdelazim says, "and to say that the current struggle against the Jews is the one announced by the Prophet Muhammad in the signs of the Hour, for that is a sort of anticipation. Yet one must not on that account suspend jihad, in the expectation that the Mahdi will appear."[59]

Jihad is the key idea of Abdelazim's pamphlet; indeed, it is administered there as a sort of antidote to Gamaleddin's aberrant and malignant suppositions. The jihadist message is underscored by the image on the book's cover (see Plate 9) of a decapitated soldier, no doubt an American, covered in his own blood. Whereas Shaykh Hawali, unable to interest a publisher in his book, had been obliged to distribute copies of *The Day of Wrath* either illicitly or via the Internet, Abdelazim had found a mass-market outlet thanks to the commercial opportunism of Dar al-Aqida, which succeeded in identifying a new audience for an even more revanchist interpretation of the end of times.

The same year a Beirut house, Dar Ibn Hazm, published a volume called *The Revelation of Grace in the Signs of the Hour, Battles, and Turmoil,* enlivened by the catchy subtitle "Vision of the Future of the Islamic World in the Light of the Qur'an and of Tradition."[60] Its author was Mahmud al-Walid, an Iraqi born in Ramadi and now living in Dubai. While stressing at the outset that knowledge of the Hour is forbidden to everyone except Allah himself, Walid numbered "the siege of the people of Iraq" among the signs of the Hour. "Western oppression," he added, "is intensifying today, and rubs salt in the wounds of Muslims by besieging them materially, morally, scientifically, and alimentarily."[61] This unambiguous accusation was all the more serious as it came from an Islamist exile who could hardly be suspected of sympathizing with the regime of Saddam Hussein.

Despite his profound anti-Westernism, Walid sees the principal cause of the rise of apocalyptic "tribulations" *(fitan)* among Muslims in their "having strayed from the path of Allah." Owing to the "denial of Islam" that now prevails, "humanity is ruled by two heads: the Crusader Satan head, represented today by America, and the Jewish Satan head, represented by the dominance of Jews in the world and the establishment of their state on the land of Palestine." What is more, the "Western camp" is none other than the hated "Byzantines" *(Rūm),* sworn enemies of Islam in the eschatological traditions, which must therefore be read with this equivalence in mind. Walid explicitly acknowledges his indebtedness to Shaykh Hawali in mocking the apocalyptic pretensions of Western leaders, and urges his readers to beware the rallying of the Jews to the Antichrist, "their leader and savior." He reproaches Gamaleddin for his reliance on the Christian concept of Armageddon, for this amounts to playing the game of Islam's adversaries: "The West believes in the battle of Armageddon, its leaders subscribe to it and treat it as a question of doctrine, whereas it is only a superstition and a pure illusion from the point of view of Muslim teaching."[62]

Less militant, but every bit as troubling, was another work published in Lebanon, this time by a Syrian author, Usama Yusuf Rahma, who claimed to clarify "the sequence of events to come in the light of prophetic tradition."[63] The cover of *The Hour Approaches* (2003) presents the sinister juxtaposition of an open Qur'an and the two airplanes heading toward the World Trade Center (Plate 10). The Western invasion of Iraq will inevitably follow that of Afghanistan, Rahma says, for "when the black banners suddenly appear on the snow-capped peaks of Khurasan, turmoil *[fitna]* will erupt on the Euphrates."[64]

Even though Shaykh Hawali, a very radical voice in Islam, had condemned the attacks of 11 September, Rahma found a justification for al-Qaida's strikes by locating them in an apocalyptic calendar of regrettable, but necessary, discord and strife—necessary because they portend the end of the world. Rahma went further and refused to find in favor either of bin Laden, whom he honored with the title of "shaykh," or of the religious authorities, which had unanimously stigmatized the terrorism of al-Qaida. On the one hand, he reproached Shaykh Usama bin Laden for denigrating his detractors by accusing them of being in the pay of their respective governments, "which, at bottom, is true of only a few of them," but, on the other, he denied the 'ulama the right "to condemn a man for the simple reason that he excited the wrath of the United States and that he humiliated them as no empire has ever been humiliated in history."[65]

Despite the appearance of neutrality, the implicit endorsement of bin Laden's tactics is unmistakable. The same bias is found in the writings of no less influential a representative of the radical messianic tendency than Muhammad Isa Dawud. In addition to accusing "Talmudic organizations" of having perpetrated the 11 September attacks, as we have seen, Dawud denounced the legal actions brought against the al-Qaida leader, remarking that "Usama bin Laden has many enemies who have the means to distort reality as they wish."[66] He protested also against the "non-Islamic puritanism" that named Mullah Omar as the Antichrist on the ground that the leader of the Taliban is a one-eyed man who appeared in Khurasan. To the contrary, Dawud argued, it was America that manipulated the fighting there, from India and Pakistan,[67] and that, above all, was preparing the invasion of Iraq to seize control of "the gold of the Euphrates" that had been announced in an apocalyptic hadith.[68]

Dawud's anti-Semitic and anti-American rage was undiminished in his latest work, *The Treasure of the Euphrates* (see Plate 7), composed in the autumn of 2002 and published at the height of the United Nations debate over the Iraq question. No doubt was possible in this matter: "Such is the secret, O nation of Islam: after having detected the Euphrates' mountain of gold, America decided to invade Iraq and to change its regime." Dawud seemed to take the expression "gold of the

Euphrates" literally, declining to interpret it, as other apocalyptic pamphleteers were to do, as a metaphor for Iraq's tremendous oil wealth. Israel and the United States had, he believed, devised a plan for "drying up the Euphrates" with the support of the United Nations' system of "smart sanctions" against Saddam Hussein's regime; and Turkey, incited by "the Jews,"[69] participated in the conspiracy as well, through its unilateral program of dam construction on the Upper Euphrates.

"President Bush's announcement of a new Crusade in the East is anything but a slip," Dawud advises his readers, for "the Americans frankly consider themselves God's representatives on earth, [and believe that] their actions therefore correspond to divine will." Together, America and Israel constitute the "United States of the Antichrist," and "a strike against Iraq is essential in order to proclaim [the establishment of] Greater Israel." Moreover, although the objective of "the impending invasion" will indeed be "to plunder Iraq," this war will not necessarily remain "limited." Dawud is convinced that Egypt is itself a target of military maneuvers that, in addition to Iraq, will also involve Syria, Arabia, and Sudan: "America wishes not only to break the will of Iraq, but that of every Arab nation."[70]

Dawud had dedicated his previous book, *Before the Destruction*, to President Mubarak personally. More modestly, but no less tellingly, he now dedicated *The Treasure of the Euphrates* to the Egyptian minister of defense, Field Marshal Muhammad Hasayn Tantawi, and to Mubarak's closest advisor, Usama al-Baz. Still more revelatory is the admiring biography of the author by a retired general, Abdelgalil Muhammad Mogahed, that was placed at the end of the new book as a sort of epilogue—proof that radical messianic ideas had resonated well beyond the working class, traditionally the main audience for apocalyptic speculation.

. . .

Whereas the excitement aroused by the approach of the year 2000 in fundamentalist Christian circles had provoked a more or less sarcastic response from Muslim pamphleteers, now, two years after the millennium, the apocalyptic landscape in the world of Islam had changed as a result of the events of 11 September and the intervention of Western nations in Afghanistan. Among the consequences were these:

- Conservative Islamic authors continued to produce canonical interpretations and authorized commentaries, but with the

emergence of an increasingly popular and inventive literature
they found themselves on the defensive. Gamaleddin, by desert-
ing their ranks, became the new symbol of the radical messianic
genre, whose unbridled anti-Semitism henceforth fueled belief in
an inevitable and ultimate confrontation with America, and with
the West in general.

- The implicitly anticlerical dimension of radical messianic writing
  was confirmed by strong disagreement over the limits of acceptable argumentation between the leading authors, all of them
  laymen, and the religious authorities, which, having produced a
  multitude of lessons and refutations to no apparent effect, was
  finally obliged to call the late Shaykh Shahrawi to the rescue.

- *The Day of Wrath* by Shaykh Safar al-Hawali, a Saudi, constituted the founding document of a new apocalyptic sensibility
  that objected to facile reliance on an overly prescriptive eschatological calendar and sought to turn against Christian Zionism
  the words of its own prophets. At the heart of this increasingly
  powerful movement, born in Arabia, lay the idea of jihad.
  Shaykh Hawali's followers, whose writings were initially disseminated via the Internet and later, after 11 September, published in
  Egypt and Lebanon, may be described as global jihadists to the
  extent that they display a considerably greater tolerance for the
  terrorism of al-Qaida than Hawali himself.

- From 11 September onward, writers of various persuasions
  placed Iraq at the center of their prognostications. Some authors
  saw the siege imposed on Iraq as a harbinger of the Hour; others
  considered it inevitable that the "anti-Islamic crusade" inaugurated in Afghanistan would be continued in Iraq.

The extension to Iraq of what the American government called
the global war against terror proved to be an extraordinary source of
encouragement to apocalyptic speculation in the Islamic world in the
years that followed. But this mode of conjecture already preoccupied
a broad range of intellectuals: conservative Islamic thinkers, typically
associated with either the clerical hierarchy or the various chapters of
the Muslim Brotherhood; radical messianics, whose unalterable hostility toward the West was largely inherited from militant nationalist
movements; and global jihadists, who developed an ideology consistent
with the belligerent and, since the events of 11 September, increasingly

influential pronouncements of al-Qaida. The new apocalyptic literature, by harnessing the rhetoric and the images of both Muslim and Christian tradition, was able to distort and redirect sacred prophecy for its own purposes, and, with the invasion of Iraq, to reach a new and larger audience while at the same time strengthening the plausibility of its forecasts.

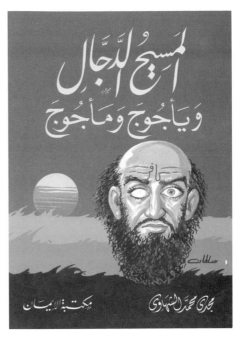

1. Said Ayyub, *The Antichrist* (Cairo, 1987).

2. Magdi Muhammad Shahawi, *The Antichrist and Gog and Magog* (Cairo, 1992).

3. Okasha Abdelmannan al-Tibi, *The Whole Truth about the Antichrist* (Cairo, 1991).

4. Muhammad Izzat Arif, *Does the Antichrist Rule the World?* (Cairo, 1997).

5. Muhammad Isa Dawud, *The Hidden Links between the Antichrist, the Secrets of the Bermuda Triangle, and Flying Saucers* (Cairo, 1994).

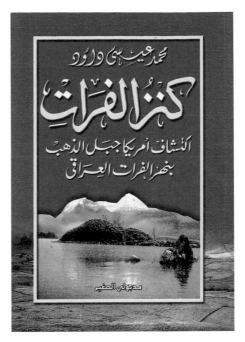

6. Muhammad Isa Dawud, *The Surprise* (Cairo, 2001).

7. Muhammad Isa Dawud, *The Treasure of the Euphrates* (Cairo, 2003).

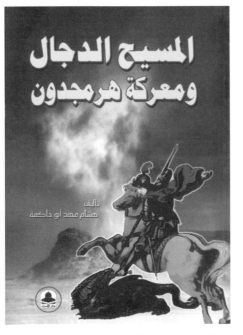

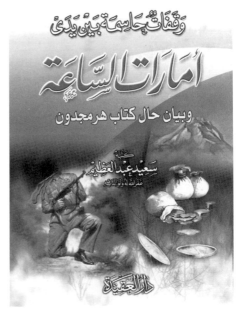

8. Hisham Muhammad Abu Hakima, *The Antichrist and the Battle of Armageddon* (Amman, 2002).

9. Said Abdelazim, *The Signs of the Hour* (Cairo, 2002).

بوادر ظهور المهدي ونزول السيد المسيح عليهما السلام
وسيناريو الأحداث المستقبلية في ضوء الأحاديث النبوية
من الآن وحتى قيام الساعة

أسامة يوسف رحمة

10. Usama Yusuf Rahma, *The Hour Approaches* (Beirut, 2003).

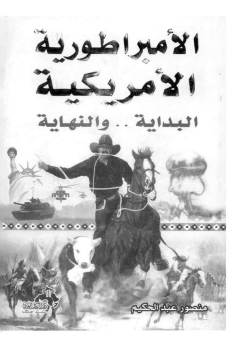

11. Mansur Abdelhakim, *The American Empire* (Cairo, 2005).

12. Mansur Abdelhakim, *New York and the Empire of Fear* (Cairo, 2006).

13. Ahmad as-Saqqa, *The Return of the Awaited Messiah for the Iraq War* (Cairo, 2003).

14. Ahmad as-Saqqa, *The Beginning and the End of the People of Israel* (Cairo, 2004).

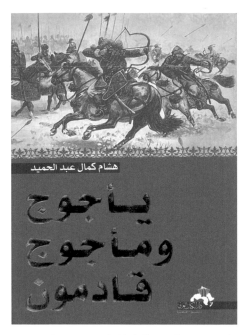

15. Hisham Kamal Abdelhamid, *Gog and Magog Are Coming* (Cairo, 2006).

16. Mustafa Murad, *The End of the World* (Cairo, 2003).

17. Muhammad Nidal al-Hafez, *The Reality between Prophecy and Politics* (Damascus, 2005).

18. Muhammad al-Wakid's translation of John Hogue's *Nostradamus: The New Millennium* (Damascus, 2006).

الدكتور بلال نعيم

مسيرة الزمان

(عج)

حتى صاحب الزمان

19. Bilal Na'im, *The March of Time Up Until the Master of the Age* (Beirut, 2006).

أحمـدي نجـاد

والـ... العالمية المقبلة

شـادي فقيـه

بعض قادة الحرس:

أحمدي نجاد هو قائد قوات المهدي التي ستحرر القدس.

بعض العلماء قالوا له..

ان المشروع النووي مرتبط بظهور الامام المهدي فلا تتهاون فيه..

20. Shadi Faqih, *Ahmadinejad and the Forthcoming World Revolution* (Beirut, 2006).

زوال إسرائيل

نبوءة قرآنية

أم صدف رقمية

بسام نهاد جرار

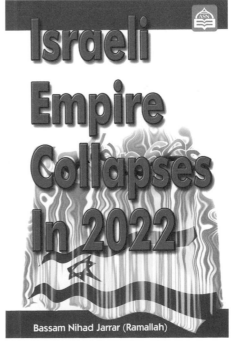

Israeli Empire Collapses In 2022

Bassam Nihad Jarrar (Ramallah)

21a–b. Bassam Jarrar, *The Disappearance of Israel in 2022* (Beirut, 1995), published in English as *Israeli Empire Collapses in 2022* (Kuala Lumpur, 2002).

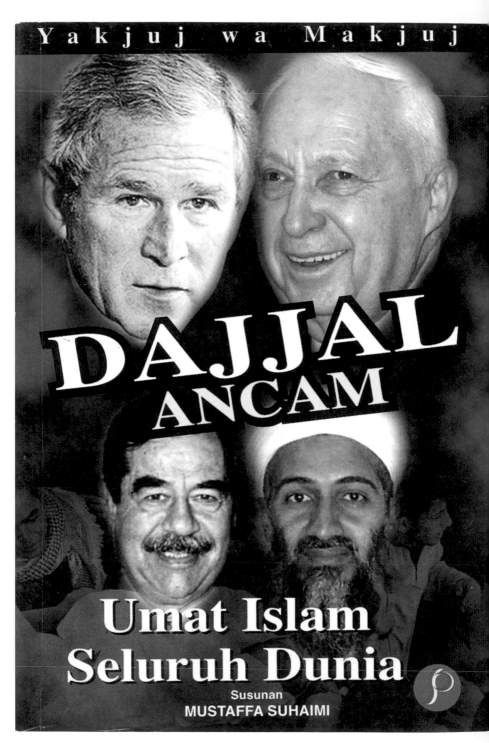

22. Mustafa Suhaimi, *Gog and Magog: The Antichrist Threatens the Islamic Nation throughout the World* (Kuala Lumpur, 2007).

CHAPTER 7

The Beginning of the End in Iraq

The Anglo-American invasion of Iraq in March 2003 changed the very nature of apocalyptic propaganda in Islamic nations. What had developed fifteen years earlier as an anti-Semitic species of fiction now became an obsessive style of paranoid interpretation, an irrational technique for making sense of a world in which hostile and infidel forces ran wild. The characterization of the invasion as a new crusade met with practically unanimous approval in circles where Christian Zionism was perceived to be a far more formidable enemy than Israel by itself. Coming after the strike against Afghanistan, the assault on Iraq unleashed a vast wave of urgent speculation about the pre-positioning of the forces of the Antichrist and the Mahdi between Khurasan and Greater Syria.[1] What in retrospect seemed to amount almost to an age of artisanally manufactured millenarianism now gave way to doomsaying on a mass scale, flooding retail book outlets from Casablanca to Djakarta and providing a new and disturbing index of social perceptions and anxieties in the Islamic world.

THE ABDELHAKIM PHENOMENON

At this juncture the powerful Dar al-Kitab al-Arabi (The House of the Arab Book), based in Cairo with a branch office in Damascus, decided to enter the booming market for apocalyptic literature. Its star author turned out to be Mansur Abdelhakim, a modest Egyptian lawyer whose first book, published in 1994, had gone virtually unnoticed.[2] A decade later he threw himself into a frenzy of activity, churning out some twenty titles in the space of three years. This staggering rate of production dwarfed the output of the genre's Egyptian pioneers, while at the same time deepening even further the delusional and vindictive aspect of their thinking.

In only a few months Abdelhakim managed to conquer a substantial audience, from the shopping centers of the Gulf to the traditional bookstores of the Levant and street stalls from Alexandria to Amman. The covers of his books—showing a beleaguered Statue of Liberty (Plate 12), satanic high priests, and rampaging cowboys (Plate 11)—were eye-catching, and their format of three hundred or so pages filled an intermediate niche in the market between popular booklets and Dawud's weighty tomes on the Antichrist. Collections of Abdelhakim's works were methodically built up for marketing purposes, among them *The Events of the End of Times* (in four volumes), a series of four books on Iraq, Greater Syria, New York, and Hijaz advertised under the title "The Countries and the Cities That Have Made the World Tremble," and *Who Secretly Rules the World?* (in three volumes). This arrangement did not exclude the independent promotion of individual books, notably *The American Empire* (Plate 11), whose subtitle ("The Beginning and the End") echoed the title of one of Ibn Kathir's apocalyptic treatises.

Abdelhakim describes his geopolitical vision in these terms:

> The American wars are religious crusades meant to hasten the coming of the "Messiah," or Jewish Mahdi.[3] The American [military] presence near Israel is intended to help bring about the victory of this Jewish Messiah, but also to confront the Mahdi awaited by the Muslims, Sunni and Shi'i alike, whose arrival will precede that of the Jewish Messiah, heir to the throne of David. The American administration and the neoconservatives believe in the biblical prophecies. Both Bushes, father and son, like Reagan before them, are convinced that the awaited Mahdi will appear in the East to do battle with the enemies of Islam and to liberate the al-Aqsa Mosque. This is why they have established themselves in Iraq, in the region nearest to where he will appear, in order to be in the best possible position to fight him there.[4]

In other words, the apocalyptic sequence of events leading to the end of the world is now unfolding, and believers must prepare themselves for the manifestation of the various signs of the Hour: "We live in an era of worldwide Jewish terrorism," for "the war waged by the Israeli Mossad prepares the way for the Antichrist to emerge."[5] With the invasion first of Afghanistan, and then of Iraq, "the Third World War has begun and can no longer be stopped."[6]

Abdelhakim exculpates bin Laden of all responsibility for the attacks of 11 September, which were instead the work of "a group of the American state apparatus charged with implementing the policy of President Bush." This plotting is under the control of the Antichrist himself. His right arm is "Freemasonry, a Jewish organization that rules the world behind the scenes at the behest of the Antichrist."[7] These Judeo-Masonic conspirators are themselves the heirs of the Knights Templar, who Abdelhakim anachronistically claims ravaged Jerusalem in 1099;[8] nearer our own time, their dark intrigues were responsible for the abolition of the caliphate by Atatürk in 1924.[9] The dollar bill betrays the Antichrist's control over the United States, since it is his omniscient eye that looks out from the Masonic pyramid pictured on the back. As for "the American Revolution and [the nation's] independence from the English, this was the doing of Rothschild."[10]

American society, Abdelhakim says, is prey to every kind of vice, "drugs, dependency, school violence, AIDS, sex, racial discrimination, and other crimes."[11] But all this is the inevitable heritage of a conquest that "exterminated" the majority of the country's eighteen million indigenous inhabitants.[12] The support of the United States for Israel is perfectly natural as well, since Israel has a comparable record of barbarism toward native populations. The "Judeo-Christian alliance" in America encourages the formation of "violent fundamentalist militias," foremost among them the "army of God" that targets abortion clinics.[13] The "Zionist infiltration of Christianity" is made possible by a distorted reading of the books of Ezekiel, Zechariah, and John,[14] and reinforced by the media power of televangelists such as Pat Robertson, Jimmy Swaggart, and Jerry Falwell.[15] Thanks to them, the American president (the "sultan of fear") is able to carry out "an old colonial policy under a new concept."[16]

More originally, Abdelhakim claims that the Antichrist is based in the Formosa (rather than the Bermuda) triangle,[17] where he uses his supernatural powers to exploit extraterrestrial technologies. Thus, for example, the ass on which the Antichrist is said by some hadiths to ride is, in fact, a flying saucer. What is more, whereas Satan is "the worst devil of jinns," the Antichrist is "the worst devil of men."[18] His Judeo-Masonic agents work tirelessly to bring about "the advent of a unified world government presided over by the Jewish Antichrist, with the restoration of the temple of Solomon and the throne of David."[19] As for

the United Nations, it is nothing more than a "Judeo-American organization of world control," just like the GATT, the IMF, and the stock
market.[20] "The two arms of the Antichrist," Abdelhakim observes, "are
communism and liberal capitalism."[21]

In his apocalyptic battle with the Mahdi, the Antichrist, unable to
gain entry to Mecca and Medina, will establish himself in Bahrain. The
fighting will start up in Syria, and then spread to the two holy places
defended by the Mahdi, who will have been proclaimed caliph in Mecca.
In saying this, Abdelhakim endorses the belief, held by some Sunni, that
the Mahdi will be the last of the twelve caliphs called "rightly guided"
(al-rāshidūn)—a claim that echoes the Shi'i belief in a mystical line of
twelve imams, of whom the Mahdi would be the last one.[22] No mercy
will be shown in this final battle, which will end only with "the end
of the Jews." Concurring in the hadith about the stones and trees that
denounce the Jews hiding behind them, Abdelhakim calls attention to
a particular kind of tree, the gharqad, which alone will remain silent.
The reason, he says, is that the Israelis have planted this species in massive numbers in order to prevent the other trees from denouncing them
when the hour comes.[23]

Moreover, according to Abdelhakim, "the first nuclear war occurred
in Iraq before the Flood," of which it was the immediate cause, and it
is "the Jews' thirst for vengeance against the people of Babylon" that
motivated the invasion of Iraq in the spring of 2003. This desire for
vengeance transformed the war into a "crusading religious duty" with
"missionaries in the wagon trains of the American army" and "priority
given to the plunder of history" (a reference to the pillage of the country's archaeological treasures).[24] The "American Mongols" have turned
out to be as barbaric as Gog and Magog, those accursed descendants of
Noah (through Yaphet) who have launched, not seven, but fully sixteen
devastating invasions—most recently against the caliphate of Baghdad
in 1258. Just as their hordes were finally turned back on that occasion
by the Mamluks of Cairo, so too will Egypt once again stand up to them
at the end of times.[25] For the moment, these monstrous tribes have gone
underground. One of their number happened to appear in the French
countryside in 1992, but "the secret of these creatures" was suppressed
following direct American intervention.[26]

In support of his paranoid theories, Abdelhakim draws freely on
the prophecies of Nostradamus—the inspiration for his "scenario of
the end of times"—which he also cites in connection with the Sufyani
and the Mahdi.[27] Every now and again Abdelhakim mentions Christian

apocalypses, but clearly he prefers the classic texts of Western anti-Semitism; indeed, the title of one of his books derives from the idea of a "chessboard" popularized by the conspiracy theorist William Guy Carr, for whom human history is no more than a chess game in which the players' moves are orchestrated by unseen Jewish grandmasters.[28] In the matter of 11 September, Abdelhakim quotes at length from the French journalist Thierry Meyssan's book 9/11: The Big Lie (2002) to deny the reality of al-Qaida's attacks.[29] But Abdelhakim also takes literally the plot of the political thriller by Larry Collins and Dominique Lapierre, Is New York Burning? (2005), in which he detects the signs of impending American doom, and trawls through the Book of the Dead of pharaonic Egypt in search of the earliest portents.[30] His eclecticism is omnivorous.[31]

Not only has the scenario for the apocalyptic wars to come already been imagined, it has been adapted for the screen in the form of Arnold Schwarzenegger's Terminator films.[32] Abdelhakim sees the offensive mounted by Israel against Hizbullah in Lebanon during the summer of 2006 as the "general repetition" of a basic confrontation that soon, as the result of an Israeli attack on nuclear installations in Iran, will be played out on a far larger scale. This conflagration will be all the more impossible to prevent as it will have been encouraged by "evangelists" and "fundamentalists" in the United States, eager to throw the entire Middle East into apocalyptic turmoil in order to realize their "biblical prophecies."[33]

DIVERSIFICATION STRATEGIES

Dar al-Kitab al-Arabi naturally hoped that the astonishing productivity of its most profitable author could be made to continue. Its able Syrian director, Walid Nassif, nevertheless sought to strengthen the house's dominant position in the apocalyptic market by diversifying in two directions: on the one hand, by acquiring the services of a leading clerical figure, in order to capture a larger share of the conservative Islamic audience; on the other, by urging other radical messianic authors to show greater enthusiasm in embracing the cause of anti-Semitism and, more generally, to give their imagination even freer rein.

Shaykh Mahmud al-Gharbawi was well qualified to help win over conservative readers. An Egyptian civil servant in the Ministry of Waqfs, the government's department for Islamic affairs, Gharbawi held the rank of Inspector of Mosques and made his home in Giza, a suburb of

Cairo. In 2004 he brought out three works with Dar al-Kitab al-Arabi: *The Antichrist, The Awaited Mahdi,* and *The Major Grace,*[34] which were marketed together as a collection entitled "Prophecies of the End of Times in the Qur'an and the Traditions."

The first title in the series included a preface by Mansur Abdelhakim himself, and so profited from the star-power of the house's best-known author. Although Shaykh Gharbawi was not reluctant to cite, in addition to Abdelhakim, radical messianic figures such as Dawud and Tawila, he relied for the most part on a more classical exposition of the relevant Qur'anic sources and established traditions, showing a particular fondness for Nu'aym ibn Hammad. This time-honored method allowed Gharbawi to avoid the risk of controversy associated with the interpretation of current events. Nevertheless he confidently dismissed the possibility that the Sufyani was Saddam Hussein, which seemed all the more remote since, so far from leading the fight against "the Americans, the British, and the Jews," Saddam had been captured in December 2003.[35] Gharbawi's apocalyptic outlook was hardly exciting, but it was also more reassuring than Abdelhakim's Dantean flights of fancy, and in any case nicely filled a gap in Dar al-Kitab al-Arabi's editorial program.

At the same time Nassif was working to expand the house's radical messianic list. He was quick to sign up Ahmad Hijazi as-Saqqa, a graduate of al-Azhar also known as Ahmad Ahmad Ali as-Saqqa, who had recently been let go by a rival Cairo publisher, Dar al-Bayan al-Arabi (The House of the Arab Declaration).[36] Saqqa's *The Return of the Awaited Messiah for the Iraq War* (2003) examines the American invasion in the light of Judeo-Christian apocalypses (George W. Bush having identified Saddam with Nebuchadnezzar, who, in a dream interpreted by the prophet Daniel, saw a statue with a head of gold and feet of clay) and concludes that this "extremist fundamentalist conflict" had been conceived for the purpose of furthering "the dissemination of Christianity" (Plate 13).[37] The Iraq War will not be the last, because America is ruled by the principles of the Talmud, "which allows the killing of every non-Jew." The true objective of this "religious war," then, is "the annihilation of Islam." Tellingly, President Bush's "grandfather" published a book of insults against the Prophet Muhammad in 1830.[38]

Saqqa describes at length the "religious foundations" of the American "crusade against Islam" and "Bush's war for the return of the Messiah." Paul Wolfowitz, Deputy Secretary of Defense, and Richard Perle, advisor to the president—both Jews, Saqqa is careful to point out—played a major role in bringing about the conflict. But it was the televangelist network, controlled by Pat Robertson, Jimmy Swaggart, and Jerry Falwell, and equipped with "two hundred television stations and fifteen hundred radio stations," that was primarily responsible for rallying support for the invasion of Iraq. Almost twenty-five years earlier, Ronald Reagan had told the televangelist Jim Bakker: "Ours will be the generation that witnesses the battle of Armageddon."[39]

Exacerbating this fundamentalist crusade, Saqqa claimed, was the "Jews' thirst for vengeance against the Arabs" in general, and "against Iraq" in particular.[40] His anti-Semitic paranoia became intensified still further in a second book, *The Beginning and the End of the People of Israel*,[41] published in 2004 in Cairo and Damascus, but written five years earlier. Not content to convict the Jewish people of every imaginable vice, Saqqa predicts their extinction at the hands of the Muslims, symbolically illustrated on the book's cover by a star of David pierced by a sword dripping with blood (Plate 14). Christian apocalypses are endlessly quoted, and forcibly subjected to numerological manipulation. Thus, for example, 666, the number of the Beast according to Saint John, is made by Saqqa to correspond to "Muhammad ibn Abdallah in Mecca"—a discovery that he claims won the approval of a dean of faculty at al-Azhar.[42] Later the same year Saqqa published *The Day of the Lord, Called Battle of Armageddon* (2004), a repugnant volume devoted to the inevitable and ultimate extermination *(ibāda)* of the Jews.[43]

Shortly afterward, in 2006, Dar al-Kitab al-Arabi further augmented its list by reissuing two recent works by an Egyptian radical messianic pamphleteer named Hisham Abdelhamid.[44] The first, *Gog and Magog Are Coming* (Plate 15), whose predictions had attracted little notice on its initial appearance eight years before, was thought to have gained in interest as a result of intervening events. Looking to the past, Abdelhamid argued that the Two-Horned One was a Yemeni sovereign, rather than the pagan Alexander the Great; and, to the future, that Gog and Magog will circumvent the ancient wall built between two mountains to contain them by flying over it, and that they will then swoop down upon Jesus and his partisans, parachuting from a squadron of warplanes. But before considering this cataclysmic battle in detail, Abdelhamid lays out an apocalyptic scenario in six stages: first, the "reunion of the Jewish diaspora on the land of Palestine," followed by an attempt "to make Jerusalem its capital by controlling the neighboring states"; then, the successive collapse of the British, German, and Russian empires to the advantage of the United States, now engaged in an implacable struggle against Islam; control of the world by America, via the United Nations;

the rise of Europe once more as a major and independent power, identified with the Byzantium of the apocalyptic hadiths; merciless combat between Europeans and Muslims, with the Muslims triumphing and seizing control of the Vatican; and, finally, the "emergence of the Antichrist in a flying saucer, attended by his devils, from the Bermuda Triangle" to lead a counteroffensive of the remaining Jewish, European, and American forces, whose destruction will mark the definitive victory of Islam.[45]

The second volume by Abdelhamid, *The Appearance of the Antichrist Draws Near*, republished in 2006,[46] sought to communicate the same sense of urgency as *Gog and Magog Are Coming*. Abdelhamid had been deeply impressed by a performance given by the magician David Copperfield before the pyramids of Giza, which he interpreted as evidence of the "secret government of the world on behalf of the Antichrist." In the Book of Ezekiel he finds incontrovertible proof of the existence of flying saucers, whose base of operations in the Bermuda Triangle serves as "the throne of Satan, the seat of the kingdom of the jinns, and the research center of the Antichrist." Furthermore, all the "scientific and religious signs demonstrate that the creatures of the flying saucers are devils in the army of the Antichrist." Elsewhere, in a text strewn with clumsy sketches and amateurish illustrations of scenes from science fiction, Abdelhamid frets over the spread of "satanic worship in Egypt through rock and black metal" and darkly concludes that "sex, sports, drugs, and films are Zionism's principal instruments for giving effect to the protocols of the Antichrist."[47]

To complete its encircling maneuver in the apocalyptic market, Dar al-Kitab al-Arabi now had only to acquire a manuscript by an indisputably conservative author, someone who, unlike Shaykh Gharbawi, was untainted by radical messianic associations. This objective was achieved in early 2007 with the publication of *The Arrangement of the Events Leading Up to the Hour* by a layman named Muhammad Abdelhalim Abdelfattah.[48] Hewing closely to orthodox teaching, Abdelfattah was careful to distinguish the minor signs of the Hour, most of which have already occurred, from the major signs, which are still to come. Thus he placed in the first category the fire in Hijaz, locating it during the medieval period, and in the second the apocalyptic fire that will hasten the gathering *(al-hashr)* of humanity on the Last Day, the tenth of the ten major signs.[49]

Abdelfattah concludes his book with the message that "research on the signs of the Hour, their study, their learning, and their teaching figure among the most important matters of our time . . . in order to strengthen faith in [people's] hearts, encourage more virtuous behavior, and prepare the entry into the other world."[50] In the meantime apocalyptic publishing prospered marvelously well, especially at Dar al-Kitab al-Arabi. Smaller firms tried to reap some of the millenarian harvest for themselves by publishing the sort of softcover booklet that had been popular a generation earlier, as Dar al-Muslim (The House of the Muslim) did with *The Antichrist and Gog and Magog.*[51]

THE SWAN SONG OF AN OLDTIMER

The international success of Mansur Abdelhakim's books placed Muhammad Isa Dawud in the unfamiliar position of having to scramble to preserve his share of the apocalyptic market, both in Egypt and elsewhere in the Middle East. The reputation he had built up by publishing some forty titles in a little more than twenty years offered no guarantee that he could meet the challenge posed by a new generation of still more radical messianic authors. The fact that *The Surprise* had come out immediately after 11 September and that his *Treasure of the Euphrates* had slightly preceded the American invasion of Iraq did, of course, bolster his claim to have a gift for anticipating events, and certainly few other pamphleteers of the previous generation enjoyed his advantages in seeking to maintain their position in a highly competitive environment. But in Dawud's latest books neither of the things that had made him famous—the baroque zeal with which he recounted the missions of UFOs dispatched by the Antichrist from the Bermuda Triangle and the fiery eloquence with which he conjured up the end of the world—was much in evidence.

Increasingly Dawud fell back on the obsessive anti-Semitism that had permeated and nourished his earlier works. In *The Messiah Made in Israel* (2005) he labored to show that an "international organization of parties hostile to the Mahdi" was working to undermine Muslim faith in His coming. At the heart of this global plot, he holds, is the Israeli intelligence service, Mossad, which now was trying not "to collect military or political information, but to destroy a belief." Dawud reviews the list of pretenders to the title of Mahdi, interspersing their portraits with photographs of women taken from the Israeli press—further proof of a Zionist conspiracy having close and unsuspected links to Yemeni Judaism. While acknowledging that Sunni and Shi'i share the same faith in the Mahdi, Dawud accuses the Meccan insurgents in 1979 of having violated all the values of Islam.[52] He calls them Kharijites, in reference to the dissidents who seceded from Shi'ism in the seventh century, taking up arms against the caliph, 'Ali.

Dawud was no more inspired when he wrote *The Temple* (2006), an attempt, in the words of its subtitle, to illuminate "H-Hour and the Next Stage of Zionism." The entire book is summed up in its introduction: "There can be no authentic Israel without Jerusalem. This is what Zionism believes. And there can be no Jerusalem without the Messiah. And the Messiah will not appear until the Temple of Solomon has been rebuilt. This temple is the essential and decisive point of transition from the diaspora of the past to the reunion of the present, as well as to [Jewish] rule over the whole world. And by their declarations regarding the new Middle East, the Jews look forward to the moment when these conditions will be fulfilled." A new plot is therefore underway, this time to destroy the al-Aqsa Mosque in Jerusalem. Recalling Napoleon's promise to reunite the Jews in Palestine, Dawud places the question in historical perspective while at the same time emphasizing that the "Jewish habit of deceit" gained its full force only "in unison with America." For it is American money that is responsible for "financing . . . the catastrophe to come," when a "red cow" will be worshiped in the temple built upon the ruins of al-Aqsa.[53]

SPOTLIGHT ON AMERICA

The invasion of Iraq relegated direct conflict with Israel to a position of secondary importance for many apocalyptic authors, who were now committed to exposing the mechanisms of Christian Zionist domination. In 2003, the Lebanese journalist and political advisor Muhammad Sammak published an article in the Egyptian daily *Al-Ahram* on "the religious foundations of American policy" that Ahmad as-Saqqa reprinted in its entirety in a book published later the same year.[54] There Saqqa addressed the subject of the exorbitant power of the televangelists, famously attributing to them two hundred television stations and fifteen hundred radio stations, figures that were subsequently to recur throughout the apocalyptic literature.[55] Sammak, for his part, developed these arguments further in *Religion in American Decisionmaking* (2005), stressing the influence of Jerry Falwell, but also of Pat Robertson, who claimed that "God's wrath" had struck down Itzhak Rabin—and that it will strike down anyone else who attempts to divide Jerusalem, the capital of Israel.[56] In general, Sammak finds, the American media "inculcated hatred and detestation of Islam even before the tragedy of 11 September."[57]

The following year another Egyptian author, Abdel Tawab Abdallah Husayn, took an even more fanatic line in a work entitled *The Destruction of America at Our Gates* (2006), which he dedicated "to the sovereigns and presidents of the Islamic nation." Citing at length Meyssan's *9/11: The Big Lie,* Husayn argues that the public understanding of this moment is based on a huge deception.[58] "The United States," he says, "has become an authentic police state" that now seeks to impose "American law on the world." Moreover, "the offensive against Iraq is only the beginning of an armed aggression against the [entire] Arab nation," with bin Laden serving as "pretext" and "argument" in a systematic campaign of "lies." After a detailed review of the Bin Laden Group's extensive financial interests in various American firms, Husayn concludes that the head of al-Qaida is an agent of the United States.[59]

This "new Crusader war" is the work of "extremist Christian Zionism," convinced that the return of the "Second Coming of the Messiah" is finally at hand. Husayn begins by denouncing the Freemasons, who have long been in the service of the Antichrist, and then patiently works his way through the modern register of obscure forces unmasked by a tradition of anti-Semitic paranoia that extends from *The Protocols of the Elders of Zion* to the chessboard of William Guy Carr—forces that prepared the way for the current "Third World War" between Christian Zionism and the Arab-Muslim world. In Husayn's retelling, however, Christian apocalypses are deployed in support of the conclusion that a major earthquake, the fruit of divine wrath, will suddenly devastate the United States. In the aftermath of this, the Muslim conquest of France and Spain will precipitate the formation of an "Islamo-European coalition" that will deliver the fatal blow to America.[60]

Anti-American rage encouraged other pamphleteers to follow Gamaleddin's example and cross over, as he had done in 2002, from the conservative Islamic camp to the radical messianic side. The Egyptian shaykh Ali Abdelal al-Tahtawi, whose book about Jesus and the Antichrist, *The Encounter of the Two Messiahs,* was published two years later, now joined his voice to the chorus of those who abominated "the triple union constituted by the Antichrist, the Jews, and the new Crusaders . . . to destroy the Muslims."[61] Whereas his countryman Abdelfattah Gamal flatly predicted "the fall of the American empire,"[62] the Jordanian polemicist Mokhtar Meslati, while cataloguing the many vices of American society with revulsion and laying particular stress on the sexual deviance of several famous televangelists, most notably Jimmy Swaggart,[63] argued that the United States can yet escape disintegration by embracing the Muslim path—hence the title of his book, *America Is Wasting Away and Islam Is Its Savior.*

The inexorability of war with the United States was taken for granted even by authors as apolitically minded as the Egyptian Mustafa Murad, in *The End of the World* (2003) ("With the strike against America on 11 September 2001, the conflict between Muslims and Christians has begun") (Plate 16), and the Lebanese author Haytham Hilak, in *The End of Humanity* (2004) ("American greed in Iraq is not limited to oil, it is obsessed by all the riches of Iraq").[64] This state of affairs, in Hilak's view, is a consequence of "the particular hostility of Protestantism, represented by America, Great Britain, and the Netherlands, toward Muslims and Arabs, and [of] their well-known support for the Jews."[65]

THE ARAB DISCIPLES OF NOSTRADAMUS

We have seen that the prophecies of Nostradamus gradually gained a prominent place in Arab apocalyptic obsessions. The events of 11 September, supposed to have been foretold by the French seer, gave his predictions renewed vigor.[66] Whole books were devoted to putting them in a properly Muslim eschatological context. One of the first was a volume by a Lebanese author, Sharafeddin al-A'raji, called *The Prophecies of Nostradamus: An Islamic and Analytical Vision of History and of the Future* that discusses the "affairs of Palestine" and the "offensive of the allies against Iraq."[67]

The Damascus house Al-Awael ("The Beginnings"), a pioneering presence in the Syrian apocalyptic market since its publication of Muhammad Munir Idlibi's *The Antichrist Invades the World* in 1998, brought out *The Reality between Prophecy and Politics* by Muhammad Nidal al-Hafez seven years later. The book's subtitle places Nostradamus on the same level as the Bible, the Gospels, and the Qur'an, and the cover shows a map in which Palestine is linked to Iraq by a sinister red dotted line leading to the Euphrates, the easternmost extent of Israel's purported expansionist designs (Plate 17). Hafez maintains that Nostradamus, in addition to having prophesied the 11 September attacks and the invasion of Iraq in 2003, also foresaw the irresistible Islamic awakening *(al-sahwa al-islamiyya)* under the direction of a leader who appears in Mecca. "These writings prove that the Islamic nation will establish itself as a great power," he says, "and will expand over a vast territory, including a part of Western Europe, even though Nostradamus was aware of the deceit and cleverness of the Jews."[68]

Al-Awael carried on in this vein with a translation into Arabic of *Nostradamus: The New Millennium*.[69] The author, an American charlatan with divinatory ambitions of his own named John Hogue, had already written a dozen books examining Nostradamus's forecasts. In 1997 Hogue collected the ten "centuries" of Nostradamus's verses under the title *The Complete Prophecies*, which he claimed to predict the advent of the papacy, the United States, and Iraq.[70] The 2002 edition of Hogue's book on the new millennium, regularly updated in the same spirit since its original publication in 1987, now laid great emphasis on 11 September and the role of the Antichrist, who, it turns out, might be any one of three people: Saddam Hussein, Usama bin Laden, or George W. Bush. Exceptional care was lavished on the Arabic edition in the way of design and illustration, with Hitler sharing the cover with the three candidate Antichrists (Plate 18), and Muhammad al-Wakid's introduction and commentary attached eschatological significance to the terrorist activities of al-Qaida.[71]

Al-Awael's editorial program was not limited to Nostradamus. It, too, offered a sampling of Western anti-Semitic literature, publishing two commentaries on *The Protocols of the Elders of Zion*.[72] To Muhammad Munir Idlibi it entrusted the job of translating into Arabic three volumes of the conspiratorial theories of Jim Marrs, an American specialist in extraterrestrials and "psychic warfare."[73] Echoing Marrs's interest in the "hidden history" that he saw linking the Trilateral Commission, the Freemasons, and the Great Pyramids,[74] Idlibi's annotated edition of Marrs's works was marketed under the title *Who Governs America and the World?*[75]

Also in Damascus, though with a rival publisher, Shaykh Muhammad Isam Arar al-Hasani brought out in 2006 a short book called *The Appearance of the Antichrist, Messiah of Aberration*. The author of an earlier pamphlet on the signs of the Hour, Shaykh Hasani revitalized the genre by sensationally reporting three recent sightings of the Antichrist, the sworn enemy of Islam, and predicting two more. The first occurred in Kuwait and coincided with the outbreak of the Iran-Iraq war, disastrous for all Muslims (Syria having been the only Arab country to refuse to support Saddam Hussein against the Islamic Republic); the second took place in Afghanistan (more precisely, in Taloqan), and the third in Iraq. A fourth appearance will occur in Iran, probably in Isfahan but possibly in Ahwaz. As for the Antichrist's fifth and final appearance, Allah alone knows the time and the place, for it will signify "the return of the Islamic caliphate, the fall of Constantinople to the Muslims and their eventual conquest of the rest of the world." America has placed itself in the service of the Antichrist, creating a "favorable climate" for his machinations by its occupation of Afghanistan and Iraq, as well as by its control of Kuwait, Qatar, and Arabia "behind the scenes." All the while "the invasion" *(al-ghazū)* of "European, Jewish, Crusader, and Freemasonic thought, the worst [possible] nightmare for Islam," continues.[76]

Faced with this rising tide of radical messianic literature, Syrian authorities reacted with relative restraint. In 2005, the Ministry of Information published *Beware, O Muslims,* an essay on the "Crusader colonial war" arguing that the motivations for "Western aggression" sprang from classical imperialism rather than militant millenarianism.[77] A private publisher, Dar al-Mahabba, had sought to assuage conservative Islamic anxieties the year before by issuing Ahmad al-Khattab's *The Voyage in the Hereafter* (2004), a familiar litany of the signs of the Hour introduced by the director of the Islamic Studies Center in Damascus.[78]

PALESTINIAN PROGNOSTICATIONS

Palestinian millennialists, for their part, carried on a tradition of Qur'anic interpretation concerning the inevitability *(hatmiyya)* of the disappearance of Israel, associated with Shaykh Tamimi, that seemed almost sober by comparison with the rabid enthusiasm of Egyptian and Syro-Lebanese apocalyptics. In 2005, Khalid Helu's *The Order of Allah Has Come and No One Can Anticipate It* (marketed with the subtitle "From Babylon to Jerusalem, Qur'anic Prophecies") appeared simultaneously in "occupied Palestine" and Jordan. Helu describes his book as an "attempt to overcome [my] lack of science and knowledge by immersing [my]self in the science and knowledge revealed in the Qur'an," with particular attention to the fifth and seventeenth chapters, "The Feast" and "The Night Journey."[79] A literalist approach of this sort left little room for personal speculation, though Helu does permit himself the luxury of predicting the final defeat of the "enemies of Allah." And although his book falls squarely under the head of Qur'anic commentary *(tafsīr),* being introduced by an expert in this subject on the faculty of Islamic law at the University of Jordan in Amman, Helu does not hesitate to heap scorn on the holy "trinity" *(thālūth)* of wealth, power, and Israel that he claims is worshiped by Zionism in both its Jewish and its Christian forms.[80]

Another Palestinian author, Khalil Husayn Jabir, had to assume most of the publication costs for *The Third Corruption of the Sons of Israel and Their End Are Inevitable According to the Qur'an, the Bible, and the Gospels* (2006). The first "corruption" *(fasād)* of the Jewish people began with the exodus from Egypt and lasted until the exile in Babylon, and the second ended with the destruction of the temple. The third will be concluded shortly. Adopting the method proposed by Shaykh Hawali, who calculated a twilight period of forty-five years beginning with the occupation of East Jerusalem in 1967, Jabir confidently expects to see the "beginning of the end" of Israel in 2012. Jabir also cites Samuel Huntington and Francis Fukuyama, in addition to *The Protocols of the Elders of Zion,* and reserves a place of honor for Jerry Falwell and his Moral Majority among the objects of his abuse. Stressing that in the minds of "59 percent of Americans, the events described in the Apocalypse of John will [definitely] occur," Jabir nonetheless cannot quite bring himself to disagree with a remark attributed to Falwell in 1999: "The coming of the Messiah should occur in the next ten years and the Antichrist, who is already among us, is a Jewish man."[81]

A third author, Shaykh Bassam Jarrar, whose 1995 book took its title from his claim that Israel would disappear in 2022, returned to Palestine from exile in southern Lebanon to resume his activities as a preacher in suburban Ramallah. There Jarrar founded the Nun Center for Qur'anic Studies and Research in order to pursue his growing interest in literalist analysis through numerological investigation.[82] In 2004 he published *Visions in the Wise Book of Allah,*[83] which marked his abandonment of apocalyptic. What is more, the Hamas movement no longer showed any interest in helping to escalate millenarian speculation; even an Islamist jurist devoted only two pages to the Antichrist in a work published two years later under the title *The Hadiths of Revolt*—a reference to the tribulations that already had given rise to all manner of delusional anxiety. Generally speaking, inhabitants of the West Bank and Gaza seemed less fond of apocalyptic imaginings than people in neighboring countries.[84] Radical messianic bestsellers could be purchased in Palestine, though not uncommonly they were sold in a plain unmarked wrapper.[85]

THE RAMPARTS OF THE GULF

The scale of Levantine apocalyptic production attracted imitators in the Gulf, both within the clerical hierarchy and among a largely autodidact population of lay authors. The need for doctrinal restoration was most keenly felt in Saudi Arabia, of course, where eschatological manuals listing hundreds of officially approved scriptural references enjoyed a sudden popularity. Notable among such works was *The Encyclopedia of the End of Times,* published in Riyadh in 2003 by Abdallah ibn Sulayman al-Mashaali, son of a religious dignitary of the kingdom and himself a high-ranking official in the Ministry of Justice.[86]

Several years later a professor at the Islamic University of Medina named Zein al-Abidin ibn Gharamallah al-Ghamidi sought to recenter eschatological debate on the ambient corruption of the age—a phenomenon held to be pregnant with ultimate meaning. Ghamidi examines the various aspects of *herj,* an obscure term found at the heart of one apocalyptic hadith that no longer can be seen as referring only to murder, he says;[87] it refers also to a host of related aberrations: "the mixing of the sexes, . . . the rising rate of divorce, the spread of lying, the increase in time spent sleeping, and [the abundance of] uninhibited dreams."[88] No less grave a threat to the moral order is posed by radical messianic deviations, vigorously dismissed in another treatise containing a preface by the imam of the Holy Mosque of Mecca.[89] A third manual evokes the hallowed memory of Muhammad ibn Abdel Wahhab (1703–1787), founder of Wahhabism and the tutelary figure of the Saudi kingdom, again as part of a campaign to extinguish messianic dissidence.[90]

A striking feature of all these treatises of moral rearmament, disseminated and encouraged by the Saudi authorities, is the frequency with which they quote Sayyid Qutb,[91] the leading Egyptian figure of contemporary Islamism, hung in Cairo in 1966, whose extreme reluctance to engage in millenarian speculation we have already noted. But Saudi publishers also hastened to reissue the works of a defunct 'alim named Shaykh Saadi (1888–1957). Although he had grown up in the cradle of Wahhabism, Saadi's teaching was associated with the relative tolerance of the city of Unayza—relative by comparison with the provincial capital of Burayda. It is notable that his writings on the Antichrist and Gog and Magog were published in Dammam, on the eastern coast of the kingdom,[92] rather than in Riyadh or Jidda, the usual sources of this kind of literature; and that one of Saadi's disciples, Shaykh Uthaymin, composed a booklet on the "turmoil" *(fitna)* in the mind of his teacher.[93] The following year, the head of the department of Qur'anic commentary *(tafsīr)* at the University of Medina arranged for the publication of a critical edition of a 1969 treatise on the Antichrist by the late dean of the faculty of Islamic law at Umm al-Qura University in Mecca, and a house in Riyadh published an eschatological commentary on the medieval author al-Andalusi, composed by a Moroccan shaykh from Tetouan and introduced by his teacher in Tangier.[94] All this effort of reissuing older works and bringing out new volumes of commentary and compilation was intended not only to strengthen conservative Islamic resistance to messianic appeals, but to protect believers against jihadist temptation as well.

Also in 2004, a government official named Hamdi ibn Hamza Abu Zeid undertook to radically revise traditional views of the Two-Horned One in a book published at his own expense.[95] Far from being a mere pamphleteer, more or less mistrusted by the authorities like so many Egyptian apocalyptics, Abu Zeid was a high-ranking civil servant, born in Yanbu but resident in Riyadh, where he sat on the Consultative Council (Majlis al-Shura), the most powerful representative body in the kingdom of Arabia, and served as a general director of the Ministry of Finance and vice president of the Saudi chapter of the Red Crescent. Thanks to his many connections, Abu Zeid was able to see to it that his book was long displayed on book racks in the principal shopping centers of the country.

Abu Zeid showed greater originality than his predecessors in arguing that the Two-Horned One was neither Alexander the Great, nor a Persian emperor, nor a Yemeni sovereign, but actually the ancient Egyptian pharaoh Amenhotep IV (known as Akhenaten, reigned 1352–1336 B.C.E.). Akhenaten was famous not only for having taken Nefertiti as his wife, but also for having promoted the cult of the sun god Aten to the exclusion of other gods—thus, in the view of many historians, laying the basis for monotheism. Abu Zeid claims, without adducing a shred of evidence, that Akhenaten quietly left the valley of the Nile, leaving the throne to his son-in-law Tutankhamun, and embarked for the Maldives. Sailing eastward as far as the Kiribati archipelago in Oceania, then turning back to the north and going on to China, Akhenaten settled in the Zhou kingdom, where he urged that a Great Wall be constructed in order to repel Mongol invasions. This inventive rereading of the myth of Gog and Magog is enlivened by color maps and photographs of the author in China and in the Kiribati islands, which seem to have stimulated Abu Zeid's curiosity by reason of their location on the international date line—and of the presence of Muslim believers there.[96]

In 2004, an official in the Ministry of Religious Affairs in the United Arab Emirates named Shaykh Mahir Ahmad al-Sufi brought out the first volume in an ambitious series of ten works, published in Lebanon under the title *Encyclopedia of the Hereafter*. Shaykh Sufi's Beirut publisher managed to persuade a number of prestigious figures from throughout the Arab world to contribute prefaces, among them Shaykh Said Ramadan al-Buti, a figure of immense prestige in Damascus and beyond; Shaykh Akrama Salim Sabri, imam of al-Aqsa and mufti of Jerusalem; Shaykh Mahmud Ashur, formerly the vice-rector of al-Azhar; and Dr. Faruk Hamada, professor of Islamic sciences at the University of Rabat. The Emirian vice minister of religious affairs and the editor of the Islamic review *Al-Manar* in Abu Dhabi jointly coordinated promotion and publicity, which were aided also by the elegant design of these paperback books.

Shaykh Sufi's exposition of eschatological material is reliably orthodox, though between the major and minor signs of the Hour he usefully introduces an intermediate category of "middle signs" *(al-ʿalāmāt al-wustā)*. And unlike other conservative Islamic authors, he has the virtue of not trying to evade certain contradictions in the apocalyptic calendar. The announced "conquest" *(fath)* of Constantinople, for example, runs up against the fact that Istanbul has been an Islamic city for more than five centuries. Sufi acknowledges this difficulty, but reminds his readers that "the unknowable" *(al-ghayb)* is a divine privilege, and that "no one knows when the Hour will come"; after all, Constantinople may fall back into Christian hands, as happened in the case of Muslim Andalusia—thus permitting a new conquest by Islam. As for Gog and Magog, Sufi admits it is hard to see where "these thousands" of creatures could possibly be hidden, but he extricates himself by adroit casuistry: "We all believe in jinns, but where are they? The fact that not one of them has been seen does not make [their existence] any less established in the Qur'an."[97]

The University of Sharjah, another institutional guardian of conventional religious wisdom in the United Arab Emirates, sponsored the publication in 2005 of a treatise on the Mahdi by one Adel Zaki. Zaki takes as his point of departure the many hadiths on this subject, dismissing at the very outset the doubts raised by Ibn Khaldun regarding their validity ("Ibn Khaldun was not a scholar of the hadith"). Notwithstanding his thoroughgoing defense of Sunni orthodoxy, the author generously devotes some twenty pages (out of more than four hundred) to the Shiʿi perception of the Mahdi, if only to point out the error of this view. For the Mahdi will first lead a jihad against the schismatics of Islam *(al-bughā)* before turning against "the Jews and the Antichrist," not to mention "the Byzantines *[Rūm]*, who will attack the Muslim countries."[98] Today, in the emirate of Sharjah itself, television delivers a considerable audience to the Egyptian preacher Omar Abdelkafi

Shahhata, whose ruminations on the hereafter *(dār al-ākhira)* have also been made available for purchase in a box of thirty-two videocassettes.

. . .

Amid the confused mass of apocalyptic writings that appeared in the wake of the American invasion of Iraq, a number of ominous developments stand out fairly clearly:

- A new generation of radical messianic authors has adopted the principal element of the global jihadist propaganda inspired by the writings of Shaykh Hawali, namely, the designation of Christian Zionism as the chief enemy of Islam.
- Just as the "Crusader" occupation of Iraq is considered to be an extension of the Jewish plundering of Palestine, America is perceived as the more or less willing instrument of Israel, and therefore of the "Judeo-Crusader" Antichrist.
- The Egyptian component remains dominant in apocalyptic production, with respect both to publishers and authors; the majority of Ayyub's epigones reside, like him, in Cairo, or else in one of its suburbs.
- Saudi Arabia has brought the full measure of its ecclesiastic influence to bear on publishing decisions in that country in order to ensure a regular flow of conservative Islamic works, hoping in this way to compensate for what it sees as the notorious failings of the Sunni hierarchy elsewhere in the Middle East.
- In addition to the works of Western anti-Semitism that have long been in general circulation, Christian apocalypses and American televangelists are now major sources of validation for paranoid scenarios of all kinds, including conspiracy theories.

The millenarian surge that gathered impetus following the American invasion of Iraq is as puzzling as it is incontestable. It is notable not least for the disturbing evidence it provides of intellectual degradation and the power of systematic obscurantism. In stark contrast to the conservative Islamic literature, whose references are rooted in classical tradition and whose prophecies reach indefinitely far into the future, the most recent radical messianic bestsellers are anchored in current events and depend increasingly on Western sources: Christian apocalypses are placed on the same level as the Qur'an and the prophetic traditions of

Islam, anti-Semitic pamphlets are ascribed gnostic significance, and all manner of statistics and news stories culled from the American press are regarded as authoritative (especially insofar as they confirm suspicions of widespread lawlessness and moral perversion). Global jihadists have sought in their turn to push this tendency to its logical extreme by turning the lethal weapons of an imaginary enemy against Christian Zionism itself.

It was less the fall of Saddam Hussein than the prolongation of the American occupation of Iraq that triggered the explosive growth of this mass literature. Large sections of the Sunni population in the Middle East turned away from the usual forums for political analysis, and even from militant propaganda, in order to wallow in the paranoid vision of a world in which Islam's chronic weakness became the surest guarantee of its ultimate triumph. National and partisan allegiances gave way to an unshakeable conviction in an imminent and apocalyptic combat between the three Abrahamic religions. The most fantastic hodgepodges of ideas were credited, with the result that the confrontation between, on the one hand, the upholders of Sunni orthodoxy and, on the other, the diabolical alliance of Judeo-Crusaders, Judeo-Protestants, and Judeo-Masons came to seem inevitable. European Catholics were doomed either to be converted to Islam or defeated by its conquering legions. The loyalty of Shi'a and other schismatics became a matter of the gravest suspicion.

There is nothing harmless about this intensifying delirium, for it is saturated with a profound sense of resentment and vindictiveness. Whereas the first generation of modern apocalyptics was often reduced to wild speculation, the messianics of the third millennium distill their venomous bile with the self-assurance of those for whom the future—and the end—of the world is obvious. America, unalterably hostile to Islam and fundamentally Machiavellian, is damned and fated to die a dreadful death; Islam is truth, irresistible power, and everlasting victory.

And yet, despite its undoubted importance and its undeniable prosperity, apocalyptic literature in the Sunni world remains a compensatory phenomenon. However deeply it may inform the thinking of ordinary people, for the moment at least it seems not to exert a great influence on political decisionmaking—no doubt in part because of its novel and massive reliance on non-Islamic sources and authorities. This is by no means the case, however, in the Shi'i world, where the resurgence of apocalyptic militancy unfolds against a background of ancient political resentments, still vividly remembered.

CHAPTER 8

The Grand Return of the Shi'i Mahdi

Shi'i traditions furnish an inexhaustible source of apocalyptic inspiration to believers convinced that the return of the Hidden Imam is imminent. An abundant literature is disseminated on this subject, primarily from the holy city of Najaf in Iraq, but also from Lebanon. The Islamic Republic of Iran had inherited from its founder, Ayatollah Khomeyni, an enduring distrust of messianic elation. With the election of Mahmud Ahmadinejad as president in June 2005, however, all official hindrance to the spread of millenarian ideas in that country was removed. The uprising of the Mahdi Army in Iraq, and indeed the war between Israel and Hizbullah during the summer of 2006, must therefore be understood as the consequence, at least in part, of mounting eschatological expectations.

THE MARTYR AYATOLLAH OF NAJAF

During the 1970s Ayatollah Muhammad Baqir al-Sadr became the symbol of the Islamist revival among the Shi'i community in Iraq. Sadr transformed his seminary in Najaf into a center of militant thought, breaking with the political quietism of Ayatollah Abul Qasim al-Khui, the supreme authority of Iraqi Shi'ism between 1971 and 1992. We have seen that Ayatollah Khomeyni, during his exile to Najaf in the 1960s, consulted regularly with Sadr. No sooner had Khomeyni devised the principle of *vilayat-e-faqih*, which was to form the theoretical basis for the Islamic Republic, than Sadr made this principle his own and sought to work out, as a practical matter, how an Islamic society and economy might function.[1] This far-reaching inquiry opened the way in turn for a rethinking of traditional Shi'i ideas of the Mahdi.

In 1977, Ayatollah Sadr composed an essay of fifty or so pages that was meant to serve as a preface to a fuller treatment of the problem. But this brief statement proved to be so popular that it was immediately published as an independent booklet, and later as an introduction to scholarly works on the subject.[2] Written in a simple and accessible style, in the hope that it would appeal as much to ordinary readers as to theologians, the essay consists of eight studies (bahth), four of them devoted to the "miracle" of the Mahdi's longevity, two to the mystery of the occultation, and two to the personal role of the Mahdi in the apocalyptic events to come.

Ayatollah Sadr declares at the outset that the Mahdi is "a man of flesh and bone, who lives among us, who sees us, who sees our hopes and our suffering, who shares our sorrows and our joys, who grieves to witness executions, poverty, and oppression (zulm), while impatiently awaiting the right moment to come to the aid of all victims of oppression, plunder, and poverty, and to overcome oppressors." To explain the longevity of the Mahdi, who was born in 869 and who has been in occultation since 941, Sadr formulates a novel premise: "The sphere of logical possibility is greater than that of scientific possibility, which in its turn is greater than that of practical possibility."[3]

From this the ayatollah deduces that "the prolongation of human longevity by several centuries is logically and scientifically possible, and even though it does not yet appear to be a practical possibility, science is moving in the direction of its realization over the long term."[4] Thus it is that

> the only two men [to have been] assigned the task of emptying humanity of its corruptness and of reconstructing [the world] were endowed with longevity on a scale incommensurate with [that of] nature. The first was Noah, who [carried out this task] in the past: the Qur'an says that he lived for nine hundred and fifty years among his people and that, thanks to the Flood, he was able to reconstruct the world. The second is the Mahdi, who has until now lived more than a thousand years among his people and who will [carry out the task] of reconstructing the world in the future.[5]

Having considered the question of the Mahdi's longevity, Ayatollah Sadr turns to the matter of the disappearance of the twelfth imam. He stresses the importance of the transition between the Lesser Occultation, entered into when the imam was a child and lasting into old age, and the Great Occultation, which began when he had already been alive for more than seventy years. Though he is still present in the world, the Mahdi has become both invisible and inaccessible. Sadr does not venture an opinion as to the date of his reappearance, but he notes that the present moment is propitious for two reasons: first, because of the "feeling of exhaustion [nafād] [that] has come into being and [now] is taking root in mankind"; and second, because of the "objective conditions of modern material life, which may be more favorable to the realization of the message on a planetary scale [now] than during the Lesser Occultation, owing to the decrease in distances [between people] and the increase in the possibility of interaction among [them]."[6]

Having thus clarified the circumstances surrounding the Mahdi's grand return, Sadr nonetheless recognizes that "the military forces and instruments that the Mahdi will have to face [are bound to] grow in proportion as he postpones the day of his reappearance." Even so, he asks, "what is the use of developing strength in its material form if it is associated with an inner psychological defeat and the rupture of the spiritual core of the man who possesses it?"[7] Pointless though infidel resistance may be, there is no doubt that an apocalyptic confrontation between the twelfth imam and the forces of godlessness will take place.

In 1977, when Sadr wrote these lines, the Ba'th party's prohibition of the observance of Ashura, the holy day of atonement and fasting celebrated on 10 Muharram, provoked serious unrest in the holy cities of Iraq. The harsh repression with which it was answered caused many religious officials to flee Iraq, the majority of them taking refuge in Lebanon. Among these senior figures was Ayatollah Hasan Shirazi, who published in Beirut an *Encyclopedia of the Sayings of the Imam Mahdi* that displayed perfect fidelity to the teachings of Ayatollah Sadr.[8] The triumph of the Islamic Revolution in Iran two years later revived Shi'i agitation in Iraq. Muhammad Baqir al-Sadr appointed a close associate, Mahmud Hashemi, as his personal representative to Khomeyni,[9] and issued a public statement on the implications of the present situation. Although Ayatollah Sadr did not believe that a revolutionary movement in Iraq was likely to succeed, his fatwa prohibiting membership in the Ba'th Party pushed the test of wills to the limit. Called upon to issue a retraction, Sadr held firm and paid for it with his life in April 1980, when he was executed by the personal order of Saddam Hussein.

The government's determination to silence internal dissent played a part in the decision, in September of the same year, to invade Iran. The ensuing conflict took a very heavy toll on the Shi'i clergy in Iraq, with Saddam Hussein moving quickly to subject Najaf and Karbala to his ruthless control. The assassination of Ayatollah Hasan Shirazi in Lebanon by a Ba'thist commando did not prevent other high-ranking figures from going into exile abroad, either in the Shi'i sanctuary of Sayyida Zeinab, on the outskirts of Damascus, or in the southern suburbs of Beirut, where they joined forces with Ayatollah Muhammad Husayn Fadlallah, a native of Najaf who had been living in Lebanon since 1966, as well as two Lebanese former students of Ayatollah Sadr, Abbas Mussawi and Hasan Nasrallah.[10] It was here that a revolutionary faction emerged in protest against the readiness shown by Amal,[11] the dominant Shi'i resistance movement in Lebanon, to compromise with Israel. The shock of the Israeli invasion in June 1982 brought about a final rupture with Amal, and the formation by a small band of radical fighters, with the support of Iran and Syria, of the Party of God—Hizbullah.

Memories of Muhammad Baqir al-Sadr, the "Martyr Ayatollah," remained vivid in the minds of Hizbullah's founders, and his conception of the Mahdi was to make its influence felt in Shi'i circles in both Iraq and Lebanon. Ayatollah Fadlallah adopted Sadr's line of reasoning with regard to the supernatural longevity of the Mahdi: "Miracles are certainly not impossible, nor can they be denied by scientific arguments. It can never be proved that the causes and agents that manifest themselves in our world are uniquely the ones that we can see and know. Thus it is possible that in one or several members of humanity causes and agents are at work that permit them a very long life of several thousand years."[12]

LEBANESE MILLENARIAN THOUGHT

The Shi'a of Lebanon, who constituted a large majority in the southern part of the country, had long benefited from the dispensations of a powerful religious order created by the Safavid throne in the sixteenth century to help establish Shi'ism as the state religion of Iran. In particular, the central region of southern Lebanon, known as Jabal Amel, was permitted to train clerics in schools comparable to the seminaries of Iraq. But by the late twentieth century the luster of this tradition had been badly tarnished, with Qum asserting its primacy in the aftermath of the Islamic Revolution over the holy city of Najaf, now under the murderous tyranny of the Ba'th Party.

It was against this background that lay figures interested in apocalyptic speculation were able to circumvent the dogmatic authority of the clergy in southern Lebanon. In 1979, a man living in a suburb of Tyre named Kamel Sulayman finished a massive volume entitled *The Day of Deliverance,* which, predictably enough, began by reviewing the relevant sayings found in the two canonical anthologies of Bukhari and Muslim, recognized in common with Sunni tradition, and then those of the successive Shi'i imams. But Sulayman referred also to three of the four Christian Gospels (Luke, John, and Matthew), Paul's letters to the Thessalonians, and the Apocalypse of John, in addition to the Book of Zechariah.[13] His conclusions sometimes went beyond those of earlier authors. Thus, for example, with regard to the vexed question of the Mahdi's longevity, Sulayman draws up a list of persons who have lived on earth for more than a thousand years. Apart from Noah, previously mentioned by Ayatollah Sadr, Sulayman names ten others, among them the Two-Horned One, whom he generously credits with an age of three thousand years.[14]

Sulayman furthermore holds that the cycle of apocalyptic battles was inaugurated with the founding of the state of Israel. It must be kept in mind that southern Lebanon had repeatedly been subject to raids by the Israeli army, which during its first invasion in March 1978 established a "security belt" on Lebanese territory, leading Amal's founder, Imam Mussa al-Sadr, to characterize Israel as the embodiment of "absolute evil" *(sharr mutlaq)*. This sort of demonization of the Jewish state encouraged Sulayman in his turn to condemn "the Israeli turmoil *[fitna]* that has penetrated every Arab nation in an accumulation of catastrophes," and to identify Israel not only with the Byzantines *(Rūm)*, who occupy Palestine in apocalyptic tradition, but also with the Banū al-Asfar, the infidel people with whom it is prophesied the Muslims will conclude a short-lived truce before the Great Battle.[15]

In a later edition of *The Day of Deliverance,* published in 1995, Sulayman extended his theory of apocalyptic geopolitics by identifying the Americans with the "Turkic races" of eschatological tradition. Washington's ambition, he says, is to control the Arabian Peninsula; its strategy depends initially on encircling Baghdad and establishing a headquarters on the banks of the Euphrates.[16] Echoes of the Gulf War of 1990–1991, in which Kuwait was liberated by an anti-Iraqi coalition led by the United States, are readily detected in these belated predictions. Yet Sulayman manages to give his prophecy a historical dimension by invoking the ambiguous figure of the Sufyani. Emerging from his Syrian sanctuary, the Sufyani will succeed in neutralizing Israeli-American aggression. But his true purpose will be to aggravate existing conflicts among Muslims, by hurling himself first upon Iraq, and then upon Arabia. A counteroffensive launched by the faithful will nonetheless overwhelm the Sufyani and his troops, who will meet with a crushing defeat near Lake Tiberias.[17] Seemingly exhausted by so many battles yet to come, Sulayman runs through the apocalyptic sequence of events associated with the Antichrist in a mere dozen pages or so,[18] and then abruptly concludes his treatise.

In the meantime a Beirut publisher, Dar al-Hadi (The House of the Guide), had brought out a late work by Said Ayyub,[19] as well as translations of several Iranian ayatollahs, and now looked for a way to enlarge its presence in the Shi'i apocalyptic market in Lebanon. The result was *The Day of Resurrection and the Relativity of Time: Between Science and the Qur'an,* by Sayyid Husayn Najib Muhammad—a daring attempt to reconcile modern physics and the return of the Mahdi that, by taking into account the acceleration of time, was able to warn against "the neglect *[ghafla]* that prevents the coming of the Day of Resurrection from being recognized."[20] Two years later Dar al-Hadi issued Bilal Na'im's *The March of Time Up Until the Master of the Age* (Plate 19), a still more exciting volume that postpones the return of the Mahdi until a momentous series of penultimate events has come to pass, including the "collapse of America, weakening and destruction of Israel, advent of the Jews' ally, the Sufyani, to seize control of Syria and possibly Iraq [as well], appearance of the Yemeni and the Khurasani to combat the Sufyani."[21] Supplementing Dar al-Hadi's apocalyptic list were a reissue of *The Battles and Signs of the End of Times* by Shaykh Hamdani, first published in Beirut in 1958, and a biography of the Hidden Imam.[22]

THE MAHDI ARMY IN IRAQ

Following Ayatollah Muhammad Baqir al-Sadr's assassination in 1980, his cousin and student Muhammad Sadiq al-Sadr inherited the family's political legacy. Sadiq al-Sadr was the author of a treatise on the Mahdi published three years earlier with a preface by the ayatollah,[23] and the popularity and influence of his teaching steadily grew in Najaf. When the Grand Ayatollah Khui died in 1992, he moved quickly to fill the vacuum of spiritual power that emerged within the Shi'i community of Iraq,[24] breaking with the traditional quietism of the clerical leadership and calling for a commitment to social reform. He went further in April 1998, ordering that the Friday prayers suspended by the grand ayatollahs of Iraq until the Mahdi's return be reinstated, with the result that these weekly gatherings soon acquired an overtly political character. Moreover, in addition to criticizing Najaf's ruling caste for its resistance to change, he contested Ayatollah Khamenei's claim to speak on behalf of all Shi'a, both inside and outside Iran.[25] This disruptive behavior having at last come to be considered an intolerable nuisance by Saddam Hussein's regime, Sadiq al-Sadr was assassinated, along with two of his sons, in February 1999.

A third son, Muqtada al-Sadr, was twenty-five years of age at the time of his father's murder. An undistinguished student at a seminary in Najaf, and married to one of the Martyr Ayatollah's daughters, Sadr was known for his shy and humble demeanor. Yet despite his willingness to adopt the sober dress of the mullahs, he belonged to the so-called embargo generation, which had endured both Ba'thist repression and the privations that followed from the international sanctions imposed on Iraq. Like other young men his age he felt a hatred for the regime; and, like them, his attitude of defiance was sharpened by the conviction that foreign powers had connived not only in abandoning Iraq to its fate, but also in willfully compounding its suffering. When the American army toppled Saddam Hussein in April 2003, looting became widespread in a country on the verge of chaos. Muqtada (as his followers familiarly called him) approved this pillage on the condition that the canonical tribute *(khums)* be paid to the imams who had given him their support.[26] His fatwa aroused the indignation of the religious hierarchy, but it also strengthened Muqtada's popularity among the poorest members of society, notably in the immense Shi'i suburb of Saddam City, in Baghdad, promptly renamed Sadr City.

At the urging of the major Shi'i party leaders who were now gradually returning from exile, the chief U.S. civil administrator, Paul Bremer, denied Muqtada a place in the new government. The young mullah responded by forming the Mahdi Army, a militia numbering a few thousand fighters who were deployed at once in Sadr City and in the south. In Shi'i eschatology, as we have seen, the army of the Mahdi is also known as the "army of wrath" for its implacable and brutal hostility toward oppressors. This explicit reference to the apocalyptic heritage struck fear into the hearts of Muqtada's Shi'i adversaries, who found themselves charged with collaboration with the infidel occupier. The symbolism of the moment was both powerful and deliberate: just as his father had ignored official prohibitions in reinstating Friday prayers, so too Muqtada had made jihad, likewise suspended until the return of the Hidden Imam, lawful in the name of the Mahdi;[27] and just as Sadiq al-Sadr had encouraged Shi'a to pray alongside Sunnis, so too Muqtada reached out to Sunni insurgents who rose up against the United States. In doing this he set himself apart from the supreme authority of Iraqi Shi'ism, Ayatollah Sistani, as well as from Shi'i political leaders and their Iranian protector.

In 2004, the Mahdi Army waged a violent struggle against American troops, first in April and May, and then in August and September. The dead and wounded were counted in the thousands, and the destruction, especially in the holy cities, was immense. Muqtada al-Sadr and his men held out in Najaf for three weeks inside the mausoleum of the first imam, 'Ali, while Ayatollah Sistani was conveniently hospitalized in London. Despite the eagerness of the clerical authorities to be rid of Muqtada, Sistani was eventually obliged to negotiate terms of surrender with him. Having managed to transform military defeat into a political victory, the rebel mullah obtained from the American overlord what he wanted, namely, recognition of his right to play a part in Iraqi politics. The Sadr faction won twenty-three seats in the elections to the constituent assembly in January 2005, and thirty-two seats in the legislative elections of December 2005. Notwithstanding Muqtada's claim to be uninterested in the details of ministerial appointments, his followers fought fiercely over portfolios, prerogatives, and budgets.

Political recognition helped the Mahdi Army to recruit new members, and its ranks soon swelled to tens of thousands.[28] Now by far the most powerful militia in Iraq, it lost no time in mercilessly pursuing Ba'thists and other "terrorists" whom Sadr had singled out for punishment. Nor did his followers shrink from imposing their vision of moral order through armed actions, arguing that the Mahdi Army was "the means on which the Hidden Imam depends in order to bring about justice."[29] Deprived of a stable, centralized source of funds, the militia was not always able to enforce discipline in its ranks, however, and its members often had to buy their weapons themselves. The fragmented structure of authority in the higher echelons had the effect of reinforcing the arbitrary power of local militia commanders, very much dreaded by the Sunni population in the still mixed neighborhoods of the capital and in the center of the country. The chief element of Muqtada's appeal was political, and derived from his intransigent nationalism, which took the form of an uncompromising demand for the withdrawal of American forces, a refusal to tolerate Iranian interference,[30] and an unwavering commitment to the unity of Iraq.

Even during the deadly siege of Najaf, in August 2004, Muqtada mobilized few of the symbolic resources of the Mahdi, preferring to exploit the more classic theme of the martyr, so closely associated with his family. Like his father before him, he covered his shoulders with a shroud of mourning in order to advertise his own willingness to make the supreme sacrifice. And although he was accustomed to use the term *dajjāl* in connection with President George W. Bush,[31] it was less the satanic figure than the imposter (the primary meaning of the Arabic word) whom he denounced, on account of Washington's unwillingness to announce a timetable for the withdrawal of its troops from Iraq.[32] Many Sadrist militants failed to notice this nuance, however, and identified the American forces with the battalions of the Antichrist, further magnifying their leader's stature.[33] Muqtada, for his part, did nothing to correct this misapprehension, which permitted him in turn to disregard the doctrinal reprobation of the grand ayatollahs—and also to destabilize rival militias.

The anniversary of the Mahdi's birth, 28 August 2007,[34] provided Sadr's fighters with the opportunity to confront and destroy their progovernmental rivals in what later came to be known as the Battle of Karbala. The authorities were forced to impose a cease-fire in the holy city and to empty it of tens of thousands of pilgrims, many of whom were killed during the clashes. Just before this explosion of violence, the Mahdi Army had seized control of the police headquarters in Basra, only very recently evacuated by the British Army despite its strategic importance to the security of the state. All of this well served Sadr's purpose in claiming for his soldiers the aid and sanction of the Mahdi, while accusing the Shiʻi leadership of being in league with the Anglo-American infidels.

Faced with a sudden and menacing upsurge of millenarian populism, the religious hierarchy of Najaf could no longer persevere in a policy of quietist passivity. Even Ayatollah Sistani warned that "awaiting the Imam of the Age does not mean that all Muslims and Shiʻa must fold their arms and do nothing to advance [the cause of] Islam, [that they can] just wait for his appearance. . . . Each Muslim has a duty to sacrifice himself in the name of Islam and always to be ready to welcome the expected Messiah, in such a way as to avoid all contradiction with His purposes and to be able to stand behind Him and take part in the combat against His enemies."[35] Nevertheless, as a theoretical matter, the point of equilibrium between faith in supreme designs and activism in the name of these same designs was difficult to determine precisely. As clerical leaders cast about for a workable policy, and as the holy cities of Iraq were attending to the wounds inflicted by the Mahdi Army, the Islamic Republic of Iran was experiencing its own outburst of messianic fervor.

THE LIMITS OF STATE-SPONSORED MILLENNIALISM

Ayatollah Khomeyni had succeeded for the most part in neutralizing the millenarian impulses of his allies. Earlier we noted his longstanding and complicated relationship with the Hojjatieh, the ultraconservative sect based in Qum whose militant intolerance had deep roots in messianic belief. From the earliest days of the Islamic Revolution, supporters of the regime and members of the Hojjatieh contended with one another rhetorically, the one side invoking the Supreme Guide, the other the Hidden Imam.[36] In 1983, the Hojjatieh was officially threatened with dissolution. Although the group complied by suspending all its activities, its adversaries objected to the survival of pockets of Hojjatieh influence in the state apparatus.[37]

It was not until the death of Ayatollah Khomeyni in 1989 and the uncertainty surrounding his succession that the Hojjatieh was able to engineer a return to favor with the support of Ayatollah Mesbah Yazdi. Born in 1934, and settled in Qum from 1960 onward, Yazdi had remained very much in the background during the Islamic Revolution. This half-heartedness, though it did not go unnoticed at the time, nonetheless enabled him to escape the factional struggles that tore apart Khomeyni loyalists. In the meantime his teaching at the Haqqani theological college *(madrasa)* in Qum had influenced a whole generation of officials serving the new regime. Yazdi threw his support behind Ayatollah Khamenei, despite the fact that Khamenei's candidacy aroused great misgivings among the clerical hierarchy of Qum. The gamble paid off. Having gained the favor of the new Guide of the Revolution, he was promptly made the head of the Khomeyni Foundation for Education and Research, dedicated by Ayatollah Khamenei in Qum in 1995, and with the election two years later of the reformist candidate, Muhammad Khatami, as president of the republic, Yazdi became the voice of the conservative reaction, issuing stern warnings about the temptations of "pluralism" and the dangers of "secularism."[38]

In 2003, Ayatollah Yazdi actively supported Mahmud Ahmadinejad during his successful mayoral campaign in Teheran. The new mayor's rivals attacked him for his millenarian beliefs and accused him of having distributed a map indicating the itinerary of the Mahdi's return.[39] At this juncture the Hojjatieh stepped forward and mounted a propaganda offensive urging the faithful to prepare for the return of the Hidden Imam, explaining Ahmadinejad's selection for this purpose by the Mahdi himself, and emphasizing the religious duty to vote (and to make others vote) for him during the presidential campaign of June 2005.[40] Ahmadinejad was the first chief of state of the Islamic Republic who did not come from the clerical hierarchy. In the aftermath of his election, popular expectations of his ability to translate messianic belief into official policy ran high, but so long as real supreme power remained in the hands of the Guide of the Revolution, Ayatollah Khamenei, Ahmadinejad had no choice but to make the fullest possible use of the powers of the presidency of the republic in order to appeal over his head to the people.

The president's public declarations concerning the imminence of the return of the Hidden Imam and his determination to instruct the country beforehand became more frequent.[41] He claimed to have been suffused with a halo of light during his speech before the General Assembly of the United Nations, in September 2005—proof, he said, of the Mahdi's support for his international message.[42] More important still, in symbolic terms, was the formal allegiance to the Mahdi sworn by Ahmadinejad and his ministers.[43] This document, signed on the occasion of the first meeting of the new government, was carried by the Minister of Culture and Islamic Guidance, Mohammad Hossein Safar-Harandi, to the shrine at Jamkaran, near Qum, and thrown into the holy well in which millions of pilgrims deposit their requests to the Hidden Imam.[44]

Ahmadinejad's government paid a quite particular attention to Jamkaran, and generously financed its restoration, despite the fact that the mosque's mystical aspect and its special link with the twelfth imam were persistently denied by the majority of senior Shi'i clerics. Ahmadinejad's messianism resonated with those—and they were many—who held to the belief, strongly tinged with superstition, that the Mahdi would emerge from his occultation through the well of Jamkaran.[45] In this same populist spirit, the head of state made generous gifts to the poor during the celebration of the anniversary of the Mahdi's birth, the fifteenth day of the Muslim month of Shaaban. But it was above all his avowed conviction that believers must not passively await the Mahdi's return, but instead work actively to help bring it about, that brought Ahmadinejad into conflict with the highest authorities of Shi'ism, whether they subscribed to the Khomeynist principle of *vilayat-e faqih* or whether they rejected any human attempt to fathom divine intentions. Even if it was not expressly anticlerical, this frank expression of millenarian commitment constituted an unmistakable gesture of defiance toward the caste of the ayatollahs, recalling the position adopted by the Hojjatieh in the scholastic quarrels of Qum and responding to popular disenchantment with the religious establishment.

The chief of state's adversaries saw his messianic impulses as evidence of irresponsibility, if not actually of megalomania. In the December 2006 elections to the Assembly of Experts, which has the authority to appoint the Guide of the Revolution (and therefore, in this case, Ayatollah Khamenei's successor), Ahmadinejad's supporters met with a serious setback. Ayatollah Yazdi finished only in sixth place, far behind Ayatollah Rafsanjani, a former president of Iran, who was elected with an overwhelming majority in Teheran.[46] Although the voters were evidently dissatisfied with Ahmadinejad's calamitous handling of affairs of state, he persisted in sounding apocalyptic themes,[47] for this allowed him to go on castigating the Mahdi's enemies for their arrogance without attacking the United States and Israel as directly as he had done in the past. Thus, for example, in 2007, Ahmadinejad chose the anniversary of the Mahdi's birth in order to rejoice in the fact that the United States had become "prisoners of their own quagmire" in Iraq.[48]

Shortly after the December 2006 elections, the government radio posted on its website a summary of a series of twelve programs on the Mahdi that repays closer examination.[49] Entitled "The World Is Moving toward Illumination" and produced under the nominal auspices of the Supreme Guide, Ayatollah Khamenei, these programs deliver an angry indictment of the Christian Zionists and their control over Hollywood (especially loathed by the series' official sponsors for films such as *The Matrix*). The day will soon come when, along with Communism, the traces of "liberal democratic civilization . . . will have to be sought in the history museums." And, of course, the architect of universal justice will be the Mahdi, who may be expected to appear on one of the two following dates: Ashura, in a year when it falls on a Friday, the anniversary of the Imam Husayn's martyrdom in 680, or during the spring equinox, when it is celebrated under the name of Nowruz as the Iranian New Year.[50]

The creators of this series have little to say about the circumstances of the Christian Zionists' defeat, and mention only in passing that the Antichrist will be hung in Kufa. Their apocalyptic account, which bears for the most part upon the conflict between the Mahdi, based in Mecca, and the Sufyani, master of Syria and the brutal conqueror of Iraq, amounts to this: the Sufyani's assaults upon Arabia will be repulsed; Najaf and the rest of Iraq will be liberated by an Iranian hero; and the Mahdi will crush the Sufyani in Jerusalem and establish his earthly capital in Kufa. One of the characteristics of the global government of the Mahdi, the series claims, will be "the incredible development of science and technology," and—a sign of the harmony now restored by the Master of the Age—"women will be able to travel without fear from Iraq to Syria with their jewels."[51]

This scenario bears the distinctive marks not only of Shiʻi mysticism, but also of Iranian ethnocentrism. The idea that the Mahdi should return on the first day of the Persian new year is profoundly foreign to Arab culture. No less disturbing is the notion that Syria should yield its privileged place in classical tradition to Iraq, or that the Sufyani should supplant the Antichrist as the chief villain of the piece, being vanquished in Palestine by the Mahdi (a more important event in the Shiʻi schema than the killing of the Antichrist, also in Palestine, by Jesus). Finally, the deliverance of Iraq by an Iranian leader represents a radical reversal of the apocalyptic sequence, with the Antichrist now emerging in Isfahan. Taken together, these subversive elements show the extent to which vague messianic longings had become part of the very identity of the Islamic Republic. Millenarian propaganda was nevertheless to find a new and still more promising outlet in Lebanon, where Ayatollah Khamenei's disciples were more numerous than in Iran itself.[52]

AHMADINEJAD AND THE FORTHCOMING WORLD REVOLUTION

This arresting phrase forms the title of an Arabic work published in 2006, in Beirut, and distributed outside Lebanon, not coincidentally, by the Iranian Cultural Center of Damascus. A radiant President Ahmadinejad is shown on the cover next to two distraught American soldiers, their faces daubed with camouflage paint (Plate 20). The subtitle leaves no doubt about the book's message: "Ahmadinejad is the head of the Mahdi's forces, which will liberate Jerusalem. . . . The nuclear program is associated with the appearance of the Imam Mahdi." Written by a Lebanese publisher named Shadi Faqih, the book represents an attempt to go beyond Persian narcissism, which the author regards as the main obstacle to exporting a militant messianism.

In order to appreciate what this world revolution involves, it is helpful first to consider the seventeen signs *(ʻalāma)* associated with the appearance *(zuhūr)* of the Imam Mahdi. The first fourteen are these:

1. "The reunion of the Jews in Palestine";
2. "The appearance of a man in Qum," which is to say the Ayatollah Khomeyni;

3. "[The assembly of] the military and media forces of the Imam before [his] appearance," which is to say the Guardians of the Revolution in Iran, the Mahdi Army in Iraq, and Hizbullah in Lebanon;

4. "The founding of the Islamic Republic in Iran as the first preparation for the state of the Imam";

5. "The combat of the black turbans against the enemies of Islam before his appearance," the black turban being the Shi'i insignia of the descendants of the Prophet, worn in this case by Ayatollahs Khomeyni and Khamenei in Iran, Baqir al-Sadr in Iraq, and Hasan Nasrallah in Lebanon;

6. "The fighting by one party at the gates of Jerusalem," in this instance Hizbullah, the party of God;

7. "The entry of Western forces into Iraq";

8. "The martyrdom of the Pure Soul [al-nafs al-zakiyya] in Najaf with eighty faithful"[53]—a reference to the death in August 2003 of Ayatollah Baqir al-Hakim, faithful ally of Iran and head of the Supreme Council of the Islamic Revolution in Iraq (SCIRI), killed in Najaf in a suicide attack ordered by the Jordanian jihadist Abu Musab al-Zarqawi; here Ayatollah al-Hakim is identified with the Pure Soul, the martyred envoy of the Mahdi according to certain Shi'i traditions having deeply revolutionary implications;

9. "The transfer of [Islamic] science from Najaf to Qum," which is to say the relocation, from the holy city in Iraq to the intellectual seat of the Islamic Republic of Iran, of the principal seminaries for training the Shi'i religious elite;

10. "The establishment in Iraq of an Islamic government faithful to Iranian precursors," which is to say the government in Baghdad of Prime Minister Nuri al-Maliki, a Shi'i Islamist who had long lived in exile in Iran;

11. The growing fear of natural catastrophes;

12. The intersection with the Earth's orbit of a comet, which will alter existing weather patterns;

13. The appearance of the Khurasani, identified with Ayatollah Khamenei, the man who will restore the Mahdi's banner to him;

14. The appearance of Shuaib ibn Saleh, identified with President Ahmadinejad, the leader of the Mahdi's armies.[54]

These fourteen signs, Faqih says, are incontestable and consummated events that underscore the imminence of the Mahdi's return. For this return actually to occur, however, three further signs remain to be fulfilled. First, the United States and Israel will provoke a coup d'état in Damascus in order to install there the perfidious government of the Sufyani, "who will consolidate his influence in Syria, Iraq, Jordan, and Lebanon, and whose forces will penetrate Hijaz in order to crush, in Medina, the revolt [of the Mahdi's followers]."[55] Next will come the Battle of the Calls between the Imam's followers and Satan's henchmen, who will be humiliated in the eyes of the world. Finally, the assassination of the Mahdi's representative in Medina will incur the wrath of the Imam and rapidly bring about his appearance.[56]

Even accepting that the ascendancy of the Islamic Republic, assisted by its allies in Iraq and Lebanon, may have eschatological significance, most Muslims would find the identification of Ayatollah Khamenei and President Ahmadinejad with the two key figures of the Mahdi's entourage simply extraordinary. In Faqih's telling, the imminence of the world's end is palpable and the influence of the Hojjatieh manifest, Ayatollah Yazdi being emphatically presented as the "intellectual guide" of the Guardians of the Revolution. Ominously, messianic import is attached to the "Iranian nuclear bomb," for it is "directly related to the question of the [Mahdi's] appearance." A peaceful nuclear program is an inalienable right of Teheran, and "it is possible that a military program has been underway for a long while, even if the seal of secrecy must be observed until the appearance of the Imam Mahdi."[57]

HIZBULLAH AND THE END OF TIMES

Ahmadinejad and the Forthcoming World Revolution was published by Shadi Faqih's own firm in Beirut, Dar al-Ilm (The House of Knowledge), whose books are sold mainly in the Biqa' and in southern Lebanon, the two regions of the country having a majority Shi'i population. Faqih went on to edit and publish a series of eight short and very affordably priced books devoted to the Mahdi. These pamphlets, whose illustration is as colorful as it is provocative, were likewise offered for sale outside Lebanon by the Iranian Cultural Center of Damascus, which distributed the rest of Dar al-Ilm's list without, however, officially endorsing its publications. Faqih took great care to note that neither his own book nor the series of pamphlets on the Mahdi in any way involved Hizbullah, and that he assumed sole responsibility for their contents.

This disclaimer was all the more necessary as the pamphlets conferred apocalyptic stature on Shaykh Nasrallah, the secretary general of Hizbullah, by identifying him with the Yemeni.[58] We saw earlier that the emergence of this figure, the Mahdi's scout, is reckoned to be one of the five major signs of Shi'i eschatology.[59] Thus it was that the war of the summer of 2006, described by Hizbullah as a "divine victory" over Israel, was sanctified by the grace of the Hidden Imam: "The fire did not burn the mujahedin, it burned their enemies"; "phantoms and monsters" joined forces against the invaders; sixty resistance fighters were able to stand up to five thousand adversaries, and so on.[60] Similarly, the missiles that enabled Hizbullah to strike Haifa and the north of Israel were "a gift of God" and a "miracle." Even Zulfiqar, the legendary sword of the Imam 'Ali, was placed at Hizbullah's disposal in order to decimate the aggressors. Still further proof of the supernatural character of such interventions was provided when two Hizbullah combatants, equipped with the wings of angels, swooped down from the sky upon their enemies.[61] There could not be the least doubt, then, that this war was "the introduction to the [Mahdi's] appearance."[62]

The sense of messianic urgency was heightened by the publication later that year, in 2006, of a booklet whose title summarily informs readers that they are now living in the age of the Mahdi's appearance.[63] Ayatollah Yazdi's authority is invoked in support of this claim, and also to make it clear that the Hidden Imam has appointed Ahmadinejad to the presidency of the Islamic Republic. The signs of the Hour, already enumerated in *Ahmadinejad and the Forthcoming World Revolution*, are rehearsed again—only now this irresistible succession of events has been expanded by two further episodes: the killing in June 2006 of Abu Musab al-Zarqawi, the al-Qaida in Iraq leader, who is identified with the satanic executioner of faithful pilgrims because of his repeated attacks against Shi'i places of worship; and the accession to the Saudi throne in August 2005 of King Abdallah, styled the last sovereign of Hijaz, whence the Mahdi will soon emerge.[64]

Still more crucial, however, was Shaykh Nazrallah's transformation into the apocalyptic figure of the Yemeni, completing a very political trinity in which Ayatollah Khamenei served as the standard bearer of the Mahdi and Ahmadinejad as the commander of his armies. America, already massively committed in Afghanistan and Iraq, and now faced with a divinely sanctioned coalition of forces, finds itself obliged to "divide the region up into a federation of confessional provinces, in order to maintain the chaos in those places, and then to fuel an ethnic and sectarian war." Exploiting "differences among the Arabs and their weakness" is an integral part of this diabolical plan, as well as intensifying dissension among Sunnis and Shi'a, already exacerbated by the "fatwas of Wahhabi shaykhs excommunicating [takfīr] the Shi'i Hizbullah." As for the establishment of American bases in the Gulf, it is aimed primarily at preventing the appearance of the Mahdi in Mecca and at neutralizing his followers.[65]

But all this maneuvering will come to naught, for the infidels will be swept away by the Hidden Imam—though he will not reappear until a "major ballistic capability" has been achieved. The cycle of apocalyptic battles has already been inaugurated in southern Lebanon, where, just as the popular hadith had predicted, the trees and stones alerted Hizbullah to the Jews who were hiding behind them.[66] The Great Battle (al-malhama al-kubrā)—in which the seventy thousand mujahedin of the Yemeni, Nazrallah, will be joined by the armies of Iraq and Iran and carry out, under the direction of the Mahdi, the "conquest [fath] of Palestine" and Jerusalem—draws near.[67]

Perhaps Shadi Faqih's opinions are indeed his alone, as he claims. But it is quite a different matter in the case of Shaykh Naim Qassim, a former chemistry professor who since 1991 has been the deputy secretary general of Hizbullah and its official historian.[68] In early 2007, only a few months after the war against Israel, Qassim considered it an opportune moment to publish a book called Mahdi the Savior.[69] In the clear, pedagogic style for which he is known, Qassim once again reviews the signs justifying the belief that "we are living in the era of the [Mahdi's] appearance." Since "the spread of oppression and corruption announce the deliverance [faraj]," he reasons, Western decadence and Israeli-American aggression must increase as the Mahdi's return approaches. Henceforth, then, it is incumbent upon Hizbullah to conceive of its struggle as part of "the movement of the appearance [harakat al-zuhūr]," and to aspire to "hasten the deliverance and the appearance."[70]

Qassim associates the theme of the "black banners" of Khurasan with "the march of Iran launched by the holy Imam Khomeyni and directed by Imam Khamenei," celebrates "the strengthening of the presence of the modern banner in the East, so that the law, this standard of rectitude, raised in Iran—that is, the state of Islam—may be defended," and praises "the security [inspired by] the existence of the Guide Khamenei (may Allah protect him) and the desire that grows with the approach of the [Mahdi's] appearance." In so doing Qassim casts Hizbullah's organic allegiance to the Islamic Republic of Iran in apocalyptic terms, while honoring his fighters as the undaunted defenders of an Islam threatened on all sides at "the end of times." The conflict with Israel is described with somewhat greater uncertainty, however: "Only Allah knows [Allah a'lam] whether the predictions will be fulfilled in our current confrontation with the Zionists, but we hope that it will be thus." Qassim manages to dispel the sense of ambivalence by citing a well-known tradition: "Work for the here-and-now as if you had to live forever, and strive for the hereafter as if you were to die tomorrow."[71]

In order to emphasize his self-conferred dignity as a cleric, Shaykh Qassim makes it a point never to quote President Ahmadinejad, and he is very careful to avoid any mention of the nuclear controversy. But apart from the prudent formula "Only Allah knows," his apocalyptic forecast scarcely differs from that of Shadi Faqih. In modern Khurasan the black banners of the Islamic Republic defy the world's arrogance; strife (fitna) rages in the land of Shām, where Hizbullah—the Party of God—holds the front line against the enemies of the faith; and it is on the holy land of Palestine that the Antichrist will be put to death, either by the Mahdi or by Jesus.[72] The promotion of this brand of partisan millenarianism by a high official of Hizbullah suggests the extent to which apocalyptic ideas have penetrated the minds of radical Shi'a in Lebanon.

THE MESSIANIC BLOODBATH OF NAJAF

In 2007, the anniversary of the martyrdom of the Imam Husayn, known as Ashura, fell on 28 January. We saw earlier that Shi'i tradition generally envisages the return of the Mahdi to take place during Ashura in an even year of the Muslim calendar.[73] The celebration of Ashura that 1,428th year after the Hegira was marked in Najaf by a terrifying bloodbath in which several hundred or more armed members of a millenarian sect called Soldiers of Heaven (jund al-samā') went to their deaths. The precise details of this tragedy remain obscure; until now only the official Iraqi version, strenuously supported by Washington (and, as it happens, Teheran), has been accepted. Nevertheless a few basic facts seem no longer to be in doubt.

First, it has been shown that the Iraqi Mahdist movement responsible for the assault in Najaf is profoundly nationalist and anti-Iranian.[74] The movement had first come to the attention of authorities as a result of its agitation in Iraqi refugee camps in Iran, and then later because of its attack on the Iranian consulate in Basra. It is clear, too, that the Soldiers of Heaven are hostile to Shi'i religious authorities, and in particular to

Ayatollah Sistani, a native of Iran who has resided in Najaf since 1952. Yet the sect did not play a major role in the Battle of Najaf in August 2004, when the Mahdi Army succeeded in weakening the authority of the interim government endorsed by Sistani.

The Soldiers of Heaven carried on a venerable millenarian tradition in Najaf. It is here, not far from Kufa, the Mahdi's future capital in Shi'i eschatology, that the Imam 'Ali is buried. Southern Iraq has historically been a fertile ground for Shi'i dissidence, for two reasons: first, the conversion to Shi'ism of whole tribes goes back no further than the nineteenth century,[75] with the result that official dogma has relatively shallow roots in the region; second, this area has more recently seen the development of the Shaykhiya, a Shi'i school that denies the moral magisterium of the ayatollahs, claiming instead to have a direct relationship with the Hidden Imam.[76] In 1998, an engineer from Basra named Ahmad al-Hasan announced that he had been designated by the Hidden Imam himself as his "representative" (wassī),[77] denounced the "errancy" of the religious seminaries of Najaf, and organized a militia known as the Supporters of the Imam Mahdi (Ansār al-imām al-mahdī).

Five years later, following the American invasion of Iraq, Hasan condemned the "occupation by the infidels, Crusaders, Jews, and Buddhists," which he saw as "one of the signs of the emergence of the Imam Mahdi." He then proclaimed "revolution against the oppressors" and "defensive jihad" against the "American Satan," promising all those who resisted him that they would perish "by the sword, or die in the shadow of the sword." And although he was a native Iraqi at the head of a movement of Iraqis, Hasan chose for himself the epithet "the Yemeni," evidently in reference to the Mahdi's precursor on Earth in the Shi'i apocalypse.[78] Claiming to be supported in this mission by the archangels Gabriel, Michael, and Asrafil (the last of whom will sound the trumpet of the Last Judgment), he credited himself with performing "miracles," notably the mystical discovery of the authentic tomb of Fatima, daughter of the Prophet Muhammad and wife of the Imam 'Ali. And it was also in the name of the Mahdi that Hasan called upon Ayatollah Khamenei and all other Muslim leaders to yield their power to him. For the sect's symbol he had selected a five-pointed star enclosing the two-headed sword of the Imam 'Ali, Zulfikar; later this became a six-pointed star, emblazoned in its center with the name of Ahmad al-Hasan.

These claims created confusion in the minds of some believers in Najaf, who referred the matter to the judgment of Ayatollah Kadhem Husayni Haeri, an Iraqi by birth who saw himself as continuing the work of Ayatollah Muhammad Baqir al-Sadr in Qum. Ayatollah Haeri dismissed the allegations of the Supporters of the Imam Mahdi, calling them a blameworthy innovation *(bid'a)*.[79] Indifferent to such anathemas, Hasan continued to recruit new members for his sect, staging parades on Shi'i holidays and excoriating all those ayatollahs who denied that the end of the Great Occultation was at hand. One of the Yemeni's lieutenants put the number of his followers at five thousand.[80] The most radical of the Supporters of the Imam Mahdi were settled, together with their families, in a camp at Zarga, north of Najaf. This was the group that soon was to become infamous under the name of the Soldiers of Heaven.

On 28 January 2007, the Iraqi government announced that it had moved quickly to put down a messianic insurrection in Najaf inspired by the Yemeni, Ahmad al-Hasan, and carried out by a force of seven hundred Soldiers of Heaven from the Zarga camp.[81] The insurgents' plan had been to invade the holy city on this day, Ashura of the Islamic year 1428, putting Sistani and the other three grand ayatollahs to death and proclaiming a new era in the name of the Mahdi. Instead the authorities acted first, seizing the headquarters of the Supporters of the Imam Mahdi in Najaf shortly before the attack began. Contrary to the government's account, then, the main part of the fighting took place not in Najaf itself, but in Zarga, where the Mahdists were quickly encircled and then massacred.

Another inaccuracy of the official version of events has to do with the alleged need to resist the challenge to internal stability posed by al-Qaida and foreign mujahedin.[82] This, after all, was the justification given by the U.S. military for committing a sizable contingent alongside Iraqi security forces. Yet al-Qaida was absent from the region of Najaf, where its hostility to Shi'ism prevented it from attracting local support, all the more since foreign combatants were scarcely welcome in an area where nationalist feeling bordered on xenophobia. Far more important in fueling the violence was the assassination at a checkpoint of the chief of an anti-Sistani tribe, the Hatami, whose members took up arms to avenge his killing.[83] A neighboring and allied tribe, mostly from Zarga, the Khazaali, was drawn into the confrontation as well.[84]

Fighting continued with renewed intensity the next day, 29 January. The official tally for these two days of fierce combat was "263 terrorists killed,"[85] as against only ten members of the Iraqi security forces, perhaps a few more. Two American soldiers were said to have died in a helicopter crash. In the event U.S. firepower was employed unsparingly, at a level not seen since the second siege of Falluja in November 2004.[86] The American press reported much higher casualty figures, according to which four hundred or more Mahdists were killed; one Arab daily claimed that five hundred Mahdists had died.[87] Whatever the actual number of fatalities may have been, it is certain that no one in the Zarga camp survived, the women and children having all perished in the assault alongside the insurgents.[88] The governor of Najaf released a video recording of the weapons and heavy armament seized in the camp,[89] citing them as justification for the devastating and indiscriminate character of the assault. Ahmad al-Hasan, for his part, denied all responsibility for the uprising and implicitly disavowed the Soldiers of Heaven.[90]

In retrospect, the fact of a messianic rebellion by a more or less heavily armed group of trained fighters seems undeniable. The apocalyptic rhetoric of the Yemeni, his repeated incitations to violence, and the enlistment of his most devoted followers in constituting a paramilitary force all support the view of a failed millenarian insurrection. Apart from two local tribes that were caught up in the spiraling violence, the Soldiers of Heaven found themselves isolated in the face of a vigorous Iraqi-American offensive, powerless to prevent their stronghold from being destroyed. The confusion that reigned at the time in and around Najaf contributed to a sense of incomprehension elsewhere in the country, or perhaps merely a lack of interest—though at least one-and-a-half million pilgrims were gathered in Karbala, only thirty-five miles to the north, to take part in the rites of Ashura and to honor the Imam Husayn, and some fifty people were killed in three separate attacks meant to disrupt Ashura ceremonies in Baghdad and in Kurdistan. It seems plain that the increasing frequency of violence in Iraq helped to make the horror of the bloodshed in Najaf less keenly felt than it otherwise would have been.

Even allowing for the residual uncertainty that still surrounds this event, comparison with the messianic uprising of 1979 in Mecca is instructive. The preparation of the Sunni insurgents was more thorough, and their military discipline superior, allowing them to withstand a prolonged siege, whereas the Zarga camp was overrun in fewer than two days. In both instances the resort to Western reinforcements, French in the case of Mecca, American in the case of Najaf, was decisive. In the case of Najaf, however, the government was encouraged in its hardline attitude by a neighboring regime that was resolved to destroy a sect known to be hostile to it. In Iraq, the fatal enemy of a rebel Shi'i messianic movement turned out to be not the local authorities, but instead a foreign Shi'i government having messianic pretensions of its own.

THE YEMENI LIVES ON TO FIGHT ANOTHER DAY

Ahmad al-Hasan, far from being eliminated as a political force by the massacre of the Soldiers of Heaven, continued to energetically pursue his campaign of apocalyptic mobilization and recruitment. His first move after Najaf was to produce an attractively designed newspaper, *Al-sirāt al-mustaqīm* (The Path of Rectitude), that printed testimonials from various Shi'i figures declaring their allegiance to the Yemeni. These statements were mimeographed and distributed throughout the southern part of the country, where each new reader was called upon to expand the paper's circulation by making ten copies. A millenarian "library" including titles such as *Jihad Is the Gateway to Heaven* was made available to his followers as well, and an Internet site, which opens onto an image of the six-pointed star of the Supporters of the Imam Mahdi, was created to spread the good word in Arabic, Persian, French, English, German—and Chinese.

Hasan's growing influence in southern Iraq was accompanied by a considerable radicalization of the sect's rhetoric. America, said to be "at war with Allah," is clearly identified with the Antichrist; but it is also the Beast *(al-wahsh)* spoken of by the prophet Daniel, which "devours" and "tramples" other nations. It is America, moreover, that trained and protected the "satanic" Wahhabis, that trained bin Laden and his men in Afghanistan, and that urges them to perpetrate the worst crimes against the Muslim faithful. Al-Qaida, for its part, is directly associated with the end of the world. As for the "so-called Iraqi government," it is hardly more worthy of respect than Shi'i religious leaders, defamed as ayatollahs of "aberration and treason, of occupation and tyranny." In the face of such "corruption," Hasan describes his movement as "the army of divine wrath" and "the army of justice."[91]

Accordingly, the Supporters of the Imam Mahdi resolved to make a show of force during the commemoration of the next year's Ashura. On 18 January 2008, there were very serious clashes with the Iraqi security forces. In Basra, millenarian rebels seized at least two vehicles belonging to the police, and in Nassiriya attacked four police stations before retreating to the Sahliyya neighborhood. Several high-ranking officers were killed during the fighting, which came to an end the next day after a night of sporadic gunfire. By the government's accounting, eighteen policemen died together with fifty-three militia members. Responsibility for the sudden explosion of violence no doubt lay with the followers of the Yemeni. Whereas a year before Ahmad al-Hasan had sought to distance himself from the apocalyptic bloodbath of Najaf, now he celebrated the sacrifice of his "martyrs" and swore mercilessly to avenge their deaths. Although Muqtada al-Sadr's Mahdi Army dominated the paramilitary landscape at this juncture, the Yemeni's commandos had made an appointment with destiny in the great struggle for control of southern Iraq. Between Baghdad and Basra, armed millenarianism lay in wait for its enemies.

. . .

The contrast between the gradual and convoluted growth of Sunni millenarianism, driven as much by commercial opportunism as by ideology, and the inherently political character of Shi'i messianism, centered on the figure of the Mahdi, is obvious. Within both of the families of Islam, however, apocalyptic writing—largely the province of lay authors in each case—posed a serious threat to the authority of the religious hierarchy. The American invasion of Iraq in 2003, crucial in catalyzing Sunni energies, was no less vital in stimulating Shi'i activism, and in particular the formation of the Mahdi Army in opposition to the American Antichrist. The emergence of a belligerent messianism in the Shi'i world was the result of a number of convergent developments:

- Although Muqtada al-Sadr surely did not believe himself to be the Mahdi, any more than Hasan Nazrallah genuinely imagined that he was the Yemeni, neither one of them was in the least inclined to restrain apocalyptic speculation that promised to strengthen their appeal at the expense of the gerontocracy directed by the ayatollahs.

- The mixture of populism and messianism, manifest in the maneuvering by which Sadr and Nazrallah managed to negotiate a place in mainstream political life for their militias, played an even greater role in the election of President Ahmadinejad, which amounted to a grand wager on mass piety against clerical elitism.

- The Shi'i hierarchy, despite having been divided since 1979 between supporters of *vilayat-e faqih* and upholders of political quietism, was nonetheless agreed on the necessity of suppressing all expressions of millenarian anxiety, until the Supreme Guide, Ayatollah Khamenei, tacitly approved the overtly messianic appeals made by his chief of state after 2005.

- Messianic dissidence was able to attract independent support only by exploiting a crisis in the Shi'i system of political and military control, as in southern Iraq, where the crushing of the revolt by the Soldiers of Heaven in Najaf did not prevent Ahmad al-Hasan from recruiting a new generation of fanatical henchmen.

- The holy cities of Iraq erupted in violence in 2007 on two dates associated with messianic eschatology: in January, on the day of the expected return of the Mahdi to Najaf, during Ashura; and in August, on the anniversary of his birth in Karbala—as if the apocalyptic calendar buckled under the weight of paramilitary millenarianism.

- Owing to the close connection between militant Shi'i communities in Iran, Iraq, and Lebanon, apocalyptic messages were able to circulate among them very rapidly, especially in moments of armed confrontation, such as the one with Israel during the summer of 2006.

Amid the welter of events and ideas described in this chapter and the two preceding ones, nothing is more striking than the almost total absence of agreement among Sunnis and Shi'is regarding the ultimate fate of mankind. Whereas the paternalism of Muslim orthodoxy fails to conceal a very widely shared ignorance of Shi'i doctrines of salvation, followers of the Hidden Imam, for their part, are increasingly encouraged to overlook the traditional apocalyptic combat between Jesus and the Antichrist in favor of the challenge brought against the Mahdi by the Sufyani, a satanic figure associated both with Syria and with Sunnism. Far from reconciling the two great families of Islam, contemplation of the end of the world serves only to deepen misunderstandings, when it does not also intensify hatreds.

CHAPTER 9

Diasporas of the Apocalypse

The final state of the world according to Islam, revealed in Arabic to an Arab prophet, was shaped by Arab (or Arabized) traditionists and subsequently dramatized by contemporary Arab pamphleteers. In recent years even Shi'i messianism, tinged by Persian narcissism during its transit through the Islamic Republic of Iran, has been purified and radicalized by Arab militants. But the Arab nation represents only a fifth of the world's Muslim population. We need, then, to examine the revival of apocalyptic outside the Arab geographical and linguistic area, both in the Muslim communities of Western countries and in the nations of Indo-Malaysian Islam.

THE LAST HOUR IN FRENCH TRANSLATION

Islamic writings in the French language are, at bottom, less apocalyptic than eschatological. The first title in this vein was published in 1996 on the island of Réunion in the Indian Ocean, home to one of France's oldest Muslim communities, most of its members having come there from the province of Gujarat in India.[1] *The Signs of the End of the World,* by a native author named Ahmad Lala Anas, is a classic presentation of the minor and great signs of the Hour whose only innovation consists in the introduction of an intermediate category of "middle signs" falling between the "distant" and "near" signs of the Resurrection.[2] Anas changed course a few years later with a book entitled *Is Man Descended from the Apes?* (2001).[3] His approach to the theory of evolution is fairly open-minded and draws upon the teachings of the medieval theologian al-Ghazali (1058–1111), who had raised hopes of a reconciliation between Sufi mysticism and Sunni orthodoxy.

The following year Anas's new publisher in Paris, Tawhid, brought out a book by Muhammad Benshili called *The Coming of the Mahdi according to Muslim Tradition.* The description on the back cover well summarizes Benshili's aims in this work: "Although pious Muslims are innumerably many, one cannot help but notice that the men of stature who are so sorely needed today are quite absent. Some now place their hopes in [another] man, the Mahdi, whose coming Muhammad predicted. Each person, whether he be Sunni, Shi'i, or Sufi, awaits [the Mahdi] in accordance with his own convictions. One thing is certain: the Hour is near, enthusiasm is great, and the man will appear."[4]

Benshili nevertheless concedes that "the chronological order of all the events relating to the advent of the Mahdi and his reign remains very vague," and recalls Ibn Khaldun's prejudice against hadiths concerning the Mahdi.[5] For the most part he expounds the arguments made by the four other grand masters of the medieval apocalypse, Ibn 'Arabi,[6] al-Qurtubi, Ibn Kathir, and al-Suyuti. While Benshili makes a point of showing respect for Shi'i sensibilities, he does not refrain from emphasizing the contradictions among the various Twelver traditions. The Sufyani, for example, is prophesied to be the first of the Mahdi's enemies who will raise an army against him. "Nevertheless," Benshili observes, "it is not possible to determine if he will send two armies against the Mahdi or only one, nor if he himself will be swallowed up with his troops or [will] remain [instead] in Damascus." The only thing of which one may be sure, Benshili says, is that the coming of the Mahdi will be preceded by the "degradation of the values of the Muslim community"—this at a time when "the greater part of the Middle East will be in the throes of insurrection."[7]

The same sentiment of the tragic imminence of the end of the world animates another Muslim author working in France, Muhammad Karimi Almaghribi, in *The Omens of the End of the World:* "The Hour approaches, its minor signs have manifested themselves and only a few more remain; next will come the major signs, which will succeed one another like pearls dropping from a broken necklace." Among the "false prophets" who have paved the way for the Antichrist the author mentions not only the Baha'is and the Ahmadiyya, but also Mahmud Muhammad Taha, a prominent intellectual and proponent of modernization who was executed in Khartoum by the order of the Sudanese dictator Jaafar Muhammad Nimeiri in 1985. Additionally, Karimi Almaghribi heralds the appearance of "special police forces at the end of times," who will support "the unjust governors" with "whips resembling a cow's tail." He has more to say than other commentators, too, about the Beast, one of the last signs of the Hour: "It is a four-legged animal [that] will come out from Tihama [the coastal region of western Yemen on the Red Sea], or from Mount Safa [one of the hills surrounding Mecca]; it will gallop like a horse; whoever pursues it shall not overtake it and whoever flees from it shall not escape it; it is armed with the rod of Moses and the seal of Solomon."[8]

Still less plausible is a book published in Beirut in 2007 by Buhafs Abdeljalil, a retired Algerian schoolteacher, called *The Apocalypse of Armageddon*. It is meant as a refutation of misguided astrological conjectures, but also as a demonstration of the "eschatological convergence [between] the Apocalypse of John and Qur'anic revelation." The crushing of the modern state of Israel is held to be inevitable as a result of "the battle of the Apocalypse that will take place at Armageddon, in Palestine, before the last times. The destiny of this arrogant political entity—prideful of its military power, and of the protection given it by certain allied nations of this world—inescapably looms over it, for it will not have been able to live in peace with its Arab neighbors."[9]

The number of original works written in French remains limited by comparison with the sizeable amount of translation from Arabic into French being done in Lebanon. In 1994, Abdeljalil's Beirut publisher, al-Buraq, brought out in France a book called *The Great Signs of the End of the World,* by the Egyptian shaykh Abdallah al-Hajjaj.[10] Another publisher in Beirut, Dar al-Kutub al-Ilmiyya (The House of Scientific Books), translated *The Awaited Mahdi* by Yusuf ben Yahia al-Sulami in 2004, and the following year *The Omens of the Hour* by Azzedin Husayn al-Shaykh, which had originally been published in 1993 in Saudi Arabia.[11] All of these works are classic examples of the conservative Islamic genre. Sulami, in particular, insists on recounting the horrifying details of the Sufyani's ravages: "He will seize two children named Hasan and Husayn and crucify them on the door of the mosque. . . . He will go out from [his lair], a spear in his hand, and seize a pregnant woman and give her to one of his men, ordering him to violate her in the street. The man will comply. Then [the Sufyani] will slit open the belly of this woman and the fetus will fall out." With the approach of the Last Hour, "massacres will occur, strife and great misfortunes, and [those who survive] will envy the bones that have been turned into dust."[12]

French houses were not idle in the meantime. Essalam translated and published in Paris the minor works of the late Egyptian cleric Muhammad Metwalli Shahrawi, among them *Al Geib: The Invisible World* and *The End of the World.*[13] A decade earlier, La Société Universelle had issued *Death and the Final Judgment* by Fdal Haja, a volume notable for its anti-Shi'i overtones and stern warnings: "Blindly imitating the Jews and the Christians, who do not believe in the prophecy of Muhammad (peace and blessings be upon him), in their way of life, their morals and their passions, and preferring them to the Muslims, is another sign of the Hour."[14] Annotated collections of hadiths,[15] together with the basic writings of Ibn 'Arabi, al-Qurtubi, Ibn Kathir, and al-Suyuti,[16] have recently been made available in French as well, in the form of small, slender books with a minimal scholarly apparatus.

The appearance in 2006 of a translation of a thesis in Islamic law defended by Yusuf al-Wabil in 1983 at the University of Mecca called *The Signs of the End of Times,* under the imprint of the Brussels house Al-Hadith, deserves special mention. In addition to the great signs of the Hour, all still to come, Wabil enumerates fifty-nine minor signs, of which the fifty-fourth—involving "combat against the Jews"—is everywhere censored in the Belgian edition, the phrase having been whited out or the relevant pages excised.[17] In this case, in other words, the publisher took the initiative of literally erasing all apocalyptic passages having an anti-Semitic implication.

By and large, works composed in French or translated into French belong to the corpus of traditional writings (even the fanatical Abdeljalil is seldom prone to the outbursts common to radical messianic authors), and respond more to a demand for guidance in eschatological matters than to a taste for apocalyptic fantasy. The self-censorship enforced by a Belgian publisher and its French distributors nevertheless provides refreshing evidence of a willingness to combat the sort of anti-Semitism that is regularly encouraged by the Egyptian houses that dominate the apocalyptic market.[18]

THE MYSTICAL APOCALYPSE OF THE CONVERTED

The primordial role of Jesus in the Muslim apocalypse has long oriented the spiritual itinerary of converts to Islam who brought with them the influence of their Christian upbringing. It is partly for this reason that the triumph of faith over impiety represented by Jesus's anticipated return to slay the Antichrist has been more or less literally interpreted. The Algerian shaykh Khalid Bentunes, guide of the Sufi Allawiya order, whose tolerant mysticism attracts many Western converts, lays great stress on this aspect of the last days: "In the Muslim consciousness, the return of Jesus is a hope, the end of an apocalyptic cycle at the heart of which are found the seeds of renewal. From that time on men will join together to work on behalf of humanity and to strike down evil. . . . In Muslim esotericism [Sufism], there are stations [spiritual degrees] for each prophet mentioned in the Bible and in the Qur'an. The station of Jesus is a special one, and among the most high. His teaching liberates a pure spirituality having no fixed boundaries in time and space."[19]

This glorification of Jesus is also an essential part of the vision of Islam's future urged by Shaykh Muhammad Hisham Kabbani, the representative of the Sufi Naqshbandiyya order in the United States, president of the Supreme Islamic Council of America, and editor of *Muslim Magazine*. Whereas Muslim pamphleteers routinely describe the White House as one of the darkest dens of evil in the world, Shaykh Kabbani boasts of having been invited to meet with George W. Bush there in November 2004,[20] and insists that "Jesus, on his return, will personally correct the erroneous representations and interpretations [that have been made] concerning him. He will affirm the authentic message that he brought in his time [on earth] as a prophet, for he never claimed to be the son of God." Shaykh Kabbani is particularly unforgiving toward Saudi Wahhabism, which "promotes its warped cult through massive propaganda campaigns, through preachers in mosques, and through the Internet and television." Fundamentalist Islam casts its teaching in apocalyptic terms, he believes, in the hope that "once the whole world has been corrupted, at the end of times, these ignorant young people [who have embraced Wahhabist ideas] will come to speak in the name of Islam." Weakened by the morbid decadence of conservative doctrines, Islam will find its salvation in the many converts it will have made: "The Prophet predicted, fourteen centuries ago, that the Western peoples would convert to Islam in the last days, and this is what we are witnessing today. Despite all the obstacles they face, massive numbers of Westerners are now adopting Islam, by the grace of Allah."[21] Accordingly, Sufi eschatology attaches great value to the messianic role of Western converts in producing an apocalyptic literature that is primarily intended for a Western readership.

Thus, for example, a French scholar named Didier Ali Hamoneau contributed a preface and commentary to a new edition of al-Suyuti's

Return of Jesus published in Paris in 2000.[22] In this work he finds a "basis for Islamo-Christian dialogue" that will "prepare us to welcome with dignity the one whom the world awaits, our messiah Jesus, who will rid the world of imposters and establish on earth a golden age even before the Last Judgment." Hamoneau defends Sufi intelligence against fundamentalist obscurantism: "The return of Jesus will unquestionably constitute a trial for overly rigid and dogmatic minds. . . . In reality, the self-styled 'fundamentalists' are only the victims and toys of the governments of the Western materialistic world (more atheistic than [it is] Christian)."[23] Yet this mystical interpretation in no way seeks to diminish the horror of the apocalypse:

> The Antichrist will represent the worst trial that humanity has ever experienced. Next to him, Nero, Hitler, Stalin, Mao, and their like are dwarves, even though they were considered in their time—and rightly so—to be minor Antichrists, which in fact they were insofar as they were forerunners and mentors of the apocalyptic Swine. Moreover, to [help believers] understand this kind of demon, God also created in the past as many minor local Mahdis—this before the advent of the grand Mahdi, who will be to Jesus as Aaron was to Moses and as 'Ali to the Prophet Muhammad, may divine blessing and peace be upon them.[24]

Hamoneau's account of the apocalypse mentions a "collection of hadiths translated and compiled by Sidi Abdallah Penot."[25] The reference is to a book entitled *The Signs of the End of Times in Islamic Tradition* that was published in Lyon by an author better known as Dominique Penot.[26] The two hundred and nine hadiths it contains place great emphasis on al-Qurtubi's vision of the advent of the Mahdi in the Muslim West, though Penot acknowledges that "the fact that al-Qurtubi was an Andalusian may explain his hope of seeing [the Mahdi] appear in the Maghrib, whereas Ibn Kathir . . . , an 'Easterner,' envisaged his appearance in the Mashriq."[27] Penot's indebtedness to al-Qurtubi is made clear, too, by his endorsement of a particularly repellent hadith concerning the extermination of the Jews after the death of the Antichrist: "God will put the Jews to flight and nothing of what He has created will conceal a Jew in these times without His causing it to speak; not a tree, a stone, a wall, nor a beast will not say: 'O servant of God, O Muslim, here is a Jew, come kill him!'"[28]

Penot devotes a chapter of his collection to "Jesus, son of Mary, Christ of the Parousia."[29] One of the authorities explicitly cited in this connection is Shaykh Anwar Shah Kashmiri (1873–1933), the chief theologian of the Pakistani branch of the Deoband School of Islamic

Sciences (Darul Oolum Deoband). Kashmiri's extensive commentaries on the authentic collections of Bukhari and Muslim were published in Arabic by his students in abridged form; the Urdu edition of his commentary on Bukhari alone runs to thirty-two volumes. The Arabic version of Kashmiri's *Descent of the Messiah*, quoted by Penot, reports one hundred and one traditions on the apocalyptic role of Jesus.[30] Prepared under the auspices of the mufti of Pakistan himself, Shaykh Muhammad Shafi, this text went through several successive editions, appearing first in 1965 in Aleppo, then in 1981 (reissued 1992) in Beirut, and finally in 1982 (reissued 2005) in Cairo. It was through the medium of Arabic, then, that the views of this fundamentalist Sunni thinker came to exert an influence on French-language Islamic eschatology.[31]

One recent book stands out from the rest. In *The Prophecies of Islam* (2006), Jean Ezéchiel wholeheartedly subscribes to the logic of the Muslim apocalypse, finding in it a tragic resonance with current events:

> After the attacks of 11 September 2001, the Americans expressed a great anger, indisputably legitimate, against the authors of this aggression and against the religion in the name of which they acted. This wrath made them go to war in two Muslim countries: Afghanistan and Iraq, which led in turn to tens of thousands of victims. And this is only the beginning. Before the Americans are appeased, millions of Muslims will probably lose their lives. . . . Ancient prophecies of the tradition have been awakened. Indeed, Iraq, the future native land of the Antichrist, is a gate of hell that, once opened, will be difficult to close again.[32]

Ezéchiel is convinced that, faced with the prospect of raging conflict, Islam may be unable to avoid adopting a pacifist approach: "In the event America refuses to show forgiveness and make peace, the Muslim people will have no recourse but to [embrace] prayer and non-violence." Refusing to say whether he is "a Christian who fraternizes with the Muslims or a Muslim who fraternizes with the Christians," this author calls for nothing less than a "spiritual revolution."[33]

THE HARUN YAHYA MULTINATIONAL

The Turkish pamphleteer Adnan Oktar, born in 1956 in Ankara, has acquired a worldwide celebrity over the last two decades under the pen name of Harun Yahya. His dozens of short, vividly illustrated books are sold in cheaply priced editions in many European languages (English, French, German, Spanish, Italian, Russian, Portuguese, Polish, Dutch, Danish, Albanian, Bulgarian, and Serbo-Croatian), to say nothing of their translation into Arabic, Urdu, Kazakh, and Malay. Formerly a student of art and philosophy in Istanbul, Harun Yahya makes no claim whatever to clerical authority. He nonetheless has taken it upon himself to mount a massive campaign of proselytization aimed at the Western public, advertising boxed sets of "Islamic morality" (ten books accompanied by as many multilingual DVDs) and "special offers for children" on his online sales site www.bookglobal.net.

Fiercely opposed to the theory of evolution, Yahya has promoted a muscular form of creationism in books such as *The Evolution Deceit, The Creation of the Universe, The Disasters Darwinism Brought to Humanity, The Miracle of Creation in DNA, The Collapse of the Theory of Evolution in Twenty Questions, The Miracle of Human Creation,* and *The Miracle in the Ant.* In January 2007, he became the talk of France when he tried to donate hundreds of copies of his *Atlas of Creation* to secondary schools and universities, apparently with the intent of reaching faculty and students alike.[34] Although shipments were quickly blocked through the prompt intervention of the Ministry of Education, Yahya boasted afterward of having caused "panic in France, the cradle of materialist ideas."[35] A few months later he attempted the same maneuver in the United States, only this time on a far larger scale that included scientific museums and members of Congress—a wildly expensive initiative that aroused both acerbic and perplexed reactions in the American press.[36]

Harun Yahya is constantly at pains to emphasize that "the day of judgment, contrary to what many believe, is approaching now, not in some distant future."[37] He distinguishes two apocalyptic phases. The first is "a period during which all people will suffer material and spiritual problems. Following this, the Earth will enter into a period of salvation called the 'Golden Age,' which will be characterized by generosity and kindness owing to the reign of the true religion. With the end of the Golden Age, there will be rapid social collapse and people will begin to await the Day of Judgment."[38] This scenario, which includes the 1979 uprising in Mecca, the oil wells set on fire in Kuwait in 1991, and the great Turkish dam built to reduce the flow of the Euphrates, is notable for its highly original view of Gog and Magog. Their invasion, Yahya says, threatens to involve "the malicious use of television network transmission towers." The Two-Horned One will create an electromagnetic field, however, in the form of a dam, that will be capable of "jamming the television programs transmitted by Gog and Magog."[39]

In the matter of apocalyptic speculation, and much else, Harun Yahya shows himself to be a dutiful disciple of the Kurdish Islamist Said

Nursi (1878–1960), to whose monumental commentary on the Qur'an, *Risale-i Nur,* he often recurs. Known as "Bediuzzaman" (Wonder of the Age) to his followers, Nursi attacked both Atatürk's secular reforms and Communism while nourishing a virulent hostility toward Freemasonry. Yahya inherited this hatred,[40] but his emphasis on the importance of the role to be played by Jesus at the end of the world permitted him to cultivate an ecumenical image, in the name of all believers, Muslim and Christian alike, joined in combat against the reviled materialism propagated by the Masons. Nursi, for his part, had left no doubt about the task assigned to "Muslim Christians." Though they are considered to be Christians, their "zeal and abnegation" will soon cause them to be justly regarded as Muslims, for "they will strive to unite the authentic religion of Jesus with the message of Islam and, by destroying the society established by the Antichrist, they will save mankind from atheism."[41] Since 1975, Nursi has been published in Istanbul by Sözler, which subsequently opened an office in Cairo for paperback translations into Arabic; in 2004, *The Signs of the Hour and the Questions of the Great Antichrist and of the Sufyani*[42] became the twenty-fifth volume to appear in an on-going series of Nursi's works, available in all of the major cities of the Arab world. Sözler now has branches in Germany (Asya Verlag in Cologne) and the United States (Nur Publishers in Phoenix) as well, in addition to publishing its list in Russian, French, Persian, Albanian, Uzbek, and Kirghiz.

In the meantime, though he acknowledges Said Nursi as his master, Harun Yahya has been busy assisting his own circle of disciples, collectively known as "Nurjus," in implementing a worldwide communications strategy. The like of their apocalyptic antirationalism is found in other, less gifted Turkish pamphleteers who have also been translated into French. Adem Yakup, in *The Prophet Jesus* (2004), predicts the "extermination of antireligious movements by Jesus and the Christians" in the last days, for "Christians and Muslims will be able to form a grand alliance; Jesus will kill the Antichrist, emblem of all the atheistic currents of thought, and thus eliminate them." Moreover, Yakup holds, Jesus will be supported in this battle by "mujahedin."[43] Two other Turkish authors, Ismail Buyukcelebi and Resit Haylamaz, less extreme in their views than Yakup but no less attached to the teachings of Shaykh Nursi, cautiously attempt in *Jesus: His Mission and His Miracles* (2005) to read the confrontation between Jesus and the Antichrist in metaphorical terms: "What is insinuated here, perhaps, is that the idea of atheism will be shattered and a victory won for faith."[44]

ABOMINATORS OF THE JEWISH KING

The theme of an apocalyptic alliance between Christians and Muslims against the Jewish Antichrist evidently involves at least some degree of anti-Semitism. In *Dajjāl, the Antichrist* (1997), by Ahmad Thomson,[45] this antagonism acquires a virulent and obsessive dimension. Thomson, a British convert to Islam, born in Zambia, is concerned to establish the lethal villainy of Ashkenazi Jews, whom he sees as the spiritual fathers of both Zionism and Communism. What is more, he identifies them with the monstrous races of Gog and Magog, noting that they are "intimately linked with the appearance of the Dajjal [Antichrist], since many of them today are in high positions of control in the various interlinking systems which together make up the kafir [infidel] system, that is, the Dajjal system." This "ruling elite" has long concealed itself under the guise of Freemasonry, Thomson holds, stressing that *The Protocols of the Elders of Zion* constitutes "a partial, yet informative, outline of the freemasonic blueprint for world control." And "although Hitler was aware of the freemasons' bid for world control, he did not have access to the only viable alternative to . . . the Dajjal system—that is, trust in Allah." Since Islam alone could have saved Nazi Germany from the scheming of the Freemasons, its collapse was inevitable. But Islam itself is also vulnerable to the *kafir* banking system, currently the Antichrist's principal weapon for plundering the Muslim peoples of their wealth.[46]

Also in 1997, the year that Thomson published his pamphlet in London, Mohammad Yasin Owadally brought out in Delhi *Emergence of Dajjal: The Jewish King*.[47] This slender volume, likewise written in English and printed in very large characters, is illustrated with hand-drawn sketches of the future itinerary of the Antichrist, which will lead him to his death in Lod—presently the site, Owadally points out, of "the airport of the Zionist state." "The Jews," he says, "are waiting impatiently for the coming of the Dajjal, their beloved king. Dajjal will surely appear: he will take possession of the whole world from east to west. He will summon all creatures to his obedience. He will emerge between Iraq and Syria and will raise great fuss and mischief right and left in every direction. Dajjal will be tall, so tall that his head will be above the clouds. In the deepest parts of the sea the waters will not get beyond his heels. He will rule the whole world for forty days." Owadally does not exclude the possibility that "the current problem between the Muslims and the Jews regarding the Bayt-ul-Maqadiss [holy places] and Jerusalem will actually be the cause for the emergence of Dajjal," whose coming "will be without the least doubt disastrous for the Muslims"—though they will nonetheless manage to reconquer Jerusalem "on the eve of the [Last] Hour."[48]

In addition to a dozen other pamphlets on topics ranging from Noah's ark to King Solomon and the patience of Job, Owadally devoted a separate work to Gog and Magog. Although originally published in India, an edition later appeared in Malaysia, where the house of A.S. Noordeen also helped it to reach a substantial readership online.[49] In 2002, again in Kuala Lumpur, Owadally brought out with Noordeen an English translation of an apocalyptic booklet by the Palestinian Islamist Bassam Jarrar that first appeared seven years earlier, *Israeli Empire Collapses in 2022* (Plate 21b).[50] His preface to this work is awful in its vindictiveness. "What the Jews are doing now," Owadally says, "is the zenith of corruption and barbarism. The mass slaughtering of innocent people. The Jews are massacring Muslims, bombarding their land, buildings under the *carte-blanche* pretext [sic] of terrorism."[51]

The following year, in 2003, Noordeen published a pamphlet called *The Inevitable Victory: The Coming of Jesus,* whose stated purpose is to denounce "the crimes of the Jews" past and present, throughout the world, and their "greatest conspiracy, [the] 11 September attack."[52] The author, an Iranian Shi'i, vents his anti-Semitic and Holocaust-denying rage under the cover of a pseudonym, Gholam al-Mahdi ("Slave of the Mahdi"). The current decadence of Islam, he holds, is a matter of eschatological fate, no less than the alliance of Christians and Jews against Islam. At the end of times, however, "at the final battle between Good and Evil described as Armageddon in the Bible," the Mahdi will appear and pray with Jesus in Jerusalem.[53]

EASTERN APOCALYPSES

Owadally's local and international success encouraged the development of apocalyptic publishing in Delhi. Aftar Shahryar, author of *Dajjal: The Final Deception and Signs of Qiyamah* (2003),[54] explicitly acknowledged the influence of Ahmad Thomson and justified his undertaking by reference to "the rapid succession of events in the beginnings of the new millennium. Almost all these events were related to or affected Muslim countries and societies—September eleven, Afghanistan, Iraq, and many more." There was a pressing need, then, to "enlighten our readers about the conspiracies, machinations, and deceptions of the Dajjal with the hope that each believer will defeat such deceptions individually and collectively"—all the more because the "clear and immediate danger" has grown since the launching of the "great Crusade" in Iraq.[55] Published a few months after the fall of Saddam Hussein, Shahryar's book was distributed by a network of firms stretching from the Persian Gulf to Great Britain and the United States.[56]

Shortly afterward, in 2005, looking to profit from the increasing demand for apocalyptic insight, another Delhi publisher, Idara, reissued a book by a Pakistani author named S. Bashir ud-din Mahmood that had first appeared almost twenty years earlier under the title *Doomsday and Life after Death.*[57] Mahmood displays extreme caution in deciphering the ultimate fate of the universe as seen through the Holy Qur'an (as the book's subtitle describes his intention): rather than place the coming end of the world at a distance of some few centuries from now, he relocates it on the far side of a more reassuring horizon of ten thousand years. On the other hand, Mahmood shows greater courage in rejecting the prevailing conception of the Antichrist as a cunningly manipulative and political creature, regarding him instead as an allegory of high technology and of scientific breakthroughs diverted to serve "evil ends."[58] Idara carried on in the same vein the next year, publishing a volume of selected writings by Ibn Kathir under the comfortably familiar title of *Dajjal the False Messiah.*[59]

Another Indian author to rise to prominence, though by a more conventional route than either Owadally or Shahryar, was a former director of the Islamic Studies Center, Dar al-Amana, in the southern province of Kerala named Siddheeque Veliandoke. Subsequently he moved to Riyadh, establishing an Arabian branch of Dar al-Amana. Nonetheless it was in Toronto, and in English, that Veliandoke published *Doomsday, Portents, and Prophecies* (1998), a methodical presentation of what he reckoned to be the sixty-three minor signs and eleven major signs of the Last Hour. With no apparent concern for either anachronism or inconsistency, Veliandoke writes, for example, that "the Zionists planned the defeat of the Muslims during the Crusades," and that in the early twentieth century "Jews and Christians collaborated to eliminate the Turkish caliphate."[60] Five years later, in 2003, he had the honor of seeing himself published in Arabic, in the capital of the Saudi kingdom. The numbering of the apocalypse had changed in the meantime, for he now counted seventy-five minor signs and nine major signs. Among the latter class of indications he points in particular to "the meetings and treaties concluded by the enemies of Islam to destroy its religion and its people."[61] Rather than grasp the outstretched hand of the infidels, Islam must cut it off—or else perish.

These authors well illustrate in their differing ways the spread of Muslim millennialism from the Persian Gulf westward to North America, on the one hand, and eastward to the Malay Peninsula, on the other. Malaysia itself constitutes a textbook case in the globalization of the Islamic apocalypse. In addition to the publication of English-language works by Owadally, an Indian, a number of Arab authors were translated into Malay after 11 September, including representatives of both the radical messianic camp (Muhammad Isa Dawud and Amin Gamaleddin)[62] and the conservative Islamic camp (Muhammad Metwalli Shahrawi and Muhammad Kheir Ramadan Yusuf).[63] These translations have been accompanied by the appearance of a number of original works in Malay as well.[64]

Pustaka Syuhada (House of the Martyrs) is remarkable among Kuala Lumpur publishers for its sponsorship of radical messianic translations. Its list includes a collection of apocalyptic hadiths that features an image of the World Trade Center in flames on the cover,[65] and several pamphlets by Abdullah Azzam (1941–1989), the mentor of bin Laden and theoretician of global jihad. But other houses have been active in this line as well. Very shortly after Ahmad Thomson was translated in Kuala Lumpur, in 2007,[66] a local author named Mustaffa Suhaimi brought out a book under the imprint of Progressive Publishing House called *The Antichrist Threatens the Islamic Nation throughout the World* that quotes at length from Thomson in its conclusion.[67] The cover of the book (Plate 22) juxtaposes photographs of George W. Bush, Ariel Sharon, Saddam Hussein, and Usama bin Laden.

Finally, as we saw earlier, Harun Yahya's works are available in Malay-language editions. Yet they have enjoyed only mixed success in Malaysia, despite being prominently displayed in the shopping centers of Kuala Lumpur and in airport newsstands; indeed, they cannot be found in Islamist bookstores, even in the eastern state of Kelantan, where radical booksellers are accustomed to showcase apocalyptic works by local authors and by Arab authors in translation. In a country whose population is two-thirds Muslim, and whose government seeks to advance what it calls a civilizational form of Islam *(islam hadhari)*, one therefore encounters every possible attitude toward apocalyptic temptation: wariness, enthusiasm—and serene indifference.

THE FINAL CALL OF THE BLACK MUSLIMS

In the United States, beginning in the early 1930s, Elijah Muhammad (1897–1975) helped to found a movement known as the Nation of

Islam whose principles could not have been less in agreement with those of Muslim orthodoxy.[68] Through his own newspaper, as well as sermons and books, most notably *Message to the Blackman in America* (1965),[69] Elijah Muhammad elaborated a doctrine of communal separatism and black counterracism on the basis of a quite fantastic cosmogony. The black race, he claimed, was descended from the tribe of Shabazz, which appeared on earth sixty trillion years ago.[70] Having in the meantime made themselves masters of the Nile Valley and of the holy city of Mecca, these Arabo-Africans faced the prospect of extinction around 4000 B.C.E. following the birth of Yakub, a demoniacal being who used grafts to modify their genes ("germs") and, by gradually lightening their skin pigmentation, created the white race—the source of Shabazz's subsequent misfortunes. Exiled with sixty thousand of his followers on the island of Patmos in the Aegean Sea, Yakub managed to consolidate the forces of white subversion, with the result that its poison spread, reaching as far as Mecca. "Yakub's race of devils" was then expelled into the barbarous lands of Europe, but this was not enough to neutralize the white menace. The black nation was eventually subjugated, and, according to Elijah Muhammad, it will remain in this condition for a period of six thousand years. At the end of this time it will produce the Mahdi, also known as "the second Jesus," who "will remove and destroy the present, old warring wicked world of Yakub (the Caucasian world) and set up a world of peace and righteousness" in which the supremacy of the aboriginal race will be restored for eternity.[71]

Elijah Muhammad's vision of the world was absolutely heretical from the point of view of orthodox Islam. His followers described themselves not simply as Muslims, but as Black Muslims. Nor did Muslim communities in the United States consider the members of his movement to be coreligionists.[72] The revolutionary agitator Malcolm X, for many years a pillar of the Nation of Islam, broke with Elijah Muhammad in 1964. After making his pilgrimage to Mecca, Malcolm could not find words harsh enough to condemn the errors of his former teacher.[73] Malcolm was soon ostracized by the Nation of Islam and replaced in all of his duties by Louis Farrakhan, whom he had personally recruited and converted. Thus the betrayal of Elijah Muhammad by Malcolm X was answered by Farrakhan's betrayal of his own mentor. In February 1965, Malcolm X was shot down in a hail of gunfire. The Nation of Islam denied all responsibility for his assassination.

Louis Farrakhan served as the organization's official spokesman until Elijah Muhammad's death in 1975. Temporarily obliged to defer to Elijah's son, Wallace Muhammad, Farrakhan found a way to take over the movement in 1981 by shrewdly exploiting both his charisma and his talent for invective.[74] Despite recurrent controversies, notably in connection with his anti-Jewish tirades,[75] Farrakhan's ability to attract new followers was undiminished. He was able, too, to inspire African-Americans who did not subscribe to the tenets of the Nation of Islam, as the march of hundreds of thousands of black protesters on Washington, first in 1995 and then again a decade later, was to demonstrate in dramatic fashion. Earlier he had transformed a former Greek Orthodox church in Chicago into the seat of the Nation of Islam, renaming it Mosque Maryam in honor of the mother of the "prophet Jesus," and the discipline and efficiency insisted upon by the Black Muslims increasingly made themselves felt throughout the country in black communities ravaged by delinquency and drugs. Gang lords and rap music notables made no attempt to hide their respect for Farrakhan.[76]

The apocalyptic dimension of Farrakhan's rhetoric is unmistakable. Just as Elijah Muhammad referred to the prophecy of Ezekiel in announcing a "battle in the sky" and the "Great Wheel,"[77] Farrakhan in 1985 had a "vision-like experience" in which he was abducted by a UFO and learned of America's plans for war. At first he believed it was a premonition of the U.S. raid on Tripoli in April 1986, but later came to see it as the sign of eschatological conflict on a wholly different scale.[78] On a visit to Baghdad in January 1991, during the Iraqi occupation of Kuwait, Farrakhan warned against "the war of Armageddon which is the final war."[79] The lightning victory of the American-led coalition did not undermine his confidence in an apocalyptic outcome, however, for he interpreted the burning oil wells in Kuwait as proof that this conflict was at bottom only a "prelude to the Great Battle."[80] In the newspaper of the Nation of Islam, *The Final Call*,[81] Farrakhan announced that "when God comes, His presence in the world will be a declaration of war. For it is written that God will tear out the heathen, root and branch."[82]

In July 2001, Farrakhan called upon the United States to prepare itself to confront "God's wrath," saying "This world is not good, for Allah's enemy rules it. When Allah comes to judge a world that is led by America, its name will be at the head of the nations that must disappear."[83] His tone did not soften after 11 September. In December 2001 he enjoined President Bush not to "involve America in the greatest of all wars, the War of Armageddon, in which no nation will be left out," and the following October he called upon the American president to abstain from all intervention in Iraq, on pain of bringing "Divine Wrath on the

American people and on American cities."[84] The tsunami of December 2004 seemed to him to be "a sign of the end of this system of things." There will be "earthquakes in diverse places, pestilence and famine," he prophesied, adding that, "unfortunately, the worst is yet to come."[85]

The American stalemate in Iraq and Washington's threats against Iran led Farrakhan to sound the alarm once more. Interviewed in March 2007 on the pan-Arab television station Al-Jazira, he declared that "the time for warnings is past . . . I have warned President Bush, I have warned his people, and I have warned my own people. The time for warnings is behind us, the time of Allah's punishment is at hand."[86] Less than a month later, this time on the occasion of the Easter service at Mosque Maryam in Chicago, Farrakhan's message had lost none of its urgency:

> Muslims are going to be persecuted [in the United States]. Black people and others who oppose the war will be persecuted. . . . This is not as much a war against terrorism as it is a war against Islam. . . . As this war gets hotter and hotter, Allah (God) will be bringing down more of His Wrath on the United States, which will be seen in the unusual weather the country is now experiencing. . . . Muslims, we have to now think more deeply into what we believe. If our belief system can be shaken again, then the War of Armageddon will have claimed us as its victims.[87]

These maledictions issue directly from Elijah Muhammad's confident forecast four decades earlier of the "fall of America."[88] For more than a half-century the Nation of Islam's vengeful millenarianism has been part of a broader attempt to establish the movement as a countersociety within the United States. To some extent, then, its apocalypticism is a peripheral phenomenon, unaffected by the forces that are shaking the foundations of the Muslim world. But even though the heretical cosmogony of the Black Muslims forbids any doctrinal alliance with Islamic messianism in either its traditional or radical forms, Farrakhan's repeated invocations of "the Wrath of Allah" since 2001 have met with an undeniably sympathetic response in the Middle East, diffused throughout the region by the satellite television channel Al-Jazira.

THE VIRTUAL APOCALYPSE

The enormously powerful resources of the Internet as a medium for broadcasting messianic messages have gone largely untapped. For the moment, at least, the easily portable pamphlet and the bulkier but more imposing treatise remain preferred formats for apocalyptic literature.

Of all the authors I have mentioned up to this point, the only one to have systematically put his writings online is the Palestinian Bassam Jarrar, no doubt in hopes of overcoming his isolation on the West Bank. Even Harun Yahya, who oversees a cyberarchipelago of some twenty websites, attaches great value to the physical distribution of his works, in both hardcover and paperback. For publishing houses in the Middle East that are riding the radical messianic wave, conventional methods of production and distribution are still immensely profitable; and the privileged status of the book, its abiding nobility and prestige in Muslim culture, continue to attract obscure academics and ambitious clerics.

Two English-language websites give some idea of the place occupied by the apocalypse in the virtual community of believers. Probably the most popular site of contemporary Islam is www.islamonline.net, based in Dubai and very frequently visited in its Arabic version. It is concerned mainly to provide spiritual and moral guidance, and pays practically no attention to eschatological matters, except in relation to the probable timing of the Last Judgment and the duty of all Muslims to prepare themselves for it with a clear conscience. The second site, www.islaam .com,[89] is linked to islamonline.net, as well as to the website of the Saudi government's Ministry of Religious Affairs; but it is clearly also aimed at Muslims in North America and Europe, even if for the time being only a French version is supported in addition to English. The writings it makes available by a vast range of religious authorities, from the legalistic hierarchy to authors in the vanguard of Islamist protest, serve a proselytizing purpose as well.[90]

This expansive orientation leads islaam.com to lay emphasis on the figure of Jesus, particularly in his apocalyptic aspect,[91] and to declare that "the Muslim nation is more worthy of Jesus than the others."[92] Otherwise the "Judeo-Christian alliance in Palestine" is denounced, the Bible dismissed as a "corrupt text," and "the Jews" accused of seeking to "submit all of humanity to Israel" and, once the time has come, to the Antichrist.[93] The future conquest of Rome by the Muslims is regarded as inevitable.[94] In order to ward off the prophetic threat of the destruction of Mecca by an Abyssinian, Islam must be promoted in East Africa.[95] Only the Mahdi will be able to put an end to the current "tyranny," in which apostate Muslim regimes collaborate with the infidel powers, and to install a universal caliphate.[96] Earthquakes, uncontrollable epidemics, and heat waves are only the first of many divine punishments to be visited upon the "enemies of Islam" and the "secular world."[97] At least five extracts from the work of the Indian author Siddheeque Veliandoke have been posted on islaam.com, in addition to Shaykh Hawali's *The Day of Wrath*, the founding document of the global jihadist version of contemporary apocalypse.

By juxtaposing a variety of eschatological accounts, from the most conservative to the most radical, islaam.com helps to popularize the latter at the expense of the former while giving the impression of evenhandedness. This tacit encouragement of increasingly rabid apocalyptic speculation can also be detected in Arabic-language discussion groups *(muntadā)*, notably the very popular www.alsaha.com (the Public Place).[98] A few such forums specialize in millenarian topics. Al-Malāhim wa al-Fitan, which borrows its name ("Battles and Trials") from the apocalyptic lexicon, reminds visitors to its home page that the "party of Allah" will triumph over the "party of Satan."[99] A millennialist community in the Kuwaiti desert, established in 1991 by its self-proclaimed messiah, Al-Husayn al-Luhaydi, has equipped itself with an ambitious website that offers several related discussion groups, and even a "Library of the Mahdi" where readers may consult works such as *The Authentic Gospel* and *Bin Laden at the Gates of Hell*.[100] In this case the sect's presence in cyberspace amounts to a way of circumventing the vow of isolation *(i'tizāl)* initially sworn by its disciples, which over the years they have found increasingly difficult to bear.

So far I have mentioned only Sunni authors and writings. It should not be overlooked, however, that Shi'i religious authorities have made a very substantial investment in web-based communications in an attempt to reassert their claim to dogmatic legitimacy and to heighten their visibility in a highly competitive environment. Each of the grand ayatollahs has set up a personal website, often multilingual,[101] on which he discusses eschatological and other questions. In this undertaking the ayatollahs have been aided abroad by the work in Montreal of Abbas Ahmad al-Bostani. For more than a decade Bostani has been editing and translating approved Shi'i works into French, which are then published under his own imprint, La Cité du Savoir (The City of Knowledge), and disseminated in electronic form as well via www.bostani.com.[102] Visitors to this site are warned against the dangers of excessive messianic enthusiasm: "The believer must resign himself to awaiting the appearance of the Imam without seeming to be in too much of a hurry. . . . The fact of being eager or impatient to see the Mahdi appear may encourage the believer to put his faith in the first false messiah who proclaims himself the 'awaited guide,' for example, which would lead him into error, and lead into error all those who follow him in this path."[103]

· · ·

The renewed interest in the grand masters of the medieval apocalypse is plain to see in contemporary Islam. It grows out of a curiosity about last things that is natural in the case of a robust and growing religion, and naturally liable to be intensified by the unrest that can be observed in so much of the world today. Nevertheless it is striking that the millenarian anxiety to which this impulse gives voice is very much less pronounced in Muslim lands lying beyond its epicenter in the Middle East, no matter that the Internet now makes it possible to transmit the wildest conjectures to the ends of the earth in an instant. It is striking, too, that Jesus should occupy a central place in apocalyptic accounts originating outside the Middle East, and this in a way that serves to distinguish them from one another: to Sufis, Jesus offers a means of strengthening the commitment of Western converts who have been captivated by the mystical tradition of Islam; to Harun Yahya and Shaykh Nursi's other disciples, a means of proselytization; and to Black Muslims, a way of rebutting the charge of illegitimacy brought against the Nation of Islam by Protestant evangelical churches in the United States.

A troubling linguistic divergence is nonetheless apparent within this diaspora of apocalypses. Whereas French-language writings are firmly of the conservative Islamic type, constituting in effect a sort of apologetic vulgate, the anglophone literature lays great stress on the message of radical messianism, indeed on the duty of global jihadism. And whereas vigilance against anti-Semitic slander is customary in Paris and Brussels, the worst Judeophobic clichés are tolerated in London and Toronto.[104] Paradoxically, then, the preaching of hatred for the Jewish race, first disseminated in pamphlet form in Europe in the early twentieth century and subsequently reinvigorated by apocalyptic propagandists in Arab lands, is now undergoing a revival in the English-speaking world.

CHAPTER 10

The Armageddon of Jihad

The counterapocalypse envisioned by Shaykh Hawali was both popularized and neutralized by the events of 11 September. It was popularized because, as we have seen, the idea of global jihad and the designation of Christian Zionism as Islam's principal enemy became the vehicle of mass propaganda, above all after the invasion of Iraq. But it was also neutralized, because Shaykh Hawali's unambiguous condemnation of the attacks on New York and Washington broke the organic link between Saudi Islamist dissent and the ideological warfare waged by al-Qaida.

Usama bin Laden now sought to promote a vision of conflict with America that held out the prospect of protracted struggle rather than any assurance of immediate apocalyptic resolution. Al-Qaida's mission was to create a Muslim territory that, once purged of all rival influences, could be dedicated exclusively to jihad, and then, from this "Jihadistan," to export subversion throughout the world. In accordance with a plan devised by bin Laden's deputy and al-Qaida's chief theoretician, the Egyptian-born Ayman al-Zawahiri, America—the "distant" and absolute enemy of the hadiths—had to be lured into ill-advised military campaigns in the Islamic world whose failure could be counted on to stir up popular anger and destabilize the "near enemy," which is to say those Muslim states that collaborate with the West. Zawahiri's main strategic objective, both before and after 11 September, was to seize power in Mecca and Medina, where the caliphate abolished in 1924 by Atatürk would at last be reestablished.

For a long while this strategy succeeded in insulating al-Qaida, both internally and in its conduct of foreign relations, against contamination by apocalyptic ideas. Only many years after the insurrection in Mecca did bin Laden confide to his companions in Peshawar that he had been slow to appreciate Juhayman al-ʿUtaybi's purpose in launching it.[1] What captured his imagination, however, was not ʿUtaybi's millenarian rhetoric, but rather his revolutionary outlook. The tribute to ʿUtaybi published in 1989 in Peshawar by Abu Muhammad al-Maqdisi[2] likewise ignored the messianic motivations of the uprising in Mecca in the hope of broadening the appeal of the jihadist movement.

Out of the mass of al-Qaida documents seized after the fall of the Taliban emirate, only one letter, dating from May 1994, briefly ventures onto millenarian terrain. Sent from Afghanistan to bin Laden and two of his lieutenants, then in Khartoum, this "Letter about Jihad in the Caucasus" was composed by Mustafa Hamid, an Egyptian jihadist better known as Abu Walid. Eight years older than bin Laden, Abu Walid was a well-respected veteran of the Afghan war who had led the Arab contingent during the siege of the government compound near Khost in 1990–1991. Described by American counterterrorism experts as "pragmatic,"[3] Abu Walid was known for a straightforward, unsentimental prose style that reflected his mastery of English.

In the middle of this letter, and for no obvious reason, Abu Walid suddenly lapses into the apocalyptic register:

> In the new phase that is about to begin, or has actually already begun, Israel needs Armageddon, the nuclear holocaust that will wipe out Western civilization in its entirety and prepare the way for the descent of the Antichrist and for his rule over the world from Jerusalem. . . . The direction of Moscow is the intermediate objective. The ultimate objective is Jerusalem for the Army of the Mahdi, whom the armies of Khurasan will choose and to whom they will pledge their allegiance. The essential thing is that both the intermediate and the ultimate objectives will appear after the unleashing of Armageddon by the Jews. This allows us to have a more realistic understanding of the battles of the end of times as they are described in prophetic tradition, for the instruments of war will be swords and horses.[4]

This passage is all the more obscure as Abu Walid makes no attempt to integrate it into the argument he develops in the rest of the letter. It may only have been a momentary aberration, the inadvertent epiphany of a hardened warrior overcome by the messianic aura of his adopted Khurasan.

Apart from this surprising and apparently unmotivated expression of personal belief, al-Qaida, so far as one can judge from its internal correspondence, was for many years impervious to apocalyptic temptation. As late as January 2003, the Center for Islamic Studies and Research (Markaz al-Dirasat wal-Buhuth al-Islamiyya), an ally of the jihadist movement, was still openly ridiculing messianic prophecies. "Allah," it bluntly reminded the faithful, "has not permitted our community to know the identity of the Mahdi prior to his appearance."[5]

Here again, however, the American invasion of Iraq liberated anxieties that had long been suppressed. Not only did an anti-Western reading of the hadith about "the gold of the Euphrates" now seem irresistible to many Muslims, the awakening of Shi'i millenarianism, in both Iraq and Iran, could not fail to provoke a reaction among those Sunni jihadists who were most devoted to combating America and its heretical allies. Thus, for example, the Iraqi branch of al-Qaida sought to nullify the messianic pretensions of the Mahdi Army by accusing Muqtada al-Sadr's soldiers of belonging to the "Army of the Antichrist." The dizzying implications of this descent into the vortex of apocalyptic alarm were soon to be brought out in an exceptional document published by one of the high commanders of global jihad.

THE REVELATION OF ABU MUSAB AL-SURI

Mustafa Setmariam Nasar, born in Syria in 1958, joined the Muslim Brotherhood at a very young age, when it was engaged in armed struggle against the Ba'thist regime of Hafez al-Assad. The dismantling of its clandestine network forced him to go into exile in Jordan, and then in Iraq, where he trained other Islamist fighters in the use of explosives and urban guerrilla warfare tactics. The Hama massacre in 1982 sounded the knell for the Syrian Muslim Brotherhood. Nasar took steps to distance himself from it, and after brief stays in France and Spain joined the Arab mujahedin in Afghanistan in 1987. There he adopted the nom de guerre Abu Musab al-Suri (the Syrian)—an allusion to the Prophet's personal emissary, Mus'ab ibn 'Umayr, sent to Medina in 621, who died a martyr's death four years later at Uhud.

Working as both a political lecturer and a technical instructor in the jihad training camps in Pakistan, Abu Musab al-Suri's reputation continued to grow. From his Syrian experience he developed a radical critique of traditional Islamism and became close to Abdallah Azzam, the theoretician of global jihad who was assassinated in 1989. The following year Abu Musab al-Suri lived and taught in an Afghan camp near Khost, alongside Abu Walid. With the fall of Kabul to the mujahedin, in 1992, Abu Musab returned to Spain, settling first in Grenada, where he had previously acquired Spanish citizenship through marriage. Two years later, in 1994, he left Andalusia for England and quickly distinguished himself as one of the fiercest propagandists in "Londonistan," particularly for his support of Algerian jihad. In the fall of 1997 he returned again to Afghanistan to assist the Taliban regime and collaborate with al-Qaida. In addition to directing his own training center for Arab mujahedin (the al-Ghuraba camp in Kargha, near Kabul) independently of bin Laden's organization, Abu Musab al-Suri supervised instruction in explosives, and indeed in chemical weapons, at the al-Qaida facilities in the village of Darunta, outside Jalalabad.

The collapse of the Taliban after November 2001 threw Abu Musab al-Suri back into the life of nomadic exile he had known in his youth. During the years of doubt and uncertainty that followed, hunted by agents of various intelligence services throughout Iran, Iraq, and Pakistan, he composed a massive 1,600-page treatise of worldwide subversion, *The Call to Global Islamic Resistance* (2004).[6] In this work, advertised as "Your Guide on the Path of Jihad" and covering every domain of al-Qaida's activities, from doctrinal precepts to political propaganda and operational methods, Abu Musab al-Suri stands revealed as a disillusioned observer of the jihadist scene and a severe critic of both Usama bin Laden and Ayman al-Zawahiri, whom he reproaches for having recklessly precipitated the destruction of the Taliban sanctuary by launching the 11 September attacks. As against al-Qaida's adventurism and centralized elitism, which in his view renders it vulnerable at its very core, Abu Musab al-Suri proposes a distributed network model of decentralized resistance that reflects and responds to the aspirations of ordinary Muslims. By granting operational autonomy to local cells, he holds, it will become possible for jihadists to regain the initiative and advance the cause of an authentically global struggle.

Abu Musab al-Suri's primary concern, then, is to place his technical expertise in designing explosive devices and communications systems in the service of a decentralized and genuinely transnational approach to terrorism. Yet a distinctive and unmistakable millenarian impulse animates his arguments on behalf of jihad. "The earth is filled with oppression and injustice," he writes, "and events lead on from one another toward the appearance of the Mahdi. . . . For jihad is an obligation *[farīdha]* until the advent of the Hour. The community that fights for what is true and just will be victorious . . . and it will persevere until the last of its members fights the Antichrist, a constant command of our religion."[7] What is more, this duty has become more urgent since 11 September: "The twentieth century is past, and we have now entered the twenty-first to find that most people seem prepared to follow the Antichrist."[8]

Brooding upon the rout of al-Qaida and the Taliban in Afghanistan, Abu Masab al-Suri bitterly regrets "the end of this chapter of the jihadist movement . . . one of the most promising chapters for revitalizing jihad in the [very] region where the Prophet had predicted the raising of the black banners of the Mahdi." Hounded by his enemies across the Iranian and Pakistani borderlands of Khurasan, Abu Musab al-Suri was driven to contemplate the messianic heritage of his native land, the Shām of classical accounts. It was there that the modern "crusades" took root two centuries earlier with the rise of European imperialism in the Middle East,[9] and it is there, he prophesied, that the crusaders will be defeated and driven back. Relentlessly pursued, racked by loneliness and a gnawing sense of abandonment, he desperately searched for a way to regain the path of the masses. Whereas bin Laden and Zawahiri reasoned in terms of a protected territorial base of operations, Abu Musab al-Suri attached absolute priority to refounding the jihadist movement on the basis of popular and broadly distributed support. In his increasingly frantic attempt to formulate a message that would appeal to the greatest possible number of Muslim believers, Abu Musab al-Suri wound up succumbing to millenarian temptation—and plunging into the apocalyptic abyss.

The final one hundred pages of *The Call for Global Islamic Resistance* are devoted to the "most important prophetic indications, reported in tradition *[sunna],* on the end of times." At this juncture, however, Abu Musab al-Suri sets himself the utterly novel task of collating and analyzing all the hadiths that concern jihad. And while he endeavors to uphold the rigorous standards of the classical compilations, he breaks with their method by mentioning not only "sound" traditions, but also "weak" ones—for, he says, "each [kind] may influence events in the future." He also decides to exclude hadiths heralding events that occurred between the death of the Prophet Muhammad and the present time, such as the fire of Hijaz (to which, in agreement with Abdelfattah, he assigns the date of 1256), in order to concentrate on events that have yet to take place, since "Allah predicts the future."[10] There is nothing in the least theoretical about this exercise in apocalyptic exegesis. It is meant instead as a guide for action: "I have no doubt that we have entered into the age of battles and tribulations *[zāman al-malāhim wal-fitan]*. The reality of this moment enlightens us as to the significance of such events. . . . We will be alive, then, when Allah's order comes. And we shall obey what Allah has commanded."[11]

Abu Musab al-Suri's argument is complicated, and involves an apocalyptic sequence of three phases: ruin (of the virtue of the 'ulama and of the faithful), signs (of the advent of the Day of Judgment and of the Mahdi), and battles (against the Byzantines, against the Antichrist, and, finally, against Gog and Magog). With the approach of Armageddon, Abu Musab al-Suri enlarges the universe of citations to tradition by introducing increasingly doubtful hadiths. At the head of each chapter he places quotations from the two "authentic" collections, Bukhari's taking precedence over that of Muslim, and regularly cites Abu Dawud and Ibn Hibban. From time to time he mentions Ibn Kathir and al-Suyuti as well, but he entirely neglects the three other masters of the medieval apocalypse: al-Qurtubi, presumably because of his bias in favor of the Muslim West; Ibn 'Arabi, because of his Sufi deviance; and Ibn Khaldun, because of his repugnant rationalism.

Abu Musab al-Suri's preferred authority is Nu'aym ibn Hammad, the great chronicler of the trials *(fitan)* to come who died in 843 in an 'Abbasid jail in Iraq—perhaps owing to a suspicion that a similar fate awaited him. But the wandering jihadist is preoccupied above all by the central role reserved for his homeland at the end of the world. It is self-evident to him that the "country of Shām"—Greater Syria, including Lebanon, Palestine, and Jordan—looms as the apocalyptic theater par excellence, and that al-Qaida's strategic conception of global jihad must be reoriented to take into account this final clash.

It would be tedious to accompany Abu Musab al-Suri in his review of the relevant texts. Certain hadiths are emphasized, especially when they carry an injunction to jihad or call down curses upon the Jews.[12] There is a section on irremediable decadence, divided into three chapters, which reveals that "the rules of Islam will be destroyed one by one. When one rule is destroyed, people will cling to the next one, and so on. The first rule to be destroyed will concern the government and the last will have to do with prayers." During this period of decline and decay, which the author identifies with the present age of darkness, "people will gather in the mosques and none of them will be faithful." Muslims will kill one another, for their spirit will have been transformed into the "dust of persons who are no longer what they believe." This is why the most noble jihad will consist in opposing the unjust sultan, for the apostasy of tyrants will be widespread and the violence of their police will be terrible. But worst of all will be the corruption of Islam and the betrayal of the scholars: "The people will follow the uneducated and ask them to issue fatwas; these will be fatwas without foundation and each person will be lost"; the "time will come when people without merit will read the Qur'an . . . , [when] mosques will be open to pronounce words absent from the Qur'an and tradition"; there will be "corrupt princes, immoral ministers, and depraved believers who will abandon prayers to follow their desires and . . . their kings will make the pilgrimage [to the Ka'ba] to amuse and entertain themselves."[13]

The first of the signs of the Hour mentioned by Abu Musab al-Suri is "the discovery [in the bed of] the Euphrates of a mountain of gold over which people will fight. For every hundred of them ninety-nine will die, but each will believe that he is the one who will survive [and carry away the gold]."[14] Other natural resources will come to light, in particular near Hijaz, and men will commit every kind of misdeed in order to seize control of one of them, even though its deceptive luster, more radiant than that of gold itself, will quickly vanish. This imitation gold will moreover be called "Pharaoh," from the name of the tyrant of Egypt at the time of the prophet Moses—an allegorical reference, apparently, to the mirage of oil in our own time, reinforced by a sinister prophecy about "the defilement of the Qur'an and the contraction of time."[15]

Abu Musab al-Suri looks with favor upon a hadith that speaks of the restoration of Islam by an armed force "coming from the east." This will be the vanguard of the Mahdi, known by its black banners and led by Shuaib ibn Saleh, whom every believer will join "even [if it means] marching in the snow." The Sufyani, whose face is scarred by smallpox, will rise up against it in Damascus and ravage Palestine, Egypt, and Hijaz, proceeding as far as Mecca, where he will kill the "Pure Soul." Yet it is also at Mecca that the Mahdi will appear, and he will reconquer Damascus after eighteen years, rallying to Islam all the Jews whom he has encountered in the meantime. Abu Musab al-Suri furthermore approves a particularly questionable hadith—condemned, he notes, in Egypt—according to which Muslims who have been were chased out of Andalusia will traverse the Strait of Gibraltar, just as Moses had crossed the Red Sea in ancient times, take control of Cairo, convert their enemies, and win over to their side fellow Muslims from Upper Egypt as well as Ethiopians.[16]

This digression nonetheless does not distract Abu Musab al-Suri's attention from the greatest of all battles (al-malhama al-kubrā), to be fought in the first instance against the Byzantines *(Rūm)*, who are identified with the contemporary Western powers. Events will unfold in the following manner: "The Arabian Peninsula will be preserved [from harm] until the destruction of Armenia, Egypt will be preserved until the destruction of the [Arabian] peninsula, Kufa will be preserved until the destruction of Egypt, the city of impiety *[madīnat al-kufr]* will be conquered only after the great wars, and the Antichrist will appear only after this conquest."[17] The concentrically expanding path of apocalyptic devastation will then close in upon Palestine, the sanctuary of Judeo-Crusader "impiety," where the ultimate confrontation with the Byzantines will take place in and around the city of Acre. Abu Musab al-Suri endorses all the accepted traditions concerning Jesus and the Antichrist, notably among them the homicidal hadith about the stones and trees that denounce the Jews hiding behind them.[18] But he innovates in supplementing it with a related saying, according to which the concealed presence of "impure Christians" will also be betrayed in the same fashion.[19]

Abu Musab al-Suri relies on the authority of Nu'aym ibn Hammad in recounting the second of the three climactic battles. The people of Shām will flee the advance of the Antichrist and his tens of thousands of Jewish partisans, finding refuge on the hills of Balqa overlooking the east bank of the Jordan River. There they will be encircled by their satanic pursuers, who will cut off all access to food and water. The Muslims will nonetheless manage to break the siege, cross over the Jordan, and regain Jerusalem, where "they will be blessed by its fruits and eat their fill of the bread and oil of the holy land." The Antichrist, harassed by two angels who denounce his lies, will attempt to follow, but at this juncture Jesus will descend from heaven and strike him down.[20]

To this fresco of apocalyptic combat on the Jordan, crowned by two brief paragraphs summarily narrating the devastation caused by Gog and Magog and the circumstances of their demise, Abu Musab al-Suri appends his last will and testament by way of conclusion. Here he implores his fellow warriors to give no credit to anything he might say in the event that he were to be captured—as indeed he was, in Pakistan, not quite a year after *The Call to Global Islamic Resistance* was posted online on jihadist websites.[21] At that point, however, he disappeared from sight altogether: the United States withdrew his name from its list of wanted terrorists without, however, confirming his very probable detention in American custody. Whatever may have become of Abu Musab al-Suri, his belated embrace of apocalyptic prophecy can be expected to shape the course of terrorism in unforeseeable ways.

AN APOCALYPTIC TALE IN SEARCH OF AN AUTHOR

So far only a few elements of messianic symbolism seem to have been used—and then only intermittently—as instruments of recruitment to the cause of jihad. One thinks, of course, of the famous black banners of Khurasan, heralds of the forward troops of the Mahdi, which have been assimilated with more or less conviction to the emblems of the Taliban and its self-styled Islamic emirate. During the winter of 2006–2007, a jihadist group called Supporters of the Mahdi *(ansār al-Mahdī)* was broken up in Morocco, where the presence of members of the military in its ranks was understandably felt to give reason for concern. Shortly afterward the disruption of an al-Qaida cell, this time in Saudi Arabia, revealed that its members had sworn an oath of allegiance to their leader, a veteran of the Afghan jihad, at the foot of the Ka'ba in Mecca. The imitative character of this oath, recalling the one sworn to the Mahdi in the apocalyptic scenario, is by no means innocent. But in this case we are dealing with the isolated exploitation of a stereotype, albeit a powerfully suggestive one, rather than the sudden emergence of a millenarian dynamic.

Shaykh Hawali's defection after 11 September deprived global jihad of an authoritative figure who could impart clerical legitimacy to its vision of the world and of its end. The self-proclaimed "shaykhs" of al-Qaida, whose religious credentials were as dubious as they were unimpressive, reacted by toying with vague ideas of revolution. This left messianic evangelism in the hands of a familiar group of more or less radical pamphleteers until Abu Musab al-Suri arrived, after a long and painful intellectual journey, at a conception of apocalypse that suddenly gave meaning and purpose to all the present torments of the jihadist movement.

Unlike Hizbullah, al-Qaida has no Shadi Faqih or other fellow traveler to whom it can look in order to place its age of armed struggle within an apocalyptic order of battle. Nor is there any evidence to suggest that either bin Laden or Zawahiri has the least interest in such a thing; for them, the mere imitation of a prophetic gesture is enough to satisfy whatever limited ambitions they entertain in the way of harnessing the power of religious symbolism. And, for the moment at least, Abu Musab al-Suri's wager on the effectiveness of messianic appeals in generating mass support for global jihad has not been rewarded.[22] It is possible, of course, that other figures may one day find themselves plunged into the vertiginous spiral of apocalyptic speculation, especially if they share Abu Musab al-Suri's vision of a terrorism that is both individual-ized and globalized. After all, as the Syrian showed, from waging war against the Judeo-Crusaders to fighting the Antichrist is but a single step. Fortunately, it is not a short step. And although no one is prevented from taking it, the group dynamics that must come into existence if humanity is to reach the millennium have so far not taken shape.

. . .

We now know that Timothy McVeigh, the author of the terrorist mas-sacre of April 1995 in Oklahoma City,[23] was strongly influenced by an ostensibly harmless culture of belief in hidden plots and conspiracies. "Predictions of violence made on the basis of beliefs alone," the politi-cal scientist Michael Barkun points out, "are notoriously unreliable. Inflammatory rhetoric can come from otherwise peaceable individuals. It does appear, however, that apocalypticists are more likely to engage in violence if they believe themselves to be trapped or under attack. Both conditions are as much the product of their own perception as of out-side forces."[24] Transposing this analysis of radical millenarianism in the United States to global jihad, it is tempting to regard Abu Musab al-Suri as the harbinger of just such a transition from beliefs to action, only on a far grander scale than Oklahoma City.

Up until now, the jihadist fuse has not been brought into contact with an explosive millenarian charge. No inevitability pushes human-ity in the direction of catastrophe, even if the popular fascination with disaster may seem somehow to favor a sudden leap into mass horror. And yet, coming after the gold of the Euphrates, widely interpreted in the wake of the American invasion of Iraq as a sign of the Hour, a fire in Hijaz may be all that is needed to set in motion a new cycle of eschatological tension, inaugurating an age of widespread fear and expectation that the end of the world is at hand. If an inflammatory and incandescent event of this sort were to occur, the chance that global jihad might undergo an apocalyptic mutation would give grounds for genuine apprehension.

Epilogue

Through the Looking Glass—and Beyond

The ten-nation confederacy assembles with the intent to wipe the Jews off the map. While the Antichrist is with his armies at Armageddon, the invading forces from the east destroy his capital city of Babylon, which is in present-day Iran. Instead of moving eastward to protect his capital city of Babylon, the Antichrist will move his forces south to the city of Jerusalem. The Jews will resist, but the Antichrist will prevail. There will be devastating loss of life. After he has captured Jerusalem, the Antichrist will disperse his armies to the south in an attempt to capture and kill Jews who are hiding in the outlying areas. When the forces of the Antichrist descend on the Jews in the wilderness, the Jews will turn back to God. Two-thirds of the Jews will have been killed during the tribulation. . . .[1]

This description of the apocalyptic extermination of the Jewish people is not the work of a Muslim pamphleteer. It appears on an American Internet site, frequently visited by Protestant millenarians. Earlier we saw that paranoid obsessions about UFOs, Freemasons, and even Ninja Turtles are shared by Christian and Islamic messianics alike. But no Muslim authority has gone as far as the late Reverend Jerry Falwell concerning the Antichrist. In January 1999, the founder of the Moral Majority declared that the Antichrist was a Jewish male, living on earth today, and preparing to reveal himself within ten years.[2]

The Antichrist is so intimately associated with Protestantism in the United States that one of its leading historians hardly thinks it an exaggeration to describe the fascination with naming the Antichrist as "an American obsession."[3] As for the Beast, militant fundamentalists have successively ascribed its attributes to unsubjugated Indians, unassimilable Jews, scheming Catholics, and debauched Socialists; during the cold war, anti-Communist propagandists unhesitatingly identified the Soviet Union and Maoist China with the doomsday peoples Gog and Magog. In 1974 one of the first apocalyptic bestsellers appeared, John Walvoord's wildly popular *Armageddon, Oil, and the Middle East Crisis*.[4] However successful the works of Mansur Abdelhakim and Muhammad Isa Dawud may have been, the print runs of their messianic pamphlets fall far short of the tens of millions of copies sold in the United States by Walvoord's book and its ilk.[5]

A 2002 *Time/CNN* poll revealed that 59 percent of Americans believe that the events announced in the Book of Revelation, and particularly the battle of Armageddon, will, in fact, occur; 25 percent of those interviewed were convinced that the Bible foretold the catastrophe of 11 September.[6] The United Church of God, founded in 1995, subsequently broadcast an apocalyptic interpretation of al-Qaida and of the "global war against terror."[7] An American academic recently expressed alarm that "the idea that the 11 September attacks were planned by the White House is gaining ground" in the United States; and a growing number of Americans believe in the hidden control of events by "dark powers, for whom the occupants of the White House are nothing more than water-carriers."[8]

Conspiracy theories prospered in the Muslim world as well after the attacks against the World Trade Center and the Pentagon. Indeed, 11 September may well be a pivotal date in the comparative development of Christian and Islamic apocalypses. Messianic expectations in the United States, already aroused by the approach of the year 2000, were now deepened by fears that almighty America might be faltering in the face of a "clash of civilizations," and sharpened by the rise of more or less militant Islamophobia.[9] For Muslim millenarians, 11 September was but the first stage in an escalating spiral of horror and violence, in which the brutality of Western intervention in Afghanistan was to be exceeded only by the savagery of the invasion of Iraq. America, the implacable and satanic enemy of Islam, had brought war to the very lands of apocalyptic conflict—confirming the imminence of the Great Battle.

In retrospect, the designation of Christian Zionism as Islam's chief adversary can be seen as the decisive move in placing present-day conflicts in eschatological perspective. Not only did the profound trauma of the occupation of Iraq, the devastation of its cities, and the plunder of its heritage come to overshadow the interminable Palestinian tragedy by reason of their dramatic intensity; they also allowed Islamist ideologues to reduce Jewish Zionism to a localized messianic phenomenon whose capacity for harm remains limited, even if no compromise with Israel is conceivable. The menace of Christian Zionism, on the other hand, as the modern and American incarnation of the Antichrist, bent on the destruction of Islam, is of an entirely different order of magnitude. The United States are the embodiment of Evil, which the forces of an unprecedented jihad, announced by a tide of black banners rising in the east, will eventually succeed in crushing once and for all. For the moment, the certainty of this ultimate victory must relieve the darkness of blasphemous oppression.

Christian and Muslim enthusiasts of apocalypse all agree on one fundamental thing, namely, the extinction of the Jewish people following Jesus's reappearance on earth. A part of their race will perish in the awful din of Armageddon and the survivors will convert to the religion of the conqueror—Islam in the view of some, Christianity in the view of others.[10] This shared interest in the physical and spiritual annihilation of Judaism introduces a curious complicity between the two millenarianisms, which in every other respect are resolutely opposed to each other. It is for this reason that the hateful message of *The Protocols of the Elders of Zion* and other Western anti-Semitic pamphlets migrates from one paranoid universe to the other and back again. Transfigured by revanchist authors on both sides of the apocalyptic divide, it ends up casting a long shadow over a single ominous panorama.

The willingness of Islamic messianism to incorporate aspects of the other Abrahamic religions manifests itself not only in the rabid recycling of Western anti-Semitism. It is also found in the unrestrained importation of Judeo-Christian apocalypses, whether from the Old Testament prophecies of Isaiah, Ezekiel, and Daniel or from the revelation of John in the New Testament. Islam feels itself justified in adopting texts whose true meaning is denied to Christians—a blinkered people of the Book who are one revelation short of the truth available to Muslims. But the plundering of infidel sources responds also to a dogmatic imperative, for there are troubling gaps in the orthodox narrative that must be filled. Reliance on doubtful hadiths cannot provide Islam with the grand millenarian work it requires. This task can only be completed by borrowing from Judeo-Christian tradition.

Another paradoxical feature of the Muslim vision of the end of the world has to do with the central place it grants to two figures who are absent from the Qur'an, the Antichrist and the Mahdi. The Beast, on the other hand, who is mentioned in the Qur'an, practically disappears from the messianic horizon of present-day Islam; or, rather, it has given way to the Beast of Christian apocalypses. The rod of Moses and the seal of Solomon no longer figure among its emblems. They have been discarded as obsolete, notwithstanding their evident dramaturgic power, and replaced by satanic horns, which, though they help to account for the Beast's ravenous appetite for destruction, also call attention to its Christian origins.

Despite the pretense of scriptural rigor, this hybrid apocalypse is a fragile construction that depends on a cynical and opportunistic attitude toward religious doctrine in both publishing and politics: publishers of mass-market apocalyptic literature, in multiplying titles whose mutually inconsistent claims about the last times show a striking indifference to the proper citation of classical sources, betray their own utter lack of conviction; and ambitious militia leaders, such as Muqtada al-Sadr in Iraq and Hasan Nasrallah in Lebanon, consciously exploit popular messianic feeling in order to assert their authority at the expense of the Shi'i clerical establishment, without allowing themselves to fall captive to apocalyptic rhetoric.

The producers, distributors, and manipulators of this very widely read literature serve as trustees of an immense fund of symbolic capital that in recent times has nonetheless only sparingly been put to use. It is very unlikely that Juhayman al-'Utaybi believed in the messianic pretensions of his brother-in-law, and in any case he was himself able to galvanize the insurgents of Mecca in the fall of 1979 even after the death of the self-proclaimed Mahdi. This relative indifference to the possibilities of apocalyptic persuasion is fairly new. Without going back even as far as the black banners of Abu Muslim in the eighteenth century, one notes the mark left on Islamic history by revolutionary movements that more or less skillfully took advantage of a millenarian dynamic. For the moment, only the Iraqi militia known as the Supporters of the Imam Mahdi has actively sought to translate the rise of eschatological anxiety into political action. Yet one day a larger and more resourceful group, eager (like Abu Musab al-Suri) to tap the energy of the "masses" as a way of achieving superiority over rival formations, may be strongly tempted to resort to the messianic gambit. An appeal to the imminence of apocalypse would provide it with an instrument of recruitment, a framework for interpreting future developments, and a way of refashioning and consolidating its own identity. In combination, these things could have far-reaching and deadly consequences.

The intrinsic opportunism of contemporary apocalyptic accounts brings them into closer contact with the mission of global jihad promoted by al-Qaida, which itself appeared on the cusp of two millenniums. Breaking with fourteen centuries of Islamic tradition, bin Laden's organization gave old ideas a new meaning—foremost among them the idea of jihad—in order to justify novel methods of depredation and domination. In much the same way, contemporary messianism rejects the claims of orthodoxy, preserving their outward forms while recasting their ultimate purpose. Just as jihad for its own sake risks dragging the world into the infernos of apocalypse, universal jihad—the struggle of all against all—assumes its place in the world-ending cycle of fitna, that age of strife and tribulation that Muhammad had prophesied for his community. And so it shall be, from the darkness of so much terrible violence, that the light of divine reconquest will soon shine forth.

It is here that the Muslim apocalyptic account cloaks itself in the traditions of Islam and diverges from its Christian counterpart. For rivers of blood will flow long before the colossal battles on the plain of Acre and on the slopes of Megiddo. In preparation for the ultimate confrontation between faith and impiety, the lands of Islam themselves must be purified not only of unjust governors and corrupt 'ulama, but also of depraved men and unchaste women. The sword of vengeance will fall upon hypocrites before being turned against infidels. Even then, the Sufyani and other champions of a warped conception of Islam will intervene to postpone the Last Hour; and since one believer's apocalypse is seldom shared by his neighbor, Sunnis and Shi'a are unlikely to obey the same Mahdi.

One last parallel between the heralds of global jihad and the harbingers of apocalypse suggests itself. Just as al-Qaida, under the cover of struggle against America, is a machine of war against Islam itself, so too radical millenarianism, while assailing the transatlantic Antichrist, has erected a scaffold on which to exact vengeance upon wayward Muslims. In the name of combat against a remote and inaccessible enemy, it is the close friend and neighbor who are to be punished instead. Truly the end of times is already at hand when brothers kill one another.

Notes

1. ARCHEOLOGY OF THE END OF THE WORLD

1. See *Encyclopédie de l'Islam*, 8 vols. plus supplements and index (Leiden: Brill/Paris: G.-P. Maisonneuve et Larose, 1960–89), 1:950. This "sign of prophecy" was a hairy mole on Muhammad's left shoulder blade. The same type of physical indication was attributed to various messianic figures of Islam, among them Tariq ibn Zyad in Andalusian mysticism; see Mercedes García-Arenal, *Messianism and Puritanical Reform: Mahdīs of the Muslim West*, trans. Martin Beagles (Leiden: Brill, 2006), 81.

2. See *Encyclopédie de l'Islam*, 1:950. In fact, the Apocalypse of Bahira is apocryphal, having been composed in 820; see García-Arenal, *Messianism and Puritanical Reform*, 12.

3. The Qur'an, 36:46, 49–54. [This quotation, and all the ones following, are taken from the fluent new English translation by M.A.S. Abdel Haleem, rev. ed. (Oxford: Oxford University Press, 2005).—Trans.]

4. Ibid., 25:22–26.

5. Ibid., 4:171. [Here the author has substituted for the "Jesus" and "Mary" of the English translation the Arabic transcription of these two names.—Trans.]

6. Ibid., 43:63. [The pronoun *hu*, construed here as referring to Jesus, can also be considered to signify the Qur'an itself; see Haleem's gloss at page 319 of the Oxford edition.—Trans.]

7. Ibid., 43:61–62.

8. Ibid., 54:1–3, 44:10–11, 27:82, 34:14. Jinns—unseen beings ranking below angels, able to assume human or animal form and capable of redirecting the course of human affairs, whether for good or for evil—were a familiar

presence in Islam: Allah "created mankind out of dried clay, like pottery, and the jinn out of smokeless fire" (ibid., 55:14–15).

9. Ibid., 84:1–5, 69:13–16.

10. Ibid., 70:8–9, 52:9–10, 50:44, 21:104, 81:1–2, 81:6. Compare this vision of apocalypse with the image in the Book of Revelation (6:14): "The sky vanished like a scroll that is rolled up, and every mountain and island was removed from its place."

11. Ibid., 18:94.

12. The Two-Horned One is also associated with a Himyarite monarch of pre-Islamic Yemen, as well as a Persian (probably Achaemenid) emperor; see Jane Dammen McAuliffe, ed., *Encyclopedia of the Qur'ān,* 6 vols. (Leiden: Brill, 2001–6), 1:61. [The rendering "Possessor of the Two Horns" is sometimes preferred in connection with Alexander, who ruled both Greece and Persia.—Trans.]

13. The Book of Ezekiel (usually transcribed in Arabic as *Hizqīl,* but also as *Dhū al-kifl)* mentions a king of Magog named Gog—this before Christian eschatology transformed Gog and Magog into two distinct and evil races; see ibid., 2:331. The theme of peoples confined to the margins of the civilized world who threaten to overrun and destroy it permeates a whole tradition of Christian writing; it is memorialized still today, though as an outgrowth of native pagan traditions, in the topography of England, where the Gog Magog Hills rise to the south of Cambridge, and in the Lord Mayor's Show, an annual procession in which the giants Gog and Magog are honored as guardians of the City of London.

14. The Qur'an, 18:98–101.

15. The two standard works on this "Great Dissension" are Henri Laoust, *Les schismes dans l'Islam: Introduction à une étude de la religion musulmane* (Paris: Payot, 1965), and Hichem Djait, *La grande discorde: Religion et politique dans l'Islam des origines* (Paris: Gallimard, 1989). I have related the history of this time of troubles from the perspective of jihad in an earlier book; see *Les frontières du jihad* (Paris: Fayard, 2006), 25–32. [The Arabic term *al-fitna* (pl. *fitan*) has the meaning in the Qur'an of a trial, of a challenge to be endured that serves to separate those who act rightly from those who do not. With reference to the social and political upheavals of the early years of Islam in the works of Burkhari and other traditionists, however, it carries instead the sense of rebellion, turmoil, or strife; see note 28 below.—Trans.]

16. *Encyclopédie de l'Islam,* 5:1221.

17. Muhammad ibn Jarir al-Tabari, *Les Omeyyades,* trans. Herman Zotenberg (Paris: Sindbad, 1983), 56–57.

18. *Encyclopédie de l'Islam,* 4:333.

19. Ibid, 5:1222.

20. See Heinz Halm, *Le chiisme,* trans. Hubert Hougue (Paris: Presses Universitaires de France, 1995), 25; also Moshe Sharon, *Black Banners from the East* (Jerusalem: Magnes Press, 1983), 117, and James Darmesteter, *Le Mahdi: Depuis les origines de l'Islam jusqu'à nos jours* (Paris: Ernest Leroux, 1885), 35.

21. *Encyclopédie de l'Islam,* 5:1223–24.

22. Ibid., 5:537, 1221.

23. Ibid., 8:676.

24. Ibid., 12:755. [The general initially dispatched by the Sufyani caliph Yazid I to put down the insurrection, Muslim ibn ʿUkba, died at the Battle of Harra in August 683 and was succeeded by al-Husayn ibn Numayr, who instituted the siege against Mecca.—Trans.]

25. The eminent Oxford Islamicist Wilferd Madelung has noted that most of the traditions linked to the Mahdi emanated from Iraq (Kufa and Basra), whereas prophecies concerning the Sufyani appeared in Syria (mainly at Homs) and in Egypt; see "The Sufyani between Tradition and History," *Studia Islamica* 53 (1986): 16.

26. A hadith is considered "correct" or "genuine" *(sahīh)* when it satisfies four conditions: continuity of the chain of transmission, uprightness of the person reporting a tradition, soundness of the reporter's authority for the tradition, and the absence of anomaly. If one or more of these conditions fails to be met, the hadith may be considered merely good *(hasan)* or plainly weak *(daʾif)*. A hadith endorsed by either Bukhari or Muslim is considered to enjoy the first of seven degrees of authenticity. See Mahboub Moussaoui, *Initiation aux sciences du hadith* (Paris: Sabil, 2003).

27. Muhammad ibn Ismaʿil al-Bukhari, *Les traditions islamiques,* trans. Octave Houdas, 4 vols. (Paris: Maisonneuve, 1977), 4:480, 485. All subsequent quotations from Bukhari's *Sahīh* are likewise taken from book 92 ("Dissension").

28. Ibid., 4:485, 477. Houdas renders *fitan* here as "passions," for which I have preferred "dissension." [Again, the sense of multiple instances of discord is implied in this context.—Trans.]

29. Ibid., 4:481, 478.

30. Ibid., 4:493. It is tempting to read the final sentence of this passage in the light of the Book of Revelation (9:6): "And in those days men will seek death and will not find it; they will long to die, and death will fly from them."

31. Bukhari, *Les traditions islamiques,* 4:494–95.

32. Ibid., 4:492. On the confusion in later accounts between this view of the "fire in Hijaz" as an apocalyptic event and the medieval record of an actual fire in the thirteenth century, see chapter 7, note 49 below.

33. Ibid., 4:477. See also the similar hadith at 4:496.

34. Abu al-Husayn Muslim, *Sahīh,* 5 vols. (Beirut: Dar Ahya al-Turath al-Arabi, 1982), 4:2226.

35. Ibid., 4:2250, 2266, 2267. The appearance of the Antichrist in Khurasan had earlier figured in the Christian Apocalypse of Ephrem (306–373 C.E.); see McAuliffe, ed., *Encyclopedia of the Qurʾān,* 1:110.

36. Muslim, *Sahīh,* 4:2257.

37. Ibid., 4:2258, 2222, 2266.

38. Ibid., 4:2221.

39. Ibid. Chapter 18 of the Qurʾan (verses 9–26) Islamizes the Christian myth of the Seven Sleepers, first promulgated in the fifth century by the bishop of Ephesus. Now called the "Companions of the Cave," the protagonists of the Qurʾanic account awaken after 309 years, fortified by an unshakable faith in Allah. This episode, dissociated from any apocalyptic context, was henceforth invoked by sailors confronted with the risk of shipwreck or, more generally, in the face of calamity.

40. Ibid., 4:2253.

41. *Encyclopédie de l'Islam*, 5:806.

42. Muslim, *Sahīh*, 4:2239.

43. *Gharqad* seems to be an untranslatable term, but it is identified in some dictionaries with another thorny bush, *al-'awsaj (Lycium arabicum)*.

44. *Encyclopédie de l'Islam*, 10:715–17.

45. Muslim, *Sahīh*, 4:2254.

46. Muslim, *Sahīh*, 4:2254. The "insects" mentioned in the first sentence are a kind of worm *(naghaf,* plural of *naghfa)*, a sometimes deadly parasite found in sheep and other bovid animals.

47. Ibid., 4:2252, 2253.

48. Ibid., 4:2261–64. This hadith is numbered 2,942 in the *Sahīh,* and 119 in the Book of Strife and Portents of the Hour.

49. The anthropologist Emma Aubin-Boltanski reports a tribal account of the emigration of the Tamimi clan, a branch of the Banū Lakhim, some going from Yemen to Iraq, others to Palestine. According to a much later descendant, Tamim al-Dari "wanted to be a priest [and] studied the true Torah"; and it was this theological background that enabled him immediately to recognize Muhammad's prophetic vocation. See Aubin-Boltanski, *Prophètes, héros et ancêtres* (Paris: École des Hautes Études en Sciences Sociales, 2004), 304–5.

50. *Encyclopédie de l'Islam*, 10:189.

51. The apparent contradiction between the relatively slight apocalyptic content of the Qur'an and the much more frequent references to the end of the world in the Islamic tradition literature led the French scholar Paul Casanova to advance the daring hypothesis that the Qur'an had been purged of its apocalyptic elements. Such references, he suggests, "were in the original [version of the] Qur'an [but] were arbitrarily eliminated from it by later recensions." See Paul Casanova, *Mohammed et la fin du monde: Étude sur l'Islam primitif,* 2 vols. (Paris: Geuthner, 1911–24), 1:69.

52. See in this connection the quite remarkable work by Jean-Robert Armogathe, *L'Antéchrist à l'âge classique: Exégèse et politique* (Paris: Mille et Une Nuits, 2005), 49–53; also Robert C. Fuller, *Naming the Antichrist: The History of an American Obsession* (New York: Oxford University Press, 1995), 14–32. Fuller argues that John's epistles and the Book of Revelation (also known as the Revelation of St. John the Divine) were due to different authors, themselves distinct from the evangelist. On Tertullian and Origen, see Romolo Gobbi, *Les enfants de l'Apocalypse: Histoire d'un mythe des origines à nos jours,* trans. Laura Brondino (Paris: Publisud, 2007), 17–21.

53. See Jorge Aguade, "La importancia del *Kitāb al-fitan*," in *Actas de las jornadas de cultura arabe e islamica* (Madrid: Instituto Hispano-Arabe de Cultura, 1981), 349–52.

54. See *Encyclopédie de l'Islam*, 8:675.

55. See ibid., 2:78.

56. Quoted in Jalal al-din al-Suyuti, *La descente de Jésus et l'apparition de l'Antéchrist,* ed. and trans. A. Desmazières, 2nd ed. (Lyon: Alburda, 2002), 140.

57. *Encyclopédie de l'Islam*, 1:117.

58. Quoted in ibid., 5:1222. Ibn Khaldun, among others, demonstrated the fragile character of this hadith's chain of transmission in his *Kitāb al-'ibar;* see 'Abd al-Rahman ibn Khaldun, *Le livre des exemples,* trans. Abdessalam Cheddadi, vol. 1 (Paris: Gallimard, 2002), 637. It is in the most sacred space of Mecca—between the eastern corner of the Ka'ba, site of the Black Stone (reputed to have been deposited in the original sanctuary by Adam himself), and the Station where Abraham contemplated the Black Stone, brought to him by the angel Gabriel—that, according to this tradition, the oath of allegiance will be administered to the Mahdi.

59. This hadith is numbered 4,282 in Abu Dawud's recension; see his *Kitāb al-Sunan,* 5 vols. (Istanbul: Dar Sahnun, 1992), 4:473.

60. See *Encyclopédie de l'Islam,* 10:15.

61. Ibid., 2:72.

62. Muhammad ibn Hibban, *Al-Ihsān bī-tartīb Sahīh Ibn Hibbān,* 10 vols. (Beirut: Dar al-Kutub al-Ilmiyya, 1987), 8:276. Ibn Hibban refers to the Byzantines as *Banū al-Asfar,* literally "the sons [or tribe] of the Yellow One"—a term earlier employed in this sense by Bukhari, among others, who styled the Byzantine emperor Heraclius as "emir of the Banū al-Asfar"; see Bukhari, *Les traditions islamiques,* 2:330, 3:283. The expression "Banū al-Asfar" later came to designate Europeans more generally; see *Encyclopédie de l'Islam,* 1:708–9.

63. See ibid., Ibn Hibban, *Sahīh,* 8:279–80, 283.

64. Quoted in Henry Corbin, *Histoire de la philosophie islamique,* rev. ed. (Paris: Gallimard, 1986), 83.

65. See Halm, *Le chiisme,* 42.

66. Quoted in Corbin, *Histoire de la philosophie islamique,* 109.

67. See Halm, *Le chiisme,* 46, 47.

68. See Mohammad Ali Amir-Moezzi, *Le guide divin dans le shi'isme originel* (Paris: Verdier, 1992), 261, 262.

69. See Henry Corbin, *L'Imam caché* (Paris: L'Herne, 2003), 37.

70. Quoted in Corbin, *Histoire de la philosophie islamique,* 111. This hadith, reported by Abu Dawud (see pages 21–22 above), nonetheless enjoyed immense popularity in Shi'i circles.

71. This letter is reproduced in the Arabic original by several authors; see, for example, Naim Qassim, *Al-Mahdī al-mukhaliss* (Beirut: Dar al-Hadi, 2007), 135.

72. The details that follow are taken from Shaykh al-Mufid, *Kitāb al-Irshād: The Book of Guidance into the Lives of the Twelve Imams,* trans. I.K.A. Howard (London: Balagha Books, 1981), 541–54.

73. Ibid., 542, 544.

74. Ibid., 548. Note Shaykh Mufid's use of the term *shi'a,* which designates both the partisans of the Mahdi and the partisans of 'Ali (that is, the Shi'a).

75. Ibid., 549, 552–54.

76. See Amir-Moezzi, *Le guide divin dans le shi'isme originel,* 286.

77. "The first [Call] will be issued by the archangel Gabriel in the name of the Imam-Mahdi and his father. In particular, he will call out: 'Know that the truth is with 'Ali and his partisans.' Each people will hear this call in its own language, and even the Virgin will hear it within her house"; quoted in Sayyed

Muhammad Redhâ al-Mutallaq, *En attendant le Mahdi,* ed. and trans. Abbas Ahmad Al-Bostani (Montreal: La Cité du Savoir, 2005), 19.

78. "Pure Soul" translates the Arabic phrase *al-nafs al-zakiyya.* For this reason his assassination has sometimes been identified with the 'Abbassid suppression in 762 of the revolt led by Muhammad ibn Abdallah, who was known by the same epithet. This is only one more illustration of the porousness of the boundary separating apocalyptic and revolutionary impulses, more or less validated by the custodians of prophetic tradition. The Pure Soul's brother, Idris ibn Abdallah, subsequently fled to Morocco, where he established the Idrisid dynasty on a messianic basis in 789.

79. See Amir-Moezzi, *Le guide divin dans le shi'isme originel,* 286–87. These five signs are presented in a slightly different order (Yemeni, Sufyani, Pure Soul, Call, and Entombment) in Jassim M. Hussein, *The Occultation of the Twelfth Imam: A Historical Background* (London: Muhammadi Trust, 1982), 26–27.

80. On the number of these warrior angels, the Qur'an speaks of "a thousand angels" (8:9), whereas the sixth Shi'i imam gives the number of 313, the same as the number of combatants at Badr; see Amir-Moezzi, *Le guide divin dans le shi'isme originel,* 293.

81. Quoted in Moojam Momen, *An Introduction to Shi'i Islam: The History and Doctrines of Twelver Shi'ism* (New Haven: Yale University Press, 1985), 169.

82. See Amir-Moezzi, *Le guide divin dans le shi'isme originel,* 294–95.

83. See Mohammed Ali Amir-Moezzi, "Fin du temps et retour à l'origine (Aspects de l'imamologie duodécimaine VI)," *Revue d'études sur le monde musulman et méditerranéen,* special issue *(Mahdisme et millénarisme en Islam),* nos. 91–94 (2000): 59.

84. Amir-Moezzi, *Le guide divin dans le shi'isme originel,* 295.

85. See Momen, *An Introduction to Shi'i Islam,* 169.

2. GRAND MASTERS OF THE MEDIEVAL APOCALYPSE

1. Ibn al-'Arabi, *Le Mahdi et ses conseillers: Une sagesse pour la fin des temps,* trans. Tayeb Chouiref (Paris: Mille et Une Lumières, 2006), 30, 31–32, 44–45.

2. Ibid., 47. [The French translation has been slightly modified; Chouiref acknowledges the obscurity of the Arabic text, noting that these events can be interpreted as taking place over a period of six (rather than seven) months.—Trans.]

3. See ibid., 35, 45, 33, 34.

4. Ibid., 77–78, 38, 46.

5. Ibid., 46.

6. See ibid., 36.

7. See Henry Corbin, *Histoire de la philosophie islamique,* rev. ed. (Paris: Gallimard, 1986), 455, 407.

8. See *Encyclopédie de l'Islam,* 8 vols. plus supplements and index (Leiden: Brill/Paris: G.-P. Maisonneuve et Larose, 1960–89), 3:733; also Miguel Asín Palacios, *La escatologia musulmana en La Divina Comedia,* 4th ed. (Madrid: Hiperión, 1984).

9. See al-Qurtubi, *Mémento d'eschatologie musulmane,* trans. Latif ibn Omar (Beirut: Dar al-Kutub al-Ilmiyya, 2002), 165–66; the original Arabic text may be consulted in the edition of *Al-Tadhkira* published in Cairo by Dar al-Hadi in 1999.

10. Al-Qurtubi, *Mémento d'eschatologie musulmane,* 167, 169, 171–76.

11. Quoted in ibid., 167.

12. Ibid., 176.

13. Ibid., 181, 182–83.

14. Ibid., 184, 186. [This church, called *Kanīsat al-dhahab* in the Arabic, is most probably Hagia Sophia in Constantinople, though al-Qurtubi does not indicate its exact location.—Trans.]

15. Al-Qurtubi, *Le Faux Messie et le retour d'Issa,* trans. Abdelkarim Zentici (Lyon: Dar al-Muslim, 2003), 57. The vehemence of the hadith authenticated by Muslim (see page 17 above) is accentuated here. [The French volume cited translates a section of the *Tadhkira* called "Al-Masīh al-Dajjāl wa nuzūl 'Issā ibn Mariam" (The False Messiah and the Return of Jesus, Son of Mary).—Trans.]

16. Al-Qurtubi, *Mémento d'eschatologie musulmane,* 197, 203, 168.

17. Ibn Kathir, *Les signes du Jour Dernier: Dans le Coran et la Sunna,* trans. Maha Kaddoura (Paris: Al-Bustane, 2005), 21.

18. Ibn al-'Arabi, *La profession de foi,* trans. Roger Deladrière (Paris: Sindbad, 1985), 81; for Ibn 'Arabi's commentary on the division into seventy-three sects, see 253–55.

19. Ibn Kathir, *Les signes du Jour Dernier,* 22, 35, 36.

20. For Bukhari, see page 15 above; for Muslim, see his *Sahīh,* 4:2220.

21. Ibn Kathir, *Les signes du Jour Dernier,* 40.

22. Ibid., 42.

23. Ibid., 51.

24. See al-Qurtubi, *Mémento d'eschatologie musulmane,* 186.

25. Ibn Kathir, *Les signes du Jour Dernier,* 90–91.

26. Ibid., 91.

27. Ibid., 81.

28. Ibid., 92.

29. Ibn Kathir, *L'exégèse du Coran,* trans. Harkat Abdou, 4 vols. (Beirut: Dar al-Kutub al-Ilmiyya, 2000), 3:816.

30. Ibn Kathir, *Les signes du Jour Dernier,* 98.

31. Ibid. Ibn Kathir embroiders here on a sibylline hadith approved by Muslim: "Dhu'l-Suwayqatayn the Abyssinian will destroy the house of Allah" (see Muslim, *Sahīh,* 4: 2232).

32. Ibn Kathir, *Les signes du Jour Dernier,* 99.

33. Ibid., 65.

34. Ibn Kathir, *L'exégèse du Coran,* 1164.

35. Ibn Khaldun, *Le livre des exemples,* trans. Abdessalam Cheddadi, vol. 1 (Paris: Gallimard, 2002), 906–7.

36. Ibid., 652.

37. Ibid., 653.

38. See ibid., 662; also page 10 above.

39. Ibid., 670.

40. Ibid., 672, 673, 675, 678.
41. Ibid., 413.
42. Ibid., 311, 310, 301.
43. E.M. Sartain, *Jalāl al-Dīn al-Suyūtī: Biography and Background* (Cambridge: Cambridge University Press, 1975), 24; see also Jalal al-Din al-Suyuti, *La descente de Jésus et l'apparition de l'Antéchrist,* ed. and trans. A. Desmazières, 2nd ed. (Lyon: Alburda, 2002), 7.
44. See al-Suyuti, *La descente de Jésus,* 13.
45. See Sartain, *Jalāl al-Dīn al-Suyūtī,* 50–52.
46. See ibid., 71.
47. See al-Suyuti, *La descente de Jésus,* 18.
48. Jalal al-Din al-Suyuti, *Les Dires du Prophète,* trans. François Cadoz (Paris, 1852); quoted in Alfred Bel, *L'Islam mystique* (Paris: Imprimerie Jules Carbonel, 1928; reprinted Paris: Maisonneuve, 1988), 96.
49. Didier Ali Hamoneau has put the number of al-Suyuti's works at five hundred sixty; see Hamoneau's introduction to al-Suyuti, *Le retour de Jésus,* trans. Mohammed Aoun (Paris: Iqraa, 2000), 9.
50. For a list of contemporary Arabic editions of this work, see al-Suyuti, *La descente de Jésus,* 156.
51. Ibid., 88.
52. Ibid., 83.
53. Ibid., 36.
54. Ibid., 68, 67; see also al-Suyuti, *Le retour de Jésus,* 73–74.
55. Al-Suyuti, *Le retour de Jésus,* 75.
56. Al-Suyuti, *La descente de Jésus,* 150, 36, 35.
57. Quoted in ibid., 38.
58. "The texts show," al-Suyuti says in *Al-Hāwī lil-fatāwī,* "that the [Muslim] community will last longer than a thousand years, but that it will not last more than five hundred years beyond that, for it is reported in various ways that the term of earthly life is seven thousand years and that the Prophet was sent at the end of the sixth millennium"; quoted in Youssef al-Wabil, *Les signes de la fin des temps* (Brussels: Al-Hadith, 2006), 60. [The Islamic reckoning of time is based upon a pure lunar cycle, so that thirty-three Muslim years are roughly equivalent to thirty-two Christian ones; see Bonnie Blackburn and Leofranc Holford-Strevens, *The Oxford Companion to the Year: An Exploration of Calendar Customs and Time Reckoning* (Oxford: Oxford University Press, 1999), 731–35.—Trans.]
59. Timothy R. Furnish has proposed the term "centennialism" to refer to the obsession of Islamic messianic movements with the turn of centuries; see *Holiest Wars: Islamic Mahdis, Their Jihads, and Osama bin Laden* (Westport: Praeger, 2005), 7.
60. See David Cook, *Contemporary Muslim Apocalyptic Literature* (Syracuse, N.Y.: Syracuse University Press, 2005), 90. [A.H. stands for *anno Hegirae* (year of the Hegira), which is to say the time elapsed since 622 C.E.—Trans.]
61. See Jean-Robert Armogathe, *L'Antéchrist à l'âge classique: Exégèse et politique* (Paris: Mille et Une Nuits, 2005), 92, 101.

3. AVATARS OF THE MAHDI

1. *Encyclopédie de l'Islam,* 8 vols. plus supplements and index (Leiden: Brill/ Paris: G.-P. Maisonneuve et Larose, 1960–1989), 2:465; see also Heinz Halm, *Le chiisme,* trans. Hubert Hougue (Paris: Presses Universitaires de France, 1995), 182.

2. See *Encyclopédie de l'Islam,* 4:688.

3. See ibid., 4:689.

4. The Mahdi's Sunni adversaries showed less respect, calling him 'Ubayd Allah (or Ubaydullah)—'Ubayd being the familiar diminutive of 'Abd.

5. See Janine and Dominique Sourdel, *Dictionnaire historique de l'Islam* (Paris: Presses Universitaires de France, 2004), 286; also Halm, *Le chiisme,* 174–75.

6. Maxime Rodinson, preface to Bernard Lewis, *Les assassins: Terrorisme et politique dans l'Islam médiéval,* trans. Annick Pélissier (Brussels: Complexe, 1982), 22.

7. See Bernard Lewis, *The Assassins: A Radical Sect in Islam* (London: Weidenfeld and Nicolson, 1967), 68.

8. Ibid., 70.

9. Ibid., 72–73; see also Farhad Daftary, *The Ismāʿīlīs: Their History and Doctrines* (Cambridge: Cambridge University Press, 1990), 386–87.

10. Quoted in Halm, *Le chiisme,* 73. As it happens, Sunni tradition also validated this hadith; see Yusuf al-Wabil, *Les signes de la fin des temps* (Brussels: Al-Hadith, 2006), 123.

11. Henry Corbin, *L'histoire de la philosophie islamique,* rev. ed. (Paris: Gallimard, 1986), 437.

12. See ibid., 446. Tusi's *Rawdat al-taslīm* is available in French as *La convocation d'Alamut: Somme de philosophie Ismaélienne,* trans. Christian Jambet (Paris: Verdier/UNESCO, 1996).

13. Quoted in Halm, *Le chiisme,* 75.

14. See ibid., 74.

15. See Sourdel and Sourdel, *Dictionnaire historique de l'Islam,* 385.

16. Ibn Battuta, *Voyages et périples choisis,* trans. Paule Charles-Dominique (Paris: Gallimard, 1992), 106–7. For the sake of clarity I have replaced "God" by "Allah" and expressly indicated that the *'asr* and *maghrib* prayers are those of afternoon and evening (sunset).

17. The geographer Yaqut cites the case, among others, of the Iranian town of Kashan; quoted in Halm, *Le chiisme,* 226. See also Ibn Battuta, *Voyages et périples choisis,* 87.

18. See *Encyclopédie de l'Islam,* 3:619.

19. Sourdel and Sourdel, *Dictionnaire historique de l'Islam,* 387.

20. *Encyclopédie de l'Islam,* 3:620.

21. See ibid. [The year of Fazlallah's death has been a subject of much dispute, but it is now believed that dates of 1401 or 1403 are based on erroneous sources.—Trans.]

22. See Halm, *Le chiisme,* 90.

23. The Bektashi brotherhood also haltingly incorporated elements of Qalandarism, another messianic offshoot of Sufism. The revolutionary impulses of this sect of wandering dervishes led one of its members in 1492 to make an assassination attempt against the Ottoman sultan Bayazid II, claiming himself to be the Mahdi; see Julian Baldick, "Les Qalenderis," in Alexandre Popovic and Gilles Veinstein, eds., *Les voies d'Allah: Les ordres mystiques dans l'Islam des origines à aujourd'hui* (Paris: Fayard, 1996), 502.

24. Orhan Pamuk, *The Black Book,* trans. Maureen Freely (New York: Vintage, 2006), 296–99, 392.

25. See ibid., 79–82.

26. See Halm, *Le chiisme,* 90; also Moojan Momen, *An Introduction to Shi'i Islam: The History and Doctrines of Twelver Shi'ism* (New Haven: Yale University Press, 1985), 102.

27. See *Encyclopédie de l'Islam,* 7:672.

28. See Corbin, *L'histoire de la philosophie islamique,* 421, and Halm, *Le chiisme,* 93.

29. See *Encyclopédie de l'Islam,* 8:794, and Halm, *Le chiisme,* 94.

30. See Halm, *Le chiisme,* 93.

31. See ibid., 101.

32. This hadith is quoted, for example, in Corbin, *L'histoire de la philosophie islamique,* 111; see also pages 21–22, 25 above.

33. See Tilman Nagel, "Le Mahdisme d'Ibn Toumert et d'Ibn Qasi: Une analyse phénoménologique," *Revue d'études du monde musulman et de la Méditerranée,* nos. 91–94 (2000): 128.

34. See Maribel Fierro, "Le Mahdi Ibn Toumert et al-Andalus," *Revue d'études du monde musulman et de la Méditerranée,* nos. 91–94 (2000): 110.

35. Quoted in Michael Brett, "Le Mahdi dans le Maghreb médiéval," *Revue d'études du monde musulman et de la Méditerranée,* nos. 91–94 (2000): 101.

36. See Fierro, "Le Mahdi Ibn Toumert et al-Andalus," 108.

37. See García-Arenal, *Messianism and Puritanical Reform,* 198–99.

38. See Mercedes García-Arenal, "Imam et Mahdi," *Revue d'études du monde musulman et de la Méditerranée,* nos. 91–94 (2000): 166.

39. See Houari Touati, "L'arbre du prophète," *Revue d'études du monde musulman et de la Méditerranée,* nos. 91–94 (2000): 146.

40. See Julia Clancy-Smith, "La révolte de Bû Ziyân en Algérie," *Revue d'études du monde musulman et de la Méditerranée,* nos. 91–94 (2000): 189.

41. Ibid., 194, 199.

42. See P. M. Holt, *The Mahdist State in the Sudan, 1881–1898: A Study of Its Origins, Development, and Overthrow* (Oxford: Clarendon Press, 1958), 38–40.

43. See Nicola A. Ziadeh, *Sanūsīya: A Study of a Revivalist Movement in Islam* (Leiden: Brill, 1958), 54.

44. See ibid., 52; also Rudolf C. Slatin, *Fire and Sword in the Sudan: A Personal Narrative of Fighting and Serving the Dervishes,* trans. Francis R. Wingate (London: Edward Arnold, 1896), 231.

45. See Holt, *The Mahdist State in the Sudan,* 73.

46. James Darmesteter, *Le Mahdi: Depuis les origines de l'Islam jusqu'à nos jours* (Paris: Ernest Leroux, 1885), 93, 99.

47. Slatin, *Fire and Sword in the Sudan,* 230.

48. See ibid., 369.

49. See also Ibn Khaldun's tribute to the integrity of Mahdi Ibn Tumart in *Le livre des exemples,* trans. Abdessalam Cheddadi, vol. 1 (Paris: Gallimard, 2002), 37.

4. DAWN OF THE FIFTEENTH CENTURY OF ISLAM

1. Shaykh Shaltut's opinion is translated in C.C. Adams, "A Fatwa on the 'Ascension of Jesus,'" *Moslem World* 34 (1944): 215. With regard to the recurrent polemic over the role of the two converted Jews, Ka'ab al-Akhbar and Wahb ibn Munabbih, in the "transmission" of hadiths, see Mohammed Ali Amir-Moezzi, ed., *Dictionnaire du Coran* (Paris: Robert Laffont, 2007), 430–32.

2. Shaykh Shaltut's biographer remarks that he was "admired for the boldness of certain of his *fatwās,*" notably the one on Jesus; see Kate Zebiri, *Mahmūd Shaltūt and Islamic Modernism* (Oxford: Clarendon Press, 1993), 14.

3. The standard work placing Qutb's thought in the context of Egyptian Islamism remains Gilles Kepel, *Le Prophète et le Pharaon* (Paris: Seuil, 1993). [Available in English as *Muslim Extremism: The Prophet and the Pharaoh,* trans. Jon Rothschild (Berkeley: University of California Press, 2003)—Trans.]

4. Born in 1897, Shaykh Shaltut was rector of al-Azhar from 1958 until his death in 1963.

5. Sayyid Qutb, *Fī zilāl al-Qur'ān,* 6 vols. (Beirut: Dar al-Shuruq, 1982), 4:2294, 2293.

6. See Abbas Amanat, "The Resurgence of Apocalyptic in Modern Islam," in Bernard McGinn, John J. Collins, and Stephen J. Stein, eds., *The Encyclopedia of Apocalypticism,* 3 vols. (New York: Continuum, 1998), 3:245.

7. Quoted in Amir Taheri, *Khomeyni,* trans. Jacqueline Carnaud and Jacqueline Lahana (Paris: Balland, 1985), 235.

8. See Yann Richard, *L'Islam chi'ite: Croyances et idéologies* (Paris: Fayard, 1991), 139.

9. See Asghar Schirazi, *The Constitution of Iran: Politics and the State in the Islamic Republic,* trans. John O'Kane (London: I. B. Tauris, 1997), 22–25. [The principle of *vilayat-e faqih* is also known in English as "guardianship of the Islamic jurist."—Trans.]

10. See ibid., 31–32.

11. See ibid., 48.

12. Although in this case there were close to five million fewer voters: 15,758,956 persons cast ballots in the referendum of 2–3 December 1979, as against 20,439,908 in the one of 30–31 March the same year.

13. *Constitution de la république islamique d'Iran, 1979–1989,* ed. and trans. Michel Potocki (Paris: L'Harmattan, 2004), 45. [French text slightly modified, following the official English version.—Trans.]

14. Ibid., 49, 39.

15. Strictly speaking, the pilgrimage occurs from the eighth to the thirteenth day of *dhū al-hijja,* the tenth day—the occasion of the great 'Aid, or Feast of

the Sacrifice *('aid al-adhā)*, during which a lamb is offered up in memory of the animal killed by Abraham—being the most important.

16. Unquestionably the most diligent study of the 'Utaybi group is Thomas Hegghammer and Stéphane Lacroix, "Rejectionist Islamism in Saudi Arabia," *The International Journal of Middle East Studies* 39 (February 2007): 103–22. I have drawn freely from their account in the discussion that follows.

17. Quoted in Rifaat Sid Ahmel, *Rasā'il Juhaymān al-'Utaybi* (Cairo: Madbuli al-Sghir, 2004), 198.

18. For the traditions reported by Abu Dawud, see pages 21–22 above.

19. See Alexei Vassiliev, *The History of Saudi Arabia* (London: Saqi Books, 1998), 396; also Lawrence Wright, *The Looming Tower: Al-Qaeda and the Road to 9/11* (New York: Knopf, 2006), 91–92.

20. Abdulaziz ibn Baz, named head of the High Council of 'Ulama in 1971, from then on unofficially discharged the duties of the grand mufti of Saudi Arabia. This authority was formally granted to him in 1993.

21. Subsequently, having been appointed president of the Permanent Committee for Scholarly Research and Fatāwā in the meantime, Shaykh Ibn Baz ruled that no one could proclaim himself the Mahdi until the signs of the Hour had come to pass. The text of this fatwa can be found in Salaheddin Mahmud, *Al-Masīh al-Dajjāl wa Ya'jūj wa Ma'jūj* (Cairo: Dar al-Ghad al-Jadid, 2005), 82.

22. See Wright, *The Looming Tower,* 94.

23. See ibid., 92, 94.

24. Lawrence Wright's very careful inquiry, parts of which first appeared in the *New Yorker,* cites an unofficial tally of four thousand dead (ibid., 94). This seems unlikely, since only a few hundred rebels took part in the uprising.

25. See Iaroslav Trofimov, *The Siege of Mecca* (New York: Doubleday, 2007), 160–65. Trofimov, a correspondent for the *Wall Street Journal,* reports that Qahtani, convinced of his invincibility, threw back all the grenades thrown by the security forces except one, which exploded and killed him on or about 25 November, leaving 'Utaybi to galvanize the surviving insurgents. Trofimov also claims that two African-Americans took part in this messianic uprising; if in fact only one of them was killed in the fighting, as he states, then the other presumably survived (see ibid., 240–41).

5. PIONEERS OF THE CONTEMPORARY APOCALYPSE

1. See Jean-Pierre Filiu, *Les frontières du jihad* (Paris: Fayard, 2006), 109.

2. In 1988, Abdallah Azzam, the Arab "imam of jihad" in Afghanistan, wrote an article on this topic entitled "Afghanistan or Khurasan?" See Gilles Kepel, ed., *Al-Qaida dans le texte* (Paris: Presses Universitaires de France, 2005), 52.

3. The first edition of this book, which was finished in July 1980, did not appear for another thirteen years; see Muhammad Salama Jabir, *Ashrāt al-sā'a wa asrāruha* (Cairo: Dar al-Salam, 1993).

4. Ibid., 8, 11, 107.

5. See Muhammad Salama Jabir, *Tanabu'hāt Nustrādāmūs, naqd wa tahlīl* (Kuwait: Dar al-Sahwa, 1996).

6. Quoted in Adel Zaki, *Al-Mahdī* (Beirut: Dar Ibn Hazm, 2005), 305.

7. Quoted in ibid., 362. This hadith, reported by Ibn Maja, is not found in either of the two canonical collections due to Bukhari and Muslim, who characterize its reliability as "weak."

8. Said Hawwa, *Al-Islām* (Cairo: Dar al-Salam, 2005), 715.

9. See Abdelmohsen ibn Hamad al-Abbad, *Al-radd ʿalā man kazaba bi-al-ahādīth al-sahīha al-wārida fī al-Mahdī* (Medina: Matbaha Rashid, 1981).

10. See Abdelhalim Abderrahman Khodr, *Mafahīm jugrāfiyya fī al-qussass al-qurʾāni qissāt Dhū al-qarnayn* (Riyadh: Imam Muhammad ibn Saʿud Islamic University, 1981).

11. Quoted in Muhammad Kheir Ramadan Yusuf, *Dhū al-Qarnayn*, 3rd ed. (Beirut: Dar al-Shamia, 1999), 34. The first edition dates from 1982, and the second from 1988.

12. Ibid.

13. See the map in ibid., 221, which gives a rough indication of this barrier's location.

14. Said Ayyub, *Al-Masīh al-Dajjāl* (Cairo: Al-Fath lil-Aalam al-Arabi, 1987), 331.

15. See, for example, ibid., 10, 11, 311.

16. Ibid., 24.

17. Ibid., 6, 5, 7.

18. Ibid., 21.

19. Ibid., 44, 47, 52, 48.

20. See ibid., 47. Maurice Bucaille (1920–1998), a surgeon and the author of *La Bible, le Coran et la science* (Paris: Seghers, 1976), opposed what he claimed to be the factual inaccuracies of Christian texts to the alleged consistency of the Qurʾan with modern science—a thesis that made his book very popular among Muslim preachers. Libya saw to its distribution in francophone Africa through the Association Mondiale pour l'Appel *(daʾwa)* Islamique, having first arranged for its publication in New Delhi in 1991 by Idara Ishaaʾat-e-Diniyat.

21. Ayyub, *Al-Masīh al-Dajjāl*, 58.

22. Ibid., 55, 58, 55, 7, 60, 61.

23. Ibid., 36, 62.

24. Ibid., 129, 63, 125, 250, 143, 125.

25. Ibid., 115, 295, 178. Reagan's remark is from 1984. Four years earlier, during the 1980 presidential campaign, he had appeared as a guest on the televangelist Jim Bakker's program, carried by the PTL (Praise the Lord) Network, and stated, "Ours will be the generation that witnesses the battle of Armageddon." Rabbi Dan Cohn-Sherbok reckons that Reagan publicly expressed his belief in Armageddon on at least seven occasions; see *The Politics of Apocalypse: The History and Influence of Christian Zionism* (Oxford: Oneworld, 2006), 165.

26. Ayyub, *Al-Masīh al-Dajjāl*, 66, 180, 181.

27. Ibid., 136, 137, 174.

28. Ibid., 172, 222, 189, 195, 185, 192, 190.

29. Ibid., 198, 199. Said Ayyub seems to relish the image of crows and birds of prey tearing apart the flesh of the vanquished enemy, for he reverts to this point in some detail at page 205.

30. Ibid., 172, 214, 221.

31. Ibid., 230–32, 237, 257, 237.

32. Ibid., 255, 261, 240 (quoting hadith), 329.

33. William Guy Carr's *Pawns in the Game*, a conspiracist tract published in the United States (and elsewhere) by the Legion for the Survival of Freedom, appeared in 1958.

34. Ayyub, *Al-Masīh al-Dajjāl*, 327, 323, 324. The expression "chosen people" is a staple of both Muslim and Christian millenarian rhetoric. The British historian Norman Cohn has shown that in Christian apocalyptic, during the Middle Ages, "the old phantasy of divine election was preserved and revitalised"; see *The Pursuit of the Millennium* (London: Secker and Warburg, 1957), 14.

35. Ayyub, *Al-Masīh al-Dajjāl*, 282.

36. The "narrow-mindedness of the Egyptian reading public" had earlier been identified as one of the structural weaknesses of the domestic market; see Yves Gonzáles-Quijano, *Les gens du livre: Édition et champ intellectuel dans l'Égypte républicaine* (Paris: Éditions du CNRS, 1998), 85, 131.

37. See Said Ayyub, *Aqīdat al-Masīh al-Dajjāl fī al-adyān* (Cairo: Dar al-Hadi, 1991), and *Ibtilā'āt al-umam* (Beirut: Dar al-Hadi, 1999). The latter book bears the subtitle, "Meditations on the Way of the Antichrist and of the Mahdi in Judaism, Christianity, and Islam."

38. Abdellatif Ashur, *Thalatha yantazaruhum al-'ālam* (Cairo: Maktabat al-Qur'an, 1987), 54.

39. Ashur, *Thalatha yantazaruhum al-'ālam*, and *Al-Masīkh al-Dajjāl, haqīqat la khyāl* (Cairo: Maktabat al-Qur'an, 1988). Note that Ashur employs here the term *masīkh*, meaning one who has been transformed (like a monster), rather than *masīh*, the annointed one (and therefore the Messiah, whether true or false). Even though the majority of Arab apocalyptic authors use the term *masīh*, the term *masīkh* is not uncommon—all the more since typing errors in poorly produced pamphlets may alone explain the almost random oscillations from one term to the other.

40. See Ashur, *Thalatha yantazaruhum al-'ālam*, 77.

41. See Abbas Amanat, "The Resurgence of Apocalyptic in Modern Islam," in Bernard McGinn, John J. Collins, and Stephen J. Stein, eds., *The Encyclopedia of Apocalypticism*, 3 vols. (New York: Continuum, 1998), 3:247. The Ahmadis initially considered Western missionaries as false messiahs, indeed as Antichrists; on this point see Jane Dammen McAuliffe, ed., *Encyclopedia of the Qur'ān*, 6 vols. (Leiden: Brill, 2001–2006), 3:139. There is a striking parallel between the anti-Baha'i campaigns, conducted in Iran beginning in 1956 by the Hojjatieh, with Khomeyni's approval (see page 71 above), and the campaigns led at the same moment against the Ahmadis in Pakistan under the moral guidance of Abu Ala Mawdudi, one of the great figures of modern Islamism. This anti-Ahmadi hatred endures still today, for example in Bangladesh, where an Islamist coalition has insisted since 2002 that they no longer be considered Muslims, but instead be stigmatized as "infidels."

42. See Muhammad Bayyumi, *'Alāmāt yawm al-qiyāma al-kubrā* (Cairo: Maktabat al-Imam, 1992), *'Alāmāt yawm al-qiyāma al-sughrā* (Cairo: Maktabat al-Imam, 1994), *Al-Mahdī al-muntazar* (Cairo: Maktabat al-Imam, 1995).

43. See Magdi Muhammad Shahawi, *Al-Masīh al-Dajjāl wa Ya'jūj wa Ma'jūj* (Cairo: Maktabat al-Imam, 1992).

44. See ibid., 11, 16, 15, 36, 51, 53, 53.

45. Ibid., 57, 70. Shahawi borrows the argument made in this connection in 1981 by the Saudi geographer Abdelhalim Abderrahman Khodr (see page 82 above), though without acknowledging it.

46. See Hassan Zakarya Fulayfil, *Haqiqa aghrab min al-khayāl: Ya'jūj wa Ma'jūj* (Cairo: Ibn Sina, 1991).

47. See ibid., 35.

48. See Okasha Abdelmannan al-Tibi, *Akbār maqal fī al-Masīh al-Dajjāl* (Cairo: Dar al-I'tisam, 1991).

49. See Okasha Abdelmannan al-Tibi, *Ahwāl al-qyāma* (Amman: Dar al-Isra, 1997).

50. See Hamza Faqir, *Ya'jūj wa Ma'jūj* (Amman: Dar al-Isra, 1994).

51. Muhammad Izzat Arif, *Nihāyat Saddam* (Cairo: Dar al-I'tisam, 1990).

52. See Gonzáles-Quijano, *Les gens du livre*, 158.

53. See Muhammad Izzat Arif, *Nihāyat al-Yahūd* (Cairo: Dar al-I'tisam, 1990).

54. Muhammad Izzat Arif, *Hal al-Dajjāl yahkum al-'ālam* (Cairo: Dar al-I'tisam, 1997), 9.

55. Ibid., 16, 10, 41, 54. Concern about the satanic powers of Ninja Turtles is not restricted to Muslim apocalyptics. At least one American Christian shares this point of view: see Peter Lalonde, *One World under Antichrist: Globalism, Seducing Spirits, and Secrets of the New World Order* (Eugene, Ore.: Harvest House, 1991).

56. See Muhammad Isa Dawud, *Indharū: Al-Masīh al-Dajjāl yaghzu al-'ālam min muthallith Bermūda* (Cairo: Al-Mukhtar al-Islami, 1991).

57. See Muhammad Isa Dawud, *Al-khuyūt al-khāfiyya bayna al-Masīh al-Dajjāl wa asrār muthallath Bermūda wa-l-atbāq al-tā'ira* (Cairo: Dar al-Bashir, 1994).

58. The protocols of the elders of Zion, in the 1905 edition of the book of this title, were associated with the Christian vision of the Antichrist; see Norman Cohn, *Warrant for Genocide: The Myth of the Jewish World-Conspiracy and the Protocols of the Elders of Zion* (London: Eyre and Spottiswoode, 1967), 66–67. An Arabic version was first published in Egypt in 1951, on the basis of the English edition brought out in 1921 in London by Victor E. Marsden, the Moscow correspondent of the ultra-conservative *Morning Post;* see Pierre-André Taguieff, *Prêcheurs de haine* (Paris: Mille et Une Nuits, 2004), 744.

59. A leading propagandist for *The Protocols of the Elders of Zion,* the Tsarist general Arthur Cherep-Spirodovich (1858–1926) himself composed a denunciation of the "Jewish conspiracy" entitled *The Secret World Government; or, "The Hidden Hand"* (New York: The Anti-Bolshevist Publishing Association, 1926).

60. See note 33 above.

61. Dawud, *Al-khuyūt al-khāfiyya,* 10, 28, 32.

62. See ibid., 37 (on the island near Yemen), 45–51 (at the court of the Pharaoh), 66–70 (Muslim's hadith), 85 (in Bermuda), 92 (the French Revolution and its aftermath).

63. See ibid., 103, 122, 151, 152. The obsession with "diabolical" UFOs was already common at the time in Western apocalyptic thought: see Hal Lindsey, *The 1980s: Countdown to Armageddon* (New York: Bantam, 1981), 32–33. The American literature on UFOs, remarks the political scientist Michael Barkun, produces "diatribes against the Masons and the Illuminati, the pope and the Jesuits, the Anti-Defamation League and the Jewish banker" and constitutes "a milieu in which *The Protocols of the Elders of Zion* are approvingly cited and obscene rituals in the Vatican are taken for granted"; see *A Culture of Conspiracy: Apocalyptic Visions in Contemporary America* (Berkeley and Los Angeles: University of California Press, 2003), 130.

. 64. On Dawud's accusation regarding the "Jewish" king of Jordan, see David Cook, *Contemporary Muslim Apocalyptic Literature* (Syracuse, N.Y.: Syracuse University Press, 2005), 136.

65. Quoted in Dawud, *Al-khuyūt al-khāfiyya*, 216. The fundamentalist minister Jerry Falwell (1933–2007), an outspoken critic of President Carter and the Camp David accords, argued that the Israeli retreat from Sinai was "contrary to the Abrahamic pact"; see Mokhtar Ben Barka, *La droite chrétienne américaine: Les évangéliques à la Maison-Blanche?* (Toulouse: Privat, 2006), 54. In 1979, Falwell founded the Moral Majority, whose members helped to elect Ronald Reagan the following year.

66. Muhammad Fuad Shakir, *Al-Masīh al-Dajjāl, Masīh al-dhalāla* (Cairo: Dar al-Bashir, 1994), 72–73; for the hadith of Tamim al-Dari's encounter with the Antichrist, see ibid., 20.

67. See Atif Lamada, *Madha tu'raf 'an al-Masīkh al-Dajjāl?* (Cairo: Dar al-Dhahabiyya, 1996).

68. See note 39 above.

69. Lamada, *Madha tu'raf 'an al-Masīkh al-Dajjāl?*, 5, 6, 93, 104–5, 100, 106, 105.

70. See Abdelmohsen ibn Hamad al-Abbad, *Al-Mahdī al-muntazar* (Cairo: Maktabat al-Sunna, 1996).

71. See Ibn Kathir, *Al-Masīh al-Dajjāl* (Cairo: Maktabat al-Sunna, 1996).

72. Amin Muhammad Gamaleddin, *Al-qwal al-mubīn fī ashrāt al-sā'a al-sughrā li-l-yawm al-dīn* (Cairo: Maktabat al-Tawfiqiyya, 1997).

73. See ibid., 101–2.

74. See ibid., 105, 106, 121, 114.

75. Ibid., 115. On the Banū al-Asfar, see chapter 1, note 62 above.

76. Gamaleddin, *Al-qwal al-mubīn fī ashrāt al-sā'a al-sughrā li-l-yawm al-dīn*, 123–24, 126, 53, 128. .

77. Ali Ali Muhammad, *Lam'āt al-bayān fī ahdāth ākhir al-zamān, ashrāt al-sā'a al-sughrā wa al-kubrā* (Amman: Dar al-Isra, 1994), 74–76. For the hadith reported by Bukhari on the "gold of the Euphrates," see chapter 1, page 15 above.

78. Abdelaziz ibn Badwa, *Al-yawm al-akhīr* (Amman: Dar Ibn Rajab, 1996).

79. Yusuf Muhammad Amr, *Min ashrāt al-sā'a al kubrā* (Cairo: Dar al-Dhahabiyya, 1997), 89–90.

80. See Jean-François Legrain, "Islamistes et lutte nationale palestinienne dans les territoires occupés," *Revue française de science politique* 36 (1986): 232.

81. See Charles Enderlin, *Paix ou guerres: Les secrets des négotiations israélo-arabes (1917–1997)* (Paris: Fayard, 2004), 636.

82. Bassam Jarrar, *Zawāl Isra'īl'ām 2022* (Beirut: Maktabat al-Biqaa al-haditha, 1995). The al-Aqsa Mosque did not exist in 621, of course, having been constructed only at the end of the seventh century; it is referred to in the Qur'an (17:1) as the "furthest place of worship" for the purpose of emphasizing the great distance of Muhammad's voyage. At the other end of the sacred esplanade *(al-haram al-sharif)* on Temple Mount in Jerusalem, the rock where Muhammad is supposed to have been raised up to heaven *(mi'raj)* stands at the center of a mosque with a gold dome known as the Mosque of Omar, or, more commonly in the West, the Dome of the Rock. The quotations from Jarrar that follow are taken from a later edition of *Zawāl Isra'īl'ām 2022*, published in Damascus in 2000 by Dar al-Chehab and subtitled "Qur'anic Prophecy and Numerological Chance."

83. Jarrar, *Zawāl Isra'īl'ām 2022* (Damascus: Dar al-Chehab, 2000), 47.

84. Ibid., 30.

85. Ibid., 67. [This is a rather puzzling remark, not least since Halley's comet has a period of slightly more than seventy-five years and was last visible from Earth in 1986.—Trans.]

86. His son Nadir Bayyud Tamimi subsequently traveled to Pakistan to carry out research on the founding myth of the Tamimi family contained in the hadith of Tamim al-Dari (see chapter 1, pages 18–19). This material formed the basis of a dissertation that he defended in Arabic in 1990 at the University of Sindh, in Hyderabad, under the title *Makānatu al-ardh al-mubāraka wa-'alāqātuha bil-sahābi Tamīm ibn Aws al-Dārī* (The Sites of the Blessed Land and Their Relationship to the Companion Tamim ibn Aws al-Dari). Nadir Bayyud Tamimi then unofficially assumed the duties of mufti for the Palestinian "mujahedin," and later founded in Amman the Council *(diwān)* of the Tamimi, dedicated to perpetuating the memory and celebrating the glory of Tamim al-Dari.

87. Assad Bayyud al-Tamimi, *Zawāl dawlāt Isra'īl hatmiyya qur'aniyya* (Cairo: Dar al-Mukhtar al-Islami, 1998; reprinted Amman: Al-Ahliyya, 2006).

88. The Qur'an, 17:4–8. [In the Oxford translation of this passage by M.A.S. Abdel Haleem, the term *wa'd* is mistakenly rendered as "warning"; following the more exact French version by Denise Masson, I have substituted "promises."—Trans.]

89. Al-Tamimi, *Zawāl dawlāt Isra'īl hatmiyya qur'aniyya*, 188.

90. For example, a commentary by the seventeenth-century imam Muhammad ibn 'Abd al-Rasul al-Husayni al-Shahrazawi al-Barzanji, *Al-ishā'a wa ash-rāt al-sā'a*, edited by Mowafiq Fawzi al-Jabir (Damascus: Dar Bashir, 1994); a second edition was published in 1995.

91. Muhammad Munir Idlibi, *Al-Dajjāl yujtah al'ālam* (Damascus: Al-Awael, 1998).

92. Ibid., 147, 154, 155, 148–49. Members of the clerical hierarchy have contributed to this literature as well. In 2001, Shaykh Abdelqader al-Arnawut brought out an annotated edition of *Al-Izā'a*, the eschatological treatise first published in the late nineteenth century by Shaykh Muhammad Sadiq Hasan Khan al-Husayni al-Bukhari al-Qannuji, with Dar Ibn Kathir in Damascus. A

leading figure of the Islamic renaissance in India during the latter part of the British Empire, Qannuji was a near contemporary, unlike Shaykh Barzanji (see note 90 above), whose work had been reissued with a new commentary seven years earlier, also in Damascus; but Qannuji's remoteness from the Arab Levant weakened the influence of his teaching, which, moreover, was impeccably orthodox. Two more commentaries on Qannuji's treatise subsequently appeared, one by Massaad Abdelhamid Muhammad Saadani (Cairo: Dar al-Qur'an, 2000), the other by Mustafa Hajiri (Beirut: Dar al-Kitab al-Arabi, 2005).

93. With the notable exception of the American religious scholar David Cook; see, among his other publications, "Muslim Fears of the Year 2000," *Middle East Quarterly* 5 (June 1998): 51–62.

6. THE HORSEMEN OF APOCALYPTIC JIHAD

1. Mustafa Abu Nasr Shalabi, *Sahīh ashrāt al-sā'a* (Jidda: Maktaba Sawadi, 2002; first composed in 1990 in Taif); Abdelhalim Abdelaziz al-Bastawi, *Al-mawsū'a fī ahādīth al-mahdī al-dha'īfa wa al-mawadhū'a* (Mecca: Maktabat al-Makiyya, 1999).

2. Al-Shafi' al-Mahi Ahmad, *Ya'jūj wa Ma'jūj,* 2nd ed. (Beirut: Dar Ibn Hazm, 2001).

3. See ibid., 310. The claim that this barrier was located at the Daryal Pass had first been made by al-Mahi Ahmad's countryman, the Egyptian geographer Abdelhalim Abderrahman Khodr (see chapter 5, page 82 above).

4. Al-Mahi Ahmad, *Ya'jūj wa Ma'jūj,* 28, 212–18, 256; also chapter 3, page 54 above.

5. Al-Mahi Ahmad, *Ya'jūj wa Ma'jūj,* 248, 271–76; see also the accompanying map.

6. Ibid., 295, 296, 298, 304, 305.

7. David Cook has well described the conceptual impasse of present-day writing on Gog and Magog; see *Contemporary Muslim Apocalyptic Literature* (Syracuse, N.Y.: Syracuse University Press, 2005), 208.

8. Gilles Kepel, ed., *Al-Qaida dans le texte* (Paris: Presses Universitaires de France, 2005), 50.

9. See Lawrence Wright, *The Looming Tower: Al-Qaeda and the Road to 9/11* (New York: Knopf, 2006), 296–98.

10. Safar ibn Abderrahman al-Hawali, *Yawm al-ghadab* (self-published on the World Wide Web, 2001), chapter 4, page 2; available via www.IslamicAwakening .com.

11. It was also in 1994 that Usama bin Laden, then living in exile in Sudan, was stripped of Saudi nationality and his assets frozen by the authorities in Riyadh.

12. Hawali, *Yawm al-ghadab,* chapter 4, page 1.

13. Ibid., chapter 2, page 3. Hawali is guilty of both exaggeration and misrepresentation: evangelicals are estimated to account for a quarter of the American population, and almost 40 percent of those who voted for George W. Bush in 2000; nonetheless only 55 percent of these voters believe that it is important to

support Israel, as against 40 percent of Americans in general. See Mokhtar Ben Barka, *La droite chrétienne américaine: Les évangéliques à la Maison-Blanche?* (Toulouse: Privat, 2006), 102, 110, 111.

14. See Hawali, *Yawm al-ghadab,* chapter 5 (entitled "The Jews Are Jews").

15. Ibid., chapter 2, page 2.

16. See ibid., chapter 9, page 9. After founding the Moral Majority in 1979, Rev. Jerry Falwell went on to become a powerful voice during Ronald Reagan's two terms (1981–1989), and a key figure promoting cooperation between the American Christian right and the Israeli Likud Party. Pat Robertson, who launched the Christian Coalition in 1988 and that same year received 15 percent of the vote in the Republican primaries against George H. W. Bush, was chief executive officer of the Christian Broadcasting Network (CBN) and hosted its hugely popular program "The 700 Club" (Ralph Reed, the director of the Christian Coalition from 1989 to 1997, served as a senior advisor to George W. Bush's election campaign in 2000). In 1991 Robertson published *The New World Order,* an apocalyptic bestseller in which a secret world government is finally defeated by the forces of restored Christianity; see Michael Barkun, *A Culture of Conspiracy: Apocalyptic Visions in Contemporary America* (Berkeley and Los Angeles: University of California Press, 2003), 53.

Falwell and Robertson both founded fundamentalist Christian universities in Virginia. In 1980 Falwell became the first Gentile to receive the Jabotinsky Medal, named after the founder of the right-wing Revisionist Zionism movement, and Robertson was awarded the State of Israel Friendship Award in 2002. Jimmy Swaggart, like Robertson a Pentacostalist, was a pioneer of American televangelism in the mid-1970s, having begun his career as a child preacher in a small Assemblies of God church in rural Louisiana.

17. Hawali, *Yawm al-ghadab,* chapter 3, page 1.

18. Ibid. This characterization of Christian Zionist doctrine is fairly close to the description of the evangelical Christian position on Israel given by academic observers; see, for example, Ben Barka, *La droite chrétienne américaine,* 177–78.

19. See Hawali, *Yawm al-ghadab,* chapter 8, page 3. The five kingdoms, Hawali says, are those of Nebuchadnezzar himself, Cyrus the Great, Alexander the Great, the Roman Empire—and Islam.

20. Ibid., chapter 8, pages 6 and 7. In identifying successive popes with false prophets, Shaykh Hawali does no more really than repeat a charge brought against the Vatican during the Reformation; see Jean-Robert Armogathe, *L'Antéchrist à l'âge classique: Exégèse et politique* (Paris: Mille et Une Nuits, 2005), 92.

21. Hawali, *Yawm al-ghadab,* chapter 8, page 10.

22. See Ben Barka, *La droite chrétienne américaine,* 179: "According to the scenario of the end of the world in the form given it by the Evangelicals, the Jews will have to accept Jesus—which is to say, to convert to the Christian religion—when he comes back to Israel."

23. Hawali, *Yawm al-ghadab,* chapter 11, page 7.

24. See ibid., chapter 13, page 1.

25. See chapter 5, page 94 above.

26. Muhammad Isa Dawud, *Ma qabla al-damār* (Cairo: Dar al-Bashir, 1999), 207. Dawud's book bears a passionate dedication to President Mubarak, the rector of al-Azhar, and the Egyptian people.

27. See Abdelwahab Abdessalam Tawila, *Al-Masīh al-muntazar wa nihāyat al-ʿālam,* 2nd ed. (Cairo: Dar al-Salam, 2002), 11, 278.

28. See Ridha Hilal, *Al-Masīh al-yahūdi wa nihayāt al-ʿālam* (Cairo: Maktabat al-Shuruq, 2000).

29. See Ben Barka, *La droite chrétienne américaine,* 172.

30. See Muhammad Isa Dawud, *Al-Mufājaha* (Cairo: Madbuli al-Sghir, 2001).

31. See Dawud, *Ma qabla al-damār,* 355.

32. Dawud, *Al-Mufājaha,* preface to the third edition (2001), pages 2, 3, and page 281.

33. See Amin Muhammad Gamaleddin, *Harmajaddūn* (Cairo: Maktabat al-Tawfiqiyya, 2001).

34. Ibid., 3, 5.

35. Ibid., 22, 24, 25.

36. Ibid., 30–31, 33, 35. General Myers became Chairman of the Joint Chiefs of Staff of the United States on 1 October 2001.

37. Ibid., 59, 66, 70, 68.

38. Ibid., 86, 96, 76, 71. [The modern city of Istanbul is habitually referred to by Muslim apocalyptics as Constantinople, since this is the name used in the hadith.—Trans.]

39. See chapter 5, page [144] above.

40. See Dawud, *Al-Mufājaha,* 590.

41. See Gamaleddin, *Harmajaddūn,* 8–9.

42. See ibid., 15. Composed during the last fifteen years of his life, the *Prophecies* of Michel de Nostradame (known as Nostradamus [1503–1566]) are divided up into ten "centuries," each composed of one hundred supposedly divinatory quatrains. Quatrain 97 of the sixth century has attracted particular attention:

> Five and forty degrees will burn
> Fire will approach the great new city
> At once a great scattered flame will leap up
> When proof will be wanted of the Normans.

Reread in the light of 11 September, the "great new city" is seen to be New York, with the "five and forty degrees" representing the forty-five minutes elapsed during the hour when the first airplane crashed into the north tower (8:45 a.m. local time). Immediately following the attacks, Nostradamus's "prediction" was featured on a number of American Internet sites; see Barkun, *A Culture of Conspiracy,* 1.

43. See Amro Gomaa, *Muthalath Bermūda* (Cairo: Nafiza, 2003).

44. See Hisham Muhammad Abu Hakima, *Al-Masīh al-Dajjāl wa maʾarakat Harmajeddūn* (Amman: Dar al-Isra, 2002).

45. Ibid., 5, 74.

46. See Abu Abdallah Mazen ibn Muhammad Sirsawi, *Kashf al-maknūn fī al-radd ʿalā kitāb Harmajeddūn* (Cairo: Maktabat al-Islamiyya, 2002).

47. Ibid., 5, 12, 24–25.

48. Ibid., 86, 104, 138–39.

49. See Khalid ibn Uthman, ʿAlāmāt yawm al-qiyāma (Cairo: Maktabat al-Safa, 2002).

50. See Abu Muhammad al-Husayn ibn Masʾud al-Farāʾ al-Bughawi, Ahwāl al-qyāma, ed. Ali Abdelal al-Tahtawi (Cairo: Maktabat al-Safa, 2002).

51. See Nuʿaym ibn Hammad, Kitāb al-fitan, ed. Ahmad ibn Shaaban and Muhammad ibn Ayyadi (Cairo: Maktabat al-Safa, 2003).

52. See Mustafa ibn al-Adawi, Al-Sahīh al-musnad li ahadīth al-fitan (Cairo: Maktaba Mekka, 2002).

53. Muhammad Ahmad Ismail al-Mokaddem, Fiqh ashrāt al-sāʾa (Alexandria: Dar al-Alamiyya, 2004), 8.

54. See Muhammad Metwalli Shahrawi, ʿAlāmāt al-qiyāma al-sughrā (Cairo: Maktabat al-Turath al-Islami, 2001).

55. See ibid., 70, 97; also chapter 1, pages 14–15 above. This "fire of Hijaz," whose glow will be visible as far as present-day Basra, is also the theme of a booklet published at about the same time by a government-sponsored institution in Kuwait; see Muhammad Ibrahim al-Shibani, Nār al-Hijāz (Kuwait City: Center for Manuscripts, Patrimony, and Documents, 2002).

56. Said Abdelazim, Amārāt al-sāʾa (Cairo: Dar al-Aqida, 2002).

57. Ibid., 16, 5, 7.

58. See chapter 2, page 36 above.

59. Abdelazim, Amārāt al-sāʾa, 8.

60. Mahmud Rajab Hamadi al-Walid, Kashf al-minan fī ʿalāmāt al-sāʾa wa al-malāhim wa al-fitan (Beirut: Dar Ibn Hazm, 2002).

61. Ibid., 16, 112.

62. Ibid., 148, 174, 242–43, 233, 244–45, 315. See, too, the apocalyptic treatise of another Iraqi author, composed in 2002 but not published until three years later in Jordan: Majed al-Bankani, Al-Masīh al-Dajjāl (Amman: Dar al-Nafaes, 2005).

63. From the publisher's description on the inside cover of Usama Yusuf Rahma, Iqtarabat al-sāʾa (Beirut: Dar Qotaiba, 2003). The book's subtitle reads: "The Beginnings of the Appearance of the Mahdi and of the Descent of the Messiah (May Peace Be Unto Them Both) and the Sequence of Events to Come in the Light of Prophetic Tradition from Now until the Last Hour."

64. Ibid., 143.

65. Ibid., 120, 121.

66. Muhammad Isa Dawud, Kenz al-Fūrat (Cairo: Madbuli al-Sghir, 2003), 229.

67. Ibid., 225, 229.

68. See chapter 1, page 15 above.

69. Dawud, Kenz al-Fūrat, 31, 61, 43, 49.

70. Ibid., 81, 119, 83, 105, 38, 56, 84.

7. THE BEGINNING OF THE END IN IRAQ

1. See Mansur Abdelhakim, Nihāyat al-ʿālam (Cairo: Dar al-Kitab al-Arabi, 2004), 135–36.

2. This first work, *Nihāyat al-'ālam qarīban* (The End of the World is Near), unfindable today, is mentioned by Abdelhakim in a later work, *Al-sīnāryū al-qādim li ahdāth ākhir zamān* (Cairo: Dar al-Kitab al-Arabi, 2004), 76. He also cites it as having been published not in 1994, but in 1995; see *Nihāyat al-'ālam,* 9.

3. Abdelhakim reproduces the Arabic translation of the call to the First Crusade issued by Pope Urban II in 1095 in *Bilād al-Shām* (Cairo: Dar al-Kitab al-Arabi, 2005), 93–95.

4. Mansur Abdelhakim, *Al-Mahdī fī muwājahat al-Dajjāl* (Cairo: Dar al-Kitab al-Arabi, 2007), 74.

5. Abdelhakim, *Nihāyat al-'ālam,* 207.

6. Abdelhakim, *Al-sīnāryū al-qādim li ahdāth ākhir zamān,* 149.

7. Ibid., 24, 25, 150.

8. See Abdelhakim, *Al-Mahdī fī muwājahat al-Dajjāl,* 122. In a previous book Abdelhakim had correctly noted that the Order of the Temple was not founded until 1118, but he nonetheless insisted on the shadowy links between the Knights Templar and the Isma'ili terrorists known as "Assassins"; see *Al-'ālam ruq'a shatranj* (Cairo: Dar al-Kitab al-Arabi, 2005), 79–84.

9. See Abdelhakim, *Al-sīnāryū al-qādim li ahdāth ākhir zamān,* 151; also *Al-'ālam ruq'a shatranj,* 118; *Nihāyat al-'ālam,* 137.

10. Abdelhakim, *Al-sīnāryū al-qādim li ahdāth ākhir zamān,* 57; Abdelhakim, *Man yahkum al-'ālam sirran?* (Cairo: Dar al-Kitab al-Arabi, 2005), 135.

11. Mansur Abdelhakim, *Al-imbirātūriyya al-amrīkiyya* (Cairo: Dar al-Kitab al-Arabi, 2005), 99.

12. Ibid., 8. Abdelhakim's figures are taken from a University of California study.

13. Ibid., 8, 131, 145.

14. Abdelhakim, *Man yahkum al-'ālam sirran?,* 11.

15. See Abdelhakim, *Al-imbirātūriyya al-amrīkiyya,* 248.

16. Abdelhakim, *New York wa sultan al-khawf* (Cairo: Dar al-Kitab al-Arabi, 2006), 97. In this work Abdelhakim goes so far as to claim that chapter 54 of the Qur'an, the cataclysmic sura called "The Moon," speaks of the misfortunes that will be visited upon New York (see ibid., 19).

17. See Abdelhakim, *Nihāyat al-'ālam,* 193; also *Al-sīnāryū al-qādim li ahdāth ākhir zamān,* 29.

18. See Mansur Abdelhakim, *Ashrāt yantaziruha al-'ālam* (Cairo: Dar al-Kitab al-Arabi, 2004), 39, 46.

19. Abdelhakim, *Al-'ālam ruq'a shatranj,* 8.

20. Abdelhakim, *Al-imbirātūriyya al-amrīkiyya,* 151, 149.

21. Abdelhakim, *Al-Mahdī fī muwājahat al-Dajjāl,* 235.

22. See Abdelhakim, *Al-sīnāryū al-qādim li ahdāth ākhir zamān,* 143, 154, 117.

23. Abdelhakim, *Ashrāt yantaziruha al-'ālam,* 106, 99. On the subject of *gharqad,* see chapter 1, page 17 above and accompanying note 43.

24. Mansur Abdelhakim, *Al'Iraq: Ardh al-nubu'āt wa al-fitan* (Cairo: Dar al-Kitab al-Arabi, 2005), 31, 83, 93. The fact that the White House spokesman had, on 15 March 2003, encouraged Saddam Hussein to read "the writing on the wall" was interpreted as a biblical injunction; see *Nihāyat al-'ālam,* 15.

25. Abdelhakim, *Al'Iraq: Ardh al-nubu'āt wa al-fitan,* 109; Abdelhakim, *Ya'jūj wa Ma'jūj* (Cairo: Dar al-Kitab al-Arabi, 2004), 11, 260.

26. Abdelhakim, *Ashrāt yantaziruha al-'ālam,* 163.

27. See Abdelhakim, *Al-sīnāryū al-qādim li ahdāth ākhir zamān,* 59–74, 89; Abdelhakim, *Nihāyat al-'ālam,* 122–27.

28. Compare Abdelhakim's *Al-'ālam ruq'a shatranj* (The World Is a Chessboard) with Carr's *Pawns in the Game;* see chapter 5, note 33 above.

29. Thierry Meyssan, *L'effroyable imposture: 11 septembre 2001* (Casablanca: EDDIF/Chatou: Carnot, 2002), quoted in Abdelhakim, *Al-sīnāryū al-qādim li ahdāth ākhir zamān,* 29–30, and *New York wa sultan al-khawf,* 188.

30. Larry Collins and Dominique Lapierre, *Is New York Burning?* (Beverly Hills, Calif.: Phoenix Books, 2005), quoted in Abdelhakim, *Al-imbirātūriyya al-amrīkiyya,* 315.

31. See Abdelhakim, *Al-imbirātūriyya al-amrīkiyya,* 23.

32. Mansur Abdelhakim, *Al-harb al-'alamiyya al-akhīra al-qādima* (Cairo: Dar al-Kitab al-Arabi, 2008), 281–83. The series consists of *The Terminator* (1984), *Judgment Day* (1991), and *Rise of the Machines* (2003). Abdelhakim was particularly impressed by the second installment.

33. Abdelhakim, *Al-harb al-'alamiyya al-akhīra al-qādima,* 263, 160.

34. Respectively, *Al-Masīh al-Dajjāl* (Cairo: Dar al-Kitab al-Arabi, 2004); *Al-Mahdī al-muntazar* (Cairo: Dar al-Kitab al-Arabi, 2004); and *Al-minna al-kubrā* (Cairo: Dar al-Kitab al-Arabi, 2004).

35. Gharbawi, *Al-Mahdī al-muntazar,* 83.

36. Saqqa had been dropped by Dar al-Bayan al-Arabi after it brought out his *Bashāra bānī Islām fī al-tūrā wa al-injīl* (The Announcement of the Sons of Islam in the Bible and the Gospels); the exact date of publication is unclear.

37. Ahmad Hijazi as-Saqqa, *'Awdat al-Masīh al-muntazar li-harb al-Irāq* (Damascus: Dar al-Kitab al-Arabi, 2003), 7–8. Curiously, the edition published the next year under the name Ahmad Ahmad Ali as-Saqqa was also advertised as the first edition. Like Abdelhakim (see note 24 above), Saqqa holds that the warning to Saddam Hussein by the White House regarding "the writing on the wall" derives from the Book of Daniel (ibid., 5); likewise "the threat of the evangelicals to Iraqi Muslims, in keeping with the fifth chapter of Daniel" (ibid., 114). For the dream of Nebuchadnezzar, see Daniel 2:31–45, discussed in ibid., 7.

38. Ibid., 10–11, 19. The reference is to the biblical scholar Rev. George Bush (1796–1859), a distant relation of the former president.

39. Ibid., 30, 39, 44, 30, 66, 68; see also chapter 5, note 25 above.

40. Saqqa, *'Awdat al-Masīh al-muntazar li-harb al-Irāq,* 88, 84.

41. See Ahmad Hijazi as-Saqqa, *Al-Bidāya wa al-nihāya li-umma Banī Isra'īl* (Cairo: Dar al-Kitab al-Arabi, 2004). "The Beginning and the End" is an implicit reference to Ibn Kathir's treatise of this name, and one that may also be detected in the subtitle of Abdelhakim's *The American Empire,* mentioned earlier.

42. Saqqa, *Al-Bidāya wa al-nihāya li-umma Banī Isra'īl,* 401–2, 421. The reference here is to Shaykh Muhammad ibn Muhammad Abu Shahba, dean of faculty of the Foundations of Religion *(usūl al-dīn)* at al-Azhar, Saqqa's alma mater.

43. See Ahmad Hijazi as-Saqqa, *Yawm al-rāb al-'azīm* (Cairo: Dar al-Kitab al-Arabi, 2004).

44. Abdelhamid had formerly been published by Dar al-Bashir in Cairo.

45. Hisham Kamal Abdelhamid, *Ya'jūj wa Ma'jūj qādimūn* (Cairo: Dar al-Kitab al-Arabi, 2006), 59, 134, 158, 161, 162.

46. Hisham Kamal Abdelhamid, *Iqtaraba khurūj al-Masīh al-Dajjāl* (Cairo: Dar al-Kitab al-Arabi, 2006); the text was first published in 1995, but reissued on this occasion in its revised 1999 version.

47. Ibid., 7, 16, 60, 162, 274, 318.

48. Muhammad Abdelhalim Abdelfattah, *Al-izā'a bi ahdāth qiyām al-sā'a* (Cairo: Dar al-Kitab al-Arabi, 2007).

49. See ibid., 132. There is chronic disagreement among apocalyptic writers regarding whether the "fire in Hijaz" is to be reckoned a minor or major sign of the Hour. The disagreement arises from a confusion between the accounts of ninth-century traditionists and medieval chroniclers: whereas Bukhari and Muslim associate an extraordinary fire in the Arabian Peninsula with the end of the world (see chapter 1, pages 14–15 above), contemporary observers reported a fire in Hijaz of exceptional magnitude in 1256. By distinguishing between this historical event and the apocalyptic one, Abdelfattah attempts to reconcile the two accounts. Abu Musab al-Suri likewise regards the fire as a minor sign (see chapter 10, page 188 below), while Muhammad Metwalli Shahrawi considers it to be a major sign (see chapter 6, page 115 above).

50. Ibid., 131.

51. Talaat Yusuf, *Al-Masīh al-Dajjāl wa Ya'jūj wa Ma'jūj* (Cairo: Dar al-Muslim, 2004).

52. Muhammad Isa Dawud, *Al-Mahdī al-muntazar, sinā'a isra'īliyya* (Cairo: Madbuli al-Sghir, 2005), 13, 9, 97, 139, 131.

53. Muhammad Isa Dawud, *Al-Heykal: Sā'a al-safr, khūtwa al-sahāniya al-qādima* (Cairo: Dar Mustafa, 2006), 9, 23, 31, 53, 124, 95. The last is an oblique reference to the Jewish belief that the birth of a red cow is a sign that the time has come to build the Third Temple in Jerusalem.

54. Saqqa, *'Awdat al-Masīh al-muntazar*, 27–29.

55. See pages 126–127 above.

56. Muhammad Sammak, *Al-dīn fī qarar Amrīka* (Beirut: Dar al-Nafaes, 2005), 44, 76. Rabin was assassinated in Jerusalem in November 1995. Robertson, a fierce opponent of the Israeli retreat from Gaza ten years later, in August 2005, likewise detected a punitive divine intent in the stroke that Ariel Sharon suffered shortly afterward.

57. Ibid., 61.

58. Abdel Tawab Abdallah Husayn, *Dimār Amrīka* (Cairo: Madbuli al-Sghir, 2006), 9, 13–15; the cover of Meyssan's book is reproduced on page 194.

59. Ibid., 17, 38, 44–45, 48.

60. Ibid., 54, 61, 64, 111, 115, 114, 132, 177.

61. Ali Abdelal al-Tahtawi, *Iltiqa'al al-masīhayn* (Beirut: Dar al-Kutub al-Ilmiyya, 2004), 227.

62. Abdelfattah Abderrahman Gamal, *Su'ūd wa sukūt al-imbirātūriyya al-amrīkiyya* (Cairo: Maktaba Jazirat al-Ward [undated]).

63. See Mokhtar Khalil Meslati, *Amrīka tahriqa nafsaha wa al-Islām huwwa al-munqidh* (Amman: Alam al-Kitab al-Hadith, 2006), 120. For a hilarious

send-up of Reverend Swaggart's sexual misbehavior, listen to the introduction of Frank Zappa's song "Stinkfoot" in the live version recorded on *Make a Jazz Noise Here* (Ryodisc, 1991–1993).

64. Mustafa Murad, *Nihāyat al-'ālam* (Cairo: Dar al-Fajr, 2003), 137; Haytham Hilak, *Nihāyat al-bashariyya* (Beirut: Dar al-Maarifa, 2004), 113.

65. Hilak, *Nihāyat al-bashariyya*, 114.

66. See chapter 6, note 42 above.

67. Sharafeddin al-A'raji, *Tanabu'āt Nostradamus* (Beirut: Dar al-Yusuf [undated]), 115, 142.

68. Muhammad Nidal al-Hafez, *Al-haqīqa bayna al-nubu'a wa al-siyāssa* (Damascus: Al-Awael, 2005), 20–22, 23.

69. See Muhammad al-Wakid, *Nostradamūs: Al-alfiyya al-jadīda* (Damascus: Al-Awael, 2006), an annotated translation into Arabic of John Hogue's *Nostradamus: The New Millennium* (Shaftesbury, Dorset: Element, 2002). Hogue's book was originally published under the title *Nostradamus and the Millennium* (New York: Doubleday, 1987).

70. In 2007 Hogue published an e-book entitled *Nostradamus: The War with Iran* under the imprint of Hogue Prophecy; see www.hogueprophecy.com.

71. See Wakid, *Nostradamūs: Al-alfiyya al-jadīda*, 13–16.

72. Mazin Naqib, *Al-qutl min asfār al-yahūd wa brūtūkūlāt hukamā' sahyūn ila fāris bilā jawād* (Damascus: Al-Awael, 2004); Raja Abdelhamid Arabi, *Adhua 'ala brūtūkūlāt hukamā' sahyūn* (Damascus: Al-Awael, 2005).

73. Jim Marrs came to prominence in 1989 with his book *Crossfire* on the assassination of President Kennedy, which to a large degree inspired Oliver Stone's film *JFK* (1992). Marrs went on to write *Alien Agenda* (1997) and *Rule by Secrecy* (2000), both bestsellers. His conspiracy theories acquired a more markedly anti-Semitic cast after 11 September, however, and he found himself obliged to pay for the publication of his next book, *The War on Freedom* (2003). Even if *The Protocols of the Elders of Zion* are a forgery, Marrs argues, they nonetheless contain a hidden truth; see Michael Barkun, *A Culture of Conspiracy: Apocalyptic Visions in Contemporary America* (Berkeley and Los Angeles: University of California Press, 2003), 147.

74. Jim Marrs, *Rule by Secrecy: The Hidden History That Connects the Trilateral Commission, the Freemasons, and the Great Pyramids* (New York: HarperCollins, 2000).

75. Muhammad Munir Idlibi, ed. and trans., *Man yahkum Amrīka wa al-'ālam sirran?*, 3 vols. (Damascus: Al-Awael, 2003–2004).

76. Muhammad Issam Arar al-Hasani, *Zuhūr al-Dajjāl* (Damascus: Al-Matba'a al-Dimashqiyya, 2006), 107, 109, 110, 115, 123, 232, 233.

77. Muhammad Uthman Uthman, *Intabahu ya muslimūn* (Damascus: Ministry of Information, 2005), 23, 25; see also 88, where Uthman cites Guillaume Dasquié and Jean-Charles Brisard, *Ben Laden: La vérité interdite* (Paris: Denoël, 2001), to emphasize the American interest in exploiting the oil reserves of Afghanistan (and Central Asia) well before 11 September 2001.

78. Ahmad al-Khattab, *Rihla al-akhīra* (Damascus: Dar al-Mahabba, 2004). Note that the author is a native of Hama, a bastion of Sunni traditionalism; the Islamic Studies Center is directed by Muhammad Habash, a Muslim cleric and

member of the Syrian parliament. In this connection see also Abdelrahim Mardini, *Rihla ilā dār al-ākhira* (Damascus: Dar al-Mahabba [undated]).

79. Khalid Helu, *Atā amr Allāh fala tasta'jilūhu* (Amman: Dar al-Isra, 2005), 18. The sense of this apparently paradoxical title is that although Allah has decided the fate of the world, believers must wait for his grand design to be revealed. Shaykhs Jarrar and Tamimi had earlier emphasized the significance of the seventeenth chapter of the Qur'an; see chapter 5, pages 100 and 101 above.

80. Helu, *Atā amr Allāh fala tasta'jilūhu*, 17, 375.

81. Khalil Husayn Jabir, *Banū Isra'īl wa al-afsād al-thalath wa nihayatuhum* (Amman: Mataba' al-Dustur al-Tijariyya, 2006), 131–32, 50, 51, 52. Jabir's quotation of Falwell is a good example of the profound ambivalence that Christian televangelists inspire in Muslim apocalyptic authors, who despite their revulsion at the hideous depravity of American morals nonetheless feel obliged to acknowledge the rightness of the televangelists' predictions. Some Muslim apocalyptics, following the example of Hawali, have managed to resolve the contradiction by standing fundamentalist Christian eschatology on its head: their Messiah is our Antichrist. The like of this ambivalence is also found in the discourse of radical imams who celebrate bin Laden and the 11 September attacks while at the same time holding that they were a CIA-Jewish plot.

82. Nun *[nūn]* corresponds to the letter N and to the first letter of "number" in both Arabic and English. The Nun Center has its own website, www.islamnoon.com.

83. Bassam Jarrar, *Nazariyyāt fi kitāb Allāh al-hakīm* (Ramallah: Nun Center for Qur'anic Studies and Research, 2004).

84. Ma'mun Fa'iz Jarrar, *Ahādith al-fitan* (Amman: Dar al-Aalam, 2006), 82–83. There is a striking contrast in this regard between Ramallah and Amman, where a major downtown bookstore stocks Usama Nayim Mustafa's *'Alāmāt al-sā'a al-kubrā* (Amman: Dar al-Isra, 2005), among other such works.

85. In Ramallah, for example, Muhammad Isa Dawud's *Ma qabla al-damār* (Cairo: Dar al-Bashir, 1999) is available in a plain gray cover under the title *Al-Masīkh al-Dajjāl wa al-harb al-qādima* (The Antichrist and the Coming War), with no mention of the publisher; the date of publication is given as 2002–2003.

86. Abdallah ibn Sulayman al-Mashaali, *Majmū' akhbār ākhir al-zamān* (Riyadh: Dar al-Muslim, 2003). Note that Mashaali validates the hadith about trees having been endowed with the power of speech in order to denounce the Jews hidden behind them, with the exception of the *gharqad*—"for this is the tree of the Jews" (ibid., 70); see chapter 1, note 43 above.

87. See chapter 1, page 14 above.

88. Zein al-Abidin ibn Gharamallah al-Ghamidi, *Fiqh ta'āmul ma'aal-fitan* (Riyadh: Dar al-Fadhila, 2006), 82.

89. See Fahd ibn Abdelaziz al-Fadel, *Ashrāt al-sā'a al-kubrā* (Riyadh: Dar Tayyiba, 2004), 12.

90. See Muhammad Abdelwahhab al-Aqid, *Al-fitna* (Riyadh: Adhwa al-Salaf, 2005), 210.

91. See, for example, al-Fadel, *Ashrāt al-sā'a al-kubrā*, 156. Another author who quotes Qutb is Umar Sulayman Abdallah al-Ashqar, one of the pioneers of Kuwaiti Salafism who now teaches at Zarqa University in Jordan; see his

Al-qyāma al-soghrā (Amman: Dar al-Nafaes, 2004), 302. Ashqar, a native of Palestine who moved to Kuwait in 1966, is a veteran of the apologetic (and therefore conservative Islamic) genre, having published a three-volume work entitled *Al-Yawm al-Akhīr* in 1988.

92. See Ahmad ibn Abderrahman ibn Uthman al-Qadi, ed., *Fitna al-Dajjāl wa Ya'jūj wa Ma'jūj*, by Shaykh Abderrahman ibn Nasser ibn Abdallah Saadi (Dammam: Dar Ibn Juzi, 2003).

93. See Muhammad ibn Saleh Uthaymin, *Al-fitna* (Riyadh: Dar al-Qassim, 2003).

94. See Muhammad ibn Khalil Harath, *Fasl al-maqāl* (Cairo: Dar al-Sharia, 2004); Abdallah Abdelmo'men al-Ghomari al-Hasani, ed., *Ashrāt al-sā'a*, by Abdelmalik bin Habib al-Andalusi al-Maliki (Riyadh: Adhwa al-Salaf, 2005).

95. See Hamdi ibn Hamza Abu Zeid, *Dhū al-Qarnayn wa Ya'jūj wa Ma'jūj* (Riyadh: [self-published], 2004).

96. See ibid., 522, 530, 532.

97. Mahir Ahmad al-Sufi, *Ashrāt al-sā'a* (Beirut: Al-Maktaba al-Asriyya, 2006), 64–65, 145.

98. Adel Zaki, *Al-Mahdī* (Beirut: Dar Ibn Hazm, 2005), 12, 187–205, 122, 408. Like Mahir Ahmad al-Sufi's *Encyclopedia of the Hereafter*, this work was published in Lebanon to guarantee its distribution beyond the United Arab Emirates.

8. THE GRAND RETURN OF THE SHI'I MAHDI

1. See Pierre-Jean Luizard, *La question irakienne* (Paris: Fayard, 2002), 102. Luizard perceptively describes the complicated state of Shi'i authority in Najaf: "When Khomeyni appeared as a new *marja'-e taqlīd* [literally, model for emulation], a certain confusion set in, with a majority of Iraqi Islamists obeying him in political matters, but following the opinions of Khui in matters of daily life" (ibid., 186).

2. Muhammad Baqir al-Sadr's essay, first published alone in 1977, was originally intended as the preface to an encyclopedia *(mawsū'a)* on the Mahdi composed by his disciple and cousin, Muhammad Sadiq al-Sadr. A Lebanese house later had the idea of attaching the ayatollah's text to a treatise published in Najaf in 1964 by Shaykh Abdelhadi al-Fadhli: see Muhammad Baqir al-Sadr and Abdelhadi al-Fadhli, *Al-Imām al-Mahdī* (Beirut: Dar al-Murtada, 2004).

3. Ibid., 103, 111.

4. Ibid., 114.

5. Al-Sadr and al-Fadhli, *Al-Imām al-Mahdī*, 117–18. Noah, it will be recalled, is considered a prophet of Islam: "We sent Noah out to his people. He lived among them for fifty years short of a thousand. . . . " (Qur'an 29:14).

6. Al-Sadr and al-Fadhli, *Al-Imām al-Mahdī*, 149.

7. Ibid.

8. Ayatollah Hasan Shirazi, *Mawsū'at kalīmāt al-imām al-Mahdī* (Beirut: Hayat Muhammad al-Amin, 2001).

9. In the event, Mahmud Hashemi did not return to Iraq. He stayed in Iran, where in 1982 he became the first president of the Supreme Council of the Islamic Revolution in Iraq (SCIRI), the pro-Iranian opposition in exile. Later he

took Iranian citizenship under the name Mahmud-Hashemi Shahrudi, and in 1999 was named head of the judicial system by Ayatollah Khamenei.

10. Nasrallah and Mussawi seem to have met each other in Najaf, where they studied with Ayatollah Sadr from 1976 to 1978.

11. Amal means "hope" in Arabic; used in Lebanon as an acronym, it stood for "Brigades of the Islamic Resistance."

12. Quoted on the Lebanese website http://francais.bayynat.org.lb/Infail libles/ImamElMahdi.htm.

13. See Kamel Sulayman, *Yawm al-Khalāss*, 6th rev. ed. (Beirut: Al-Alami, 1995), 393–95, 470, 633, 526.

14. See ibid., 123.

15. Ibid., 504, 505; on the identification of the Banū al-Asfar with the Byzantines, see chapter 1, note 62 above.

16. See ibid., 498, 505, 521, 501.

17. See ibid., 584, 540, 575, 621.

18. See ibid., 622–32.

19. Said Ayyub, *Ibtilā'āt al-umam* (Beirut: Dar al-Hadi, 1991).

20. Sayyid Husayn Najib Muhammad, *Yawm al-qiyāma* (Beirut: Dar al-Hadi, 2004), 113.

21. Bilal Na'im, *Masīrat al-zamān hatta sāhib al-zamān* (Beirut: Dar al-Hadi, 2006), 101.

22. See Muhammad Husayn Taw'i Hamdani, *Al-malāhim wa 'alā'im ākhir al-zamān* (Beirut: Dar al-Hadi, 2004); Mahmud Mussawi, *Hayāt al-Imām al-Mahdī* (Beirut: Dar al-Hadi, 2006).

23. Muhammad Sadiq al-Sadr, *Mawsū'āt al-Imām al-Mahdī* (Beirut: Dar al-Taaruf, 1982; originally published in Iraq in 1977).

24. See Luizard, *La question irakienne*, 186–87.

25. See "Iraq's Muqtada Al-Sadr: Spoiler or Stabilizer?" *International Crisis Group Middle East Report*, no. 55 (11 July 2006), 4.

26. See ibid., 8.

27. On the "Shi'i way of jihad" in general, and the Mahdi Army in particular, see Jean-Pierre Filiu, *Les frontières du jihad* (Paris: Fayard, 2006), 218–26.

28. Estimates vary from 60,000 to 150,000 members; many Sadrist militiamen were mobilized only on a part-time basis.

29. This formula by a member of the Mahdi Army is quoted in "Iraq's Muqtada Al-Sadr," 20.

30. See ibid., 16.

31. See, for example, the speech read in Muqtada al-Sadr's name in Parliament by the deputy Liqa' al-Yassin, in Baghdad on 29 April 2007, and quoted the following day in Juan Cole's blog, "Informed Comment" (www.juancole .com/2007_04_01_juancole_archive.html).

32. Earlier that same month, on 16 April 2007, this lack of a timetable for American withdrawal had been used to justify the resignation of five Sadrist ministers from the government.

33. See "Iraq's Muqtada Al-Sadr," 17.

34. This date corresponds to 15 Shaaban 1428, or the 1,173rd anniversary of the Mahdi's birth according to the Muslim calendar.

35. Quoted on Ayatollah Sistani's official website, www.najaf.org.

36. See Abbas Amanat, "The Resurgence of Apocalyptic in Modern Islam," in Bernard McGinn, John J. Collins, and Stephen J. Stein, eds., *The Encyclopedia of Apocalypticism*, 3 vols. (New York: Continuum, 1998), 3:257; also Yann Richard, *L'Islam chi'ite: Croyances et idéologies* (Paris: Fayard, 1991), 139–40.

37. See Asghar Schirazi, *The Constitution of Iran: Politics and the State in the Islamic Republic* (London: I.B. Tauris, 1997), 129.

38. Thomas Fourquet, "Le chiisme élitiste de l'ayatollah Mesbah Yazdi," *Maghreb-Machrek*, no. 190 (Winter 2006–2007): 47.

39. This according to the Hatef website, which has close links to former president Rafsanjani; quoted in A. Savyon and Y. Mansharof, "The Doctrine of Mahdism," *MEMRI Report*, no. 357 (May 2007): 5.

40. In the first round, on 17 June 2005, Ahmadinejad received 19.5 percent of the votes, as against 21.5 percent for Rafsanjani, who had been president from 1989 to 1997. But he came out ahead in the second round, on 24 June, with 62.2 percent of the votes, as against 35.3 percent for Rafsanjani. See the report in the 22 September 2006 issue of *Le Monde*.

41. For the sources of Ahmadinejad's statements in the Iranian press see Savyon and Mansharof, "The Doctrine of Mahdism," 9. Note also, in his Christmas 2006 wishes to the Christian community, Ahmadinejad's mention of Jesus's imminent return alongside the Mahdi (ibid., 3).

42. See Jean-Pierre Perrin, "Ahmadinejad: Le début de la fin?" *Politique internationale*, no. 15 (Spring 2007): 53.

43. The idea of swearing an oath of loyalty to the Mahdi is very significant in Shi'i eschatology. One invocation of the Messiah, for example, prescribed by the sixth of the twelve imams, mentions "a pact, a contract, an oath of allegiance tied to my neck [*'ahdan wa 'aqdan wa bay'atan lahu fī 'unqi]*"; see Sayyed Mohammed Redhâ al-Mutallaq, *En attendant le Mahdi*, ed. and trans. Abbas Ahmad al-Bostani (Montreal: La Cité du Savoir, 2005), 69.

44. See Perrin, "Ahmadinejad: Le début de la fin?" 53; also "L'inspirateur caché d'Ahmadinejad," *Le Monde*, 22 September 2006.

45. According to Shi'i tradition, the Mahdi is to reappear in Mecca. In Jamkaran, a great gathering takes place every week on Tuesday, for the Hidden Imam is supposed to examine the petitions from his believers on the evening of that day. Other sources advise that the Mahdi will reappear at the al-Sahla mosque in Kufa.

46. See "En Iran, les proches du président Ahmadinejad essuient leur premier revers électoral," *Le Monde*, 19 December 2006.

47. See Savyon and Mansharof, "The Doctrine of Mahdism," 5.

48. Quoted in an Agence France-Presse dispatch from Teheran dated 28 August 2007.

49. This 22-page document, dated 1 January 2007, was available online at http://english.irib.ir/IRAN/Leader/illumination.htm until June 2007.

50. See ibid., 7, 9, 15, 6. In this case, it is emphasized, Nowruz will have to coincide with the twenty-fifth day of the Muslim month of Dhu al-Qa'da. The introduction of the Persian calendar in the apocalyptic sequence is a sign of the profound Iranization of eschatological forecasting in the Islamic Republic.

51. Ibid., 6, 3, 1.

52. There are no reliable statistics regarding the number of people who pledge their allegiance to one or another *marja'-e taqlīd* (figure to be emulated), but the grand ayatollahs of Qum and Najaf are undoubtedly more popular among Shi'a than the Guide of the Revolution, whose ascendancy is as recent as it is controversial. The Lebanese exception is explained mainly by the activism of Hizbullah, which proclaims its loyalty to Ayatollah Khamenei.

53. See chapter 1, page 27 above and accompanying note 78.

54. Shadi Faqih, *Ahmadinejad wa al-thawra al-'ālamiyya al-muqbila* (Beirut: Dar al-Ilm, 2006), 59–70.

55. Ibid., 77.

56. See ibid., 79. Faqih, identifying the Battle of the Calls with modern propaganda warfare, refers to "a great media defeat."

57. Ibid., 204, 121–22, 131.

58. See Shadi Faqih, *Anta al'ān fī 'asr al-zuhūr* (Beirut: Dar al-Ilm, 2006), 21; *Al-Imam al-Mahdī wa al-intisār* (Beirut: Dar al-Ilm, 2006), 5–6. The myth of the Yemenite origin of the Shi'i tribes of Lebanon is also marshaled in support of this identification of the Hizbullah leader with the Yemeni.

59. See chapter 1, page 27 above.

60. Faqih, *Al-Imam al-Mahdī wa al-intisār*, 15, 12, 17. The idea that supernatural forces intervened alongside Hizbullah's fighters is also developed in Shaykh Yūsuf Mūsa Ridā, *Malhamat al-nasr al-Ilāhī* (Beirut: Dar al-Mahajjah, 2009), 835–44.

61. Faqih, *Al-Imam al-Mahdī wa al-intisār*, 19, 9, 10.

62. Shadi Faqih, *Al-wa'ad al-sadīq* (Beirut: Dar al-Ilm, 2006), 4.

63. The Arabic title is given above at note 58 and in the note immediately following.

64. See Faqih, *Anta al'ān fī 'asr al-zuhūr*, 1, 14, 16.

65. Faqih, *Al-wa'ad al-sadīq*, 8, 10, 12, 17.

66. Ibid., 18, 15. For the hadith, also quoted in Faqih, *Ahmadinejad wa al-thawra al-'ālamiyya al-muqbila*, 122, see chapter 1, page 17, and chapter 2, page 36 above.

67. Faqih, *Al-wa'ad al-sadīq*, 27.

68. See Naim Qassim, *Hizbullah: The Story from Within*, trans. Dalia Khalil (Beirut: Saqi Books, 2005).

69. Naim Qassim, *Al-Mahdī al-mukhaliss* (Beirut: Dar al-Hadi, 2007). The director of Dar al-Hadi, Salah Ezzedine, has close ties to Hizbullah, and his house has published a good number of Shi'i apocalyptic writings. Ezzedine was also a wealthy financier until his arrest in September 2009 on charges of fraudulent bankruptcy. The losses of investors who unwisely placed their trust in him have been reckoned at as much as $1 billion—earning Ezzedine the nickname "the Lebanese Bernie Madoff."

70. Ibid., 178, 139, 102, 9.

71. Ibid., 181, 110, 182, 136.

72. See ibid., 191.

73. See chapter 1, page 26 above.

74. See the interview with Vali Nasr in *Newsweek*, 1 February 2007.

75. On this belated, and sometimes superficial, process of conversion, see Yitzhak Nakash, *The Shi'is of Iraq* (Princeton: Princeton University Press, 1994), 25–48.

76. The Shaykhiya remains very well established in Basra, where it can count on the support of its own militia. See "Where Is Iraq heading? Lessons from Basra," *International Crisis Group Middle East Report*, no. 55 (25 June 2007): 2, 10.

77. Regarding the views of Ahmad al-Hasan, see the very large number of statements published on his website (www.almahdyoon.org), from which the quotations that follow are taken.

78. See chapter 1, page 27 above.

79. Ayatollah Haeri took care to post this condemnation on his website (www.alhaeri.org/iraq/right-iraq.html), accessible until June 2007. A representative of the Iraqi cleric spoke more bluntly, describing Ahmad al-Hasan in January 2006 as "mentally ill"; see "Iraq's Muqtada Al-Sadr: Spoiler or Stabilizer?" *International Crisis Group Middle East Report*, 16.

80. See "Akhtalafat al-riwayyāt fī shakhsihi wa ahdāfihi al-syāsiyya wa ma'arakatihi fī al-najaf," *Al-Hayat*, 31 January 2007, and "Ashūra dām wa jamā'atun shī'iyya tanfī silatiha bi ma'arakati al-najaf," *Al-Jazira*, 31 January 2007.

81. See the Agence France-Presse dispatch from Najaf dated 29 January 2007.

82. See the Reuters dispatch of 29 January 2007.

83. See "Dans l'enfer mystique de Najaf," *Libération*, 12 February 2007. This tribe is often referred to by the plural form of its name, Hawatem.

84. See the International Press Service dispatch of 1 February 2007.

85. Quoted in the Agence France-Presse dispatch from Baghdad of 30 January 2007.

86. See "Dans l'enfer mystique de Najaf," *Libération*, 12 February 2007.

87. See "Bombs Kill Dozens of Ashura Pilgrims," *Washington Post*, 30 January 2007; "Akhtalafat al-riwayyāt fī shakhsihi wa ahdāfihi al-syāsiyya wa ma'arakatihi fī al-najaf," *Al-Hayat*, 31 January 2007.

88. See "Dans l'enfer mystique de Najaf," *Libération*, 12 February 2007. Even assuming the highest casualty figure to be correct, it would follow from the original government estimate of seven hundred insurgents that almost a third of this number survived; but no one disputes that the camp was destroyed and its occupants annihilated. However this may be, there is reason to doubt the official accounting of the slaughter.

89. See "Bombs Kill Dozens of Ashura Pilgrims," *Washington Post*, 30 January 2007.

90. See Reidar Visser's analysis in blogs dated 29, 30, and 31 January 2007 on www.historiae.org.

91. All the remarks quoted in this paragraph, due to Hasan or his spokesman, were posted online at www.almahdyoon.org.

9. DIASPORAS OF THE APOCALYPSE

1. The Mosque of Saint-Denis de la Réunion was founded in 1905 and the one dedicated to Saint-Pierre in 1913, whereas the Great Mosque of Paris did not officially open its doors until 1926.

2. Ahmad Lala Anas, *Les signes de la fin du monde* (Saint-Denis de la Réunion: Nouvelle Imprimerie Dionysienne, 1996). No direct relationship can be detected between Anas and the Emirian author Mahir Ahmad al-Sufi, who also employs the category of "middle signs" (see chapter 7, page 138 above).

3. Ahmad Lala Anas, *L'homme descend-il du singe?* (Paris: Tawhid, 2001).

4. Muhammad Benshili, *La venue du Mahdi selon la tradition musulmane,* 2nd ed. (Paris: Tawhid, 2006; originally published 2002).

5. Ibid., 14, 28; see also chapter 2, page 43 above.

6. Benshili takes due note, however, of the "anathema" *(takfīr)* issued against Ibn Arabi, notably by Ibn Taimiyya; see *La venue du Mahdi,* 127–28.

7. Ibid., 53, 57, 61.

8. Muhammad Karimi Alghribi, *Les signes précurseurs de la fin du monde* (Paris: Zeino, 2006), 4, 30, 35, 172.

9. Buhafs Abdeljalil, *L'Apocalypse de Harmagedôn* (Beirut: Al-Buraq, 2007), 70, 71.

10. Abdallah al-Hajjaj, *Les grands signes de la fin du monde,* 2nd ed. (Beirut: Al-Buraq, 2002; originally published 1994).

11. Yusuf ben Yahia al-Sulami, *Le Mahdi attendu* (Beirut: Dar al-Kutub al-Ilmiyya, 2004); Azzedin Husayn al-Shaykh, *Les signes précurseurs de l'heure* (Beirut: Dar al-Kutub al-Ilmiyya, 2005).

12. Al-Sulami, *Le Mahdi attendu,* 27–28, 36.

13. Muhammad Metwalli Shahrawi, *Al Geib: Le monde invisible* (Paris: Essalam, 1999), and *La fin du monde* (Paris: Essalam, 2002).

14. Fdal Haja, *La mort et le jugement dernier* (Paris: Universel, 1991), 75, 77–78.

15. Zerruk Sherif-Zahar, *Prophéties et signes de la fin du monde* (Montreuil: Orientica, 2005).

16. Ibn 'Arabi, *Le Mahdi et ses conseillers,* ed. and trans. Tayeb Chouiref (Paris: Milles et Une Lumières, 2006); al-Qurtubi, *Le Faux Messie et le retour d'Issa,* ed. and trans. Abdelkarim Zentici (Lyon: Dar al-Muslim, 2003); Ibn Kathir, *Les signes du Jour Dernier,* ed. and trans. Maha Kaddoura (Paris: Al-Bustane, 2005); al-Suyuti, *Le retour de Jésus,* ed. and trans. Didier Ali Hamoneau (Paris: Iqraa, 2000), and *La descente de Jésus et l'apparition de l'Antéchrist,* ed. and trans. A. Desmazières (Lyon: Alburda, 2002).

17. Yusuf al-Wabil, *Les signes de la fin des temps* (Brussels: Al-Hadith, 2006). On pages 19 and 405, the phrase "combat against the Jews" has been whited out; pages 243–46, where the fifty-fourth minor sign of the Hour is discussed, were simply removed from all copies of the book prior to publication. By the time a second edition had been issued, by Al-Hadith in 2009, these problematic passages had disappeared altogether.

18. More typical, however, is an Arabic-language DVD documentary, distributed in France by Société FMPI, "The Coming Deluge *[al-tūfān al-qādim],* Signs, and Warnings of God." Scenes of natural catastrophe follow one after another for more than an hour, against a background of chanted passages from chapter 54 of the Qur'an ("The Moon") and interspersed remarks by the Egyptian shaykh Muhammad Rawi. Earthquakes are described as the "signs of Allah" *(ayāt Allāh),* and storms and floods as the "soldiers of Allah" *(jund Allāh).*

Particular attention is given to the tsunami of December 2004 and its terrifying toll of human lives. Whereas Western tourists were caught unawares by the storm, lounging in their bungalows, half-naked, alcoholic drinks to hand, the faithful—shown praying in a devastated mosque the day after the catastrophe—survived. Far worse cataclysms are considered to be inevitable, and scenes are borrowed from Roland Emmerich's science fiction film *The Day after Tomorrow* (2004) showing New York engulfed, and the Statue of Liberty toppled, by the rampaging waters. Plainly this undubbed documentary is addressed to a nervous audience of Muslim viewers desperate for reassurance, and no one else.

19. Khalid Bentunes, "La place de Jésus dans l'islam" (27 July 2007), at http://oumma.com (bracketed phrases in the original). In the same vein, though in this case the message is intended for initiates of the Nematollahi order, see Javad Nurbakhsh, *Jesus o los ojos de los sufíes* (Madrid: Darek-Nyumba, 1996), 52–55.

20. President Bush invited American Islamic leaders and Muslim members of the foreign diplomatic corps to a dinner celebrating Ramadan on 11 November 2004. See the communiqué and photograph of Bush shaking hands with Kabbani at www.islamicsupremecouncil.org.

21. Shaykh Muhammad Hisham Kabbani, *The Approach of Armageddon?* (Washington, D.C.: Islamic Supreme Council of America [ISCA], 2003), 237, 163, 211.

22. See note 16 above.

23. Al-Suyuti, *Le retour de Jésus,* 25, 31, 133.

24. Ibid., 20.

25. See ibid., 19.

26. Dominique Penot, *Les signes de la fin des temps dans la tradition islamique,* 2nd ed. (Lyon: Alif, 1996; originally published in 1992).

27. Ibid., 88, 96, 108–9.

28. Ibid., 151. For the validation of a comparable hadith by Muslim, see chapter 1, page 17 above, and by al-Qurtubi, chapter 2, page 36 above.

29. Penot, *Les signes de la fin des temps,* 149.

30. The hadith quoted above by Penot, on the extermination of Jews whose presence had been betrayed by the stones and the trees, is the thirteenth hadith in Kashmiri's collection; see *Nuzūl al-masīh,* 6th ed. (Cairo: Dar al-Salam, 2005), 151. This collection is also cited in Andrés Guijarro, *Los signos del fin de los tiempos en el Islam* (Madrid: EDAF, 2007), 18.

31. Kashmiri campaigned against the dissident Ahmadiyya sect (see chapter 5, page 90 above and accompanying note); the Deobandi school is described as fundamentalist in Cyril Glassé, *Concise Encyclopedia of Islam* (San Francisco: Harper & Row, 1989), 96.

32. Jean Ezéchiel, *Les prophéties de l'Islam* (Paris: Alphée, 2006), 197, 223.

33. Ibid., 201, 225, 224.

34. See "Attaque ciblée contre la théorie de l'évolution," *Libération,* 6 February 2007.

35. See the announcements page of www.harunyahya.com.

36. A richly illustrated work printed on gloss coated stock, *The Atlas of Creation* is priced at $100 on Harun Yahya's website; one estimate puts the

total cost of the American distribution operation at several million dollars. See "Islamic Creationist and a Book Sent Round the World," *New York Times*, 17 July 2007. See also the Reuters dispatch dated 8 June 2007 and "Turkish Creationism Takes Root," *Washington Times*, 9 June 2007.

37. See www.dayofjudgment.com, one of the many websites affiliated with Yahya's eponymous site.

38. Harun Yahya, *Les signes de la fin des temps et le Mahdi* (Paris: Les Calligraphes, 2006), 8.

39. Ibid., 41, 43, 36–37, 62.

40. See Yahya's site www.globalfreemasonry.com.

41. Quoted in Adem Yakup, *Le Prophète Jésus* [no translator indicated] (Paris: Essalem, 2004), 111.

42. Said Nursi, *Ashrāt al-sā-a wa masā'il al-Dajjāl al-akbar wa al-Sufyāni* (Cairo: Sözler, 2004).

43. Yakup, *Le Prophète Jésus*, 113, 107, 105.

44. Ismail Buyukcelebi and Resit Haylamaz, *Jésus: Sa mission et ses miracles*, ed. and trans. Serif Gunay and Kafiha Karakus (Izmir, Turkey, and Somerset, England: The Light, 2005), 23.

45. Ahmad Thomson, *Dajjal, the Antichrist* (London: Ta-Ha Publishers, 1997). Originally written in 1980 and given the title *Dajjal, the Naked King*, it received its definitive form only with the publication of this edition seventeen years later; see the preface.

46. See ibid., 63, 15, 59, 82, 80, 142–43.

47. Mohammad Yasin Owadally, *Emergence of Dajjal: The Jewish King* (Delhi: Adam Publishers, 1997); a revised edition appeared in 2001.

48. Ibid., 70, 12, 17, 31.

49. Muhammad Yasin Owadally, *The Story of Yajuj-wa-Majuj and the Wall* (Kuala Lumpur: A.S. Noordeen [n.d.]). See www.online.islamicstore.com.

50. See chapter 5, pages 99–100 above.

51. Bassam Jarrar, *Israeli Empire Collapses in 2022*, trans. Mohammad Yasin Owadally (Kuala Lumpur: A.S. Noordeen, 2002), vi.

52. Gholam al-Mahdi, *The Inevitable Victory: The Coming of Jesus* (Kuala Lumpur: A.S. Noordeen, 2003), 193, 258.

53. Ibid., 194, 230, 235, 236, 314–16, 309, 313.

54. Aftar Shahryar, *Dajjal: The Final Deception and Signs of Qiyamah* (Delhi: Islamic Book Service, 2003), 3–4.

55. Ibid., v, vii, 57, 26.

56. Shahryar's book was distributed in the United States by IBS (based in Hicksville, New York), in the United Kingdom by Al-Azhar Academy (in London), and in the Gulf states by Al-Munna (in Sharjah and Dubai).

57. S. Bashir-ud-Din Mahmood, *Doomsday and Life after Death* (Delhi: Idara, 2005), 107–8. The first edition appeared in Islamabad in 1987, and a second revised and expanded edition in 1991.

58. Ibid., 106, 99.

59. Ibn Kathir, *Dajjal the False Messiah* (Delhi: Idara, 2006).

60. Siddheeque M.A. Veliandoke, *Doomsday, Portents, and Prophecies*, 2nd ed. (Toronto: Al-Attique, 2001), 248.

61. Siddheeque M.A. Veliandoke, *Al-fitan wa ashrāt al-sā'a* (Riyadh: Diyaa al-Watan, 2003), 123–24.

62. Muhammad Isa Dawud, *Dajjal akan muncul dari kerajaan jin di segitica Bermuda* [no translator indicated] (Kuala Lumpur: Pustaka Syuhada, 1997); *Imam Mahdi, di ambang pintu*, 2 vols., trans. Symasuddin Ali Nasution (Kuala Lumpur: Pustaka Syuhada, 2003); *Sihir perkalang perkahwinan* [no translator indicated] (Kuala Lumpur: Pustaka Syuhada, 2004). Amin Muhammad Gama-leddin, *Umur umat Islam kedatagan dan munculnya dajjal* [no translator indicated] (Kuala Lumpur: Pustaka Syuhada, 2006); *Perang Armageddon kedatangan imam Mahdi* [no translator indicated] (Kuala Lumpur: Pustaka Syuhada, 2006).

63. Muhammad Metwalli Shahrawi, *Tazkirah peringatan hari akhirat* [no translator indicated] (Kuala Lumpur: Jasmin, 2007); Muhammad Kheir Rama-dan Yusuf, *Iskandar Zulkarnayn*, 2 vols. [no translator indicated] (Kuala Lumpur: Jasmin, 2002).

64. See, for example, Ahmad Muhammad, *Menyekat kemaraan ya'juj wa ma'juj* (Kuala Lumpur: Al Falah, 2004); and Ahmad Ali Zamzam, *Kiamat hampir tiba* (Kedah: Khazanah Banjariah, 2005).

65. Syahrin Nasution, *50 hadis menceritakan dunia akhir zaman* (Kuala Lumpur: Pustaka Syuhada, 2003). For the translations of Dawud and Gama-leddin, see note 62 above.

66. Ahmad Thomson, *Dajjal raja yang tidak berpakaian* [no translator indicated] (Kuala Lumpur: Al-Shafa, 2007). *The Protocols of the Elders of Zion* was reissued the year before under the name of Victor Emile Marsden (1866–1920), who had made the first English translation, and under another title, *World Conquest through Jewish Government* (Kuala Lumpur: Masterpiece, 2006). Mathias Chang, a Chinese Catholic lawyer, published two conspiracy best-sellers in rapid succession: *Future Fast Forward: The Zionist Anglo-American Empire Meltdown* (Kuala Lumpur: Thinker's Library, 2005); and *Brainwashed for War, Programmed to Kill* (Kuala Lumpur: Thinker's Library, 2006).

67. See Mustaffa Suhaimi, *Yakjuj wa makjuj: Dajjal ancam umat Islam seluruh dunia* (Kuala Lumpur: Progressive Publishing House, 2007), 186–87.

68. For an account of the genesis and doctrine of the Nation of Islam, see Gilles Kepel, *À l'ouest d'Allah* (Paris: Seuil, 1994), 29–54. [An English version was published by Stanford University Press as *Allah in the West* in 1997.—Trans.]

69. Elijah Muhammad, *Message to the Blackman* [sic] *in America* (Chicago: Muhammad Mosque of Islam No. 2, 1965).

70. See ibid., 31.

71. Ibid., 112–13, 119, 111.

72. See C. Eric Lincoln, *The Black Muslims in America*, rev. ed. (New York: Kayode, 1991), 235. Comparison may also usefully be made with the heresy of the Ahmadiyya; see ibid., 244.

73. See Kepel, *À l'ouest d'Allah*, 47.

74. See ibid., 74.

75. See ibid., 88–91.

76. See Mattias Gardell, *In the Name of Elijah Muhammad: Louis Farra-khan and the Nation of Islam* (Durham, N.C.: Duke University Press, 1996), 293–301. The Jungle Brothers, a rap group associated with Farrakhan, delivered

this apocalyptic refrain in 1989: "In days 2 come is your prophetized fate/The name of the game is RAPTURE."

77. Muhammad, *Message to the Blackman in America*, 290.

78. Farrakhan mentions this experience in his 1 December 2001 letter to President George W. Bush, posted online by the Nation of Islam (www.noi.org).

79. Quoted in Gardell, *In the Name of Elijah Muhammad*, 162.

80. Tynetta Muhammad, quoted in ibid., 163.

81. A Spanish-language edition is published online as well.

82. Quoted in *The Final Call*, 8 February 2005.

83. From a sermon preached on 1 July 2001 at the Mosque Maryam in Chicago, reprinted online at www.finalcall.com but no longer found there.

84. Letters of 1 December 2001 and 30 October 2002, posted online at www.noi.org/statements.

85. Statement of 28 December 2004, reprinted online at www.finalcall.com.

86. From an interview broadcast on Al-Jazira on 18 March 2007.

87. From Farrakhan's 8 April 2007 sermon "The War of Armageddon," posted in three parts at www.finalcall.com; the lines quoted here are from the third part.

88. "America is falling, her doom is sealed. I compare the fall of America with the fall of ancient Babylon"; see Muhammad, *Message to the Blackman in America*, 273.

89. The citations in notes 91–97 below are taken from this site.

90. This is particularly true in the case of Saudi Arabia, where the writings of the late mufti Abdelaziz ibn Baz are found alongside the opinions of two leading figures of the Islamist "awakening" *(sahwa)*, Shaykh Salman al-Auda and Shaykh Safar al-Hawali.

91. See "The Descent of Jesus, Son of Mary, as Portrayed in the Qur'an," by Shaykh al-Humaydi, and "Jesus Will Descend at the End of Time," by Ali Abu Lauz.

92. From Yahia Adil Ibrahim, "The Truth about Jesus (Part One)."

93. From Alia Amir, "Christian and Jewish Beliefs regarding the Return of the Messiah and Plots against Masjid Al-Aqsa."

94. From Ali Hijazi, "Muslims' Victories before the Dajjal's Appearance," and Suhaib Hassan, "50 Signs of the Day of Judgment."

95. From Ali al-Tamimi, "Sit and Wait?"

96. From Ali Hajizi, "Al-Mahdi."

97. From Abdullah Hakim Quick, "Hot Times in North America"; see also Shaykh Salih al-Hamrani, "The Earthquakes."

98. This link may be accessed via the section of www.alsaha.com devoted to Islamic topics.

99. See http://alfetn.com.

100. The site, www.almahdy.net, may also be accessed via www.alsaffah.net.

101. See in this regard the very thorough article by Stephan Rosiny, "Internet et la *marja'iyya*," *Maghreb-Machrek*, no. 178 (Winter 2003–2004): 59–74.

102. For example, Muhammad Baqir al-Sadr, *Le Mahdi ou la fin des temps*, ed. and trans. Abbas Ahmad al-Bostani (Montreal: La Cité du Savoir, 1999).

103. Sayyed Mohammed Redhâ al-Mutallaq, *En attendant le Mahdi*, ed. and trans. Abbas Ahmad al-Bostani (Montreal: La Cité du Savoir, 2005), 48–49.

104. Ahmad Thomson's *Dajjal, the Antichrist* was published and distributed by Ta-Ha Publishers in London in 1997. Ten years later the sale and promotion of this "bestseller" was being handled by Al-Attique in Toronto. According to its website www.al-attique.com, Thomson's book "attempts to relate current events and trends in the world to the prophecies contained in the Qur'an and Sunna." Ahmad Thomson has published many other books as well, among them *Jesus: Prophet of Islam* (New York: Tahrike Tarsile Qur'an, 2003), a revised edition of a work originally composed by Muhammad Ata Ur-Rahim.

10. THE ARMAGEDDON OF JIHAD

1. See Lawrence Wright, *The Looming Tower: Al-Qaeda and the Road to 9/11* (New York: Knopf, 2006), 94; also chapter 4, page 77 above.

2. See Abu Muhammad al-Maqdisi, *Al-kawāshif al-jāliyya fī kufr al-dawla al-sa'ūdiyya* (The Evident Outrage of the Impiety of the Saudi State), published illegally. Five years earlier in Kuwait City, again illegally, Maqdisi had published *Millat Ibrāhīm* (The Community of Abraham), a long commentary on Juhayman al-'Utaybi's first open letter, which, having been circulated prior to the "revelation" of the Mahdi's identity, gave no indication of apocalyptic motivation; see Gilles Kepel, ed., *Al-Qaida dans le texte* (Paris: Presses Universitaires de France, 2005), 239–40. Also in Peshawar in 1989, Abu Muhammad al-Maqdisi (born Isam al-Barqawi) became the mentor of the young Jordanian jihadist Abu Musab al-Zarqawi (born Ahmad al-Khalayla).

3. See the 2007 report of the Harmony Project of the Combating Terrorism Center, U.S. Military Academy at West Point, "Cracks in the Foundation: Leadership Schisms in al-Qa'ida from 1989–2006," www.ctc.usma.edu/aq/aq3.asp, 3.

4. A slightly different and less reliable English translation of this passage is posted online by the Combating Terrorism Center, U.S. Military Academy at West Point, www.ctc.usma.edu/aq/pdf/AFGP-2002-600053-Trans.pdf; the lines quoted are found on pages 55–56 of that document, which correspond to pages 29–30 of the Arabic version also posted there. It is worth remarking that although the Jerusalem of the Antichrist and the Jerusalem of the Mahdi are the same city, Abu Walid refers to the former by its Hebrew transcription *(Urshalīm)* and to the latter by its "holy" Arabic name *(al-Qods)*.

5. Quoted in Reuven Paz, "Global Jihad and the United States: Interpretation of the New World Order of Usama bin Laden," *PRISM Series of Global Jihad* 1 (March 2003). The short-lived Center for Islamic Studies and Research had only a virtual existence, operating under the direction of Shaykh Yusuf al-Ayyiri on behalf of al-Qaida via www.alneda.com until July 2002 and www.drasat .com until late 2003.

6. Mustafa Setmariam Nasar (called Abu Musab al-Suri), *Al-da'wa lil-muqāwama al-islāmiyya al-'ālamiyya*. This work first appeared in December 2004 in two parts: *Part I: The Roots, History, and Experiences; Part II: The Call, Program and Method* (place and publisher unknown). Regarding the subsequent online edition, see notes 7 and 21 below.

7. Ibid.; this quote is found on page 62 of the Arabic version that was published via a now-defunct website in January 2005. The hadith that "jihad will

continue until the last man of my community fights the Antichrist" is cited several times by Abu Musab al-Suri; see ibid., 684, 1012, 1139.

8. Ibid., 100.

9. Ibid., 788, 549.

10. Ibid., 1517, 1518. On the dispute surrounding the fire in Hijaz, see chapter 7, note 49 above.

11. Ibid., 1518.

12. See ibid., 1523, 1531, 1532, 1544, 1554 (injunctions to jihad); 1524, 1555 (curses on the Jews).

13. Ibid., 1525, 1529, 1530, 1532, 1536, 1537, 1541, 1543, 1556.

14. Ibid., 1546. The theme of this hadith, validated by Bukhari (see chapter 1, page 15 above), is carried over almost without alteration in the formulations of Muslim and Ibn Kathir (see chapter 2, pages 38–39).

15. Ibid., 1551, 1553.

16. Ibid., 1560, 1569, 1561, 1568, 1565, 1567, 1571, 1575, 1581.

17. Ibid., 1581. The identity of the "city of impiety" is unclear, but other evidence suggests it may be Istanbul ("Constantinople").

18. See ibid., 1583–84, 1547; for the hadith confirmed by Muslim, see chapter 1, page 17 above.

19. Ibid., 1554.

20. Ibid., 1598.

21. See Brynjar Lia's meticulously researched biography, *Architect of Global Jihad: The Life of al-Qaida Strategist Abu Mus'ab al-Suri* (London: Hurst/New York: Columbia University Press, 2008), 1, 7. Lia places the online publication of *The Call to Global Islamic Resistance* in January 2005, and gives the date of Abu Musab al-Suri's capture as 31 October 2005, in Quetta (though there is some evidence it may have occurred earlier; see 344–45).

22. See Farhad Khosrokhavar, *Quand al-Qaïda parle: Témoignages derrière les barreaux* (Paris: Grasset, 2006). This fascinating book of interviews with jihadists imprisoned in France reveals no particular susceptibility to apocalyptic thinking.

23. On 19 April 1995, McVeigh, an extreme right-wing militant and veteran of the war of liberation in Kuwait, used a truck filled with explosives to blow up the Federal Building in Oklahoma City, killing one hundred sixty-eight people. He was executed on 11 June 2001 at the age of thirty-two. On McVeigh's heroism in the Gulf, where he was a member of General Schwarzkopf's security detail during the cease-fire negotiations and won eight military decorations, see Mark S. Hamm, *Apocalypse in Oklahoma: Waco and Ruby Ridge Revenged* (Boston: Northeastern University Press, 1997), 146–49.

24. Michael Barkun, *A Culture of Conspiracy: Apocalyptic Visions in Contemporary America* (Berkeley and Los Angeles: University of California Press, 2003), 169.

EPILOGUE

1. Extract from the notice concerning Armageddon ("ABCs of Prophecy") on the Christian website Rapture Ready; the location of Babylon in Iran is deliberate; see www.raptureready.com/abc/armageddon.html.

2. See "Falwell: Antichrist May Be Alive," *Washington Post,* 16 January 1999; also Michael Barkun, *A Culture of Conspiracy: Apocalyptic Visions in Contemporary America* (Berkeley and Los Angeles: University of California Press, 2003), 43, for Falwell's reaction to the controversy aroused by his remarks. Yet almost twenty years earlier, in 1980, Pat Robertson had made much the same claim: "There is a man alive today, approximately twenty-seven years old, who is now being groomed to be the satanic messiah"; quoted in Robert C. Fuller, *Naming the Antichrist: The History of an American Obsession* (New York: Oxford University Press, 1995), 166.

3. Thus the subtitle of the book by the religious scholar Robert Fuller, just cited.

4. See John F. Walvoord, *Armageddon, Oil, and the Middle East Crisis: What the Bible Says about the Future of the Middle East and the End of Western Civilization,* rev. ed. (Grand Rapids, Mich.: Zondervan, 1990). In its first two editions (another was issued by Tyndale House in 2007 under the title *Armageddon, Oil, and Terror*) the book sold more than two million copies. Walvoord, who died in 2002, is still revered by Christian apocalyptics as the "father of modern biblical prophecy"; see www.leftbehind.com.

5. Hal Lindsey's *The Late Great Planet Earth* (Grand Rapids, Mich.: Zondervan, 1970) has sold more than eighteen million copies, with translations into forty-four languages; see Dan Cohn-Sherbok, *The Politics of Apocalypse: The History and Influence of Christian Zionism* (Oxford: Oneworld, 2006), 163. The *Left Behind* series of apocalyptic fiction by Tim LaHaye and Jerry Jenkins has sold some sixty-five million copies, with seven of the volumes reaching the first position on the *New York Times* bestseller list; see www.leftbehind.com.

6. See "Apocalypse Now," *Time,* 23 June 2002. This poll, like Falwell's 1999 remarks about the Antichrist, is grist for the mill of Muslim pamphleteers such as Khalil Husayn Jabir; see chapter 7, page 135 above.

7. See *The Good News Magazine,* published online by the United Church of God (www.gnmagazine.org), which devoted several editions of its Web TV program "Beyond Today" (www.beyondtoday.tv) to this subject as well. It also distributes free of charge a booklet entitled *The Middle East in Bible Prophecy,* with attack helicopters and the dome of a mosque on the cover.

8. Quoted in Alexander Cockburn, "Le complot du 11-Septembre n'aura pas lieu," *Le Monde Diplomatique,* December 2006.

9. See Samuel P. Huntington, "The Clash of Civilizations," *Foreign Affairs* 72 (Summer 1993): 22–49. Two years earlier, Franklin Graham, son of Reverend Billy Graham, had said: "The God of Islam is not our God, and Islam is a very pernicious and wicked religion"; for this and other Islamophobic quotations, see Ibrahim Warde, "Il ne peut y avoir de paix sans l'avènement du Messie," *Le Monde Diplomatique,* September 2002.

10. Joel C. Rosenberg, one of the most popular authors of apocalyptic evangelism, boasts of having publicly called upon one of his Jewish critics to convert to Christianity before it is too late; see www.christianitytoday.com/tc/2007/mayjun/7.38.html?start=2. Hal Lindsey, for his part, declares that God will save 144,000 Jews at the end of the world and make them his most zealous evangelists; see Cohn-Sherbok, *The Politics of Apocalypse,* 154.

A Contemporary Muslim
Apocalyptic Bibliography

Al-Abbad, Abdelmohsen ibn Hamad. *Al-radd 'alā man kazaba bi-al-ahādīth al-sahīha al-wārida fī al-Mahdī* (The Reply to the Lie about the Authentic Hadiths Concerning the Mahdi). Medina: Matbaha Rashid, 1981.

———. *Al-Mahdī al-muntazar* (The Awaited Mahdi). Cairo: Maktabat al-Sunna, 1996.

Abdelazim, Said. *Amārāt al-sā'a* (The Signs of the Hour). Cairo: Dar al-Aqida, 2002.

Abdelaziz, Najwa Husayn. *Al-Masīh al-Dajjāl wa Ya'jūj wa Ma'jūj* (The Antichrist and Gog and Magog). Cairo: Maktabat al-Safa, 2000.

Abdelfattah, Muhammad Abdelhalim. *Al-izā'a bi ahdāth qiyām al-sā'a* (The Arrangement of the Events Leading Up to the Hour). Cairo: Dar al-Kitab al-'Arabi, 2007.

Abdelhakim, Mansur. *Al-sīnāryū al-qādim li ahdāth ākhir zamān* (The Impending Scenario of the End of Times). Cairo: Dar al-Kitab al-'Arabi, 2004.

———. *Nihāyat al-'ālam* (The End of the World). Cairo: Dar al-Kitab al-'Arabi, 2004.

———. *Ya'jūj wa Ma'jūj* (Gog and Magog). Cairo: Dar al-Kitab al-'Arabi, 2004.

———. *Ashrāt yantaziruha al-'ālam* (The Signs Awaited by the World). Cairo: Dar al-Kitab al-'Arabi, 2004.

———. *Al'Iraq: Ardh al-nubu'āt wa al-fitan* (Iraq: Land of Prophecies and Insurrections). Cairo: Dar al-Kitab al-'Arabi, 2005.

———. *Bilād al-Shām* (The Land of Shām [Syria]). Cairo: Dar al-Kitab al-'Arabi, 2005.

———. *Al-'ālam ruq'a shatranj* (The World Is a Chessboard). Cairo: Dar al-Kitab al-'Arabi, 2005.

———. *Man yahkum al-'ālam sirran?* (Who Secretly Rules the World?) Cairo: Dar al-Kitab al-'Arabi, 2005.

———. *Al-imbirātūriyya al-amrīkiyya* (The American Empire). Cairo: Dar al-Kitab al-'Arabi, 2005.

———. *New York wa sultan al-khawf* (New York and the Empire of Fear). Cairo: Dar al-Kitab al-'Arabi, 2006.

———. *Bilād al-Hijāz* (Hijaz). Cairo: Dar al-Kitab al-'Arabi, 2006.

———. *Al-Mahdī fī muwājahat al-Dajjāl* (The Mahdi Confronted by the Antichrist). Cairo: Dar al-Kitab al-'Arabi, 2007.

———. *Al-harb al-'alamiyya al-akhīra al-qādima* (The Next and Last World War). Cairo: Dar al-Kitab al-'Arabi, 2008.

Abdelhamid, Hisham Kamal. *Ya'jūj wa Ma'jūj qādimūn* (Gog and Magog Are Coming). Cairo: Dar al-Kitab al-'Arabi, 2006.

———. *Iqtaraba khurūj al-Masīh al-Dajjāl* (The Appearance of the Antichrist Draws Near). Cairo: Dar al-Kitab al-'Arabi, 2006.

Abdeljalil, Buhafs. *L'Apocalypse de Harmagedôn*. Beirut: Al-Buraq, 2007.

Abu Hakima, Hisham Muhammad. *Al-Masīh al-Dajjāl wa ma'arakat Harmajeddūn* (The Antichrist and the Battle of Armageddon). Amman: Dar al-Isra, 2002.

Abu Zeid, Hamdi ibn Hamza. *Dhū al-Qarnayn wa Ya'jūj wa Ma'jūj* (The Two-Horned One and Gog and Magog). Riyadh: [self-published], 2004.

Al-'Alami, Ali Korani, *Asr zuhūr al-Mahdi* (The Age of the Appearance of the Mahdi). Beirut: Dar al-Mahajja, 2004.

Amr, Yusuf Muhammad. *Min ashrāt al-sā'a al-kubrā* (Some of the Great Signs of the Hour). Cairo: Dar al-Dhahabiyya, 1997.

Anas, Ahmad Lala. *Les signes de la fin du monde*. Saint-Denis de la Réunion: Nouvelle Imprimerie Dionysienne, 1996.

Al-Aqid, Muhammad Abdelwahhab. *Al-fitna* (The Rebellion). Riyadh: Adhwa al-Salaf, 2005.

'Arabi, Raja Abdelhamid. *Adhua 'ala brūtūkūlāt hukamā' sahyūn* (Understanding *The Protocols of the Elders of Zion*). Damascus: Al-Awael, 2005.

Al-A'raji, Sharafeddin. *Tanabu'āt Nostradamus* (The Prophecies of Nostradamus). Beirut: Dar al-Yusuf [undated].

Arbawi, Nabil. *Bermūda* (Bermuda). Cairo: Dar Salaheddin, 2000.

Arif, Muhammad Izzat. *Nihāyat Saddam* (The End of Saddam). Cairo: Dar al-I'tisam, 1990.

———. *Nihāya al-Yahūd* (The End of the Jews). Cairo: Dar al-I'tisam, 1990.

———. *Al-Mahdi and the End of Time*. London: Dar al-Taqwa, 1995.

———. *Hal al-Dajjāl yakhum al-'ālam?* (Does the Antichrist Rule the World?). Cairo: Dar al-I'tisam, 1997.

———. *Ākhir zamān, nuzūl al-Masīh* (The End of Times, the Descent of the Messiah). Cairo: Dar al-Bayan al-'Arabi, 2004.

Al-Arnawut, Abdelqader, ed. *Al-izā'a* (The Dissemination), by Muhammad Sadiq Hasan Khan al-Husayni al-Bukhari al-Qannuji. Damascus: Dar Ibn Kathir, 2001.

Al-Ashqar, Umar Sulayman Abdallah. *Al-Yawm al-Akhīr* (The Last Day). 3 vols. Kuwait: Maktabat al-Falah, 1988.

———. *Al-qyāma al-soghrā* (The Minor Signs of the Resurrection). Amman: Dar al-Nafaes, 2004.

———. *Qissass al-gheyb* (Stories of the Invisible). Amman: Dar al-Nafaes, 2007.

Ashur, Abdellatif. *Thalatha yantazaruhum al-'ālam* (The Three Whom the World Awaits). Cairo: Maktabat al-Qur'an, 1987.

———. *Al-Masīkh al-Dajjāl* (The Antichrist). Cairo: Maktabat al-Qur'an, 1988.

Ata, Muhammad Abdelqader. *Al-Masīkh al-Dajjāl* (The Antichrist). Cairo: Dar al-Fajr, 1999.

Al-Auda, Sulayman ibn Muhammad. *Al-Tatar* (The Mongols). Riyadh: Dar Tayyiba, 2005.

Ayyub, Said. *Al-Masīh al-Dajjāl* (The Antichrist). Cairo: Al-Fath lil-Aalam al-'Arabi, 1987.

———. *Aqīdat al-Masīh al-Dajjāl fī al-adyān* (The Doctrine of the Antichrist in the Religions). Cairo: Dar al-Hadi, 1991.

———. *Ibtilā'āt al-umam* (The Trials of Nations). Beirut: Dar al-Hadi, 1991.

Al-Balagh Foundation. *Imam al-Mahdī* (Imam Mahdi). Teheran: Balagh, 2000.

Al-Bankani, Majed. *Al-Masīh al-Dajjāl* (The Antichrist). Amman: Dar al-Nafaes, 2005.

Al-Bastawi, Abdelhalim Abdelaziz. *Al-mawsū'a fī ahādīth al-mahdī al-dha'īfa wa al-mawadhū'a* (The Encyclopedia of Weak and Fabricated Hadiths concerning the Mahdi). Mecca: Maktabat al-Makiyya, 1999.

Bayyumi, Muhammad. *'Alāmāt yawm al-qiyāma al-kubrā* (The Greater Signs of the Day). Cairo: Maktabat al-Imam, 1992.

———. *'Alāmāt yawm al-qiyāma al-sughrā* (The Smaller Signs of the Day). Cairo: Maktabat al-Imam, 1994. [An English translation was published in Riyadh by Darussalam in 2005.]

———. *Al-Mahdī al-muntazar* (The Awaited Mahdi). Cairo: Maktabat al-Imam, 1995.

———. *Nunu'āt al-nabī* (Prophecies of the Prophet). Cairo: Dar al-Hadi, 2002.

Benshili, Muhammad. *La venue du Mahdi selon la tradition musulmane.* 2nd ed. Paris: Tawhid, 2006 [originally published 2002].

Buyukcelebi, Ismail, and Resit Haylamaz. *Jésus: Sa mission et ses miracles,* ed. and trans. Serif Gunay and Kafiha Karakus. Izmir, Turkey, and Somerset, England: The Light, 2005.

Chouiref, Tayeb, ed. and trans. *Le Mahdi et ses conseillers,* by Ibn 'Arabi. Paris: Milles et Une Lumières, 2006.

Dawud, Muhammad Isa. *Indharū: Al-Masīh al-Dajjāl yaghzu al-'ālam min muthallith Bermūda* (Beware: The Antichrist Has Invaded the World from the Bermuda Triangle). Cairo: Al-Mukhtar al-Islami, 1991.

———. *Al-khuyūt al-khāfiyya bayna al-Masīh al-Dajjāl wa asrār muthallath Bermūda wa-l-atbāq al-tā'ira* (The Hidden Links between the Antichrist, the Secrets of the Bermuda Triangle, and Flying Saucers). Cairo: Dar al-Bashir, 1994.

———. *Ma qabla al-damār* (Before the Destruction). Cairo: Dar al-Bashir, 1999.

———. *Al-Mufājaha* (The Surprise). Cairo: Madbuli al-Sghir, 2001.

———. *Kenz al-Fūrat* (The Treasure of the Euphrates). Cairo: Madbuli al-Sghir, 2003.

———. *Al-Mahdī al-muntazar, sinā'a isra'īliyya* (The Messiah Made in Israel). Cairo: Madbuli al-Sghir, 2005.

———. *Al-Heykal: Sā'a al-safr, khūtwa al-sahāniya al-qādima* (The Temple: H-Hour and the Next Stage of Zionism). Cairo: Dar Mustafa, 2006.

Desmazières, A., ed. and trans. *La descente de Jésus et l'apparition de l'Antéchrist,* by al-Suyuti. Lyon: Alburda, 2002.

Ezéchiel, Jean. *Les prophéties de l'Islam.* Paris: Alphée, 2006.

Al-Fadel, Fahd ibn Abdelaziz. *Ashrāt al-sā'a al-kubrā* (The Great Signs of the Hour). Riyadh: Dar Tayyiba, 2004.

Faqih, Shadi [also called Faris]. *Al-Imam al-Mahdī wa al-intisār* (The Imam Mahdi and Victory). Beirut: Dar al-Ilm, 2006.

———. *Anta al'ān fī 'asr al-zuhūr* (You Are Now Living in the Age of the Mahdi's Appearance). Beirut: Dar al-Ilm, 2006.

———. *Al-wa'ad al-sadīq* (The Faithful Promise). Beirut: Dar al-Ilm, 2006.

———. *Ahmadinejad wa al-thawra al-'ālamiyya al-muqbila* (Ahmadinejad and the Forthcoming World Revolution). Beirut: Dar al-Ilm, 2006.

Faqir, Hamza. *Ya'jūj wa Ma'jūj* (Gog and Magog). Amman: Dar al-Isra, 1994.

Fulayfil, Hassan Zakarya. *Haqiqa aghrab min al-khayāl: Ya'jūj wa Ma'jūj* (A Reality Beyond Imagining: Gog and Magog). Cairo: Ibn Sina, 1991.

Gamal, Abdelfattah Abderrahman. *Su'ūd wa sukūt al-imbirātūriyya al-amrīkiyya* (Grandeur and Decadence of the American Empire). Cairo: Maktaba Jazirat al-Ward [undated].

Gamaleddin, Amin Muhammad. *Al-qwal al-mubīn fī ashrāt al-sā'a al-sughrā li-l-yawm al-dīn* (The Revelation of the Minor Signs of the Hour). Cairo: Maktabat al-Tawfiqiyya, 1997.

———. *Harmajaddūn* (Armageddon). Cairo: Maktabat al-Tawfiqiyya, 2001.

Al-Ghamidi, Zein al-Abidin ibn Gharamallah. *Fiqh ta'āmul ma'a al-fitan* (Islamic Law regarding the Treatment of Insurrections). Riyadh: Dar al-Fadhila, 2006.

Al-Gharbawi, Mahmud. *Al-Masīh al-Dajjāl* (The Antichrist). Cairo: Dar al-Kitab al-Arabi, 2004.

———. *Al-Mahdī al-muntazar* (The Awaited Mahdi). Cairo: Dar al-Kitab al-Arabi, 2004.

———. *Al-minna al-kubrā* (The Major Grace). Cairo: Dar al-Kitab al-Arabi, 2004.

Gomaa, Amro. *Muthalath Bermūda* (The Bermuda Triangle). Cairo: Nafiza, 2003.

Guijarro, Andrés. *Los signos del fin de los tiempos en el Islam.* Madrid: EDAF, 2007.

Al-Hafez, Muhammad Nidal. *Al-haqīqa bayna al-nubu'a wa al-siyāssa* (The Reality between Prophecy and Politics). Damascus: Al-Awael, 2005.

Haja, Fdal. *La mort et le jugement dernier.* Paris: Universel, 1991.

Hajiri, Mustafa, ed. *Al-izā'a* (The Dissemination), by Muhammad Sadiq Hasan Khan al-Husayni al-Bukhari al-Qannuji. Beirut: Dar al-Kitab al-Arabi, 2005.

Al-Hajj Ahmad, Yusuf. *'Alāmat yawm al-qiyāma* (The Signs of the Day of Resurrection), with commentary by Yusuf Nabahani. Damascus: Maktaba Marzuk, 2001.

Al-Hajjaj, Abdallah. *Les grands signes de la fin du monde.* 2nd ed. Beirut: Al-Buraq, 2002 [originally published 1994].

Hamdani, Muhammad Husayn Taw'i. *Al-malāhim wa 'alā'im ākhir al-zamān* (The Battles and Signs of the End of Times). Beirut: Dar al-Hadi, 2004.

Hamoneau, Didier Ali, ed. and trans. *Le retour de Jésus,* by al-Suyuti. Paris: Iquaa, 2000.

Harath, Muhammad ibn Khalil. *Fasl al-maqāl* (The Definite Article). Cairo: Dar al-Sharia, 2004.

Al-Hasani, Abdallah Abdelmo'men al-Ghomari, ed. *Ashrāt al-sā'a* (The Signs of the Hour), by Abdelmalik bin Habib al-Andalusi al-Maliki. Riyadh: Adhwa al-Alaf, 2005.

Al-Hasani, Muhammad Isam Arar. *Zuhūr al-Dajjāl* (The Appearance of the Antichrist). Damascus: Al-Matba'a al-Dimashqiyya, 2006.

Al-Hawali, Safar ibn Abderrahman. *Yawm al-ghadab* (The Day of Wrath), 2001. Available via www.IslamicAwakening.com.

Hawwa, Said. *Al-Islām* (Islam). Cairo: Dar al-Salam, 2005.

Helu, Khalid. *Atā amr Allāh fala tasta'jilūhu* (The Order of Allah Has Come and No One Can Anticipate It). Amman: Dar al-Isra, 2005.

Hilak, Haytham. *Nihāyat al-bashariyya* (The End of Humanity). Beirut: Dar al-Maarifa, 2004.

Hilal, Ridha. *Al-Masīh al-yahūdi wa nihayāt al-'ālam* (The Jewish Messiah and the End of the World). Cairo: Maktabat al-Shuruq, 2000.

Husayn, Abdel Tawab Abdallah. *Dimār Amrīka* (The Destruction of America at Our Gates). Cairo: Madbuli al-Sghir, 2006.

Ibn al-Adawi, Mustafa. *Al-Sahīh al-musnad li ahadīth al-fitan* (The Authentic Compilation of the Hadiths on Rebellion). Cairo: Maktaba Mekka, 2002.

Ibn Badwa, Abdelaziz. *Al-yawm al-akhīr* (The Last Day). Amman: Dar Ibn Rajab, 1996.

Ibn Shaaban, Ahmad, and Muhammad ibn Ayyadi, eds. *Kitāb al-fitan* (The Book of Dissension), by Nu'aym ibn Hammad. Cairo: Maktabat al-Safa, 2003.

Ibn Uthman, Khalid. *'Alāmāt yawm al-qiyāma* (The Signs of the Day of Resurrection). Cairo: Maktabat al-Safa, 2002.

Idlibi, Muhammad Munir. *Al-Dajjāl yujtah al-'ālam* (The Antichrist Invades the World). Damascus: Al-Awael, 1998.

Idlibi, Muhammad Munir Idlibi, ed. and trans. *Man yahkum Amrīka wa al-'ālam sirran?* (Who Governs America and the World?). 3 vols., selected works of Jim Marrs. Damascus: Al-Awael, 2003–2004.

Jabir, Khalil Husayn. *Banū Isra'īl wa al-afsād al-thalath wa nihayatuhum* (The Third Corruption of the Sons of Israel and Their End Are Inevitable according to the Qur'an, the Bible, and the Gospels). Amman: Mataba' al-Dustur al-Tijariyya, 2006.

Al-Jabir, Mowafiq Fawzi, ed. *Al-ishā'a wa ashrāt al-sā'a* (The Propagation and the Signs of the Hour), by Muhammad ibn 'Abd al-Rasul al-Barzanji. 2nd ed. Damascus: Dar Bashir, 1995.

Jabir, Muhammad Salama. *Ashrāt al-sā'a wa asrāruha* (The Signs of the Hour and Their Secrets). Cairo: Dar al-Salam, 1993.

———. *Tanabu'hāt Nustrādāmūs* (The Prophecies of Nostradamus). Kuwait: Dar al-Sahwa, 1996.

Jarrar, Bassam. *Zawāl Isra'īl'ām 2022* (The Disappearance of Israel in 2022). Beirut: Maktabat al-Biqaa al-Haditha, 1995; published in English as *Israeli Empire Collapses in 2022*, trans. Mohammad Yasin Owadally (Kuala Lumpur: A S. Noordeen, 2002).

———. *Nazariyyāt fi kitāb Allāh al-hakīm* (Visions in the Wise Book of Allah). Ramallah: Nun Center for Qur'anic Studies and Research, 2004.

Jarrar, Ma'mun Fa'iz. *Ahādith al-fitan* (Hadiths of Revolt). Amman: Dar al-Aalam, 2006.

Jibrin, Abdallah ibn Abderrahman. *Fitan adha zamān* (The Strife of the Present Age). Riyadh: Dar al-Watan, 1999.

Kabbani, Shaykh Muhammad Hisham. *The Approach of Armageddon?* Washington, D.C.: Islamic Supreme Council of America (ISCA), 2003.

Kaddoura, Maha, ed. and trans. *Les signes du Jour Dernier,* by Ibn Kathir. Paris: Al-Bustane, 2005.

Karimi Almaghribi, Muhammad. *Les signes précurseurs de la fin du monde.* Paris: Zeino, 2006.

Kashmiri, Anwar Shah. *Nuzūl al-Masīh* (The Descent of the Messiah). 6th edition. Cairo: Dar al-Salam, 2005 [originally published 1982].

Al-Khattab, Ahmad. *Rihla al-akhīra* (The Voyage in the Hereafter). Damascus: Dar al-Mahabba, 2004.

Khodr, Abdelhalim Abderrahman. *Mafahīm jugrāfiyya fi al-qussass al-qur'āni qissāt Dhū al-qarnayn* (The Concepts of Geography in the Qur'anic Account of the Two-Horned One). Riyadh: Imam Muhammad ibn Sa'ud Islamic University, 1981.

Lahham, Said. *'Alāmāt al-sā'a* (The Signs of the Hour). Beirut: Dar al-Fikr al-Lubnani, 1991.

Lamada, Atif. *Madha tu'raf 'an al-Masīkh al-Dajjāl?* (What Is Known about the Antichrist?). Cairo: Dar al-Dhahabiyya, 1996.

Al-Mahdi, Gholam. *The Inevitable Victory: The Coming of Jesus.* Kuala Lumpur: A.S. Noordeen, 2003.

Al-Mahi Ahmad, Al-Shafi'. *Ya'jūj wa Ma'jūj* (Gog and Magog). Beirut: Dar Ibn Hazm, 1996; 2nd ed., 2001.

Mahmood, S. Bashir-ud-Din. *Doomsday and Life after Death.* 2nd rev. ed. Delhi: Idara, 2005 [originally published 1987].

Mahmud, Salaheddin. *Al-Masīh al-Dajjāl wa Ya'jūj wa Ma'jūj* (The Antichrist and Gog and Magog). Cairo: Dar al-Ghad al-Jadid, 2005.

Mahri, Abderrazak. *Le Jour dernier et les signes de la fin du monde.* Paris: Ennour, 2009.

Mardini, Abdelrahim. *Rihla ilā dār al-ākhira* (Voyage to the Hereafter). Damascus: Dar al-Mahabba [undated].

Al-Mashaali, Abdallah ibn Sulayman. *Majmū' akhbār ākhir al-zamān* (The Encyclopedia of the End of Times). Riyadh: Dar al-Muslim, 2003.

Meslati, Mokhtar Khalil. *Amrīka tahriqa nafsaha wa al-Islām huwwa al-munqidh* (America Is Wasting Away and Islam Is Its Savior). Amman: Alam al-Kitab al-Hadith, 2006.

Al-Mokaddem, Muhammad Ahmad Ismail. *Fiqh ashrāt al-sā'a* (The Islamic Law of the Signs of the Hour). Alexandria: Dar al-Alamiyya, 2004.

Muhammad, Ahmad. *Menyekat kemaraan Ya'juj wa Ma'juj* (Digest of Illusions concerning Gog and Magog). Kuala Lumpur: Al Falah, 2004.

Muhammad, Ali Ali. *Lam'āt al-bayān fī ahdāth ākhir al-zamān, ashrāt al-sā'a al-sughrā wa al-kubrā* (Clarifications regarding the Events of the End of Times and the Signs of the Hour, Great and Small). Amman: Dar al-Isra, 1994.

Muhammad, Sayid Husayn Najib. *Yawm al-qiyāma* (The Day of Resurrection). Beirut: Dar al-Hadi, 2004.

Murad, Mustafa. *Nihāyat al-'ālam* (The End of the World). Cairo: Dar al-Fajr, 2003.

Mussawi, Mahmud. *Hayāt al-Imām al-Mahdī* (The Life of Imam Mahdi). Beirut: Dar al-Hadi, 2006.

Mustafa, Usama Nayim. *'Alāmāt al-sā'a al-kubrā* (The Great Signs of the Hour). Amman: Dar al-Isra, 2005.

Al-Mutallaq, Sayyed Mohammed Redhâ, *En attendant le Mahdi*. Ed. and trans. Abbas Ahmad al-Bostani. Montreal: La Cité du Savoir, 2005.

Na'im, Bilal. *Masīrat al-zamān hatta sāhib al-zamān* (The March of Time Up Until the Master of the Age). Beirut: Dar al-Hadi, 2006.

Naqib, Mazin. *Al-qutl min asfār al-yahūd wa brūtūkūlāt hukamā' sahyūn ila fāris bilā jawād* (Revelations regarding the Crimes of the Jews and *The Protocols of the Elders of Zion*). Damascus: Al-Awael, 2004.

Nasution, Syahrin. *50 hadis menceritakan dunia akhir zaman* (Fifty Hadiths on the End of Times). Kuala Lumpur: Pustaka Syuhada, 2003.

Nursi, Said. *Ashrāt al-sā-a wa masā'il al-Dajjāl al-akbar wa al-Sufyāni* (The Signs of the Hour and the Questions of the Great Antichrist and of the Sufyani). Cairo: Sözler, 2004.

Owadally, Mohammad Yasin. *Emergence of Dajjal: The Jewish King*. Rev. ed. Delhi: Rightway Publications, 2001 [originally published in 1997].

———. *The Story of Yajuj-wa-Majuj and the Wall*. Kuala Lumpur: A.S. Noordeen [n.d.].

Penot, Dominique. *Les signes de la fin des temps dans la tradition islamique*. 2nd ed. Lyon: Alif, 1996 [originally published in 1992].

Al-Qadi, Ahmad ibn Abderrahman ibn Uthman, ed. *Fitna al-Dajjāl wa Ya'jūj wa Ma'jūj* (The Trial of the Antichrist and Gog and Magog), by Shaykh Abderrahman ibn Nasser ibn Abdallah Saadi. Dammam: Dar Ibn Juzi, 2003.

Qassim, Naim. *Al-Mahdī al-mukhaliss* (Mahdi the Savior). Beirut: Dar al-Hadi, 2007.

Rahma, Usama Yusuf. *Iqtarabat al-sā'a* (The Hour Approaches). Beirut: Dar Qotaiba, 2003.

Ridha, Yusuf Musa. *Malhamat al-nasr al-ilahy* (The Battle of Divine Victory). Beirut: Dar al-Mahajja, 2009.

Saadani, Massaad Abdelhamid Muhammad, ed. *Al-izā'a* (The Dissemination), by Muhammad Sadiq Hasan Khan al-Husayni al-Bukhari al-Qannuji. Cairo: Dar al-Qur'an, 2000.

Al-Sadr, Muhammad Baqir. *Le Mahdi ou la fin des temps.* Ed. and trans. Abbas Ahmad al-Bostani. Montreal: La Cité du Savoir, 1999.

———. *An Inquiry concerning Al-Mahdi* [no translator indicated]. Qum: Ansarya Publications [undated].

Al-Sadr, Muhammad Baqir, and Abdelhadi al-Fadhli. *Al-Imām al-Mahdī* (The Imam Mahdi). Beirut: Dar al-Murtada, 2004.

Al-Sadr, Muhammad Sadiq. *Mawsū'āt al-Imām al-Mahdī* (Encyclopedia of the Imam Mahdi). Beirut: Dar al-Taaruf, 1982 [originally published in Iraq in 1977].

Salama, Muhammad Said. *Al-Masīh al-Dajjāl, akbar fitan fī al-ardh, wa Ya'jūj wa Ma'jūj, wa al-tūfān al-sāhiq* (The Antichrist, the Greatest of All Earthly Rebellions, Gog and Magog, and the Imminent Flood). Cairo: Maktabat al-Qodsi, 1999.

Sammak, Muhammad. *Al-dīn fī qarar Amrīka* (Religion in American Decision-making). Beirut: Dar al-Nafaes, 2005.

As-Saqqa, Ahmad Hijazi [also known as Ahmad Ahmad Ali as-Saqqa]. *Bashāra bānī Islām fī al-tūrā wa al-injīl* (The Announcement of the Sons of Islam in the Bible and the Gospels). Damascus: Dar al-Bayan al-Arabi [n.d.].

———. *'Awdat al-Masīh al-muntazar li-harb al-Irāq* (The Return of the Awaited Messiah for the Iraq War). Damascus: Dar al-Kitab al-'Arabi, 2003.

———. *Al-Bidāya wa al-nihāya li-umma Banī Isra'īl* (The Beginning and the End of the People of Israel). Cairo: Dar al-Kitab al-'Arabi, 2004.

———. *Yawm al-rāb al-'azīm* (The Day of the Lord). Cairo: Dar al-Kitab al-Arabi, 2004.

Shahawi, Magdi Muhammad. *Al-Masīh al-Dajjāl wa Ya'jūj wa Ma'jūj* (The Antichrist and Gog and Magog). Cairo: Maktabat al-Imam, 1992. [Published in English as *Beware of Dajjal and Gog and Magog* (London: Al-Firdous, 2005).]

Shahrawi, Muhammad Metwalli. *Al Geib: Le monde invisible.* Paris: Essalam, 1999.

———. *'Alāmāt al-qiyāma al-sughrā* (The Minor Signs of the Resurrection). Cairo: Maktabat al-Turath al-Islami, 2001.

———. *La fin du monde.* Paris: Essalam, 2002.

———. *'Alāmāt al-qiyāma al-kubrā* (The Major Signs of the Resurrection). Beirut: Maktabat al-Asriyya, 2006.

Shahryar, Aftar. *Dajjal: The Final Deception and Signs of Qiyamah.* Delhi: Islamic Book Service, 2003.

Shakir, Muhammad Fuad. *Al-Masīh al-Dajjāl* (The Antichrist). Cairo: Dar al-Bashir, 1994.

Shalabi, Mustafa Abu Nasr. *Sahīh ashrāt al-sā'a* (The Authentic [Collection of] the Signs of the Hour). Jidda: Maktaba Sawadi, 2002.

Shami, Abu Muhammad Jamal ibn Muhammad. *Al-'ālam yantazir thalātha* (The World Awaits Three of Them). Beirut: Dar Ibn Hazm, 1993.

Al-Shaykh, Azzedin Husayn. *Ashrāt al-sā'a* (The Signs of the Hour). Riyadh: Dar al-Hadyane, 1993.

———. *Les signes précurseurs de l'heure*. Beirut: Dar al-Kutub al-Ilmiyya, 2005.

Sherif-Zahar, Zerruk. *Prophéties et signes de la fin du monde*. Montreuil: Orientica, 2005.

Al-Shibani, Muhammad Ibrahim. *Nār al-Hijāz* (The Fire of Hijaz). Kuwait City: Center for Manuscripts, Patrimony, and Documents, 2002.

Shirazi, Ayatollah Hassan. *Mawsū'at kalīmāt al-imām al-Mahdī* (Encyclopedia of the Sayings of the Imam Mahdi). Beirut: Hayat Muhammad al-Amin, 2001.

Sirsawi, Abu Abdallah Mazen ibn Muhammad. *Kashf al-maknūn fī al-radd 'alā kitāb Harmajeddūn* (Enlightened Response to the Armageddon Book [by Gamaleddin]). Cairo: Maktabat al-Islamiyya, 2002.

Al-Sufi, Mahir Ahmad. *Al-Hashr wa qiyām al-sā'a* (The Gathering and the Arrival of the Hour). Beirut: Maktabat al-Asriyya, 2004.

———. *Ashrāt al-sā'a* (The Signs of the Hour). Beirut: Maktabat al-Asriyya, 2006.

Suhaimi, Mustafa. *Yakjuj wa makjuj: Dajjal ancam umat Islam seluruh dunia* (Gog and Magog: The Antichrist Threatens the Islamic Nation throughout the World). Kuala Lumpur: Progressive Publishing House, 2007.

Al-Sulami, Yusuf ben Yahia. *Le Mahdi attendu*. Beirut: Dar al-Kutub al-Ilmiyya, 2004.

Sulayman, Kamel. *Yawm al-Khalāss* (The Day of Deliverance). 6th rev. ed. Beirut: Al-Alami, 1995 [originally published 1979].

Tabatai al-Hassani, Sayed Muhammad Ali. *Mi'atan wa khamsa 'alāma hatta zuhūr al-imām al-muntazar* (Two Hundred Five Signs until the Appearance of the Awaited Imam). Beirut: Dar al-Balagh [undated].

Al-Tahtawi, Ali Abdelal. *Iltiqa'al al-masīhayn* (The Encounter of the Two Messiahs). Beirut: Dar al-Kutub al-Ilmiyya, 2004.

Al-Tahtawi, Ali Abdelal, ed. *Ahwāl al-qiyāma* (The Agony of the Resurrection), by Abu Muhammad al-Husayn ibn Mas'ud al-Farā' al-Bughawi. Cairo: Maktabat al-Safa, 2002.

Al-Tamimi, Assad Bayyud. *Zawāl dawlāt Isra'īl hatmiyya qur'aniyya* (The Disappearance of Israel is Inevitable according to the Qur'an). Cairo: Dar al-Mukhtar al-Islami, 1998; reprinted Amman: Al-Ahliyya, 2006.

Tawila, Abdelwahab Abdessalam. *Al-Masīh al-muntazar wa nihāyat al-'ālam* (The Awaited Messiah and the End of the World). Cairo: Dar al-Salam, 1999; 2nd ed., 2002.

Thomson, Ahmad. *Dajjal, the Antichrist*. London: Ta-Ha Publishers, 1997.

Al-Tibi, Okasha Abdelmannan. *Akhār maqal fī al-Masīh al-Dajjāl* (The Whole Truth about the Antichrist). Cairo: Dar al-I'tisam, 1991.

———. *Ahwāl al-qiyāma* (The Agony of the Resurrection). Amman: Dar al-Isra, 1997.

Uthaymin, Muhammad ibn Saleh. *Al-fitna* (The Turmoil). Riyadh: Dar al-Qassim, 2003.

Uthman, Muhammad Uthman. *Intabahu ya muslimūn* (Beware, O Muslims). Damascus: Ministry of Information, 2005.

Veliandoke, Siddheeque M.A. *Doomsday, Portents, and Prophecies.* 2nd ed. Toronto: Al-Attique, 2001 [originally published 1998].

———. *Al-fitan wa ashrāt al-sā'a* (Revolt and the Signs of the Hour). Riyadh: Diyaa al-Watan, 2003.

Al-Wabil, Yusuf. *Les signes de la fin des temps.* Brussels: Al-Hadith, 2006.

Al-Wakid, Muhammad, ed. and trans. *Nostradamūs: Al-alfiyya al-jadīda.* [Annotated Arabic translation of John Hogue, *Nostradamus: The New Millennium,* rev. ed. (Shaftesbury, Dorset: Element, 2002).] Damascus: Al-Awael, 2006.

Al-Walid, Mahmud Rajab Hamadi. *Kashf al-minan fī 'alāmāt al-sā'a wa al-malāhim wa al-fitan* (The Revelation of Grace in the Signs of the Hour, Battles, and Turmoil). Beirut: Dar Ibn Hazm, 2002.

Yahya, Harun. *Les signes de la fin des temps et le Mahdi.* Paris: Les Calligraphes, 2006.

Yakup, Adem. *Le Prophète Jésus* [no translator indicated]. Paris: Essalem, 2004.

Yusuf, Muhammad Kheir Ramadan. *Dhū al-Qarnayn* (The Two-Horned One). Beirut: Dar al-Shamia, 1999.

Yusuf, Talaat. *Al-Masīh al-Dajjāl wa Ya'jūj wa Ma'jūj* (The Antichrist and Gog and Magog). Cairo: Dar al-Muslim, 2004.

Zaki, Adel. *Al-Mahdī* (The Mahdi). Beirut: Dar Ibn Hazm, 2005.

Zamzam, Ahmad Ali. *Kiamat hampir tiba* (The End of the World Is Near). Kedah: Khazanah Banjariah, 2005.

Zentici, Abdelkarim, ed. and trans. *Le Faux Messie et le retour d'Issa,* by al-Qurtub. Lyon: Dar al-Muslim, 2003.

Index

TEXT
10/13 Sabon Open Type

DISPLAY
Sabon Open Type

COMPOSITOR
BookComp, Inc.

INDEXER
Barbara Roos

PRINTER/BINDER
Thomson-Shore, Inc.